Ernst Loew

Monographs of the Diptera of North America Prepared for the Smithsonian Institution by H. Loew Part 3

Ernst Loew

Monographs of the Diptera of North America Prepared for the Smithsonian Institution by H. Loew Part 3

ISBN/EAN: 9783741151644

Manufactured in Europe, USA, Canada, Australia, Japa

Cover: Foto ©Thomas Meinert / pixelio.de

Manufactured and distributed by brebook publishing software
(www.brebook.com)

Ernst Loew

Monographs of the Diptera of North America Prepared for the Smithsonian Institution by H. Loew Part 3

SMITHSONIAN MISCELLANEOUS COLLECTIONS.

256

MONOGRAPHS

OF THE

D I P T E R A

OF

NORTH AMERICA.

PART III.

PREPARED FOR THE SMITHSONIAN INSTITUTION

BY

H. LOEW.

WASHINGTON:
SMITHSONIAN INSTITUTION.
DECEMBER, 1873.

ADVERTISEMENT.

———·

THE present publication is Part III of a work upon the Diptera of North America, prepared at the request of the Smithsonian Institution, by Dr. H. Loew, of Guben, Prussia, well known as one of the most eminent cultivators of this branch of entomology.

The first part of this series of monographs was published in 1862, and included the families of *Trypetidæ*, *Sciomyzidæ*, *Ephydrinidæ*, and *Cecidomyidæ*. The second part appeared in 1864, and consisted principally of a monograph of the *Dolichopodidæ*. The fourth part was issued in 1869, embracing a monograph of part of the *Tipulidæ*.

They were not published in sequence, but in the order in which materials could be collected for their preparation. The original manuscript of Dr. Loew was written in German, and the Institution is indebted to Baron H. Osten-Sacken for translating it into English; and to Mr. R. A. Witthaus, Jr., of New York, for revising and correcting the proof-sheets, in the absence of Baron Osten-Sacken.

JOSEPH HENRY,

Secretary S. I.

WASHINGTON, Dec. 1873.

PHILADELPHIA:
COLLINS, PRINTER.

TABLE OF CONTENTS.

THE FAMILY ORTALIDÆ.

PART FIRST.—INTRODUCTION.

(iii)

APPENDIX

REVIEW OF THE NORTH AMERICAN TRYPETINA.

APPENDIX I.

APPENDIX II.

NOTE FROM THE TRANSLATOR.

Readers of these "Monographs" may notice discrepancies in some minor points of the terminology used in the first volume from that of the following ones. A few words of explanation are therefore necessary. The first volume was translated from Mr. Loew's German manuscript into English by a German friend of his (see Vol. I, p. v). The second and third volumes were translated either by me, or under my supervision. Although in all essentials the terminology adopted in Vol. I was followed, some changes, which I thought would be improvements, were introduced. Thus, * feat* was used for *legs*; *ovipositor*, for *borer*; *crossvein*, for *transverse vein*; *arista*, for *antennal bristle*; thus *transverse shoulder vein* came to be *humeral crossvein*, and *hinder transverse vein*, *posterior crossvein*, etc. None of these changes can give rise to any error or uncertainty.—O. S.

DIPTERA

of

NORTH AMERICA.

PART III.

THE FAMILY ORTALIDÆ,

I.

INTRODUCTION.

In the variety of forms the *Ortalidæ* are hardly surpassed by any other family of diptera; at the same time, they are hardly equalled by any in the importance of the structural differences occurring among them; hence, they may be considered as one of the most interesting families of the order. Nevertheless, but little has been done as yet for the exact definition of the limits of this family, as well as for its subdivision into smaller groups.

It would be impossible, therefore, to attempt a satisfactory description of the North American species of *Ortalidæ*, without first settling the questions of the true limits of the family, of its relationship to other families, and of the characters upon which it is established. It would also be indispensable to break the family up in subordinate groups and these groups in genera.

Of all these requirements, only one has been, as far as I can see, fulfilled, and that is, the definition of the limits between the *Trypetidæ* and the *Ortalidæ*, which I have tried to draw as well as I could, in the first volume of these monographs and in my earlier work on European *Trypetidæ*.

1

(1)

Through the successive, although disconnected, publications of several authors the systematic arrangement of the *Ortalidæ*, like that of some other families of dipters, has gradually reached a state of confusion which it is impossible to unravel without a detailed and somewhat lengthy discussion. I may be excused, therefore, if I preface the description of a comparatively small number of American species by an unusually long introductory chapter.

In order to point out the relationship of the *Ortalidæ* with other families, as well as the differences which distinguish them, it is necessary, first of all, to discover those characters which serve to define the family.

THE EUROPEAN ORTALIDÆ.

The examination of the works of Meigen, the founder of systematic dipterology, will afford a solid basis to proceed from, and I will begin with the European species which are the longest known and the best investigated.

Meigen's Genus Ortalis.

The nucleus of the European *Ortalidæ* is formed of those species which Meigen has brought together in the genus *Ortalis*, a genus which, in his acceptation, far exceeded the limits which we are accustomed to give to genera at present.

1. Characters which Meigen's species of *Ortalis* have in common.

I discovered a number of characters which the species of this genus have in common, and which also occur in many species added to the genus by subsequent authors. These common characters, to the exclusion of those which also belong to most of the neighboring families, are the following :—

Front broad in both sexes; a more or less distinctly developed small callosity runs from each corner of the vertex down the front; it bears in front of the lateral bristle of the vertex one or two distinct additional bristles; beyond this, the front is beset with only short hairs, or else quite bare; it never has the second row of bristles, nearer the orbit, which distinguishes all the genera of *Trypetidæ*.

Eyes bare, even under a strong lens; the compound microscope shows only some sparse, very short hairs.

The frontal fissure is distinct, but the frontal lunule is not pushed up as far as the front, so as to seem to form a part of it; on the contrary, it appears as the upper part of the face.

Vibrissæ, such as they appear in all the genera of *Helomyzidæ*, are not extant.

The clypeus is always distinct. The palpi are rather broad; the proboscis more or less stout.

The metathorax is larger than usual, very much projecting inferiorly and posteriorly.

The feet short and strong, rather than long and slender; middle tibiæ distinctly spurred; front and hind tibiæ spurless; the erect bristle extant in several families of the *Diptera acalyptera* on the upper side of the tibiæ, near their end, for instance in the *Sapromyzidæ* and *Sciomyzidæ*, does not occur here in any species.

The abdomen of the male has four segments, the first of which, like the first segment of the female abdomen, is formed of two coalescent segments; the diminutive fifth segment of the male abdomen forms the small, more or less imbedded hypopygium; the sometimes more filiform, in other instances tape-like, rolled up penis is of an extraordinary length.

The abdomen of the female consists of five segments; the sixth, seventh, and eighth segments are converted into a flattened, extensile ovipositor, the first joint of which surpasses the two following in breadth very much, and is often colored like the rest of the abdomen; the slender last joint of the ovipositor ends in a simple point.

The wings show the complete venation of the *Diptera acalyptera*; the auxillary vein is entirely separated from the first longitudinal vein, although it is sometimes rather approximated to it; it ends at a more or less acute angle in the costal vein, without becoming less distinct at its end; the first longitudinal vein is provided with bristles, at least at its end; the two posterior basal cells are comparatively large.

2. Species erroneously placed in the genus *Ortalis*.

The agreement of all the species placed by Meigen in the genus *Ortalis* would have been complete if *O. pœciloptera* (*fulminans* M.), *connexa*, *vibrans*, and *syngenesiæ* did not show differences, which require a special mention.

O. pœciloptera and *connexa* differ from the other species in the presence of a row of bristles on each side near the orbit, besides the bristles common to all the *Ortalidæ*. These bristles are a character so exclusively peculiar to the *Trypetidæ* that we cannot but consider those two species as belonging to that family (as I have already proved it elsewhere). They cannot, therefore, be further considered here.

Ortalis vibrans, the female of which has only four segments on the abdomen, approaches, in the absence of bristles upon the first longitudinal vein, *Palloptera* and the related genera so much, that one might be tempted to place it among the *Pallopteridæ*; but there are other genera having the first longitudinal vein bare, to which *Ortalis vibrans* is still more closely allied, and which, as I will have occasion to show hereafter, cannot possibly be separated from the *Ortalidæ*. Such being the case, *O. vibrans* has to remain in this family, and this is also justified by the large size of the two posterior cells in this species, which is a proof of its relationship to the other *Ortalidæ*. There is no doubt, at the same time, that this species is a stranger in Meigen's genus *Ortalis*.

Ortalis syngenesiæ is also distinguished from the other species of *Ortalis* by its abdomen, which has only four segments in the female; in other respects it is more related to them than *O. vibrans*; it is more closely allied to the species of the genus *Platystoma* than to the other species of Meigen's *Ortalis*.

The other European Ortalidæ.

After having thus disposed of those species placed by Meigen in the genus *Ortalis*, which have either to be entirely withdrawn from the family of *Ortalidæ*, or which can only conditionally be received in it, the next step to be taken, in order to chalk out the whole extent of the family *Ortalidæ*, is to discover such other genera as may likewise possess the characters common to the species of *Ortalis*. After this, we will have to point out such genera as possess not all, but most of those characters only, and especially the principal ones; and thus we will reach a limit beyond which only such genera will be found, as, on account of important differences from the species of *Ortalis*, cannot any more be united in one family with them. This research has also to show us which among the characters common to the above enumerated species of *Ortalis* have to be

stricken out, or at least to be modified, in order to leave, as a
residue, the true characters of the family Ortalidæ.

Here also I begin with the European fauna, as the genera
and species composing it are by far the best known.

The variously organized groups of species, within the genus
Ortalis, each bare, outside of this genus, a circle of relationship of their own.

1. Forms reminding of Ortalis lamed.

If we begin with Ortalis lamed (pulchella Melg.), we are led
at once towards Sciomyza bucephala Melg., which Macquart
has united, with several other heterogeneous species, in the
genus Otites, and for which I have later established the genus
Cormocaris.

Cormocaris brings us to Tetanops, which agrees in its principal characters with Cormocaris bucephala, quite erroneously
placed in the genus Sciomyza by Meigen. In this species, as
well as in all the European species of Tetanops which I know
of, none of the characters are wanting the presence of which
distinguishes the genus Ortalis.

The genus Tetanops again leads us towards Dorycera; the
remarkable elongation of the second antennal joint is a peculiar
character of most species of this genus, a character not to be
found in the species of Ortalis. However, the difference in the
length of this joint in different species of Dorycera sufficiently
shows that too much systematic stress ought not to be laid upon
this character; all the other characters agreeing with those of
the Ortalidæ, Dorycera must necessarily be placed in this
family.

Next to Dorycera I find the genus Adapsilia, founded by
Waga, which, like most Doryceræ, has an elongated second antennal joint. It is distinguished by a very projecting front,
very approximated antennæ, and the want of ocelli; with the
species of Ortalis it agrees in the characters already specified,
except that the first joint of the ovipositor of the female is not
flattened, as in all the species of Ortalis, but capsule-shaped,
swollen; as, however, in other respects the structure of this
ovipositor resembles that of Ortalis, Adapsilia must also be
added to the Ortalidæ. At the same time, the statement concerning the shape of the ovipositor of this family must be somewhat modified to be applicable to Adapsilia.

I know of no other European genus which, although still more distant from *Ortalis* in the direction of *Adapsilia*, would nevertheless be admissible into the family of *Ortalidæ*.

2. Forms reminding of *Ortalis syngenesiæ*.

If, in our search for forms related to *Ortalis*, we start from *Ortalis syngenesiæ*, distinguished by its four-jointed female abdomen, the genera *Ulidia*, *Timia* and *Platystoma* at once claim our attention.

Ulidia, in Meigen's sense, is not a homogeneous genus. *Ulidia demandata* is too aberrant to remain in it. Together with several exotic species allied to it, it has to form a separate genus for which *Chrysomyza*, a name already used by Fallen for *Ulidia demandata*, may be applied.

Timia apicalis, described by Meigen, is nothing but an *Ulidia*, and must be referred to this genus; the differences which appear in Meigen's statements and his figures do not exist in nature.

Timia erythrocephala, upon which Wiedemann, in the *Analecta*, has founded the genus *Timia*, differs from *Ulidia* only in its extreme glabrousness, its swollen head, much more projecting beyond the eyes in profile, and perhaps also the somewhat less developed clypeus; in all the other important characters both genera agree.

In all the species hitherto placed in the genera *Timia* and *Ulidia*, and consequently also in the species of *Chrysomyza*, the first longitudinal vein is bare. In all other respects, these species share all the characters common to the species of *Ortalis*, so that, in my opinion, their position among the *Ortalidæ* cannot well be disputed, unless we separate from this family all the species the first longitudinal vein of which is bare. Nevertheless, the relationship between the species of *Ulidia*, *Timia*, and *Chrysomyza* to *Ortalis syngenesiæ* cannot be considered as unusually close, because they differ from it, not only in the bareness of the first longitudinal vein, but also in the presence of a fifth, very much abbreviated, segment of the female abdomen.

A genus agreeing with them in the bareness of the first longitudinal vein, and most closely related to them, is the genus *Empyelocera*, introduced by me.

The genus *Lonchæa* also seems related to *Ulidia*; I will, therefore, in the sequel, explain its systematic location.

The species of *Platystoma* differ somewhat from *Ortalis* in the shape of the ovipositor: its first joint is smaller, narrower, and somewhat less flattened; generally also more withdrawn in the last abdominal segment. The hypopygium, formed by the upper half of the fifth abdominal segment, is unusually small; whether the penis has the shape of an unrolled tape or thread I cannot ascertain at present, as I have no fresh specimens at hand, but I have every reason to suppose that such is the case, as the female ovipositor, in its structure, is absolutely analogous to that of the species of *Ortalis*. The agreement of all other characters compels us to admit *Platystoma* among the *Ortalidæ*; and this genus really shows, in the four-jointed abdomen of the female, the absence of bristles on the pleura and an analogous structure of the mouth, a close relationship to *Ortalis syngenesiæ*.

I know of no other European genera which, in following the same direction of relationship, might be still more distant from *Ortalis* than the species of *Platystoma* are, and which, nevertheless, would show a sufficient agreement with the *Ortalidæ* to be placed among them. I, therefore, hold *Platystoma* to be one the more distant genera, placed on the extreme limit of the family.

6. Forms reminding of *Ortalis paludum*.

Species like *Ortalis paludum*, *luctuosa*, and others of the same group, remind of the genera *Psairoptera* and *Cephalia*.

The comparatively low head, the transversely oval eyes, and the small development of the clypeus give *Psairoptera* a very peculiar appearance; nevertheless in all the other important characters it agrees with the species of *Ortalis* so well, that its position among the *Ortalidæ* cannot be disputed, although its precise location within this family may not be very easy to determine. The relationship of *Psairoptera* with the above-named species of *Ortalis*, far from being a close one, can rather be called distant.

In *Cephalia* I cannot discover a single character which would justify its separation from the *Ortalidæ*. To place this genus among the *Sepsidæ* seems to me utterly impracticable, as the distinctive character of the latter family, the rudimentary structure of the palpi, must be maintained, unless we render the limits of the family altogether doubtful. Moreover, *Cephalia* does not show any vestige of vibrissæ which the *Sepsidæ* possess, and more than all, the structure of the ovipositor of *Cephalia* is like that of the *Ortalidæ*, and not like that of the *Sepsidæ*. *Cephalia* is more closely related to the above-named species of *Ortalis* than *Psairoptera*.

4. Forms not resembling any of Meigen's species.

A fly which possesses all the essential characters of the species of *Ortalis*, and undoubtedly belongs to the *Ortalidæ*, is the *Scatophaga fasciata* of Fabricius, erroneously placed by Meigen in the genus *Trypeta*. The *Musca octopunctata* of Coquebert, Dec. III., Tab. XXIV., is probably identical with it. The circumstance that there is no other European Ortalida resembling this species probably caused Meigen to overlook its true relationship. Similar forms are more frequent in other parts of the world, especially in America. Among them I will name *Dictya ocellata* Fabr., *Ortalis vau* Say, and *Platystoma annulipes* Macq., which, by the way, is no *Platystoma* at all.

Aciphorea not belonging to the OBTALIDÆ.

That group of genera which, on account of its peculiar, three-jointed, horny ovipositor, ending in a simple point, has been called, and not improperly, *Diptera aciphorea*, is represented in Europe, besides the *Trypetidæ* and those genera which, on the preceding pages, I have claimed for the *Ortalidæ*, only by *Lonchæa*, with the genus *Earomyia*, separated from it by Zetterstedt, and by *Palloptera* and *Toxoneura*. As it would be useless to look for *Ortalidæ* outside of the *Diptera aciphorea*, it remains for us at present to define the position of those genera with regard to the *Ortalidæ*.

The number and position of the frontal bristles, the distinctness of the clypeus, the absence of vibrissæ, and the want of the characteristic bristle on the upper side of the tibia, before its end, which is distinctive of several families, the spurred middle tibia, the spurless front and hind tibiæ, as well as the completeness of the venation, clearly prove the close relationship of these genera with *Ortalis*. They are less closely allied to the *Trypetidæ*, from which they differ in the arrangement of the frontal bristles and in the course of the auxiliary vein. All four differ from all the genera, the location of which among the *Ortalidæ* I have proved in the preceding discussion, by a much smaller size of the two posterior, usually called anal, basal cells

of the wings, and all four agree among themselves in the absence of bristles on the first longitudinal vein, and this character
they share with some of the genera placed among the *Ortalidæ*.

The genera *Palloptera* and *Toxoneura* possess moreover another
striking character, which occurs also among some few of the
genera of *Ortalidæ*, but in none to that marked extent; they have,
upon the middle of the otherwise short-pilose, thoracic dorsum, as
far as its anterior part, a series of binary bristles, distinguished
by their length, stoutness, and regular arrangement. The difference in the venation already spoken of, together with this
marked peculiarity in the arrangement of the bristles of the
thorax, seem to afford sufficient ground for excluding those two
genera from the family *Ortalidæ*. I consider them as the
nucleus of a separate family, which I call *Pallopteridæ*.

The systematic position of *Lonchæa* is more difficult to decide upon than that of *Palloptera* and *Toxoneura*. While the
venation of *Lonchæa* closely approaches these two genera, the
position of the bristles on its thorax is more like that of many *Ortalidæ*, as there are no stronger bristles on the thoracic dorsum,
anterior to the suture ; this genus stands therefore nearer to the
undoubted *Ortalidæ* than *Palloptera* or *Toxoneura*. Against
its being united with the *Ortalidæ* may be urged (not to mention the smallness of the two posterior basal cells), not so much
those characters which are common to all *Lonchæa*, as a number
of peculiarities, which do not occur among the *Ortalidæ*, and
which distinguish different species of *Lonchæa*, and are quite
proper to form the basis of a subdivision of this widespread
and rather numerous genus. As such characters I consider the
long and strong hairs upon the whole body of some species, the
long and dense pubescence of the eyes of others, the partial
coalescence of the auxiliary vein with the first longitudinal in
several, and finally the circumstance that in the females of
some species the sixth abdominal segment does not take part
in the formation of the ovipositor quite in the same manner as
among the *Ortalidæ*. I am afraid that the *Ortalidæ*, as a
family, would lose too many of their well-defined characters, if,
in order to accommodate *Lonchæa* among them, we undertook
to modify these characters in accordance with the above mentioned peculiarities of the latter genus. The nature of the

venation of the wings having proved, in so many cases, to be the
most trustworthy character for the distinction of the families of
diptera, we have to take care not to attach too little importance
to the smallness of the posterior basal cells in *Lonchæa*, cells
which, in the *Ortalidæ*, always are of a considerable size. These
reasons induce me to exclude *Lonchæa* from among the *Ortalidæ*.
Those entomologists who take the European fauna alone in consideration, will, I have no doubt, justify this course, as that
fauna does not contain any intermediate forms between *Lonchæa*
and the genera of *Ortalidæ*, but I am not quite as sure of the
approbation of those who have a wide acquaintance with the
diptera from all parts of the world, because, among the number,
forms occur which seem to be intermediate between *Lonchæa*
and the genera of *Ortalidæ* allied to *Ulidia*, and it is possible
that the discovery of a large number of such forms may, at some
future time, render the exclusion of *Lonchæa* from the *Ortalidæ*
less plausible than it appears to me now. In the first volume
of these monographs, I placed this genus in the family of the
Pallopteridæ and considered it as the typical genus of a second
group in this family. Whether this arrangement, which I for
the present retain, is satisfactory, or whether it would not be
better to take *Lonchæa* as the typical genus of a separate, small
family, intermediate between the *Pallopteridæ* and the *Ortalidæ*,
is beyond the scope of the present discussion, and may, therefore, be left for future investigation.

The genus *Earomyia* is so near *Lonchæa*, that, with regard
to its systematic position, whatever I said of the latter may be
applied to the former.

Summary of the European Ortalidæ.

From what precedes may be deduced the following list of
genera and species of European diptera, which I place in the
family of *Ortalidæ*: all the species of *Ortalis*, in Meigen's
sense, with the exception of *O. pœciloptera* and connexa;
Sciomyza bucephala; the genera *Adapsilia, Dorycera, Tetanops, Psairoptera, Cephalia, Platystoma, Timia, Ulidia, Chrysomyza, Empyelocera,* and, finally, *Trypeta fasciata.*

THE ORTALIDÆ OTHER THAN EUROPEAN.

I will now try to find the genera and species from other parts of the world than Europe, which must be placed in the family Ortalidæ.

(a.) In Wiedemann.

I begin by the Ortalidæ contained in Wiedemann's writings. Besides his species of the genus Ortalis, against the location of two of which, however, I will have to raise some doubts, and besides his Timia erythrocephala, which occurs in the southeast of Europe and in the neighboring provinces of Asia, the species of Cephalia described by him undoubtedly belong to the Ortalidæ. They differ somewhat from the European Cephalia rufipes, and belong in the relationship of those species which Rob. Desvoidy distributed among his genera Polistodes and Myrmecomyia: Mr. Macquart has established for them the genus Michogaster (better Mischogaster), which coincides with the genus Conopsidea, introduced by him at a later time.

The two Ortalis of Wiedemann, the systematic position of which seems doubtful to me, are Ortalis trifasciata and atomaria, both from Brasil, both closely related to each other, and somewhat reminding, in their general appearance, of Richardia and Rhopalomera. Both have an erect bristle before the end of the tibia, which I cannot take for anything else but the preapical bristle, wanting in all the Ortalidæ. Considering the importance which the presence or absence of this bristle has in the classification of all the Diptera acalyptera, I would be very much inclined to exclude both of those species from the family Ortalidæ, if I could assign them a fitting place in some other family. The structure of the ovipositor clearly proves that they belong in the circle of the Diptera aciphorea, but even in this wider circle the existence of their, however weak, preapical bristle assigns them a rather isolated position. The venation and the position of the frontal bristles, in which they agree with the Ortalidæ, do not allow their introduction among the Trypetidæ. They have still less connection with the Pallopteridæ. Hence, nothing remains to be done, as it seems, but to tolerate them in the family Ortalidæ, however unwelcome they may be among them, as, in consequence of their appearance, the absence of a

præapical bristle ceases to be an undoubted distinctive character
of the *Ortalidæ*. That these two species, to which several undescribed South American forms have to be added, are to form
the nucleus of a new genus is beyond question. I propose for
it the name of *Automola*.

Whether the two species of Fabricius, which Wiedemann
quotes among the species of *Ulidia*, really belong to this genus
cannot be decided without seeing the original specimens; but I
have no doubt that they belong to the *Ortalidæ*. I would suppose that *Ulidia stigma* belonged to the genus *Notogramma*, and
that *Ulidia ænea* is a *Chrysomyza*.

Wiedemann's genus *Pyrgota*, with which *Oxycephala*, Macq.
is absolutely identical, shows all the characters of the *Ortalidæ*.
It is closely allied to *Adapsilia*, the only difference being that
the antennal fovex are shorter, while in *Adapsilia* they are
parallel, and run down to the edge of the mouth; but, as in different species of *Pyrgota* these fovex vary in length, this difference has so little importance that *Adapsilia* might, without any
inconvenience, be united with *Pyrgota*.

The genus *Dacus*, in Wiedemann's writings, is a mixture of
many very different forms of diptera, most of which are *Ortalidæ* and two species are *Trypetidæ*. Two of the species of
which Wiedemann formed the first section of the genus *Dacus*,
form now, together with other species added since, the genus
Stenopterina, which Macquart established under the name of
Senopterina, and which he placed quite correctly among the
Ortalidæ. The *Dacus flavicornis*, placed by Wiedemann in the
first division as a third species, has a certain general resemblance
to the two former species; it differs, however, in the bareness of
the first longitudinal vein and in several other characters, too
much to be united in the same genus with them; nevertheless,
this species, as well as the two others, belong to the *Ortalidæ*.
Among the species of Wiedemann's second division of *Dacus*
D. succinctus must be referred to the *Ortalidæ*; it belongs in
the immediate relationship of *O. syngeneriæ*. *Dacus bicolor*
likewise belongs to the *Ortalidæ*. The remaining *Dacus* of
Wiedemann's second division are *Trypetidæ*; some of them
belong to the genus *Trypeta*, if we take it in the wider sense of
Meigen and Wiedemann; for instance, *Dacus parallelus*, *fra-*

terculus, serpentinus; the greatest part of the residue are species which may be left in the genus *Dacus.*

On the other hand, Wiedemann has placed in the genus *Trypeta* several species which do not belong to the *Trypetidæ* at all and have all the characters of the *Ortalidæ.* Such species are: *Trypeta ocellata,* which Macquart described again as a supposed new species, under the name of *Platystoma ocellata,* and upon which Rondani established later the genus *Pterocalla; Trypeta obscura,* which is very closely allied to the former, and which Macquart very improperly placed in the genus *Camptoneura,* while its place is in the genus *Pterocalla,* next to *P. ocellata;* moreover *Trypeta picta,* the typical species of the Ortalideous genus *Camptoneura; Trypeta flexa,* which may be placed in the genus *Mischogaster; Trypeta trimaculata,* redescribed by Macquart as *Colometopia ferruginea; Trypeta cyanogaster, basilaris, scutellaris,* and perhaps several others among Wiedemann's *Trypetæ,* which I have not had the occasion to compare.

Those species which Wiedemann placed in the genus *Platystoma,* with the exception of his *Platystoma decora,* really belong to that genus, and consequently to the *Ortalidæ.* *Platystoma decora,* which induced Macquart to establish the genus *Loxoneura,* is also to be placed among the *Ortalidæ.*

Tetanops sanguiniceps was described by Wiedemann from a specimen of the Berlin Museum; I have seen this species, unless my memory deceives me, not in the Berlin Museum, but in Wiedemann's collection. I found that in the structure of the head and in the venation it does not sufficiently agree with the European species of *Tetanops* to be left in the same genus with them, but, at the same time, that it undoubtedly belongs to the family of the *Ortalidæ.* I am sure that the *Dichromyia brasiliensis* of Rob. Desvoidy, described as the type of the new genus *Dichromyia,* is the same species.

The *Scatophaga birpinosa* Fab., placed by Wiedemann in the genus *Tetanocera,* differs from the other *Ortalidæ* in the venation as well as in the shape of the scutellum very much, but nevertheless, judging from Wiedemann's statements, and especially from his figure, it undoubtedly belongs in that family, where Macquart also places it in establishing for it the genus *Notacanthina.* Should we judge, however, from Macquart's

figure (in the Diptères Exotiques, II., 3, Tab. xxviii., fig. 8), we
would not place it among the *Ortalidæ*, as it shows distinctly
spurred front and hind tibiæ; these spurs, however, as well as
many other things in Macquart's figures, are probably produc-
tions of the draughtsman's fancy. In the most slovenly figure
of the same species in Macquart's *Suites à Buffon*, no such
spurs are to be found.

That *Dacus podagricus* Fab., placed by Wiedemann in *Cordylura*, does not belong to that genus, nor to the *Cordyluridæ*
in general, has been recognized long ago. For this species, as
well as for similar ones, the genus *Richardia* has been established by Rob. Desvoidy in the family of the *Ortalidæ*.

The systematic location of *Dictya externa* Fab. cannot well
be ascertained, owing to the insufficient statements of Fabricius
as well as of Wiedemann; the latter are in an insoluble contra-
diction to Wiedemann's figure in what regards the shape of
the head and the picture on the thorax; judging by the figure,
it would seem that the fly does not belong to the *Diptera acalyptera* at all.

The genus *Rhopalomera*, Wied. seems to have been by all later
authors unhesitatingly referred to the *Ortalidæ*. I look upon
this decision as far from unobjectionable, but can very well con-
ceive that a certain resemblance in the shape of the head between the species of *Rhopalomera* and *Platystoma* (with the
genera allied to it), may easily have given rise to such an
opinion. The species of *Rhopalomera* differ in a striking manner from all the *Ortalidæ* in the structure of the hypopygium of
the male, while in this respect they show a most decided leaning
towards the *Sapromyzidæ*, *Sciomyzidæ*, and the families immediately connected with them. The females are not provided with
a borer-like ovipositor, composed of elongated, retractile joints;
the metanotum is but very little developed, less than usual
among the *Ortalidæ*; the front and middle tibiæ have, on the
upper side, before their end, an erect bristle; upon the upper side
of the hind tibiæ, this bristle, in most species, is not distinctly
visible among the general pilosity of the tibia; nevertheless, it
is easily recognizable in some species, for instance *Rhopalomera
pleuropunctata* Wied. Such are the characters which, in my
opinion, not only render the location of *Rhopalomera* among
the *Ortalidæ* doubtful, but even impossible. If, among the

diptera I am acquainted with, I look for the immediate connections of *Rhopalomera*, I find them unmistakably among the
South African species of the genus *Cestrotus*, erected by me.
Before all, the striking structure of the head, reminding partly
of some genera of *Ephydrinidæ*, partly of the *Ortalidæ*, is very
much alike in both genera; this resemblance extends to the
mode of pilosity of the face, the shape of the antennæ, and the
feathery pubescence of the arista. Moreover, the small development of the metanotum, the shape of the hypopygium, and the
structure of the last segments of the female abdomen are very
much alike. Now, as the genus *Cestrotus*, through the intermediate steps of *Prosopomyia* and *Physogenis*, approaches
the family of the *Sapromyzidæ* very closely, I do not find
any serious objection to placing *Rhopalomera* in the same
family. That *Rhopalomera* is one of the extreme genera of the
family cannot be doubtful; the size of the two posterior basal
cells especially distinguishes it from all the other genera of
Sapromyzidæ in a very striking manner, and connects it with
the *Sciomyzidæ*; for this reason it would be also possible, by
slightly modifying the definition of the boundary between those
two families, to place *Rhopalomera* among the *Sciomyzidæ*.
Those who will not share either of these two views, and prefer to place among the *Ortalidæ* a genus which is far apart from
all the *Diptera aciphorea* in the structure of the ovipositor, may
locate *Rhopalomera* in the vicinity of *Richardia*, on account of
the bareness of the first longitudinal vein, the rounded end of
the posterior basal cell, and the spines on the femora.

Thus, the following diptera, described in Wiedemann's works,
belong to the *Ortalidæ*: his species of *Ortalis*; all the species
which he brings in the genera *Timia*, *Ulidia*, *Cephalia*, *Platystoma*, *Tetanops*, and *Pyrgota*; in his genus *Dacus*, the three
species in the first division, and *Dacus succinctus* and *bicolor*
in the second; in the genus *Trypeta*, *Trypeta ocellata*, *obscura*,
picta, *flexa*, *trimaculata*, *basilaris*, *cyanogaster*, and *scutellaris*;
in the genus *Tetanocera*, his *T. bispinosa*, and finally, his *Cordylura podagrica*.

(b.) In Robineau Desvoidy.

I turn now, not without reluctance, to the writings of R. Desvoidy. In his well-known *Essai sur les Myodaires* he united

the genera which we are considering under the general name of
Phytomydæ Myodinæ. This generalization may be considered
as successful, as it contains but little which is foreign, that is
which would be better placed among his *Aciphoreæ*, equivalent
to the family *Trypetidæ*, and as at the same time it excludes
but little of what really belongs to the *Ortalidæ*. The position
also which Rob. Desvoidy assigns to the *Phytomydæ Myodinæ*,
next to the *Phytomydæ Thelidomydæ*, that is, the *Micropezidæ*,
cannot but be sustained, as the latter are closely related to the
Ortalidæ. After his *Phytomydæ Thelidomydæ* Rob. Desvoidy
places his *Aciphoreæ*, that is, the *Trypetidæ*, while he would have
done better in reversing this order of his two divisions, on account of the close relationship between the *Ortalidæ* and the
Trypetidæ. The sovereign neglect of all previous publications,
the wretched manner in which most of his genera are established,
chiefly upon merely relative differences (for instance, a somewhat longer third antennal joint, a somewhat more pubescent
arista, etc.), without regard to the most striking plastic characters, the very slovenly description of many species of unknown *habitat*, etc., have, long ago, put this author's writings in
such bad repute that it would not be easy to add anything to
it. It would be unjust, however, after this fully deserved blame,
not to recognize that Rob. Desvoidy's judgment, with regard to
questions of relationship, in this case, as in many others, was a
very correct one.

The genera which he places among the *Phytomydæ Myodinæ*
are: *Dichromya, Palposya, Hexyquillia, Heromya, Myoria,
Oscinis, Blainvillia, Meckelia, Melieria, Myeannis, Strauzia,
Vidalia, Delphinia, Acidia, Myrmecomya, Polystodes, Stylophora, Herina, Myodina, Richardia, Ricellia, Boisduvalia,
Clidonia, Setellia, Chlorophora*. Concerning these genera and
their names, I will offer the following remarks:—

The genus *Dichromya* (the name ought to be improved to
Dichromyia) is adopted by Macquart in his *Diptères Exotiques*,
and placed among his *Heteromyzides*. The *Dichromyia brasiliensis* of Rob. Desvoidy is the same as the *Platystoma micro-
cera* of Macquart's *Suites à Buffon*, and was described still
earlier as *Tetanops sanguinicerps* by Wiedemann. Not being a
Tetanops this species must therefore be considered as the type
of the genus *Dichromyia*. The position among the *Ortalidæ*,

assigned to it by R. Desvoidy, I hold to be correct; with *Platystoma* it has nothing to do.

The genus *Palpomyia*, a hybrid name, being formed out of a Latin and a Greek word, and not rendered more valuable by its improvement in *Palpomyia*, is identical with *Platystoma*; the typical *Palpomyia Lalandi* is nothing else but the well-known *Platystoma asphaltina* Wied.' The generic characters given by R. Desvoidy are entirely erroneous.

Under the name of *Heryquillia* Rob. Desvoidy describes *Platystoma seminationis* Fab., and under that of *Heryquillia lugubris* the *Platystoma umbrarum* Fab.; thus, the genus *Heryquillia* likewise coincides with *Platystoma*.

The genus *Heramya*, which ought at least to be called *Heramyia*, is based upon *Sciomyza bucephala*, which R. Desvoidy did not recognize, as well as upon another species which is very like it, if not identical. Macquart united this species with *Myoris* (a name which it is difficult to explain), a genus not distinguished by a single character of any value, and with *Blainvillia* (a preoccupied name), and thus formed his genus *Otites* (a name which Latreille had already used in a broader sense); but he placed in it moreover some true *Sciomyzidæ*.

The genus *Oscinis*, as understood by R. Desvoidy, is identical with *Dorycera*; it has nothing in common with the genus of the same name to which Fallen reduced the much more comprehensive genus *Oscinis* of Latreille.

Meckelia (an already preoccupied name) and *Mellerea* (probably also a dedication name), contain species belonging to Macquart's Ortalideous genus *Ceroxys*.

The genus *Myennis* (a badly formed name), is established for *Scatophaga fasciata* Fab., which Macquart, in the *Suites à Buffon*, describes as *Ortalis fasciata*, after Rob. Desvoidy, and, for a second time, as *Tephritis fasciata*, after Meigen.

Straussia (as the genus is dedicated to Strauss-Dürkheim, the name should be spelt *Straussia*) does not belong to the *Ortalidæ* at all, but to the *Trypetidæ*; the two species described by Rob. Desvoidy are nothing else but the male and female of *Trypeta longipennis* Wied., which Rob. Desvoidy did not recognize.

Vidalia seems likewise to belong to the *Trypetidæ*; not

having succeeded yet, however, in identifying the species, I am
not positive about it.

The genus *Delphinia* is established for *Trypeta picta*, Fab.,
which Rob. Desvoidy did not recognize; the unbecoming generic
name was afterwards replaced by *Camptoneura* Macq.

The genus *Acidia* belongs to the *Trypetidæ*.

Myrmecomya (more correctly *Myrmecomyia*) and *Polystodes*
(better *Polistoides*) taken together nearly correspond to the
genus *Michogaster* (better *Mischogaster*) of Macquart, placed
by the latter among the *Sepsidæ*. The size of the palpi and
the structure of the ovipositor do not justify this location, and
the genus undoubtedly belongs to the *Ortalidæ*.

Of the position of the genus *Stylophora* in the system I
cannot judge, not knowing the species upon which it is based.

Herina (the derivation of the name is not apparent) comprises species from the relationship of *Ortalis paludum*.

The genus *Myodina* (again a name of obscure derivation) is
based upon *Ortalis vibrans*, which R. Desvoidy took for *Ortalis
urticæ*. Macquart, in the *Suites à Buffon*, very erroneously
united this genus with *Ortalis*, throwing together various very
different species. Long before Rob. Desvoidy, Kirby had used
for *Ortalis vibrans* the generic name of *Seioptera*.

Richardia is founded either upon *Dacus podagricus* Fab., not
recognized by Rob. Desvoidy, or else on some closely allied
species.

Rivellia (probably a dedication name) contains species related to *Ortalis syngenesiæ*, and among them this very species, as
usual, not recognized by Rob. Desvoidy. Macquart in the *Suites
à Buffon* unites *Rivellia* with *Herina*, while the species really
belonging to it are put in the genus *Urophora*, or even in *Platystoma*; and upon one of them, in his later works, he even es-
tablishes a new genus, *Epiderma*.

Whether the genus *Boisduvalia* really differs from the preceding only in the length of the third antennal joint seems very
doubtful; should this be the case, the separation of these two
genera would not be justified.

Clidonia is considered by the author himself as belonging to
quite a different family, in which we will not contradict him.

Setellia seems to contain *Ortalidæ* resembling *Micropezidæ* in
their general appearance.

Chlorophora may also belong there, as Rob. Desvoidy especially mentions its relationship to *Setellia.*

The following among Rob. Desvoidy's genera belong therefore to the *Ortalidæ*: *Dichromyia, Palpomyia, Hexyquillia, Heramyia, Myoris, Oscinis, Blainvillia, Meckelia, Melieria, Myennis, Delphinia, Myrmecomyia, Polistoides, Herina, Myodina, Richardia, Rivellia, Boisduvallia.* Very probably *Setellia* and *Chlorophora* have to be added to them. The systematic position of *Stylophora* is doubtful. Genera not belonging to the *Ortalidæ* are: *Straussia, Vidalia, Acidia, Clidonia.*

(c.) *In Macquart.*

During his long career as an entomological writer, Macquart has several times changed his views with regard to the classification of the *Diptera acalyptera,* as was to be expected from the great difficulty of the subject. His opinion, however, on the extent of the family *Ortalidæ* has, during that time, undergone but little change. As, strictly speaking, he is the only writer who has attempted to establish a general system of the diptera, embracing all parts of the world, I consider it as my duty to give a detailed account of his views, the more so as they differ from mine in a not unimportant manner. To attain this end I will enumerate all those of his families, with their genera, which, according to my opinion, contain genera belonging to the *Ortalidæ,* as well as to the families closely connected with them, for instance, *Palloptera, Toxoneura, Lonchæa.* In order to show the progress made by Macquart during his dipterological studies I will give this in a twofold manner, that is, first after the *Suites à Buffon* and next after the *Diptères Exotiques.* Those genera which I consider as undoubtedly *Ortalideous* I have marked with an exclamation; those doubtfully introduced into this family I have designated by an interrogation. The genera related to the *Ortalidæ,* which I have united in the family *Pallopteridæ,* I have inclosed in brackets; the same I have done with the genus *Sapromyza,* because Macquart does not separate the species of *Palloptera* from the *Sapromyzæ,* although the typical *Sapromyzæ* have no relationship whatever with the *Ortalidæ.*

The review of the part of the system above alluded to, from the *Suites à Buffon,* is as follows:—

Scatomyridæ.
  Scatophaga,
  Dryomyza,
  (Sapromyza,)
  (Toxoneura,)
  Helomyza,
  Lucina,
  Helomyza,
  Blephariptera,
  Heteromyza.

Psilomydæ.
  Orygma,
  Trigonometopus,
  Eurina,
  Psilomyia,
  | Tetanops,
  | Pyrgota,
  | Otites,
  Platycephala,
  | Dorycera.

Ortalida.
  | Herina,
  | Ortalis,
  | Ceroxys,
  Clellamia,

  | Amethysa,
  | Notacanthina,
  Rhopalomera,
  | Eurypalpus,
  | Platystoma,
  | Lonchæura.

Tephritida.
  Dacus,
  Leptoxys,
  Bactrocera,
  | Senopterina,
  Petalophora,
  Urophora,
  Terellia,
  Tephritis,
  Acinia,
  Ensina.

Sepsida.
  Sepsis,
  Cheligaster,
  Nemopoda,
  | Cephalia,
  | Michogaster,
  Diopsis.

Thyreophorida.
  Thyreophora.

Leptopodita.
  Tanypeza,
  Calobata,
  Tænioptera,
  Micropeza,
  Nerius,
  Longina,
  | Setellia.

Ulidini.
  Actora,
  Cœlops,
  Gymnopoda,
  Lipara,
  | Ulidia.

Lauxanidæ.
  Lauxania,
  Pachycerina,
  (Lonchæa,)
  (Teremyia,)
  Pterocottia,
  Celyphus.

In the *Diptères Exotiques* the corresponding part of the system assumes the following shape, about which I have only to observe that in this work Macquart brings in only those genera in which he intended to describe, or at least to mention, exotic species; the genera *Toxoneura, Lucina, Tetanops, Otites, Platycephala*, etc., although not mentioned in this list, ought, in order to render it complete, to be transferred to it from the former.

Scatomyridæ.
  Scatophaga.

Sciomyridæ.
  Dryomyza,
  Tapriguster,
  (Sapromyza,)
  Phyrgota,

  Helomyza,
  Helomyza,
  Curtonotum.

Psilomyia.
  | Rametopia,
  Ectecephala,
  | Dorycera.

Ortalida.
  | Oxyocephala,
  | Loxoneura,
  | Platystoma,
  | Camptoneura,
  | Heteroguster,
  Rhopalomera,
  | Euripalpue,

: Enicmeura,   Cardiacera,   Sepsis.
Cleitamia,   Dacus,
I Richardia,   I Meracantha,   *Diopsides.*
I Senopterina,   Baclrocera,   Diopsis.
I Herina,   Enicoptera,
: Epidesma,   Ceratitis,   *Leptopodita.*
I Coronya,   Acanthoneura,   Longina,
I Ortalis,   Urophora,   Nerius,
I Amethyaa,   I Toxura,   Cardiacera,
I Lamprogaster,   Tephritis,   Calobata,
: Euprosopia,   Terellia,   Tanopoda,
I Cœlometopia,   Acinia,   Tanypeza,
I Notacanthioa,   ? Ephonrella,   I Satellia.
I Craphicera,   Ensina.
I Plagiocephala,   *Laxronida.*
I Campigaster.   *Sepsidæ.*   (Lonchæa,)
      I Cephalia,   Laurania,
Tephritida.   I Omalocephala,   I Ulidia,
I Odontomera,   : Cacopsida,   Zygothrica,
Leptosys,   Nemopoda,   Celyphus.

In the *Diptères Exotiques*, after the families I have enumerated the *Helomyridæ* and *Geomyridæ* follow, and after them the

Heteromyrida.
Heteromyza,
Actura,
I Dichromyia,
Cœlopa.

In examining the systematic distribution, introduced by Macquart in the *Suites à Buffon*, we soon find that as early as that work, he had, if not a definite knowledge, at least a correct instinct of the true characters of the *Ortalidæ*, less correct, however, than Rob. Desvoidy, who wrote before him.

Those genera which, in that work, he united in the family *Ortalidæ* really belong to it, with the exception of *Rhopalomera* and, very probably, of *Cleitamia;* the latter genus seems to be hardly distinct from *Henicoptera*, which belongs to the *Trypetidæ.*

A double error seems to be contained in the separation of the genera *Tetanops, Pyrgota, Otites,* and *Dorycera* from the *Ortalidæ* and their combination with *Orygma, Trigonometopus, Eurina, Psilomyia,* and *Platycephala* into one family, the *Psi-*

lomyde. Their relationship with the *Ortalide* is evident.
Among the genera which Macquart places in one family with
them, *Eurina* and *Platycephala* belong to the *Oscinidæ*, each
of the others to some other dipterous family; none shows any
close relationship to the *Ortalidæ*. In the *Diptères Exotiques*
Macquart has in part corrected this error, as at least *Oxycephala*,
of the identity of which with *Pyrgota* he was not aware, is put
among the *Ortalidæ*.

A second error is that the ortalideous genus *Stenopterina*
(Macquart incorrectly writes *Senopterina*) has been placed in
his family *Tephritidæ*. In the *Diptères Exotiques* Macquart
has amended this error.

A third mistake consists in Macquart having placed in his
genus *Urophora* several species which do not at all belong to his
family *Tephritidæ*; his *Urophora quadrivittata, fulvifrons*, and
several others, are true *Ortalidæ*.

Fourthly, the position of the genera *Cephalia* and *Michogaster*
(better *Mischogastra*, or at least *Mischogaster*) among the *Sep-*
sidæ cannot be sustained. As has been observed already, we
agree with Rob. Desvoidy in considering both as true *Ortalidæ*
on account of the large development of the palpi as well as of
the structure of the ovipositor.

Neither can I, in the fifth place, agree with Macquart in put-
ting *Setellia* among his *Leptopodidæ*; I refer it also to the *Or-*
talidæ, and this once more in agreement with Rob. Desvoidy.

A sixth error is the great interval between *Ulidia* and the
other *Ortalidæ*, as well as the whole composition of the family
Ulidini. *Lipara*, with which Macquart's genus *Gymnopoda* is
synonymous, belongs to the *Oscinidæ*; *Cœlopa* and *Actora* do
not belong to the same family, neither with *Lipara*, nor with
Ulidia, nor together. In the *Diptères Exotiques* Macquart did
rightly in dropping altogether the ill-conceived family of *Ulidinæ*.

I will not expatiate here on the incorrectness of the position
of *Palloptera, Toxoneura, Lonchæa*, and *Teremyia* (established
for *Lonchæa laticornis*), as this inquiry is of no especial importance to us.

It is easy to perceive that the system is improved in the *Dip-*
tères Exotiques; but even here *Dorycera* is misplaced among
the *Psilomydæ*, together with *Eumetopia* (which belongs to the
Ortalidæ).

In his family *Trypritidæ* the genus *Odontomera* is established, which is closely related to *Cœlomctopia* on one side and *Setellia* on the other, and must therefore be transferred to the *Ortalidæ*.

The same may be said of the genus *Meracantha*, the true place of which is in the vicinity of *Odontomera*, *Setellia*, *Cœlometopia*, *Richardia*, etc.

The genus *Toxura*, judging from the published figure, also belongs to the *Ortalidæ*, and indeed in the circle of relationship of *Pyrgota*; whether the examination of the insect itself would lead to the same result I do not pretend to affirm, as I have not seen it.

The figure of the head of *Epicerella* (*Dipt. Exot.*, Suppl. iv., Tab. xxvii.) might perhaps justify the supposition that the genus belongs to the *Ortalidæ*; nevertheless I think it more probable either that the frontal bristles, characteristic of the *Trypetidæ*, were broken off in Macquart's specimen, or that they have been omitted in the drawing. Thus I do not dare to express any opinion as to the correctness of the position assigned by Macquart to this genus.

Cephalia, in the *Diptères Exotiques*, is likewise put among the *Sepsidæ* instead of among the *Ortalidæ*.

Omalocephala (better *Homalocephala*, at all events, a preoccupied name) seems to belong in the vicinity of *Setellia*, *Cœlometopia*, etc., that is, in the family *Ortalidæ*.

The genus *Conopsidea*, as Macquart informs us, is founded upon *Cephalia femoralis* Wied.; in the *Suites à Buffon*, this same and two more species gave him occasion to establish the genus *Michogaster*. If these two data be correct, as we have every reason to suppose, *Conopsidea* would be a synonym of *Michogaster*; the emendation of the incorrectly formed name *Conopsidea* thus becomes useless.

The erroneous location of *Setellia* at the end of the *Leptopodiæ* is preserved.

Ulidia is transferred to the family *Lauxanidæ*, where it is a perfect stranger.

About the systematic position of *Zygothrica* (not *Zygotricha*, as Gray, in the *Animal Kingdom*, spells, in trying to improve it), a genus already proposed by Wiedemann in his essay on *Achias*, I can only form an opinion from the statements of Wiedemann and Macquart on the typical species, *Z. dispar*, as well as from their figures. It seems to me that this species may belong to the *Drosophilidæ.* In the Berlin Museum there is a little fly which apparently belongs to this genus; I have not been able to ascertain whether this species is *Z. dispar,* but I have seen enough not to doubt in the least of its belonging to the *Drosophilidæ.*

Dichromyia is wrongly placed by Macquart among the *Heteromysidæ,* between *Actora* and *Cœlopa.* I will maintain for the present its position among the *Ortalidæ,* although I cannot deny that a better place might perhaps be found for it; however, no such place has been pointed out yet. Besides the typical species, *Dichromyia sanguiniceps,* Macquart has another species from Africa, which, as I will show hereafter, cannot well belong to this genus.

About the genera which Macquart, in the *Diptères Exotiques,* places in the family *Ortalidæ,* I will make the following remarks:—

Oxycephala, as was mentioned before, is identical with *Pyrgota.*

Loxoneura is established for *Platystoma decora.*

Platystoma ismisused for the location of a number of heterogeneous forms; whatever had broad wings, with a dark picture, among the rest a *Trypeta,* was taken by Macquart for a *Platystoma.*

Camptoneura is a true ortalideous genus, based upon *Trypeta picta* Wied., and, as observed above, identical with *Delphinia* Rob. Desv. Macquart has likewise used this genus for the introduction of species not belonging there at all, for instance, of *Trypeta obscura* Wied.

Heterogaster (a preoccupied name) is a well founded genus in the neighborhood of *Pyrgota.*

Euripalpus (a hybrid name), judging from Macquart's data, belongs to the *Ortalidæ.*

The genus *Eniconeura* (better *Heniconeura*) is said to be distinguished by its spurless middle tibiæ. If such were really the case the genus could not belong to the *Ortalidæ,* nor to any of the allied families. But in *Heniconeura fenestralis* Macq., I perceive at the end of the middle tibiæ a rather strong spur, which is closely applied to the tarsus when the latter is stretched out. There cannot be any doubt, therefore, that the genus really belongs to the *Ortalidæ*.

Richardia, in the *Diptères Exotiques*, is with good reason entirely separated from *Herina*, with which it was united in the *Suites à Buffon*.

Senopterina (I have already corrected the name to *Stenopterina*) has been placed here where it really belongs, among the *Ortalidæ*.

Herina is a mixture of heterogeneous forms, which must be generically kept apart.

Epideema is probably synonymous with *Rivellia* R. Desv. ; moreover, Macquart has placed species of the latter genus under the head of *Herina*, of *Urophora*, and even of *Ceroxys*.

Ceroxys is a rather well founded genus, established at the expense of *Ortalis* Meig. But in the *Diptères Exotiques* Macquart adds species to it which do not at all share its characters ; for instance *Ceroxys cærulea*, etc. It almost seems, in such instances, that he mistakes this genus for another.

The genus *Ortalis* is a mixture of heterogeneous species ; how is it possible to crowd together in one and the same genus such species as *Ortalis ornata* Meig., *fasciata* Fab., *connexa* Fab., *frondescentiæ* Lin., *vibrans* Lin., and even the *Ortalis dentipes* Macq., said to be provided with spurs on the hind tibiæ? Either Macquart has not known these species or he has not closely examined them, otherwise he could not possibly have committed such a mistake ; how very confused his ideas about the systematic position of these species was, appears from the fact that he described *Scatophaga fasciata* Fab. as an *Ortalis*, and for a second time as *Tephritis* and that *Dictya connexa* Fab. even appears three times in his writings, as *Cordylura*, as *Ortalis*, and as *Tephritis!* (*Dipt. Exot.*, Suppl. iv., p. 292, *Tephritis dorsalis.*)

The true characters of *Amethysa* are not to be gathered from Macquart's definition of this genus. As the name alludes to the color of the African species, upon which the genus is established, it should be improved to *Amethysa*.

Lamprogaster is a well founded genus; but the species belonging to it show considerable differences in their organization which would fully justify a subdivision in several genera. It belongs in the vicinity of *Platystoma*.

Cœlometopia seems to be founded on *Trypeta trimaculata*
Fab., which Macquart did not identify; it is closely allied to
Odontomera and *Setellia.*

Euprosopia undoubtedly belongs to the *Ortalidæ.*

Notacanthina is founded upon *Tetanocera bispinosa* Fab.

The figure of the head of *Cruphiocera* (better *Cryphiocera*)
seems to indicate that the species would be better placed in some
other part of the system, as it has strong bristles on the forehead; the other characters, however, prove that its location
among the *Ortalidæ* cannot well be called in doubt.

The position of *Plagiocephala* among the *Ortalidæ* likewise
cannot be doubted; it seems closely related to *Richardia,* which
also contains broad headed species.

Campsigaster (a frightful compound) is undoubtedly well
placed among the *Ortalidæ,* but the name cannot be preserved
in its present shape.

(d.) In Walker.

Although Macquart's publications do not always define with
sufficient precision the systematic position of the genera introduced by him, this position could, in most cases, be made out,
and moreover, the attempt, on his part, of a systematic distribution is always apparent. Walker's publications on exotic diptera
do not, unfortunately, deserve this praise. The systematic de-
partment, as well as everything else in them, is treated with the
same superficial carelessness. In most cases it would be impossible to make out, from his statements, the real place in the
system which the genera, introduced by him, must occupy, unless
they were accompanied, as is often the case, by the excellent
figures of Westwood. These usually furnish the necessary data
concerning the relationship of the new genera; they would have
done so in all cases if Westwood's attention had been directed
to the sometimes very minute characters which are used in the
classification of the diptera and especially of the *Diptera acalyptera ;* the fact that in the majority of cases these characters are
reproduced in the figures, give a most brilliant proof of the ac-
curacy of Westwood's drawings, and of his keen perception.

Walker's publications in the *List of Dipt. Ins. of the Brit. Mus.,*
and in the *Insecta Saundersiana,* do not raise our expectations
very high, as the *Ortalidæ* and *Trypetidæ* are mingled together

generally; forms such as *Camptoneura picta* Fab., *Trypeta arcuata* Walk., *T. albocaria* Walk., *T. excepta* Walk., etc., are certainly no *Trypetidæ!* In Walker's later publications, the systematic confusion is still greater. As far as I can ascertain, among the genera published in the latter, *Adrana, Brea, Valonia,* are *Ortalidæ;* the two latter belong in the vicinity of *Platystoma.* The genera *Thepura, Strumeta, Sophira,* and *Riara* belong to the *Trypetidæ.* The genus *Xangelina* is closely related to *Physogenia,* perhaps identical with it, and hence, has to be placed among the *Sapromyzidæ.* The position of the genus *Xiria* remains doubtful, even in the presence of Westwood's figure; it shows some characters which make one doubt that it belongs to the *Diptera aciphorea* at all. The genera *Duomyia* and *Chromatomyia,* which, taken together, seem to correspond to *Lamproganter* Macq., and *Zona,* which is apparently identical with *Lasioneura,* are *Ortalidæ;* Walker, in the *List of Dipt. Ins,* etc., has erroneously placed them among the *Tachinidæ,* together with *Trigonostoma,* which likewise belongs to the *Ortalidæ* (however, he corrected this error in one of his later publications.)

(r.) In Bigot, Gerstæcker, Doleschall and Saunders.

In recent times it is to Bigot and Gerstæcker that the increase of our knowledge of exotic diptera is principally due.

The genera *Terastomyia, Maria, Agastrodes,* and *Pterogenia,* established by Bigot, belong to the *Ortalidæ.* *Elassogaster* likewise, although placed among the *Helomyzidæ* by Bigot, must be referred to the *Ortalidæ.* His genus *Elaphromyia,* on the contrary, if description and figure be correct, belongs to the *Trypetidæ.*

Gerstæcker has established the ortalideous genera, *Phytalmia, Gorgopis, Toxotrypana,* and *Diacrita,* and described several new species of *Richardia* and *Mischogaster.* *Phytalmia* has a synonym in Saunders's genus *Elaphomyia (Elaphomyia Wallacei* Saund. = *Phytalmia megalotis* Gerst.; *Elaphomyia cervicornis* Saund. = *Phytalmia cervicornis* Gerst.). The genus *Gorgopis* seems, as the author himself supposes, to be synonymous with *Zygænula paradoxa,* described somewhat earlier by Doleschall. If in the genus *Toxotrypana* the outer row of frontal bristles is really wanting, and it thus should really belong to the *Ortalidæ,* the not flattened ovipositor of this genus would place it in the neighborhood of *Pyrgota*, with which it also agrees in the small development of the clypeus. However, the ocelli are fully developed, and the structure of the head is rather like that of the true species of *Dacus*, as *Dacus oleæ*, etc., so that it might perhaps be considered as a genus of this group, in which, in conformity to the striking shortness of all the hairs of the body, the lateral bristles of the front have disappeared. This supposition seems confirmed by the scutellum which has only two bristles at the tip; and the uncovered last abdominal segment of the female, which is generally wanting in the *Dacina*, or is altogether concealed under the preceding segment, is not a positive objection, as this segment is very much abbreviated and much less horny than the preceding ones, and thus can very easily be concealed in the living insect.

Among the scattered publications of various authors many forms may be found which belong to the *Ortalidæ*. I purposely omit what I know of them, especially the gradually published species of the genera already discussed by me. It is not in my power to collect the residue, and I doubt whether such a work would materially alter the limits of the family *Ortalidæ* as they have resulted from the preceding discussion.

NATURAL CHARACTERS OF THE FAMILY ORTALIDÆ.

If we ask now what we have to erase or to modify in the characters of the original genus *Ortalis*, in Meigen's and Wiedemann's sense, in order to obtain the characters defining the whole family, the answer will be that it is very little indeed. In the first place, the mention of the pilosity of the front must be modified a little, as there are genera among the *Ortalidæ* which have no other bristle before the bristles of the vertex. Next to that, the description of the structure of the feet has to be changed thus, that in most genera they are short and strong, but in some rather elongate. In the third place, the statement about the female abdomen must be modified by saying that it has generally five segments, but that the fifth is very often shortened and concealed under the fourth, and that, in some cases, it entirely disappears, and then the abdomen has only four segments. In the fourth place, the introduction of *Pyrgota* and of the related genera in the family, requires a modification in the statement about the structure of the ovipositor, which is not flattened here; the chief stress in this statement should be laid upon the remainder of the structure, which is the same in all the genera. In the fifth place, the mention of the bristles on the first longitudinal vein should not be admitted in the definition of the family.

The definition of the *Ortalidæ* can therefore be put in the following manner : Front broad in both sexes ; on both sides of the vertex a more or less developed swelling runs down the front, upon which, before the bristle of the vertex, one or two erect bristles are inserted, which, however, are wanting in some genera. Otherwise the front has only the ordinary pubescence, or is quite bare, but never provided with a second row of strong bristles along the orbit, even when the hairs on both sides of the *villa frontalis* almost acquire, in some few genera, the character of bristles. Frontal fissure distinct ; frontal lunule never pushed so far up as to appear to be a part of the front ; even in those genera in which, on account of the great curvature of the frontal fissure, as in *Œdopa*, the lunule happens to lie higher than the antennæ, it always distinctly appears as a part of the face ; in many genera it is not distinguishable from the face. The vibrissæ are always wanting. The eyes are bare. The clypeus is always distinct, of various size, usually well developed. Proboscis more or less stout. Palpi rather broad, often very broad, very seldom narrow. Metanotum larger than usual, strongly projecting posteriorly and inferiorly. Feet generally rather stout and short, in some genera, however, of a considerable, although not striking, length and slenderness. Middle tibiæ distinctly spurred ; front and hind tibiæ spurless ; no erect præapical bristle before the end of the upper side of the tibiæ. The abdomen of the male has four segments, however the first consists of two coalescent segments, which is also the case in the females ; the but little developed fifth segment represents a small, more or less imbedded hypopygium ; the tape-like or thread-like penis is of an extraordinary length, rolled up in a spiral. The female abdomen consists of five segments, the fifth of which is often very much abbreviated, sometimes wanting, so that the abdomen of the female then seems to consist of only four segments ; the sixth, seventh, and eighth segments of the abdomen are converted into the three telescope-like, extensile joints of the ovipositor, ending in a simple, hairless point ; in most cases the ovipositor is flattened, and then its first joint often differs but little in its nature

and coloring from the preceding abdominal segments. The wings
show the complete venation of the *Diptera acalyptera;* the
auxiliary vein is entirely separated from the first longitudinal
vein, although often very much approximated to it; it runs into
the costa at a more or less acute angle, without becoming indistinct at its end; the two posterior, so-called small basal cells,
are of a rather considerable size.

RELATIONSHIP OF THE ORTALIDÆ.

The great variety of forms occurring among the *Ortalidæ*
accounts for the number of their near or distant connections
among other families. A relationship of the first degree, which
finds its most distinct expression in the similarity of the structure
of the male hypopygium and of the female ovipositor, connects
them with the *Trypetidæ* and the *Pallopteridæ,* as well as these
two families with each other. All three form a very close circle
of relationship, the members of which have very similar habits.

The *Ortalidæ* differ from the *Trypetidæ* in the absence of a
second, external row of frontal bristles, and in the course of the
auxiliary vein, which, in the *Trypetidæ,* is obliterated at the
end and turns rather abruptly, at a more or less right angle, towards the costa.

From the *Pallopteridæ,* the *Ortalidæ* differ in the more considerable size of the two posterior basal cells.

A relationship of the second degree connects the *Ortalidæ* with
the *Sepsidæ* and *Calobatidæ,* as well as these families with each
other. Both differ from the *Ortalidæ* distinctly in the structure
of the male hypopygium and the want of a horny, three-jointed
ovipositor, ending in a simple, hairless point. The *Sepsidæ* differ moreover in their rudimentary palpi from the *Ortalidæ,* as
well as from the *Calobatidæ.*

With those of the closely related families which, among their
characters, have an erect præapical bristle before the tip of the
tibiæ, and, at the same time, do not have any vibrissæ, that is,
with the *Sapromyzidæ* and *Sciomyzidæ,* the *Ortalidæ* have only
a very distant relationship. I would have left it unmentioned if
the genus *Rhopalomera,* which I consider as belonging to the
Sapromyzidæ, had not been placed among the *Ortalidæ.* The
presence of an erect bristle before the end of the tibiæ, the different structure of the hypopygium in the male, the absence of an

ovipositor, similar to that of the *Ortalidæ*, sufficiently distinguish the *Sapromyzidæ* and *Sciomyzidæ*.

DIAGNOSTIC OR ARTIFICIAL DEFINITION OF THE ORTALIDÆ.

The statements about the relationship of the *Ortalidæ* prove that the following characters are sufficient to distinguish this family from all the others, in other words, to constitute its artificial definition.

Male with a rolled-up, long penis; female with a three-jointed, horny ovipositor, ending in a simple point. Front without a second lateral row of bristles. No vibrissæ. Complete venation of the *Diptera acalyptera*; auxiliary vein distinct to its very tip, ending in the costa at an acute angle; the two posterior basal cells large. The middle tibiæ alone are provided with spurs; all the tibiæ are without an erect bristle before the end of their upper side.

II.

SYSTEMATIC DISTRIBUTION OF THE ORTALIDÆ.

THE last, but not the easiest, task which it remains for me to fulfil is the systematic distribution of the family *Ortalidæ*. In attempting it, I will principally confine myself to those genera and species which I possess in my own collection. Only in exceptional instances, and with especial caution, will I allow myself to transgress the limit of what I have, or have had, before me, as the statements concerning the other genera and species which have been published are seldom complete enough to afford the necessary data for the discrimination of their position in the system.

In order to obtain a preliminary survey I first divide the *Ortalidæ* in two large divisions; to the first belong those which have the first longitudinal vein beset with bristles or hairs; to the second, those the first longitudinal vein of which is bare.

FIRST DIVISION.

ORTALIDÆ WITH A BRISTLY OR HAIRY FIRST LONGITUDINAL VEIN.

Among the European *Ortalidæ* of this division five diverging forms will easily be noticed : 1. *Adapsilia;* 2. *Ortalis* Meig., of course to the exclusion of *O. syngenesiæ* and *vibrans;* 3. *Platystoma;* 4. *Cephalia;* and 5. *Scatophaga fasciata* Fab.

All the other European genera with a bristly first longitudinal vein can be grouped around these five types, with the exception perhaps of the somewhat recalcitrant genus *Psairoptera.* The same may be said of all the exotic *Ortalidæ* of this division which I know of. Thus, the *Ortalidæ* of the first division may be naturally divided into five groups.

We will characterize these groups only after having made out the genera which belong to them, and we will proceed to the discovery of these genera by means of the principal characters which distinguish the above-mentioned five types.

(32)

Adapsilia shows a striking character, distinguishing it from all the others, in the absence of ocelli and the not flattened ovipositor.

Scatophaga fasciata with its broad and low head, the circular shape of its third antennal joint, and the considerable distance intervening between the end of the auxiliary vein and that of the first longitudinal, has a general appearance which differs from the four other types so much that for a long time the close relationship of this species with the others was, for this reason, misunderstood.

Ortalis, *Platystoma*, and *Cephalia* differ in a very marked way in the mode of insertion of the bristles upon the pleure.

Ortalis has a strong bristle immediately above the basis of the fore coxæ ; this bristle is not extant in *Cephalia* and *Platystoma*.

Cephalia has above the middle coxæ, but below the longitudinal suture of the pleure, a strong bristle, which is also present in *Ortalis*, but entirely wanting in *Platystoma*. If, for the sake of brevity, I call the first *prothoracic*, the second *mesothoracic bristle*, the difference between these three genera will be as follows : *Ortalis* has a prothoracic and a mesothoracic bristle ; *Cephalia* has the mesothoracic bristle only ; in *Platystoma* both are wanting.

First Section: Pyrgotina.

I borrow the name of this group from the genus *Pyrgota* Wied., to which *Adapsilia* is most closely related. Both genera agree in the absence of ocelli, in the projecting front, the prolonged second antennal joint, the retreating face, the comparatively but little developed clypeus, the prolongation of the first abdominal segment in both sexes, and the contraction of the following segments in the female, as well as in the capsule-shaped structure of the first joint of the ovipositor, and in several other subordinate characters.

The principal difference between these genera consists in the structure of the antennal fovea, which, in *Adapsilia*, run down in a parallel direction as far as the edge of the mouth, and are separated by a straight ridge, while in *Pyrgota* they end at some distance from the edge of the mouth, and are more or less coalescent.

The South-African genus, *Hypotyphla*, founded by me, agrees

3

with *Pyrgota* and *Adapsilia* in the want of ocelli, and resembles
Adapsilia very much in the structure of the face; but it differs in
the but inconsiderable elongation of the first abdominal segment,
in the greater length of the other segments of the female abdomen,
and especially in the long, elongated-conical, but not flattened
ovipositor.

Judging by the figure which Macquart gives of his *Toxura
maculipennis*, I must suppose with a considerable degree of probability, that it likewise belongs in this circle of relationship.

I have no doubt that the interesting genus *Toxotrypana* Gerst.,
if placed in the family *Ortalidæ*, would find its location in the
section *Pyrgotina*, on account of its not flattened ovipositor, its
hairy first longitudinal vein, and the small development of its
clypeus. The presence of ocelli, the enormous length of the ovipositor, and the elongation of the posterior angle of the anal cell
into a very long lobe distinguish this genus from the other
genera of the group in a most marked manner. I have already
alluded to the fact that this genus shows some characters which
would seem to justify its location not among the *Ortalidæ* at
all, but among the *Trypetidæ* of the group *Dacina*.

Mr. Macquart has established the genus *Heterogaster* for a
South-African species. As the name he gave to this genus was
preoccupied a long time ago, I replace it by the name of *Sphenoprosopa*. This genus is very like *Adapsilia* in the structure of
the head; in the profile it projects considerably in front of the
eyes: the middle of the face forms a high and straight ridge
descending perpendicularly; alongside of it the antennal fovea,
which are further from the middle than usual, descend perpendicularly to the edge of the mouth. The cheeks are very broad.
The oral opening is very small, the clypeus but little developed,
and the proboscis not incrassated. *Sphenoprosopa* differs from
Adapsilia, *Pyrgota*, and *Hypotyphla* by the presence of distinct
ocelli, the great elongation of the third antennal joint, which
nearly reaches the edge of the mouth, the enormous development
of the last segment of the abdomen of the male, very approximated cross-veins, very parallel longitudinal veins, and a not
acute posterior angle of the anal cell. The first and third longitudinal veins are distinctly bristly. I have no doubt that
Sphenoprosopa belongs to the *Pyrgotina*, although, on the
other hand, I must acknowledge that several of the above-

quoted characters seem to point towards a relationship with
Platystoma. But I am prevented from laying much stress upon
them by the small development of the clypeus and the not incrassated proboscis, characters which are not usual in the circle
of relationship of *Platystoma*.

The typical species of the genus *Dichromyia*, proposed by
Rob. Desvoidy, is Wiedemann's *Tetanops sanguiniceps* from
Brazil. Macquart afterwards described a second species, *Dichromyia caffra*. I cannot approve of these two species being united
in the same genus. The front of *D. caffra* is much shorter, and
anteriorly it does not project as much in the profile as in *D. sanguiniceps;* moreover the ocelli are wanting here, while the other
species has them, and the vertical diameter of their eyes is much
longer than the horizontal, while in *D. sanguiniceps* the horizontal diameter exceeds the vertical; the scutellum is convex,
and the tegulæ very large, while *D. sanguiniceps* has a flat
scutellum and small tegulæ. Whether the longitudinal veins are
beset with bristles in the same manner in both species or not,
I cannot state positively; in *D. caffra* the first and third velum
are very distinctly beset with hairs; in *D. sanguiniceps*, if I
remember right, the first vein is beset with a hardly perceptible
pubescence, but I cannot positively affirm that such is the case.
But without insisting upon this difference, the others are sufficient
to justify a generic separation. For this reason I have established
for *D. caffra* Macq. a species generally found on an offensively
smelling plant, the new genus *Bromophila*.

As to the final decision about the place of the American genus
Dichromyia, I must leave it in abeyance until I have an opportunity to examine both sexes of *D. sanguiniceps*.

The ovipositor of the species of *Bromophila* is much more retracted than in the other genera of the present group; and
although not flattened, it is not at all incrassated; unfortunately
I have not been able to ascertain on any female specimen whether
the ovipositor ends in a simple point, as it seems to me it does.
Should this not be the case, the genus would not belong to the
Ortalidæ at all. At present I cannot find a better place for it
than in the neighborhood of *Pyrgota*.

I know of no other genera belonging to the *Pyrgotina*. At
present, therefore, the section is composed as follows:—

1. PYRGOTA Wied.; 2. ADAPSILIA Wagn.; 3. TOXURA Macq.;

4. HYPOTYPHLA Lw.; 5. TOXOTRYPANA Gerst.; 6. SPHENOPHO-
SOPA, Lw.; 7. DROMOPHILA, Lw.; and 8. DICHROMYIA, R. Desv.
The final decision about the location of *Toxotrypana*, *Dromo-
phila*, and *Dichromyia* is, of course, reserved.

The characters common to these eight genera are : oral opening small; proboscis not incrassated ; clypeus but little developed ;
no bristle upon the broad cheeks, and no bristle immediately
over the fore coxæ; the first longitudinal vein hairy ; the costal
vein soon attenuates beyond the end of the third longitudinal
vein. The ovipositor is not flattened.

Second Section : Platystomina.

The name of this section is derived from *Platystoma* Meig.,
the oldest and best known genus in it.

PLATYSTOMA is represented in Europe by a number of closely
allied species which must be considered as typical. We may
entertain different views on the extent of the genus *Platystoma*,
still we would not be justified in introducing in it, as has often
been done, species which, in the majority of the most important
characters, differ from the European *Platystomæ*. In fact, most
of the exotic species, described by different authors as belonging
to *Platystoma*, do not belong to it at all.

The *Dictya decora* Fabr., identical with *Tephritis violacea*
Gray, and placed by Wiedemann among the *Platystomæ*, has the
posterior angle of the anal cell drawn out into a long lobe ; this
character at once distinguishes this species, not only from *Platystoma* proper, but from all the genera closely related to it. Macquart was right in establishing the new genus LOXONEURA for it.
Walker afterwards called it *Zona*. Judging from the figure of
the head of *Loxoneura decora*, in profile, given by Macquart in the
Diptères Exotiques, this genus must belong to the *Platystomina;*
the absence of the pro- and mesothoracic bristles, and the only
four-jointed abdomen of the female confirm the correctness of
this location ; the fore femora are spinous.

Whether the South-American *Platystoma stictica* Fab. really
belongs to *Platystoma* is very doubtful.

Only a few of the species, placed by Macquart in the genus
Platystoma really belong there, for instance, none of his American species. *Platystoma fascipennis* and *ocellata* are *Ortalidæ*,
but belong to the *Pterocallina*, not to the *Platystomina*. *Platy-*

stoma *lunulata* belongs, unless the figure of the head is entirely incorrect, to the *Trypetidæ* and not to the *Ortalidæ*. The same may be said of *Platystoma latipennis*, of which Macquart does not give the *habitat*, but which is American.

In the same way as those species of Macquart, Walker's *Platystoma australis*, from Australia, does not belong to this genus. It seems even that not one of the Australian *Platystoma* hitherto described is a real *Platystoma*, and that this genus is confined to the three old continents.

Should we even confine, as we must necessarily do, the genus *Platystoma* to those species only which agree with the European species in the formation of the head, in the venation, and in the peculiar picture of the wings, we will find species in it which show some, and not unimportant, plastic differences. To the European species, the arista of which has only a short pubescence, may be opposed African species, some of which have the arista perfectly bare, and the scutellum very much swollen, with only four bristles upon it (for instance, *Platystoma asphaltina* Wied.); others, on the contrary, with a feathery arista. The latter are again divided in species, in which, as in the European species, the scutellum has six bristles, and the femora are unarmed (for instance, *Platystoma nigronotata* Lw.); and in such the scutellum of which has four bristles, and the front femora of which, on the under side, towards the tip, are armed with a few little spines. The latter, and among them *P. pectoralis* Lw., differ moreover from the former in the usually more metallic coloring of the conspicuously broad abdomen, the upper half segments of which have a much harder consistency than in the other species; and besides, in such species, the two parts of the first abdominal segment, which represent the first two abdominal segments of other diptera, are not completely coalescent. It results from the foregoing that *Platystoma* may easily be subdivided in four smaller genera, which can be distinguished by the following characters :—

1. Arista bare; femora unarmed; scutellum swollen, with four bristles ; type : *P. asphaltina* Wied.

2. Arista with a very short pubescence; femora unarmed; scutellum moderately convex, with six bristles ; type : *P. umbrarum* Lw.

3. Arista feathery; femora unarmed; scutellum moderately convex, with six bristles; type; *P. nigronotata* Lw.

4. Arista feathery; front femora spinose; scutellum but little convex, with four bristles; type: *P. pectoralis* Lw.

As in the remaining parts of the organization there is a great deal of agreement among all the *Platystomæ*, and as at the same time the number of the described species is not large enough to require a further subdivision of the genus, we may leave it undivided for the present. Walker's genus VALONIA is closely allied to *Platystoma*. Unfortunately, I possess only a single male of *Valonia complicata* Walk., which, moreover, is not very well preserved. The structure of the head, the thorax, and the feet, as well as the venation, do not show anything which would justify a generic separation from *Platystoma*. The facts that the second longitudinal vein is a little shorter, and more curved forward, and that the small crossvein is a little nearer the end of the discal cell, are evidently not sufficient for such a course. The very much swollen and apparently only too bristly scutellum, as well as the moderate breadth and smooth surface of the upper abdominal segments, would furnish a better ground for a separation from *Platystoma*. At all events, thus much is evident, that *Valonia* does not show any distinctive characters more important than those of the four genera would be in which, as I have shown above, *Platystoma* might be subdivided.

Platystoma cincta, from Port Jackson, described by Guérin (*Voyage de la Coquille*), may be considered as the type of a separate genus, allied to *Platystoma*. Several Australian and African species are closely connected with it. If I remember right, such species are designated in the Berlin Museum by the new generic name of *Pachycephala*. But as a genus *Pachycephalus* exists already, I propose the name SCHOLASTES. Such species differ from *Platystoma* in the head being larger, the front much broader, the portion of the face between the foveæ much more excavated, and the much narrower clypeus not protruding; the occiput likewise is much less swollen, so that the head is much more closely applied to the thorax, and appears entirely sessile in the profile; the thorax is much broader and flatter; the scutellum likewise, much larger and flatter, but with six bristles; the tegulæ are as much developed as in *Platystoma*. The structure of the abdomen and of the feet, as well as the venation, do not show any important difference from *Platystoma;* still it is worthy of notice that the under side of the front femora is beset with a row of little black bristles, which in the larger species assume the shape of slender spines. The coloring of the body is generally ochre, or ferruginous-yellow, usually with black longitudinal stripes on the thorax; the picture of the wings consists of numerous black spots, which often coalesce into cross-bands. In *Scholastes cinctus* Guér., and the species from Australia allied to it, the first half of the arista is feathery, the second bare, and on the thoracic dorsum there are two rather distant rows of short, but strong bristles. The African *Scholastes,* as the type of which I consider *S. repticula* Lw., from Guinea, have the whole arista bare and no trace of rows of bristles on the thorax. These characters may afford a ground for dividing *Scholastes* in two genera, in which case the present generic name would have to remain with the genus containing *S. cinctus* Guér.

Another genus, closely related to *Platystoma,* containing, as it seems, exclusively Australian species, is the genus LAMPROGAS-TER Macq., with which *Chromatomyia* Walk. is synonymous. The structure of the thorax, of the abdomen, and of the feet, as well as the venation, are very much in agreement with *Platystoma.* The tegulæ are large, larger than those of most *Platystoma.* The structure and the arrangement of the bristles of the front are likewise similar to those of *Platystoma;* only the third antennal joint is much longer; not only are the antennal foveæ also longer, but deeper and more sharply defined, on their inside especially; the clypeus is of the same breadth as in *Platystoma,* but not projecting; the palpi usually towards their end are not as broad as in *Platystoma,* and the occiput is less swollen; the scutellum is strikingly swollen and provided with six bristles. The abdomen of all the species is of a brilliant metallic color, which the scutellum and the middle of the thorax often share with it; on the latter, however, the metallic color is generally concealed by the presence of pollinose longitudinal stripes, and of an appressed pubescence of a light color. Otherwise, the coloring of the thorax generally is brown or chestnut-red, which color, in many specimens, also extends over the scutellum; the coloring of the wings consists of a few black spots. All the known species of *Lamprogaster* have unarmed femora and a bare arista;

in general, their plastic characters are so much alike that I cannot point out any peculiarity, among the species I know of, which might give rise to a generic subdivision.

Next to *Lamprogaster* stands a genus of which *Senopterina decora* Macq., from Tasmania, may be considered as the type; I call it EUCHALCOTA. The front is of about the same breadth as in *Lamprogaster*, but is flatter and altogether furrowed-scrobiculate. The third antennal joint is still longer here; the sharply defined, deep antennal fovea are once and a half the length of those of *Lamprogaster*, and reach almost altogether as far down as the front part of the lateral edge of the mouth; the arista is beset with a short pubescence near its basis, otherwise bare; the clypeus is perceptibly narrower; the occiput is less swollen, so that the head is more closely applied to the thorax. The latter is strongly built, but not as broad in the region of the wings, and hence, of a more equal breadth; scutellum convex, but not swollen, provided with six bristles. The venation is similar to that of the preceding genera, but differs in the fourth vein being gently curved forward before its end, and in the third vein being gently bent backward, so that the first posterior cell is distinctly attenuated towards its end. The coloring of thorax and abdomen is altogether metallic. In thus defining the characters of the genus, I have taken in consideration some species from Australia, which can very well be placed in the same genus with the above named typical species; nevertheless, they show the following differences: the wings are comparatively longer and without any picture, while in *Euchalcota decora*, the cross-veins have dark borders alongside of them; there are no other bristles in front of the row of bristles along the posterior part of the thoracic dorsum, while in *E. decora*, there are some few shorter and thinner bristles immediately in front of that posterior row. There is no necessity for a generic separation yet. I cannot identify any of my species from Australia in a satisfactory manner; it may be that *Chromatomyia laeta* Walk. belongs here.

It would be difficult to explain why Macquart places *Euchalcota decora* in his genus *Senopterina*. The structure of the face and the shape of the thorax are entirely different. The comparatively narrow abdomen of the male (I have not seen the other sex) is almost the only point of resemblance.

The genus DUOMYIA, of Walker, is probably closely allied to
the above named two genera. Its definition is too insufficient
to enable us to form a trustworthy opinion. The irregularly
formed name cannot possibly be preserved.

Two species closely related to each other, belonging to the
section *Platystomina*, Macquart (in the *Dipt. Exotiques*) has described as *Tephritis cærulea*, and *strigipennis*. With several
other Australian species, very similar to them, they can be united
in a genus which may be called CELETOR. The very striking
characters of this genus are the following: The structure of the
body is *Trypeta*-like, with the exception, however, of the head.
Front of an equal breadth, very steep and long, so that the antennæ are situated much deeper than in any other genus of the
present group; the front is evenly and rather densely pilose;
the bristles of the vertex and the lateral bristles, closely approximated to them are rather stout; the ocelli are near the edge of
the vertex and closely approximated to each other; the two
bristles, which otherwise are near them, are wanting here. Antennæ short, hardly reaching beyond the middle of the face;
their third joint of equal breadth, with an acute anterior angle;
antennal arista slender, bare. Middle portion of the face concave; clypeus rather broad, projecting; proboscis stout; palpi
rather broad towards their end. Eyes very high and narrow;
cheeks broad; the lower part of the occiput strongly turgid.
Thorax strongly developed, rather of an equal breadth; scutellum turgid, overhanging the perpendicular metathorax, with six
bristles. Abdomen with four segments in both sexes, as in the
preceding genera; the last segment of the female abdomen
generally of a softer consistency. The first joint of the ovipositor flattened, always entirely protruding, suddenly attenuated
near the basis, more gradually towards the tip, thus having
an almost oval outline. Wings rather large, broad towards the
basis; the auxiliary vein lies very near the first longitudinal, its
end, however, diverges from it at an obtuse angle towards the
costa, and preserves its distinctness and stoutness to the very
tip. Otherwise, the venation is not unlike that of *Platystoma*,
Lamprogaster, etc., only the small crossvein is beyond the last
third of the discal cell, a position somewhat reminding of *Valonia*
Walk. The coloring of the body is blackish-blue, seldom verging
on greenish; the front red or reddish-brown; the lateral borders

with white pollen; wings hyaline; all the four species known to me have crossbands, connected near the anterior margin, thus forming an inverted Λ, and with a third black band, bordering the apex; moreover, near the basis of the wing there is a large spot in the shape of a band, or numerous black spots which form a kind of network, not unlike that of some species of *Ptilophora*. This difference in the picture of the wings is accompanied by some plastic differences which, if the number of species were larger, could serve for a subdivision in two genera. Those species which have the large spot in the shape of a crossband near the basis of the wings have at the same time the lateral parts of the face very broad, while they are very narrow in the species which have the picture in the shape of a network; the former have the posterior angle of the anal cell smaller, the latter larger than a right angle, so that in the former, the angle is a large acute one, in the latter, a small obtuse one. One of the species from Australia in my collection, belonging to the second group, is distinguished by the very abnormal structure of the hind tibia of the male. Among the species already published, besides the two described by Macquart, and mentioned above as typical, *Ortalis trifasciata* Doleschall, from Amboina, may likewise, perhaps, belong to the genus *Celetor*.

Macquart, in the *Diptères Exotiques*, describes as *Eniconeura violacea* a species distinguished by some peculiar characters, which undoubtedly is to be considered as the type of a distinct genus of *Platystomina*. The name *Eniconeura*, or more correctly *Heniconeura*, cannot be retained, as it has been already used by Macquart himself for a genus of *Bombylidæ*. The genus may be called CLITODOCA. According to that author it inhabits the East Indies; but this statement may perhaps be erroneous, as I have seen a fly said to be from Guinea, and in which I think I recognize Macquart's species; there is a slight difference in the picture of the wing, as represented on Macquart's figure, but the agreement of the description is perfect, and seems fully to justify my supposition. By all means the species is a *Clitodoca*. The characters of *Clitodoca* may be put down as follows: head large, almost square, with a very short longitudinal diameter; antennæ narrow, descending to the middle of the face; arista with a distinct pubescence; face concave, its lateral portions very narrow; oral opening very large, broader than long; clypeus not

disciform, but representing a swelling of the gula, and hence, reminding of a similar structure in *Loxoneura*, in which it fills the
greater part of the oral opening. Proboscis but little swollen;
palpi of a moderate breadth. Thorax very stout. Abdomen
comparatively very short and narrow, consisting of four segments. Feet long; wings very large; the end of the auxiliary
vein almost obliterate; the second longitudinal vein very strongly
bisinuate; the third and fourth strongly convergent towards
their end; the posterior crossvein very oblique; all the basal
cells very long; the anal cell has an acute posterior angle.

Among the species which Wiedemann places in the genus
Ortalis, there are three closely allied ones, which do neither belong in the genus *Ortalis*, nor in the group *Ortalina*. They
have to form a separate genus in the group *Platystomina*, which
I will call ENGISTONEURA. They are: *Ortalis moerens* Fab.,
parallela Wied., and *lugens* Fab.; *Trypeta albovaria* Walk.,
may be added as a fourth species, unless it is synonymous with
O. moerens Fab., which may possibly be the case. The following characters distinguish the genus *Engistoneura*. They are
large flies of yellowish coloring, with a very much developed
thorax, especially broad between the roots of the wings; its convexity, however, is very small; the abdomen is comparatively
small, of a metallic violet color. The structure of the head somewhat reminds of *Dacus*. The antennæ reach the middle or a little
below the middle of the face; the long arista is distinctly
feathery. The foveæ, which reach a little below the middle
of the face, are very sharply defined. Clypeus distinct; proboscis of moderate stoutness, with a but little developed mentum; palpi rather broad. Scutellum large, but little convex,
overhanging the metathorax more than in most of the other
genera of the *Platystomina*; it has six bristles. Abdomen
rather cylindrical. Feet of moderate length and not very strong;
the front femora on the under side, in the vicinity of the tip, with a
few bristle-like spines. Wings large, rather narrow towards the
base, broad towards the apex; auxiliary veins of moderate
length, turning abruptly towards the costal margin, and becoming almost obliterate; the first longitudinal vein approaches
closely to the margin beyond the end of the auxiliary vein, and
runs alongside of it as far almost as the end of the second longitudinal vein; the third longitudinal vein is strongly bent back-

ward, the fourth vein slightly forward, so that the first posterior
cell, very broad in the middle, is rather narrow at the end; the
small crossvein is beyond the middle of the discal cell; the two
posterior basal cells are of a rather considerable and equal length;
the posterior angle of the anal cell is rounded. The extensive
picture of the wings forms, in the vicinity of the apex, more or
less regular crossbands.

The genus AMPHICNEPHES, which I have established for a
North American species, will be characterized in the sequel. It
is somewhat like *Platystoma*, but distinguished by the not
swollen occiput, the flat scutellum, provided with only four
bristles, the broad wings and the striking divergency of the
longitudinal veins.

A pretty *Ortalida* from Cuba, which cannot conveniently be
placed in any of the existing genera, gave occasion for the
establishment of the genus HIMERODESSA, which I will characterize below among the other North American genera. It is distinguished by the narrowness of the marginal and submarginal
cells; moreover, the posterior crossvein is prolonged inside of
the first posterior cell.

Ortalis syngenesiæ Linn. is the type of a very well justified
genus, existing in Europe, Africa, Asia, and America, which
Rob. Desvoidy called RIVELLIA. Although the name is not
particularly well chosen, the objections against it are not serious
enough for its rejection. Besides the species described by Rob.
Desvoidy, the following belong to the genus *Rivellia*: *Trypeta
basilaris* Wied., *Dacus succinctus* Wied., *Ceroxys quadrifasciata* Macq., *Ortalis Ortorda* Walk., *Tephritis melliginis* Fitch.,
and several others. Most of them agree quite well with the species placed in the genus *Rivellia* by Rob. Desvoidy; others, however, show a very gradual transition towards allied forms, which
cannot very well be united in the same genus with the typical
Rivelliæ. Thus Macquart has established for one of them the
genus *Epiderma*. The transitions, however, are so gradual, that
it is not very easy to decide upon the best boundary for the
genus *Rivellia*. *R. viridulans* R. Desv., and all the North
American species which I know of, agree in their generic characters with *Rivellia syngenesiæ* completely; the same is the case
with *R. basilaris* Wied., and with several *Rivelliæ*, from the
southeastern region of Asia, which I possess in my collection;

the only difference shown by the latter species is a somewhat smaller length of the third antennal joint. Next to these are some South African *Rivelliæ*, for instance, *Rivellia atra* Lw., which have the third antennal joint a little shorter still; all these species, however, cannot be separated from *Rivellia*, as the diminution of the third antennal joint is a very gradual one, not affording any distinct limit for a separation.

Macquart's EPIDESMA *fascipennis*, from the Cape, is likewise but very little different from the typical *Rivelliæ*. The occiput is somewhat more convex; the third antennal joint has a somewhat sharper anterior angle, the thorax is comparatively a little smaller, and the first section of the fourth longitudinal vein shows but very little of the sinuosity, so characteristic of the true *Rivelliæ*, and which renders the anterior part of the discal cell more narrow; at the end of the convex scutellum there are two strong bristles; whether the second pair of bristles, which exists in the other *Rivelliæ*, is wanting here, or whether they were accidentally broken off in the specimen I had before me, I am unable to decide; I rather incline to favor the former supposition. If I am right, *Epidesma* would deserve to be retained as a separate genus; in the opposite case, it would be better to place *Epidesma fascipennis* in the genus *Rivellia*, because then the whole difference between them would merely consist in comparative characters.

Among the species from the southeast of Asia, there are several which are closely allied to *Rivellia*, but differ from the typical species in the greater length and lesser breadth of the marginal cell, a more straight third longitudinal vein, and a hardly perceptible sinuosity of the first section of the fourth vein; moreover, the thorax is less strongly developed, so that their stature shows some, although only a distant, resemblance to the species of *Stenopterina*. They are easily distinguished by the picture of their wings, which is very different from that of the *Rivelliæ*; it consists in a conspicuous black border along the costal margin and the apex, not unlike that of *Diacrita* and *Melanoloma*, while the *Rivelliæ*, besides the apex, which is margined with black, also have black crossbands. I propose for this genus the name of SCOTINOSOMA.

Species having the first section of the fourth longitudinal vein straight, must, most decidedly, be eliminated from *Rivellia*.

Such is a group of closely related African species, which I unite
in the genus ARDELIO. The lateral portions of their face are
distinctly broader than in *Rivellia*, the eyes not so high, and the
cheeks, for this reason, broader; the clypeus is narrower and the
thorax more strongly developed; the convex scutellum has four
bristles, like *Rivellia*. They almost show more affinity to *Platystoma* than to *Rivellia*; all the species known to me are black,
with longitudinal lines of white dust on the thorax, and their
wings have black crossbands, between which, along the costal
margin, there are black spots or streaks. The single species
show, in the length of the third antennal joint, still more considerable variations than the species of *Rivellia*, and it almost
seems that, in this respect, they might be divided in two sections,
one of which would be represented, as a type, by *Ardelio longipennis* Lw., the other by *A. brevicornis* Lw.

The genus EPICAUSTA, established by me for two African species, is less allied to *Rivellia* than to *Stenopterina*, which will
be discussed below. These species are like *Stenopterina* in their
stature, but are not so slender; the head is not unlike that of the
species of *Dacus* proper; the antennæ are not quite as long as
in *Stenopterina*; the fore coxæ are much shorter, and not so
movable; the thorax, seen from the side, is not attenuated in
front, as is the case with *Stenopterina*; the scutellum has four
bristles, as in the latter genus; the wings are conspicuously
shorter, and the last section of the fourth longitudinal vein is
much more bent forward. The small crossvein is not oblique,
as in all *Stenopterinæ*, but perpendicular. The picture of the
wings, in both of the species known to me, consists only in a
large black spot at the tip.

STENOPTERINA, a genus proposed by Macquart in the *Suites à
Buffon*, is well founded, as long as it is confined to the species
of the immediate relationship of *Dacus brevicornis* Fab. and
æneus Wied. Unfortunately the same author, in the *Diptères
Exotiques*, has entirely left out of sight the characters of this
genus, established by himself, and has introduced in it a number
of heterogeneous forms, and, at the same time, placed in the
genus *Herina* species which either belong to *Stenopterina* or
are more closely related to it than to any other genus. His
Stenopterina femorata and *immaculata*, both from Bourbon,
seem to belong rather to *Epicausta* than to *Stenopterina*;

Stenopterina decora Macq. is, as has been observed above, the typical species of the genus *Euchalcota; S. gigas, scutellaris,* and *nigripes* of Macquart, all three from Tasmania, are certainly no *Stenopterina.* There would be more ground to place in that genus the *Ortalis violacea* of Macquart, which is probably correctly identified in the Berlin Museum with *Dacus macularis* Fab. *Herina mexicana* Macq. also belongs to *Stenopterina,* and *H. calcarata* Macq., although perhaps not a true *Stenopterina,* is closely related to that genus. The three species described by Walker (*List of Dipt. Ins.*), *bicolor,* of unknown origin, *trivittata,* from the Philippine Islands, and *basalis,* from Australia, do not seem to have anything in common with true *Stenopterinæ.* A true *Stenopterina* is *S. submetallica* Lw., from Mozambique; and *Herina chalybea* Doleschall, belongs probably to the same genus.

As I will have to characterize *Stenopterina* in detail among the North American genera of *Ortalidæ,* it will suffice here to indicate the principal characters. Head resembling that of *Dacus* in structure; occiput convex, but not swollen. Front of a considerable and even breadth. Antennæ long and narrow, generally descending a little beyond the anterior edge of the mouth, which is somewhat drawn upwards; clypeus broad; proboscis stout. Thorax narrow; the pectus ascending obliquely in front, so that the thorax, seen from the side, is rather conspicuously attenuated anteriorly. Fore coxæ remarkably long, inserted unusually near the neck and very movable in this insertion. Scutellum with four bristles. Abdomen narrow; wings long and narrow; little crossvein oblique, placed beyond the middle of the long discal cell; the third and fourth longitudinal veins, in the majority of the species, are somewhat bent towards each other, so that the first posterior cell becomes narrower towards its end. In all the species I know of, the stigma, as well as a border between it and the apex, and the first basal cell, up to the small crossvein, are tinged with brown; in most species the posterior crossvein has likewise a dark border.

The next genus to be mentioned here is the genus MYSCHO-GASTER Macq., founded upon *Cephalia femoralis* Wied. *Myschogaster pernix* and *diffusus* Gerst., belong to it. It differs from *Cephalia* in the absence of a mesothoracic bristle, and in the face, which does not project inferiorly; from the following genus it is

distinguished by the first abdominal segment being beset with
bristles. This character, as well as the somewhat advanced position of the anterior ocellus, remind of the *Richardia.* The
face is rather short and somewhat excavated.

The last genus which I place among the *Platystomina* forms the
transition from this group to the *Cephalina,* and shows a good
deal of approximation to the genus *Cephalia.* As the typical species of this genus I consider *Cephalia myrmecoides* Loew. Besides the want of a mesothoracic bristle, this genus differs from
the true *Cephalia* in the fact that the first abdominal segment is
so coarctate in its middle that its anterior part forms a knot-
shaped swelling; moreover, the shape of the body is still more
slender; the wings still narrower and still more cuneiform
towards the basis, so that the anal angle and the alula disappear
entirely, whereas in *Cephalia,* there is at least a rudiment of
them. The statements which Rob. Desvoidy makes about his
genus *Myrmecomyia* render it probable that the above-mentioned
species belongs to this genus. Certainty in this case is not possible, without the comparison of the species upon which Rob.
Desvoidy established the genus. Not wishing to run the risk of
introducing a useless generic name, I prefer to use the name of
MYRMECOMYIA for my species. The pleonastic name which the
species thus obtains, *Myrmecomyia myrmecoides,* is not good,
but may be tolerated in view of the fact that nothing is more
like an ant than this dipteron.

A review of the genera which I placed among the *Platystomina* shows that, besides the bristles upon the first longitudinal
vein, and the absence of prothoracic and mesothoracic bristles,
which define this group, these genera have the following characters in common: The oral opening is very large; the clypeus
generally very much developed, and the proboscis proportionally
stout; the third antennal joint is elongate; the thoracic dorsum
bristly upon its hind part only; the female abdomen has four
segments, as the fifth is either altogether wanting, or only rudimentary and then completely hidden under the fourth segment.

Third Section: Cephalina.

I call this group after the genus which was first made known
in it. It differs from the *Platystomina* in the presence of a

metathoracic bristle, from the *Ortalina*, in the absence of the
prothoracic one. With the former it moreover agrees in the
larger size of the oral opening, the greater development of the
clypeus and the stouter proboscis; with the latter it has the
more or less distinct development of the fifth segment of the
female abdomen in common. While some of the genera show a
very close affinity to the *Platystomina* in general appearance,
others stand as near to the *Ortalina*, so that the *Cephalina* seem
to form a transition from the first to the second of those sections.

The genus CEPHALIA, introduced by Meigen, shows some
affinity to those genera of *Platystomina*, the species of which are
distinguished by their slender shape, especially to the genera
Mischogaster and *Myrmecomyia*. It necessarily must be confined to those species which, like the typical *Cephalia rufipes*
Melg., have a mesothoracic bristle. The species added later to
it, although in their general shape and their coloring they more
or less resemble the true *Cephaliæ*, do not show the necessary
agreement with them in those characters which are the most
trustworthy in the establishment of the genera of *Ortalidæ*. They
belong in the group *Platystomina* and principally in the genus
Mischogaster, in part also in the genus *Myrmecomyia*. The
genus *Cephalia*, in this narrower sense, does not contain as yet
any American species. As, for this reason, I will have no occasion to refer to it again, I will characterize it here :—

Body slender, abdomen narrow at the basis, its first segment
without any knot-shaped swelling; feet rather long and slender.
Hairs on the body extremely short; thorax with a few small
bristles on the lateral and the posterior portions only; the bristles
before the scutellum and its own lateral bristles are very short.

Antennæ long and slender; their second joint short. Face
shield-like, convex, without antennal fovea.

Palpi very broad; proboscis rather stout and mentum somewhat swollen.

Wings attenuated towards the basis in the shape of a wedge,
with a very narrow alula; the second longitudinal vein hardly
sinuose at all; the third and fourth longitudinal veins normal in
their course; the anterior basal cell of equal breadth; the first
longitudinal vein bristly towards its end only; the crossveins
rather distant from each other; the picture of the wings usually

4

consists of an infuscation of the stigma and of a black spot on the apex.

Cephalia is immediately connected with a genus embracing *Trypeta flexa* Wied. and the genera related to the latter. As this genus does not coincide with any one of the hitherto adopted genera, it must receive a new name. I call it TRITOXA, the name alluding to the peculiar picture of the wings. The *Tritoxa* differ from the *Cephaliae* in the presence of a strong bristle before the end of the fore tibiae, on their upper side, and in the presence of a weak indication of antennal fovea, especially, however, in the fact that the third and fourth longitudinal veins have an irregular course, in consequence of which the anterior basal cell is expanded before its end; moreover also in the first longitudinal vein being, to a great extent, covered with bristles and in the approximation of both crossveins to each other. The wings have a dark coloring and the picture consists of three oblique, more or less arcuated, hyaline crossbands. The other characters the genus *Tritoxa* shares with the genus *Cephalia.*

After *Tritoxa* CAMPTONEURA naturally follows. The typical species is the well-known North American species, described by Fabricius as *Musca picta*, and afterwards erroneously placed by Wiedemann in the genus *Trypeta.* Rob. Desvoidy was the first to found a new genus for it, which he called *Delphinia;* Macquart established later for the same species the genus *Camptoneura*, which thus coincides with *Delphinia.* As the name *Delphinia* cannot be retained for reasons of priority, Macquart's name must be adopted. *Camptoneura* differs from *Tritoxa* in a striking manner in the structure of the wings; they are broad, and show, on the costal margin, near the end of the auxiliary vein, a shallow, but very striking excision; the third longitudinal vein is very remarkably sinuate, and the anal cell rounded at the end. The picture of the wings has a distant resemblance to that of the species of *Aciura.*

The other genera of *Cephalina* which I know of contain species of a less slender stature than the three genera which I have just examined.

Among them the genus PIARA, founded by me for an African species, is remarkable for its close relationship to the *Platystomina.* It may be characterized as follows:—

Body rather robust, the bristles upon the vertex, upon the posterior part of the thorax and upon the scutellum long.

Antennæ of medium length; the anterior corner of the third joint acute; arista feathery. Face excavated above, and with a projecting bump below.

Oral opening broader than long; proboscis very stout.

Wings rather broad; longitudinal veins diverging; the first, third, and fifth beset with bristles; posterior angle of the anal cell not acute; the picture of the wings is not unlike that prevailing in the genus *Aciura*.

Rather closely related to *Piara* is the genus TRAPHERA, which I propose to establish with *Ortalis chalybea* Wied. for its type. It also stands very near the *Platystomina* and may easily be considered as one of them, as the mesothoracic bristle is but very little conspicuous and the fifth segment of the female abdomen is also very much abbreviated. The principal differences between *Traphera* and *Piara* lie in the structure of the head and of the wings. The head of *Traphera* is not unlike that of *Platystoma*, but the lower part of the occiput is but very little turgid; the vertical diameter of the eyes is very long, the horizontal, on the contrary, very short; the first two antennal joints are short; the third pointed oval; the arista feathery; the face is descending obliquely, excavated under the antennæ, convex below; the clypeus is very much developed, its vertical diameter rather large, the horizontal one small; proboscis very much incrassated. Thorax stout and convex; its dorsum is provided with bristles only on the sides and posteriorly. Scutellum generally with eight bristles. Wings comparatively short and broad, with bristly hairs on their anterior margin; the whole of the first longitudinal vein is strongly bristly and shows, in the vicinity of the somewhat obliterate end of the auxiliary vein, a peculiar break; the basal half of the third longitudinal vein is beset with bristles; the posterior crossvein is oblique, so that the posterior angle of the discal cell is very acute; the anal cell is rounded at the end and its posterior angle withdrawn in a peculiar manner. The wings are of a dark color, marked with pale bands starting from the posterior margin and abbreviated in front.

While both of these genera are very near the *Platystomina*, the two which we have yet to mention approach the *Ortalina*. They are: DIAGRITA, introduced by Gerstæcker, and a genus to be

adopted for *Ortalis marginata* Say, for which I propose the name
of IDANA.

Diacrita is easily distinguished from *Idana* by the shape of
the posterior angle of the anal cell, which is drawn out in a very
long lobe, and by the picture of the wings, which consists only
in a very broad dark border, extending to the very apex of the
wing. The more extended picture on the wings of *Idana* is not
unlike that of *Pteropoecila* and the posterior end of its anal cell
forms only a short angle. As both genera contain North American
species, I will have occasion to refer to them again more in detail.

Fourth Section: Ortalina.

The *Ortalina* have a prothoracic, as well as a mesothoracic
bristle, while among the *Cephalina*, the former, among the *Platystomina*, both are wanting. The *Ortalina* are also distinguished
from the two above-named groups by a smaller oral opening, a
less developed clypeus, a less stout proboscis, a less turgid
mentum and smaller palpi. In several genera, moreover, the
thoracic dorsum is beset with bristles as far as its anterior
portion. The abdomen of the female has five segments, which
brings this group nearer to the *Cephalina* than to the *Platystomina.*

The geographical distribution of the *Ortalina* is, as far as
known, confined exclusively to America and to Europe, with
those parts of Asia which belong to the faunal province of the
latter. Very striking is the great agreement between the
European and North American forms of this group. As the
knowledge of the latter is still very fragmentary, the generic
distribution of the probably numerous species which may be
discovered yet would offer great difficulties, or lead into error,
unless based upon the knowledge of the European genera. I
will give here, for this reason, a review of all the European
genera adopted at present. Besides these, however, to the
Ortalina must be reckoned the genus APOSPAEMICA, which I
propose to establish for the South American *Ortalis fasciata*
Wied. and the genus ACTOMOLA, which I have adopted above for
Ortalis trifasciata Wied. and *atomaria* Wied.

The European genera of *Ortalina* are the following:—

1. DORYCERA Meig.

Charact.—Eyes round; cheeks very broad; face very much projecting in profile; inferiorly it is very strongly retreating, carinate.

The hairs on the body have the ordinary length, or a little over the ordinary; thoracic dorsum bristly on its hind portion only.

Antennæ projecting, either of ordinary breadth and medium length, with the third joint oval; or narrow and elongate, with an elongate third joint.

The first longitudinal vein bristly at its end only.

This genus contains gray species, their faces with dark spots, and with well-marked black stripes upon the thorax; the wings are either without any picture, or it consists of blackish-gray longitudinal lines, which are more confluent towards the apex, and even, in the male of one species, form a large, black spot.

The genus may be divided into two sections, which it will be necessary, when the number of species grows larger, to separate as genera.

Sect. 1. (*Dorycera*, sensu strict.) Antennæ narrow and very much prolonged; the pilosity of the body is of an ordinary length.

Typical species: *graminum* Fab.

Sect. 2. (*Percnomatia* Lw.) Antennæ of ordinary breadth and of medium length; pilosity of the body longer than usual.

Typical species: *inornata* Lw.

2. TETANOPS Fall.

Charact.—Eyes rounded-ovate; cheeks broad. Face in the profile very much projecting, more or less retreating inferiorly.

The hairs upon the whole body extremely short; the middle of the thoracic dorsum bristly on its hind part only; the prothoracic bristles are smaller than in all the other genera of *Ortalina*.

Antennæ short, often strikingly short; their third joint oval; somewhat longer than the second.

The first longitudinal vein is bristly at its end only.

This genus contains remarkably glabrous species; there are no thoracic stripes; the first segment of the ovipositor is comparatively large; there is no picture on the wings at all, or it consists only in narrow borders along the crossveins, or in more or less faded spots at the end of the longitudinal veins, thus resembling the picture of *Ceroxys*.

Typical species: *myopina* Fall.

3. CORMOCARIS LW.

Charact.—Eyes round; cheeks very broad; face in the profile strongly projecting, very much retreating inferiorly, not carinate.

Hairs on the body comparatively long; thoracic dorsum hairy and bristly as far as its anterior portion.

Antennæ short; the rounded oval third joint hardly as long as the second.

First longitudinal vein bristly at its end only.

Gray species, the abdomen and thorax of which are without any picture, and the wings dusky and somewhat spotted along the anterior margin.

Typical species: *bucephala* Meig.

4. PTEROPŒCILA LW.

Charact.—Eyes small, rounded oval; cheeks broad; front very much projecting.

Hairs on the body of the usual length; the middle of the thorax bristly on its hind portion only.

The rounded third joint of the antennæ short; the second likewise short.

The first longitudinal vein is hairy upon its whole length.

The coloring of the body is gray; the picture of the wings is not unlike that of *Idana marginata* Say.

Typical species: *lamed* Schrk.

5. PTILONOTA LW.

Charact.—Eyes elongated oval; front but little projecting.

Thorax bristly upon its middle, as far as its anterior portion.

The third antennal joint rounded oval; the second shorter.

The first longitudinal vein bristly at its end only.

Cinereous-gray species, the thorax of which is marked with four somewhat darker longitudinal lines; the picture of the wings consists of large blackish spots; in several species these spots are so much confluent that the picture of the wings can almost be called guttate.

Typical species: *centralis* Fab.

6. ORTALIS Fall.

Charact.—Eyes rather large, elongate oval; front only moderately projecting.

Hairs on the body of the usual length; the middle of the thoracic dorsum bristly on its hind portion only.

The rounded third antennal joint short, the second of the same length with it.

Both crossveins not more approximate than usual; the first longitudinal vein bristly at its end only.

The genus *Ortalis* contains species above the average size, some of them rather large; the abdomen is banded with gray; the thorax strongly pollinose, in most species with conspicuous black, in some, with gray longitudinal stripes, in a few, without any stripes The wings are more or less spotted.

Typical species: *ruficeps* Fab.

7. SYSTATA Lw.

Charact.—Eyes rather large, elongate oval; front only little projecting.

The hairs on the body as usual; the middle of the thoracic dorsum with bristles upon its hind portion only.

The rounded third antennal joint is short; the second of equal length with it.

The two crossveins are very closely approximated; the first longitudinal vein bristly at its end only.

The species of this genus differ from those of *Ortalis* in the very close proximity of the crossveins, but agree with them in the remainder of the organization. The picture of the wings consists in bands.

Typical species: *rivularis* Fab.

8. LOXODESMA Lw.

Charact.—Eyes large, elongate: front but little projecting; face rather strongly carinate: cheeks narrower than in most other genera.

Hairs on the body as usual; thoracic dorsum with bristles upon its hind part only.

Third joint of the antennæ more or less prolonged, rounded at the tip; the second much shorter.

Both crossveins very much approximated; the first longitudinal vein bristly at its end only.

The species belonging here remind of the *Systatæ* in the striking proximity of the crossveins, differ however in other respects very much from them, and that in the same way as the species of *Pteropæctria* differ from *Ortalis*. The relation of *Loxodesma* to *Pteropæctria*, which is by far the most closely allied genus to

it, is exactly the same as that of *Systata* to *Ortalis*. The coloring and the picture of the wings resemble those of the first section
of *Pteropaectria*, only the obscure borders of the crossveins coalesce
more or less, on account of their proximity, into a single crossband.

Typical species: *lacustris* Meig.

9. PTEROPÆCTRIA Lw.

Charact.—Eyes large, elongate; front but very little projecting, face rather
strongly carinate; cheeks narrower than in most other genera.

Hairs on the body of the usual length; the middle of the thoracic
dorsum bristly on its posterior portion only.

Third antennal joint more or less elongate, rounded at the end;
the second very much shorter.

The crossveins are at the usual distance from each other; the
first longitudinal vein has bristles upon its end only.

This genus contains small, shining black species, the thorax of
which shows only a faint trace of pollen. The picture of the
wings generally consists in the dark color of the costal and subcostal cells, a more or less distinct black border of the crossveins
and a black spot on the costa, lying a little before the apex, or
upon it; in some species, however, this picture expands into four
crossbands which are connected, two and two, near the costa.

The genus is divided into two sections, which may even be
considered as separate genera. They are easily distinguished by
the picture of the wings, which is in keeping with a corresponding difference in the rest of the organization.

Sect. 1. (*Pteropaectria*, sensu strict.) with spotted, or incompletely banded, wings.

Typical species: *palustris* Meig.

Sect. 2. (*Thryphila* Lw.); bands on the wings complete.

Typical species: *frondescentiæ* Lin.

10. TEPHRONOTA Lw.

Charact.—Third antennal joint, although not excised on the upper side,
still with a sharp anterior corner.

Thoracic dorsum, upon its middle, not bristly in front of the
region of the suture.

First longitudinal vein bristly upon its end only; the fourth not
bent forward; the posterior angle of the anal cell not prolonged in
a lobe.

Tephronota begins the series of those genera, the third antennal joint of which is not rounded at the tip, but ends above in a sharp corner. It contains small species which, in the shape of their body, and especially in the structure of the head, remind of the *Pteropæciriæ* very much. But they can always be distinguished by their thorax, which is thickly covered with a gray pollen, even should the third antennal joint, in drying, have lost the sharpness of its upper corner. The picture of the wings consists either of complete crossbands, or of spots and half-bands, or even of spots only.

Typical species: *gyrans* Lw.

11. CZROXYS Macq.

Charact.—Third antennal joint distinctly excised on its upper side.

Thorax upon its middle beset with bristles as far as its anterior portion.

First longitudinal vein briefly upon its end only; fourth longitudinal vein not bent forward; the posterior angle of the anal cell not drawn out in a lobe.

Yellowish-gray or cinereous-gray species, with a thorax without stripes, and with wings having large dark spots; the arista is always distinctly pubescent.

Typical species: *crassipennis* Fab.

12. HYPOCHRA Lw.

Charact.—Third antennal joint distinctly excised on its upper side.

Thorax, upon its middle, not bristly in front of the region of the suture.

First longitudinal vein with bristles upon its end only; fourth longitudinal vein not bent forward; posterior angle of the anal cell not drawn out in a lobe.

Small, grayish-white species, with a very limited picture of the wings, generally consisting of a very narrow border of the crossveins.

Typical species: *albipennis* Lw.

13. ANACAMPTA Lw.

Charact.—Third antennal joint distinctly excised upon its upper side.

Thorax, upon its middle, not bristly in front of the region of the suture.

First longitudinal vein bristly upon its end only; fourth longitudinal vein bent forward towards its end; posterior angle of the anal cell not drawn out in a lobe.

Rather robust species having the thorax pollinose with gray, without stripes or with weak ones, a black, shining abdomen, generally with gray bands, and wings which have black cross-bands, or spots almost forming such crossbands.

Typical species: *urticæ* Lin.

14. HOLODASIA Lw.

Charact.—Third antennal joint distinctly excised on its upper side.

Thorax without bristles upon its middle, in front of the region of the suture.

First longitudinal vein bristly upon its whole length; fourth longitudinal vein curved forward at the end; posterior angle of the anal cell not drawn out in a point.

Holodasia differs from *Anacampta* (which it otherwise resembles very much) in the fact that the first longitudinal vein is bristly upon its whole extent, and not upon its end only. In this it agrees with *Pteropæxila*, from which it differs in the not projecting front, longer antennæ, the third joint of which is excised upon its upper side and pointed at the tip and in the fourth longitudinal vein being curved forward.

Typical species: *fraudulosa* Lw.

Fifth Section: Pterocallina.

At the beginning of the chapter on the Systematic Distribution of the Ortalidæ, I have pointed out *Scatophaga fasciata* as the species of this group known for the longest time and which may be considered as typical. It was described under that name by Fabricius in the *Systema Antliatorum*, was transferred by Meigen to the genus *Trypeta* and by Robineau Desvoidy to his new genus MYENNIS. It is very probably the same fly which was described by Coquebert in his *Iconographia*, Dec. III, under the name of *Musca octopunctata*, although it has nothing of the picture of the thorax shown in Coquebert's figure and which gave rise to the specific name. Although the publication of Coquebert's name is probably a little anterior to that of Fabricius, the choice of this name, based upon a non-existing character, as well as the nature of the entomological correspondence, which existed

between both authors, forbid us from giving Coquebert's name
the priority over Fabricius's.

At the same place I have also observed how very distinct a
species *Myennis fasciata* is, with its *Trypeta*-like stature, its
low head and especially the very large distance between the ends
of the auxiliary and of the first longitudinal vein; the latter
character especially is quite peculiar among the *Ortalidæ* with
a bristly first longitudinal vein.

Among the *Ortalidæ* hitherto described, the following species,
as far as known to me, show a sufficient agreement, in their
characters, with *Myennis fasciata* to be considered as belonging
to the same circle of relationship: *Trypeta ocellata* Wied., from
the environs of Bahia, Brazil; *Ortalis obscura* Wied., from
Brazil, *Ortalis vau* Say, and *Platystoma annulipes* Macq., the
two last from the United States. The numerous characters which
all these species share with *Myennis fasciata*, besides the already
mentioned peculiarities belonging to this species in particular,
are: 1, the nonmetallic coloring of the body; 2, the comparatively
low, but rather broad head; 3, the broad front; 4, the rounded,
more or less protruding eyes; 5, the round, or very short rounded-
oval shape of the third antennal joint; 6, the shortness of the more
or less concave face; 7, the small development of the clypeus; 8,
the comparatively large development of the chest; 9, the prothoracic bristle, represented by a very small hair only; 10, the middle
of the thorax, which is beset with bristles upon its hind part only;
11, the convex scutellum, provided with four bristles; 12, the very
much abbreviated fifth segment of the female abdomen, which is
very often quite withdrawn under the preceding segment; 13, the
posterior angle of the anal cell, which is drawn out in a point, or
even in a lobe.

Although the agreement in so many characters affords a distinct proof of the close relationship of these species, each of them
shows at the same time plastic differences of such an importance,
that one might be tempted to establish a separate genus for
almost every one of them. These differences principally consist
in the different shape of the wings, and in the different course
of their veins, while the rest of the organization shows a remarkable agreement.

In the shape of the wings two remarkable modifications are
worthy of notice, and may serve at some future time for a further
subdivision of this group.

The wings of *Trypeta ocellata* and *obscura* differ from the usual shape of the wings of the *Ortalidæ* by their narrowness, the parallelism of their anterior and posterior margins, their broad and rounded apex and their comparatively great length. Macquart placed the first of these species in the genus *Platystoma*, and the second, still more oddly, in the genus *Camptoneura*. Rondani has had a better eye for the plastic peculiarities of *Trypeta ocellata* and established the genus PTEROCALLA for it. I have derived the name of the present group from this well-founded genus of Rondani's, and not after Rob. Desvoidy's *Myennis*, established for *Scatophaga fasciata*, because the latter name, although much earlier in date, is a senseless malformation.

Trypeta obscura is, as Wiedemann has correctly observed in its description, a near relative of *Pterocalla ocellata*. As what occupies us now is the systematic location of only a small number of species, we can, without any hesitation, unite both of these species in the same genus, although the venation of *T. obscura* differs from that of *Pterocalla ocellata* in the second longitudinal vein being more arcuate than undulated, and in the fourth longitudinal vein being distinctly curved forward.

A small North American species, which will be described below, stands close enough to those two species in the shape of its wings and its venation to be placed in the same genus. It differs however in the second, third, and fourth longitudinal veins being quite straight, and neither wavy nor arcuate.

A most striking resemblance to this *Pterocalla strigula* is exhibited by *Trypeta ulula*, a South African species, described by me (*Berl. Entom. Zeitschr.*) after an incomplete specimen, without head. Already in describing this species, I drew attention to the fact that it differs from the ordinary venation of the *Trypetina* in the great distance intervening between the tips of the auxiliary and of the first longitudinal veins. I do not doubt now that this species is a *Pterocalla*, and that I would have recognized this earlier if I had had a complete specimen before me. Both species agree very well in all their plastic characters, especially in the shape of the wings and in the venation; the only difference which I notice in *P. ulula* is the position of the posterior crossvein, which is much steeper.

The genus *Pterocalla*, as I define it here, thus embraces all those *Pterocallina* which, in the outline of their wings, resemble

Pterocalla ocellata, so that this outline must be considered as the principal diagnostic character of this genus.

Among the numerous undescribed *Pterocallina*, which I have seen, I know of no one which may be placed in the genus *Pterocalla*, although several of them agree with the species of this genus in some one point pertaining to the venation. But none of those species has the wings of that peculiar shape which characterizes *Pterocalla*; on the contrary, the outline of the wings of all these species does not, in any marked degree, differ from that of the ordinary *Ortalidæ*. Like the species enumerated above, they have this peculiarity, that each species, although agreeing with the others in the characters belonging to the group, at the same time shows such important plastic differences, that the establishment of a series of new genera becomes indispensable. I regret not to be able to enter here into the detail of this subject, as, without plates, it is impossible to define those genera sufficiently. Thus much only will I mention, that among them there is a species which has the posterior angle of the anal cell rounded. The generic distribution of the North American species, which will be described below, does not, fortunately, require these South American forms to be taken into consideration.

Among the North American *Pterocallina*, *Ortalis vau* Say is the nearest to *Myennis fasciata* Fab. The venation, however, is different enough to prevent us from placing them in the same genus. The two crossveins in *O. vau* are less approximated, and the anterior end of the posterior one is further from the basis of the wing than the posterior end, while in *Myennis fasciata* the contrary is the case, so that the posterior crossvein of this species has a different position. Moreover, the first segment of the ovipositor of the female of *Ortalis vau* has not the conically attenuated shape which it has in *Myennis fasciata* and in many *Trypetina*; it is broader, somewhat attenuated from its middle only, like the ovipositor of the majority of the *Ortalidæ*. I consider, therefore, *Ortalis vau* as the type of a new genus, which I call STICTOCEPHALA.

To *Stictocephala vau* must be added a second North American species, which I received from Baron Osten Sacken, under the name of *Trypetis corticalis* Fitch in litt., and which will be described by me under the same name. The venation resembles

that of *S. cau* so closely that I have no hesitation in placing it
in the same genus.

There are two other North American species which I take to
be undescribed, and which also belong to *Stictocephala*. As
their wings are not pictured like those of the two preceding species, but simply banded, the difference between them seems, at
first glance, to be greater than it really is. A close examination
does not disclose any plastic difference which would justify their
generic separation from *Stictocephala*. I will describe them as
Stictocephala cribrum and *cribellum*.

The North American species described by Macquart as *Platystoma annulipes* shows, in the detail of its structure, an almost
complete agreement with the species of *Stictocephala*, but differs
so much in the outline of the wings and still more in the venation, that it cannot be placed in that genus. The difference in
the outline of the wings consists in the fact that the posterior
margin is more convex, and hence, the wings are broader; the
difference in the venation appears in the posterior angle of the
anal cell being drawn out in a very long lobe, and in the position
of the posterior crossvein, the anterior end of which is much
nearer to the apex of the wing than the posterior end. As this
species does not find a convenient place in any of the existing
genera, I am compelled to establish a new one for it, which I call
CALLOPISTRIA.

This would close the series of the few genera of *Pterocallina*,
hitherto sufficiently defined, if we had not to advert to the genus
PAALKOPTERA Wahlb., occurring in northern and central Europe,
as well as in northern Asia, a genus for which it is not easy to
find an appropriate place in the system. The species of this
genus resemble the *Ulidina* in their general appearance, and I
would not have hesitated to place them in that section, if their
third longitudinal vein was not distinctly beset with hairs. I
acknowledge that their location among the *Ulidina* is more
natural than among the *Pterocallina*. Nevertheless, I place
the genus among the latter and thus put a greater stress upon
the artificial character, derived from the pilosity of the third
vein, than upon more close and natural affinities, but which are
more difficult to explain in words. If I do this, it is because I
hold that a strict adherence to those characters, by means of
which I have tried to introduce into the systematic chaos of the

Ortalidæ a satisfactory distribution in groups, is more apt to insure the recognition within these groups of available genera, than if we should attempt to avail ourselves of affinities, which, although visible to the eye, do not admit of exact definitions.

Psairoptera finds a fitting location at the end of the *Pterocallina*, so as to be immediately followed by the *Ulidina*. The principal differences from the above-mentioned genera of *Pterocallina* consist in the posterior angle of the anal cell, which is more or less a sharp right angle, and in the much smaller distance between the end of the auxiliary vein and that of the first longitudinal. The shape of the head likewise shows not unimportant differences from the other genera of the group, and some of the species of *Psairoptera* have, moreover, the last antennal joint of a more elliptical shape.

In enumerating the most characteristic distinctive marks of the *Pterocallina*, we cannot, for the above stated reasons, lay the same stress upon *Psairoptera* as upon the other genera of this group. These characters may be summed up as follows:—

Habitus *Trypeta*-like; coloring non-metallic; head rather broad, but low, with rather protuberant eyes; face short, perpendicular, excavated in the middle; clypeus but little developed; third antennal joint round or rounded ovate; thoracic dorsum bristly upon its posterior part only; third longitudinal vein hairy; and above all, as the most important character, the unusually large distance between the end of the first longitudinal and that of the auxiliary veins.

For the *Pterocallina* from North America, hitherto known, we can add to the above-enumerated characters the posterior angle of the anal cell, which is drawn out in a long lobe.

SECOND DIVISION.

ORTALIDÆ HAVING THE FIRST LONGITUDINAL VEIN BARE.

The European genera belonging here are: SEOPTERA Kirby, TIMIA Wied., ULIDIA Meig., CHRYSOMYZA Fall., with which *Chloria* Schin. is coincident, and EMPYELOCERA Lw. They are allied enough to each other to be united in the same group.

A type, very different from the preceding genera, appears in the genus RICHARDIA Rob. Desv., which seems to be rather

abundantly represented in America and likewise belongs to this
division. A whole series of related genera, peculiar to America,
may be classed with *Richardia*: like the latter, they are all
distinguished by armed femora.

This is the reason why, in a former publication, I separated
the whole second division of the *Ortalina* in two groups, the one
with unarmed, the other with armed femora; the first I called
Ulidina, the second *Richardina*; and in the *Berlin Entom. Zeitschrift*, Vol. XI, I described the American *Ulidina* which, at
the time, were known to me. Now, however, that I have become
acquainted with a larger number of forms belonging in this
division, I incline to think that its separation in the groups
Ulidina and *Richardina* becomes more natural, if, as a distinguishing character of these groups, we assume, not the armed or
unarmed femora, but the shape of the anal cell. All the genera
having the posterior angle of the anal cell more or less pointed
belong to the *Ulidina*; those genera, on the contrary, where this
is not the case are to be placed with the *Richardina*. This
modification does not much alter the distribution of the genera
among these two groups, as all the genera with armed femora, at
present known, will, in the new distribution, be likewise referred
to the *Richardina*. Among the genera which, in the above-
quoted publication, I placed with the *Ulidina*, *Epiplatea* alone
will have to be transferred among the *Richardina*. Among the
genera of *Richardina*, enumerated below, *Stenerelma*, according
to the former mode of subdivision, would have belonged to the
Ulidina, and thus would not have been placed near *Idiotypa*,
which is closely allied to it. With the former mode of distribution, the position of the new genus *Coniceps*, based upon a North
American species, would have been a somewhat doubtful one, as
the under side of its hind femora bears a few stronger hairs, but
can hardly be called armed.

First Section: Ulidina.

The five genera of *Ulidina* represented in Europe, and
enumerated in the preceding paragraph, are not confined to this
part of the world. The European SEOPTERA vibrans also occurs
in the adjoining provinces of Asia, and is represented in America
by a species most closely resembling it. European species of

Timia, Empfelocera, and Ulidia occur in Asia together with other species, peculiar to that part of the world. Chrysomyza demandata likewise ranges over a considerable part of Asia and Africa; both countries contain besides species of this genus peculiar to them.

The South American *Ulidia stigma* Wiedemann and the Brazilian *Ulidia bipunctata* Macq. are not *Ulidiæ* at all, although they probably belong to the group *Ulidina*, the first to the genus *Notogramma*, the last to *Euxesta*. *Ulidia metallica* Bigot, from Cuba, is perhaps a *Chrysomyza*; as to the *Ulidia fulvifrons* Bigot, from the same locality, it is impossible, from Bigot's description, to come to any conclusions about its place in the system.

America seems in general to be very rich in forms belonging to the *Ulidina*. For the species which came within my knowledge I have established the genera: Dasymetopa, Oedopa, Notogramma, Euphara, Acrosticta, Euxesta, Chætopsis, Hypoecta and Stenomyia.

The species described by former authors, which belong in the circle of the above-mentioned genera, are to be found in Wiedemann partly in the genus *Ortalis*, partly in *Ulidia*. In Macquart, as far as I can ascertain, they are scattered among the *Ulidiæ* or even in *Ceroxys* and *Urophora*, which shows, on that author's part, an utter neglect of their plastic characters. The genus Eumetopia established by Macquart in his family *Psilomydæ*, does not belong to it, but to the *Ulidina*.

It is not doubtful at all that Asia and Africa, besides the genera which they have in common with Europe, harbor some genera of *Ulidina* which are peculiar to them. Gonaorta Gerstæcker, described by Dolcschall, some time previously, under the inappropriate name of *Zygænula*, probably belongs to this group. It differs, it is true, from all the known *Ulidina* very much; still the structure of the head in *Oedopa* may be indicative of an affinity.

Unfortunately I cannot give any further information concerning other exotic *Ulidina* of the old world, as I have none in my possession. The existing descriptions of a number of *Ortalidæ* which may possibly belong to the group *Ulidina*, are not accurate enough to admit of any positive conclusions.

I have not met with any *Ulidina* from Oceanica yet.

5

Second Section: Richardina.

Among all the genera of this group, RICHARDIA Rob. Desv., distinguished by its posterior femora, armed with spines, is the best and longest known. This circumstance induced me to derive the name of the section from it. It seems to be exclusively American; the *Richardia flavitarsis* Macq., from the Marquesas Islands, does not belong to this genus, and if the manner in which the auxiliary vein is represented upon Macquart's figure be only of average correctness, we may even infer that it does not belong to the *Richardina* at all. The other species which Macquart, Rondani and Gerstaecker have added to the genus *Richardia* are all natives of America. The two males of *Richardia* described by Gerstaecker are distinguished by the dilatation of their head, somewhat in the manner of *Achias*; their females are not known yet; still the analogy of *Achias* and of other genera, having a similar structure of the head, justifies us in supposing that their heads do not show any extraordinary dilatation.

The fly of unknown *habitat* which Macquart described as ODONTOMERA *ferruginea* undoubtedly belongs in the immediate affinity of *Richardia*. As I have never seen it, my knowledge of it is based exclusively upon Mr. Macquart's statements. These, however, are entirely sufficient to prove that the fly belongs in the family *Ortalidæ*, and not in the *Trypetidæ*, where Macquart places it. That it belongs to the *Richardina* I infer from the evidently very close relationship which exists between it and the *Sepsis Guérinii* Bigot from Cuba. The generic name must be changed, on account of the already existing *Odontomerus* Gravenh.

This *Sepsis Guérinii* agrees in so many characters with *Odontomera ferruginea* Macq. that one might be tempted to place it in the genus *Odontomera*. Should Macquart's statements, however, be correct, this would not be admissible, as *Odontomera ferruginea* possesses not only much stouter femora and a much more projecting front, but also an auxiliary vein which is much less approximated to the first longitudinal than in *Sepsis Guérinii*. We are compelled, therefore, to consider *Sepsis Guérinii* as a separate genus of the *Richardina*, which we will call STENOMACRA.

We have, in the next place, to mention the genus SETELLIA

It was founded by Rob. Desvoidy, and *Setellia atra* Rob. Desv. must be considered as its type. I have not seen this species, and, unfortunately, the statements of Rob. Desvoidy are not sufficient to enable me to decide whether *Setellia atra* belongs to the *Richardina* or to the *Cephalina*. In the same way, I am unable to decide whether the Brazilian species, subsequently described by Macquart as *Setellia apicalis* really belongs in the same genus with *Setellia atra*. As Rob. Desvoidy does not allude at all to the femora of his species being spinous, while Macquart's species is remarkable for all its femora being armed in a rather striking manner, it becomes exceedingly doubtful whether Macquart's species is a *Setellia* in the sense of Rob. Desvoidy's.

I do not know of any species more related to *Setellia apicalis* Macq. than that species from Colombia, South America, which Gerstaecker described under the name of *Michogaster egregius*. As its first longitudinal vein is bare and its femora are armed, it cannot possibly remain connected with the true species of *Michogaster*, but must be considered as the type of a separate genus of *Richardina*, for which I propose the name of EVOLENA.

To place *Setellia apicalis* in the genus *Evolena* is not possible; it has no stamp of a vein upon the second longitudinal vein inside of the submarginal cell, a character distinguishing *Evolena egregia*; its third and fourth longitudinal veins converge more distinctly towards their end, and the posterior angle of the anal cell is not rounded. *Setellia apicalis* will also have to be considered as the type of a separate genus, which may be called SYNTACEA. In the supposition that the first longitudinal vein of *Syntacea apicalis*, like that of its relative *Evolena egregia*, is bare, I think that the best location for this genus is among the *Richardina*. It is true that the posterior angle of the anal cell, in Macquart's figure, is almost acute; in the generic diagnosis, however, he calls the anal cell: "terminée carrement," so that the shape of this cell cannot be an obstacle to the location of the genus among the *Richardina*; and this view is supported by the spinous femora, a character common to nearly all the genera of this group. Should, however, the first longitudinal vein of *Syntacea* be hairy or bristly, then the location of the genus among the *Richardina* would be impossible.

Next to *Evolena* is the genus IDIOTYPA, which I establish for a new species from Cuba. In its general habitus it is almost like one of the more corpulent American species of *Baccha;* for instance, *Baccha capitata* Lw. The second longitudinal vein, which in *Euolena* forms a short stump inside of the submarginal cell, bears, in this genus, almost at the same place, similar stumps, not only in the submarginal, but also in the marginal cell. The most striking difference, however, lies in the structure of the feet, as *Euolena* has the four posterior femora remarkably long and slender, which is not in the least the case with *Idiotypa.*

The genus STENZELTMA, which will be characterized in the third part, treating of the North American species, is related to *Idiotypa.*

The South American species described by Fabricius once as *Scatophaga trimaculata* and another time as *Dacus flavus,* and which Wiedemann placed in the genus *Trypeta,* does not belong in this genus at all, but in the present group of the *Ortalidæ.* The description, which Macquart gave of his CŒLOMETOPIA *ferruginea,* contains so much which is entirely applicable to Fabricius's species, that I have no doubt that the latter species was the very same from which the description of *Cœlometopia ferruginea* was drawn. When Macquart says that in *C. ferruginea* the middle femora alone are armed, this statement is probably based upon an insufficient observation; when he calls the last three tarsal joints white, this seems to be a *lapsus calami,* as the figure shows nothing of the kind, and as on two of the tarsi the first joints are even represented as much paler than the following ones; the latter probably being infuscated, as they are in Fabricius's species. Should even, contrary to my supposition, Macquart's species be different from that of Fabricius, they will at all events belong to the same genus.

The *Odontomera maculipennis* of Macquart from Colombia, South America, seems very closely allied to *Cœlometopia;* Macquart's own statements show that it agrees in so many characters with *Cœlometopia trimaculata,* that it may be transferred to the same genus with it; one would even be led to suppose that it is nothing but the female of *Cœlometopia trimaculata.* With the above mentioned *Odontomera ferruginea* Macq. (not *Cœlometopia ferruginea* Macq) *Odontomera maculipennis* has too little in common to be considered as belonging to the same genus.

A pretty species from Cuba, which will be described in the

sequel, can also be placed in the genus *Cœlometopia*, although
the ocelli, which here, as well as in the latter genus, are rather
much forward on the front and close to each other, are placed
here upon a very gentle elevation, while in *Cœlometopia* the
projection which bears them is quite high.

Closely related to *Cœlometopia* is the species described by
Wiedemann as *Trypeta cyanogaster*. It is not a real *Cœlometopia*, as its posterior ocelli are less remote from the vertex and
the anterior one quite distant from them; moreover the third
and fourth longitudinal veins are parallel here and the hind
femora alone bear a few bristles, while in *Cœlometopia* all the
femora are beset with spines. For this reason *Trypeta cyanogaster* has to be considered as the type of a new genus, which
may be called MELANOLOMA. A second species of this genus,
from Brazil, has the same picture of the wings as *M. cyanogaster*,
consisting in a black border of the costal margin and of the small
crossvein.

Other Brazilian *Ortalidæ* resemble the genus *Melanoloma* in
the fact that the third and fourth longitudinal veins are parallel;
the agreement in the structure of the rest of the body, especially
of the head, is very striking. These species differ, however, in all
the femora being spinous, in the arista being distinctly pubescent,
in the still greater distance between the anterior ocellus and the
two posterior ones, in the close proximity of the two crossveins
of the wings, and in the picture of the wings, which does not
consist in a black border on the costa, but in large, crossband-
like spots. I deem it useful to introduce for such species a new
genus, which I will call HEMIXANTHA; a species of this genus,
H. spinipes, will be described below.

That *Dacus flavicornis* Wied., from Brazil, belongs in the
same circle of relationship is proved by the original specimen,
preserved in the Berlin Museum.

Before having subjected that specimen to a second and more
close examination, I would not venture to decide whether it can
be placed in any of the genera, which I have just discussed. As
far as I remember, its scutellum bears only two bristles; this
would prevent its identification with any one of those genera, as
it is very unlike just those among them which share that character
with it. Otherwise it has the same *Dacus*-like structure of the
face as most *Richardina;* the third antennal joint is elongated;

the slender arista is distinctly pubescent; the abdomen is of an equal breadth; the posterior angle of the anal cell is not acute and the fourth longitudinal vein somewhat convergent with the third; all the femora are armed.

I have also to mention the genus CONICEPS, which I find necessary to establish for a North American species. On account of the retracted posterior angle of the anal cell it must likewise be placed among the *Richardina*, although in its general appearance it is more like certain *Ulidina*, especially *Eumetopia*.

The reason why I place EPIPLATEA among the *Richardina* has been alluded to above.

Thus I have reached the limit of the genera, the location of which among the *Richardina* appears to me beyond doubt. It is certain that the number of *Richardina* which may yet remain unrecognized among the existing descriptions is far from exhausted by me; but who would venture, upon the statements of most of these descriptions, to form an opinion on the systematic location of the species which they mean to represent?

It will hardly be necessary to mention here the East Indian genus MERACANTHA. Its spinose femora may suggest the supposition that it belongs to the *Richardina*. But as this character does not belong exclusively to this group, and as the very acute angle of the anal cell of *Meracantha* does not occur among the *Richardina* in the acceptation of that group as I understand it here, I cannot consider *Meracantha* as belonging to the *Richardina*.

Besides the bareness of the first longitudinal vein and the not acute posterior angle of the anal cell, which two characters constitute the diagnosis of the *Richardina*, the following characters are common to all the genera which I have had occasion to examine in detail: a break in the costal vein immediately before the end of the auxiliary vein; the great proximity between the auxiliary and first longitudinal veins and the very small distance between their ends; finally the thoracic dorsum being beset with bristles upon its posterior part only.

III.

THE NORTH AMERICAN ORTALIDÆ.

It is a long time since I intended to publish a monograph of the North American Ortalidæ. The hope and expectation, however, of increasing in a measure my very fragmentary knowledge of this family by the addition of more species, either new or not yet seen by me, induced me to postpone for some time the completion of my work. Unfortunately, this expectation has not been fulfilled. Within the last four years, only five species were added to those previously known by me, and it became evident that if I had to wait for a tolerable increase of my acquaintance with the Ortalidæ, my work would run the risk of remaining unpublished. I let it appear, therefore, in the best shape I could give it, with the scanty materials at my command. I have no doubt that North America contains a far larger number of genera than those which came within my knowledge. In order to define, with some approximation, the systematic position of the genera of which I have not had any representatives for comparison, I have included in this monograph all the South American genera of which I possess specimens; inasmuch as it is very probable that most of them occur at least in the southern portion of North America. The striking analogy between the North American and European *Ortalina* renders it very probable that the number of genera in this group, common to both continents, is larger than it appears at present. For this reason I have deemed it useful to include in the general characters of the *Ortalina* all the data necessary for the recognition of the more difficult and less well known among the European genera.

Synopsis of the Distribution of the Family.

Division I.—First longitudinal vein bristly or distinctly hairy.
  A. Oviparitor not flattened.
    Section I. *Pyrgotina.*

(71)

B. Ovipositor flattened.

    a. Third antennal joint not circular.

        1. No prothoracic, no mesothoracic bristle.
           Section II. *Platystomina.*

        2. No prothoracic, but a mesothoracic bristle.
           Section III. *Cephalina.*

        3. A prothoracic and a mesothoracic bristle.
           Section IV. *Ortalina.*

    b. Third antennal joint circular.
        Section V. *Pterocallina.*

Division II.—First longitudinal vein bare.

    A. Posterior angle of the anal cell drawn out in a point, or, at least,
        more or less acute.

    Femora never armed.
        Section I. *Ulidina.*

    B. Posterior angle of the anal cell obtuse, rounded or retracted.

    Femora armed in most of the genera.
        Section II. *Richardina.*

FIRST DIVISION.

ORTALIDÆ WITH THE FIRST LONGITUDINAL VEIN BRISTLY OR DISTINCTLY HAIRY.

First Section: PYRGOTINA.

GEN. I. **PYRGOTA** WIED.

Charact.—Front of equal breadth, without ocelli, very much projecting in
profile.

    Antennæ drooping, second joint rather long, third more or less ovate;
arista pubescent.

    Face retreating, under the antennæ with deep foveæ, separated by a
very low ridge; they reach as far as the middle of the face, or only
a little below; lateral parts of the face very broad, still more
approximated on the lower half of the face; oral opening comparatively small; *clypeus* but little developed; *proboscis* not stout.

    Scutellum with many bristles.

---

¹ It may not be useless to refer here to Vol. I, p. xxiv, of these *Monographs*, where (fig. 1) a wing of *Ortalis* is represented. The *anal cell* is
marked *M* on the figure, and is the same as the *third basal cell*, or the
posterior one of the small basal cells. Although this synonymy is not
mentioned in the explanation of the figure (at the foot of the same page),
it may be found in the same volume, p. xx, line 19 from the top.—O. S.

Abdomen: in the male with four segments, the first of which strikingly
prolonged, the following ones considerably shorter; in the female
with five segments, the first of which very remarkably prolonged,
the following ones quite as remarkably shortened; *ovipositer* large,
not flattened, almost capsule-shaped.

Spurs of the middle tibiæ only bristle like; very weak in the species
with few coarse hairs.

Wings large; posterior angle of the anal cell acute; small crossvein
beyond the middle of the long discal cell; third longitudinal vein
curved backwards towards its end; the last section of the fourth
longitudinal vein arcuated, but little diverging from the third.

Macquart's genus *Oxycephala* is identical with *Pyrgota.*
Harris, in his Catalogue of the Insects of Massachusetts, calls
this genus *Sphecomyia.*

Real *Pyrgotæ* are known to occur with certainty in North
America only. As in Europe and Africa genera occur, which
are closely allied to *Pyrgota*, it is not impossible that Walker's
P. latipennis (List of Dipt. p. 1087) from Sierra Leone is a real
Pyrgota; however, his description is altogether silent concerning
those characters which are indispensable for the recognition of
the genus. Whether *P. pictipennis* Walker (List, etc. 1162)
belongs to this genus is very doubtful; the author himself
introduces it with a doubt, but remains silent as to the motives
of this location as well as the cause of the doubt.

The North American *Pyrgotæ* at present known may be
divided in two groups: In the first, the arista is only two-jointed,
and, at the same time, the usual bristles on the vertex, as well
as those bristles which in other genera protect the ocelli, are
present; in the other group, the arista is distinctly three-jointed,
and there are no conspicuous bristles either on the vertex, or
round the spot where, in other genera, the ocelli are placed.
Pyrgota millepunctata belongs to the first, all the other species
to the last group. Were the number of the species larger, these
characters would justify a subdivision in two genera; at present,
with the small number of species, all easy to identify, this subdivision would be useless.

1. P. millepunctata Lw. ♀.—Fusco picea, seta solennall biarti-
culata; alæ infuscatæ, guttulis numerosis subpellucidis aspersæ.

Pitch-brown; arista two-jointed; wings infuscated, dotted with numerous
pellucid spots. Long. corp. 0.36—0.43, cum terebra 0.51—0.55, long.
al. 0.49—0.55.

Syn. *Pyrgota millepunctata* Loew, Neue Beitr. II, 22, 60.
  (Oxycephala maculipennis Macq. Dipt. Exot. Suppl. 1, p. 210.   Tab.
    xxvii, f. 2.
  Sphecomyia valida Harris, Catal. Ins. Mass.

Prevailing color of the body pitch-brown, reddish-brown or
even brownish-red in less intensely colored specimens, with a
black pubescence, which is perceptibly coarser than in the following species. The occiput has, behind the vertex, a distinct black
triangle, with its point directed downwards, which is connected
with a black spot on the place where the ocelli should be; at
some distance from this triangle there is, on each side, a large
black spot, reaching from the posterior orbit of the eye almost to
the point of attachment of the head; between these spots and
the triangle the color is clay-yellow, almost wax-yellow; the
sides of the occiput are generally of a similar yellow color, but
become more infuscated towards the orbits and the cheeks, or are
tinged with brownish as far as the black spots above. The front
has a broad black stripe, which is divided longitudinally in two
by a more or less complete and more or less narrow, sometimes
more yellow, sometimes brownish, line; on both sides, near the
orbits, the stripe is margined with yellow. The ordinary strong
bristles on the vertex, the bristle placed in front of these, on
each side, near the orbit, and those bristles which are inserted in
the region of the ocelli (which here are wanting), are all present.
The first antennal joint is generally rather dark-brown, except at
the basis; the second is usually of a dirty brownish-yellow; the
third agrees in its coloring sometimes with the first, sometimes
more with the second joint; in some specimens, it is altogether
ochre-yellow; the arista is distinctly two-jointed, the first joint
short. The face is usually of a dark ferruginous-brownish coloring, often verging on ochre-yellow on the sides. The antennal
foveæ are somewhat less deep than in *P. undata*, but perceptibly
longer and separated by a higher ridge. The sides of the face
are approximated on the lower half, but not so much by far as in
P. undata, so that the middle part of the face has about double
the breadth of the other species. The oral opening is more
horizontal than in *P. undata*. The but little developed clypeus
is black, the palpi generally yellow; their shape is almost the
same as in *P. undata*. The ground color of the thorax is clay-
yellow or wax-yellow, but with very broad pitch-brown stripes,

which occupy everything but the hameci and the narrow intervals
between the stripes, so that the prevailing color is the brown
one; the middle stripe, which is of equal breadth, is longitudinally divided in two by a lighter longitudinal line; the stripe
stops at the last quarter of the thorax, however, beyond it, at
the posterior margin of the thorax, there is a brown spot; the
very broad lateral stripes are strongly abbreviated anteriorly,
attenuated and interrupted at the transverse suture; moreover,
the lateral margin has a broad brown border. Scutellum
blackish-brown, paler on the sides; the numerous bristles are
more conspicuous in this species on account of their stoutness
and their black coloring. Pleuræ pitch-brown, clay-yellowish
on the sutures. Abdomen usually blackish-brown or dark pitch-
brown, sometimes ferruginous-brown or yellowish-brown; the
first segment is about once and a half the length of the four following segments taken together. The capsule-shaped ovipositor
is of the same color as the abdomen, or somewhat paler; its
shape is nearly the same as in *P. undata*, but it is a little less
pointed; on each side, not far from the basis, it has a large, impressed spot. The color of the feet is as variable as that of the
remainder of the body; blackish-brown in more intensely colored
specimens, otherwise ferruginous-brownish; the knees are always
clay-yellow; paler colored specimens have the extreme tip of
the thighs and the tarsi of a dirty ferruginous-yellow or ochre-
yellow color. The shape of the wings is not unlike that in *P.
undata*, but towards the apex they are broader. The chief differences in the venation are the following: the little stump of a
vein on the second longitudinal vein existing in *P. undata*, is
wanting here; the discal cell is much broader, especially towards
its tip; the posterior transverse vein is nearer the margin of the
wing, much longer and more straight; the last section of the
fourth longitudinal vein is less strongly arcuated and the second
posterior cell much smaller; the posterior angle of the anal cell
is more drawn out in a point. The whole surface of the wings
has a rather uniform dark-brownish coloring; this color is variegated by numerous transparent dots of a gray-yellowish tinge;
the shape of these dots is rather irregular; they are often confluent, as often distinctly separated; round the root of the second
longitudinal vein and round the small crossvein, the dark coloring is more continuous and less interrupted by dots; the brown

is also more intense along the costal margin, than upon the remaining surface.

Hab. Carolina (Zimmerman); Washington, D. C., New York, Illinois (Osten-Sacken); Massachusetts (Harris).

Observation 1.—Mr. Macquart (Dipt. Exot. Suppl. I, p. 210) describes as *Oxycephala maculipennis* from Texas (figured on Tab. XIX, f. 13), a species which either is a *Pyrgota* or is closely allied to this genus. In several respects this species shows a decided resemblance to *P. millepunctata*, and the question as to their diversity is a very doubtful one. The conformity is especially apparent in the picture of the wings and the venation, also in the coloring of the front and even in that of the thorax. But Macquart says that the thoracic stripes are interrupted near the suture (which is also rendered in his figure); moreover, according to the figure, the posterior angle of the anal cell is drawn out in a much longer point than is the case in *P. millepunctata*. These discrepancies alone, however, with Macquart's well-known inaccuracy in description and figure, would not be sufficient to neutralize the evident analogies. A more weighty ground for doubt is to be found in the representation of the abdomen; nothing like its remarkable breadth has been observed in any known *Pyrgota*; moreover, it shows, instead of five segments, only four, the first of which is abbreviated, and the second the longest; the ovipositor hardly exceeds one-third of the length of the abdomen, while in the other *Pyrgota* it equals the abdomen in length. If these statements were based on Macquart's figure alone, I would have been inclined to think that the abdomen, wanting in the specimen, had been supplied by the imagination of the draughtsman; but this supposition does not hold good in presence of the fact, that Macquart mentions expressly, that he had a female before him; and we know that the sex of a *Pyrgota* can only be recognized by the structure of the abdomen. Macquart also says that the ovipositor is flattened, which is not in the least the case with *P. millepunctata*. These grounds seem sufficient to justify the belief that Macquart's *Oxycephala maculipennis* is a different species from *P. millepunctata*, unless we assume that Macquart's specimen had the abdomen of a different species fastened to it. Should this not be the case, there is every reason to doubt whether the species is a *Pyrgota* at all. It is rather strange that in the list of the exotic species described in Macquart's work, which is appended to his fourth supplement, *O. maculipennis* is omitted. The cause of this omission is not apparent. Should Macquart have discovered that it belonged to a different genus, he would have transferred it to that genus; but the species is altogether omitted in the list.

Observation 2.—*Sphecomyia valida* of Harris's Catalogue of the Insects of Massachusetts, is, according to a communication from Baron Osten-Sacken, nothing else but *Pyrgota millepunctata*. As a matter of course, Harris's name, being merely a catalogue name, has no claim of priority.

2. P. undata Wied. ♂ ♀.—Ex ochraceo ferrugineæ; antennarum articulus tertius secundo æqualis; seta antennalis triarticulata, articulis primis duobus subæqualibus; alarum vena longitudinalis secunda appendiculata.

Yellowish-ferrugineous; the third antennal joint equal to the second in length; arista three-jointed; its first two joints of nearly equal length; the second longitudinal vein with a stump of a vein upon it. Long. corp. ♂ 0.4—0.43; ♀ cum terebra 0.5—0.53; long. al. 0.5—0.58.

Syn. *Pyrgota undata* Wied. Auss. Zweifl. II, p. 561. Tab. X, 6.
Pyrgota undata Macq. Suites, etc., II, p. 423. Tab. XVIII, f. 23 (were mentioned after Wiedemann).
Myopa nigripennis, Gray, Anim. Kingd. Tab. 123, f. 6.
Oxycephala fuscipennis Macq. Dipt. Exot. II, 3, p. 198. Tab. XXVI, 6.
Sphecomyia undata Harris, Cat. Ins. Mass.
Pyrgota undata Guer. Stett. Ent. Zeit. xii, p. 188.

Yellowish-ferrugineous or more ochre-brownish. Front rather broad, projecting almost in the shape of a tower, and with a short, rather inconspicuous pubescence; without stronger bristles in the region of the vertex or round the place where the ocelli usually are. Antennæ yellow; the first two joints with a yellowish pubescence; the third sometimes ochre-brown, of the same length as the second. Arista distinctly three-jointed; the first two joints almost of equal length. The face very much retreating when seen in profile; the very deep antennal foveæ reach only to its middle and are separated by a very low ridge, which is usually tinged with brown; below them, the middle portion of the face is remarkably narrow, groove-like and bordered on each side by a brownish-black ridge. A brown or brownish-black, somewhat curved stripe generally extends from the middle of the inner orbit of the eyes towards the region of the antennæ.

The oral opening is cut obliquely upwards; the but little
developed clypeus is tinged with blackish; the rather broad palpi
are usually tinged with yellowish-red towards the tip, sometimes
they are altogether ferruginous. The thoracic dorsum has an
extended ferruginous-brown spot upon it, formed by the almost
complete coalescence of a broad intermediate stripe with two
broad lateral stripes, which are abbreviated in front. The metathorax and the greater part of the pleuræ are often tinged with
dark pitch-brown. The coloring of the abdomen on the first two
segments, and also at the basis and along the middle of the following ones, often becomes pitch-brown or brownish-black, this
is especially often the case in male specimens. The first
abdominal segment is very much elongated in both sexes; in the
male it is not quite as long as the three remaining segments
taken together; in the female, the last four segments are so
much shortened, that, taken together, they are much shorter than
the first joint. The capsule-shaped ovipositor is conical, bent
downward towards its end. The feet are ochre-yellowish, but
the femora brown up to the tip; the tibiæ likewise are more or
less infuscated, except the basis and the extreme tip. Wings
large, the greater portion of them is uniformly tinged with
brown, which color covers the costal, marginal, submarginal, the
first posterior and the discal cells, also the basal cells, with the
exception of a pale stripe in the anal cell, moreover, this color
forms a broad border along the inner portion of the second posterior cell, and a narrower one along the anterior margin of the
third posterior cell; within this brown coloring some specimens
do not show any paler spots, the majority, however, show, in the
submarginal cell, a little beyond the small crossvein, a rounded
or oval, almost hyaline spot, which attains sometimes a considerable size; moreover, a great many specimens show some scattered,
small, hyaline dots, not far from the end of the same cell, of the
first posterior and of the discal cells; the posterior limit of the
brown coloring has a whitish-hyaline border, which, following the
course of that limit, forms a steep curve in the second posterior
cell; in the third posterior cell it takes the shape of a gently
arched longitudinal stripe; within this border, the surface of the
wing has a uniform brownish coloring, which is perceptibly more
intense only in the region of the axillary incision; in some cases,
near the posterior side of the sixth longitudinal vein, a little

beyond the end of the anal cell, there is a small, almost hyaline
spot; the alula is almost hyaline, or infuscated towards the
posterior margin only. The second longitudinal vein, opposite
the posterior crossvein, shows a small fold, the tip of which,
directed backwards, emits a short stump of a vein; the last
section of the fourth longitudinal vein is very strongly curved;
the posterior angle of the anal cell forms a sharp, but not very
acute angle.

Hab. United States; Carolina (Zimmerman), Massachusetts
(Harris), etc.

Observation.—I am not able to compare the figure of *Myopa
nigripennis* Gray, but I do not hesitate, on Gerstaecker's authority,
to place this name among the synonyms of *P. undata.* The
synonymy of *Sphecomyia undata* Harris is based upon a statement of Mr. Walker, who seems to have received specimens from
the author.

3. P. vespertilio Gerst. ♂.—Antennarum articulo tertio prace-
dente plus dimidio breviore, rotundato ovato, fusco, arista articulo primo
brevissimo, secundo elongato: fronte oculis duplo latiore, palpis filifor-
mibus: alis vená longitudinali secundá nec fracta, nec appendiculatá,
alulá strigisque duabus marginis posterioris hyalinis.

Third antennal joint not half so long as the second, rounded oval, brown;
the first joint of the arista very short, the second elongated; front
double the breadth of the eyes; palpi linear; second longitudinal vein
of the wings without fold or stump of a vein; the alula and two stripes
near the posterior margin hyaline. Long. corp. 0.64; long. al. 0.50.

Grs. *Pyrgota vespertilio* Gerst. Stett. Entom. Zeitschr. xxi, p. 169, Tab. II,
f. 3.

Head comparatively stouter than in the preceding species;
front, when viewed from above, and taken as far as the anterior
border of the eyes, at least by one-half broader than long; the
gibbosity projecting over the eyes is not of equal breadth, as in
P. undata, but conically attenuated anteriorly; its tip is as
broadly truncated as in the other species; viewed in profile, this
projection is as high as in *P. undata*; its anterior side, however,
does not ascend in a straight line, but shows a strong convexity,
so that the tip itself is retreating. The cheeks are considerably broader and more sunken. The eyes are comparatively
smaller, the excavated upper part of the face perceptibly shorter.
The coloring on the front, especially on the inside of the eyes and

upon the gibbosity, is darker, more brown; upon the cheeks, with
the exception of the ferruginous-yellow border of the eyes,
chocolate-brown; the two black ridges, bordering the middle of
the face, are present, as in *P. undata*, but even more distinctly
marked and descending lower.   The first two joints of the
antennæ are pale ferruginous-yellow; the third joint dark-brown;
the arista ferruginous-yellow at the basis, whitish towards the
tip; the second antennal joint is not quite as long as in the preceding species, chiefly because it is but very little less drawn
out forwards above than below; the last joint is at least by one
half shorter than the second, rounded oval, ending in a blunt
point; the arista is inserted on the middle of its length, on the
outside, near the upper margin; of its two basal joints the second
has four times the length of the very short first joint.   The palpi
are slender, filiform, tinged with brown, like the proboscis.   The
thoracic dorsum shows three deep black stripes; the middle one
is very broad, begins at the anterior margin and ends some
distance before the scutellum; the lateral stripes are abbreviated
anteriorly and posteriorly; the portion of them behind the suture
is larger than that in front of it.   The greater part of the pleuræ,
a spot on each side at the posterior margin of the scutellum,
as well as the metathorax, dark-brown.   On the abdomen, the
anterior part and the middle line of the first segment are pitch-
black and somewhat shining; on each of the following three segments is a triangular spot, of the same coloring, the basis of which
is directed anteriorly, and which occupies the whole breadth of
the segment.   The upper part of the abdomen has delicate
transverse grooves, the under side on the contrary is strongly
grooved in a longitudinal direction, opaque velvet-black, with a
narrow, ochre-yellow middle line; the projecting male organ of
copulation is of a shining reddish-brown.   The feet are light
ferruginous, with yellow hairs; the femora, to the exclusion of
the tip and tibiæ, with the exception of the basis and of the extreme tip, are chestnut-brown.   The second longitudinal vein of
the wings is hardly perceptibly broken and without any vestige
of a stump; the wings in general are comparatively shorter than
in *P. undata*, darker and more evenly earth-brown; a very
delicate streak near the posterior border of the first longitudinal
vein, not far from the origin of the second vein, the whole alula
and two streaks near the posterior margin, the position of which

corresponds to the entirely discolored spots in *P. undata*, are hyaline. These two streaks have a very definite outline, and the space beyond them is as dark-brown as the remainder of the wing; the longer one is almost straight, the shorter one sickle-shaped. The halteres are pale ferruginous-yellow.

Hab. Carolina (Zimmermann).

Observation.—The above description is the reproduction of that prepared by Dr. Gerstaecker, l. c., from a single specimen in the Berlin Museum. I have had a passing view of the specimen; it is very like *P. undata.* The differences in coloring, noticed by this author, are in my opinion of but little importance, as most of them occur among the varieties of the very variable *P. undata.* More important are the plastic differences, mentioned by Dr. Gerstaecker. Although the shape of the head in different specimens of *P. undata* is variable (evidently, however, in consequence of different degrees of shrinkage in drying), although the size of the third antennal joint is subject to slight variations, and although the relative length of the first two joints of the arista is not altogether constant, it is hardly credible that all these discrepancies should reach the degree which Dr. Gerstaecker noticed in his *P. vespertilio.*

4. P. pteropherina Gerst. ♀.—Antennarum articulo tertio præcedente paulo longiore, oblongo ovata, arista brevissima, crassa: fronte oculis latiore, fortiter prolongata, palpis cochlearibus; alis latis, vena longitudinali secunda geniculata, haud appendiculata, fuscis; alula, macula duabus, postulis magnis, semilunaribus, guttisque duabus hyalinis.

The third antennal joint is somewhat longer than the preceding one, elongated-oval, with a very short, stout arista; front broader than the eyes, very much prolonged; palpi spoon-shaped; wings broad, with a second longitudinal vein which is geniculate, but has no stump of a vein upon it; coloring on the wings brown; alula, two large crescent shaped spaces on the posterior margin and two dots hyaline. Long. corp. 0.4; long. al. 0.44.

Syn. *Pyrgota pteropherina* Gerst., Stett. Entom. Zeit. xxi, p. 190, Tab. II, f. 6.

Body small, slender, pale-ferruginous, shining. Head, viewed from above, by one-third longer than broad; front broader than the eyes, but, taken as far as the anterior margin of the eyes, nevertheless longer than broad; the gibbosity only a little shorter

6

and very little attenuated anteriorly; viewed in profile, this gibbosity is less elevated than in the two preceding species; on the
contrary, it is, to its very much protruding tip, almost on the
same level with the remaining portion of the front; this causes
the anterior margin, which, with a slight convexity, is strongly
retreating, to lie almost entirely on the under side; cheeks likewise broader and descending lower than in *P. undata.* The
coloring of the head is altogether pale-ferruginous, even the black
lines, bordering the middle portion of the face, are wanting.
The antennæ likewise are altogether ferruginous-yellow; the two
apical joints are almost of equal length; the third appears a little
longer, only when viewed from the outside, along the lower
margin, because, at this point, this joint is less covered by the
second than above and on the inside; the first two joints are
beset with blackish bristles, as in the two preceding species; the
third joint is elongated-oval; the arista is inserted in the middle
of its length, near the upper margin; it is stout and very short,
shorter than the third antennal joint; the second joint of the
arista is one-half longer than the first; the styliform third joint
is but little longer than the first two taken together. Palpi
elongated, slightly curved, somewhat spoon-shaped at the tip,
pale ferruginous-yellow, with black bristles; the proboscis brown.
Thorax uniformly ferruginous-yellow; clothed, as the head, with
delicate black bristles. Abdomen of a similar color, but more
shining, beset with long black bristles, forming bunches, especially on the sides; the upper side of the first abdominal segment
is infuscated beyond the middle. The horny capsule, which
forms the end of the fifth segment of the abdomen of the female,
has, in profile, the appearance of a sparrow's bill; it is convex
above, concavo below, obtuse at the tip and somewhat shorter
than the last three abdominal segments taken together. Feet
perceptibly longer and more slender than in the two preceding
species, with dense and rather long hairs, light brown; the basal
third of the tibiæ and the tarsi pale yellowish; the hind tibiæ
are much more incrassated toward the tip than the middle ones.
Wings remarkably broad, obtusely rounded at the apex; the
second longitudinal vein strongly bent and then broken in the
shape of an angle, but without stump of a vein; ground color of
a saturate earth-brown; a trapezoidal spot, extending from the

costa to the third longitudinal vein and situated before the break
in the second vein, a round spot between both crossveins, the
alula and two large crescents on the posterior margin hyaline ;
the crescents show a pale shade of brownish towards the posterior
margin. Halteres altogether pale yellow.

Hab. Carolina (Zimmerman).

Observation 1.—The above is a translation of Gerstaecker's
description of the specimens in the Berlin Museum. The species
is distinguished enough to render the discussion of its specific
rights useless. I will only notice here, that when the author
says that the fifth abdominal segment in the female gradually
passes into the capsule-shaped ovipositor, this expression is not
to be understood literally; in the two species which I have seen,
such a transition is not visible. When the author calls the first
two antennal joints of *P. pterophorina* "beset with blackish
bristles, as in the preceding species (*P. undata* and *vespertilio*),"
I would observe that in *P. undata* this pubescence is in reality
yellow, and assumes a ferruginous or even blackish tinge only
when seen against the light.

Observation 2.—A fifth American species is described by
Macquart (Dipt. Exot. Suppl. IV, p. 281, Tab. XXVI, f. 1) as
Oxycephala fenestrata. His data are not even sufficient to
ascertain whether the species really is a *Pyrgota.* Moreover it
is not distinctly stated whether this species belongs to North
America.

Second Section : PLATYSTOMINA.

Gen. I. AMPHICNEPHES nov. gen.

Charact.—Front of medium breadth, not narrower anteriorly.
> Antenna reaching down to the edge of the mouth.
> Face excavated, without distinct antennal foveæ; occiput but little
> turgid; eyes high; cheeks narrow.
> Scutellum large, flat, with four bristles.
> Wings very broad; the longitudinal veins straight and conspicuously
> diverging; anal cell shorter than the preceding basal cell; its
> posterior angle rounded.

Small, metallic-colored species, the wings of which show a
picture not unlike that of the species of *Platystoma*, and the
general habitus of which is less like the species of *Rivellia* than

those of *Platystoma.* They are, however, easily distinguished from the latter by the narrower front, the much less turgid occiput, the larger and flatter scutellum and the much broader wings, with straight, very much diverging longitudinal veins.

1. A. pertusus n. sp. ♂ and ♀.—(Tab. VIII, f. 1) Viridis, nitidus ala nigra, guttis et fascia subapicali hyalinis.

Green, shining; wings black with hyaline dots and a hyaline crossband before the tip. Long. corp. 0.13—0.14; long. al. 0.11—0.12.

Dark metallic-green, shining. Head black; the front blackish-brown, even, rather long, but only of a medium breadth, not narrowed anteriorly; the ocelli are closely approximated to each other near the edge of the vertex; the small ocellar triangle and the little stripes running down at the corners of the vertex are of a shining blackish-green. Bristles of the vertex rather long, directed backwards; the bristle which is in front of them on each side is short; the ocellar bristles are not distinct. Antennæ reaching down to the edge of the mouth, brownish-yellow; their narrow third joint is blackish at the tip; often the greater part of its outer side is brownish. Face excavated; its lateral portions very narrow; antennal foveæ indistinct. The shining black clypeus broad. Palpi broad, shining black, with a paler border on the under side and at the tip; proboscis of moderate thickness; mentum but little swollen. Eyes much higher than broad; cheeks narrow; occiput but little turgid. Thorax very delicately transversely aciculate. Scutellum large, flat, weakly rugose, with four bristles. Abdomen more distinctly rugose. Ovipositor black, considerably extensile. Feet black, brownish-black in less mature specimens; the first joint of the front and hind tarsi and the first three joints of the middle tarsi of a dirty ochre-yellow. Halteres black, tegulæ but little developed. Wings rather broad, black, more grayish-black near the hind margin; immediately before their apex is a conspicuous, arcuated, hyaline crossband; before this band there is a moderate number of hyaline dots of regular shape, which become more sparse towards the anterior margin; five dots which are nearest to the crossband form a row, parallel to the latter; the blackish-gray coloring near the hind margin of the wings has no hyaline spots. The veins are much more straight than in *Platystoma* and very diverging;

the two posterior basal cells are rather striking for their large size; however, the anal cell, which has an obtuse posterior angle, is shorter than the basal cell lying in front of it; the small cross-vein is in the middle of the discal cell; the first half of this cell is by no means attenuated, as is the case in the species of *Rivellia*.

Hab. Carolina (Zimmerman); Washington, D. C., Connecticut (Osten-Sacken).

Gen. II. **HIMEROËSSA** nov. gen.

Charact.—Front of equal breadth, distinctly projecting in profile.
 Antenna reaching almost to the mouth, arista bare.
  Face moderately excavated, somewhat retreating below; epistome moderately turgid, eyes high; cheeks narrow.
  Scutellum convex; with six bristles.
  Wings: marginal and submarginal cells very narrow; second section of the fourth longitudinal vein straight; posterior crossvein prolonged beyond the fourth vein; posterior angle of the anal cell rounded.

As I have seen only a single species of this genus, the one which is described below, the definition of the generic character can naturally be only a provisional one. Should the peculiar prolongation of the posterior crossvein, which distinguishes *H. pretiosa*, be wanting in some allied species, it would then be necessary to omit this character from the definition of the genus; the remaining characters are amply sufficient for the purpose.

1. **H. pretiosa** n. sp. ♀.—(Tab. VIII, f. 2.) Rufo testacea, abdomine violaceo, pedibus anticis totis, posteriorumque tibiis et tarsis nigris; alæ hyalinæ, inæquali costa limbo et fascia transl subinterrupta nigro-fuscis.

Yellowish-red, with a violet abdomen; the front feet altogether, the tibiæ and tarsi of the four posterior feet, black; wings hyaline with an irregular costal border and a narrow, somewhat interrupted crossband, blackish-brown. Long. corp. 0.38, long. al. 0.3.

Yellowish-red, shining. Front darker, opaque, of equal breadth, with very indistinct traces of flat pits and a very delicate border of white pollen along the orbits; distinctly projecting in profile; the little stripes, descending from the vertex along the sides of the front, and the ocellar triangle are distinct, and somewhat more shining; the latter is somewhat larger than

usual; ocelli very near the edge of the vertex, rather large, but
little approximated; the four bristles on the edge of the vertex
rather strong; the lateral, as well as the ocellar bristles replaced
by shorter, bristle-like hairs. Antennæ of the coloring of the
body, almost reaching to the anterior edge of the oral opening;
arista bare. Face but moderately concave, somewhat retreating
on the under side, pollinose with white, except in the vicinity of
the oral opening; in the well-marked fovea this pollen is thicker
and more conspicuous; the lateral portions of the face, bordering
on the eyes, are very narrow and likewise clothed with white
pollen. Eyes much higher than broad; cheeks narrow. Clypeus
of a moderate breadth, distinctly projecting over the edge of the
mouth; palpi not very broad, almost ferruginous. Proboscis
rather stout; occiput moderately turgid. The whole thorax and
the convex scutellum shining, with a very faint trace of a reddish
metallic reflection. Scutellum with six bristles. Abdomen of a
metallic reddish-violet coloring, which, in a different light, assumes
upon the first three segments a bronze-green tinge; this is not
the case with the last segment. Front feet with the coxæ
brownish-black; on the four posterior feet the tibiæ and tarsi
alone have this coloring; the coxæ and femora have the color of
the thorax. Halteres yellowish-red, with an infuscated knob.
Wings hyaline, with brown veins, which are not in the least
sinuous; their anterior margin has a conspicuous, but unequal
brown border, which, near the apex, extends as far as the fourth
vein; from the root of the wing to the small crossvein, which is
still included in this border, it becomes gradually broader and
reaches here almost to the fifth longitudinal vein; it contracts
immediately beyond the small crossvein, to the second longitudinal vein; opposite the posterior crossvein it expands again
towards the third longitudinal vein, and runs immediately behind
this vein as far as the apex of the wing, where it suddenly turns
towards the fourth longitudinal vein, which forms the limit of this
dark border; the very steep posterior crossvein projects in an
unusual way beyond the fourth longitudinal vein; it is bordered
with brown: this border forms a narrow, perpendicular crossband, which growing paler and more indistinct, extends to the
dark border of the anterior margin, or quite near it; the costal
cell is clay-yellow, except at the basis and at the tip, which are
more brownish. The marginal and submarginal cells are re-

markably narrow; the small crossvein is in the middle of the
discal cell; the posterior angle of the anal cell is rounded and
the last section of the fourth longitudinal vein is parallel to the
third.

Hab. Cuba (Gundlach).

Gen. III. RIVELLIA R. Desv.

Charact.—*Front of equal breadth, not projecting in profile.*

Antennæ usually reaching down to the margin of the mouth; third
joint long and narrow; arista with a very short pubescence.

Face rather excavated, its lower part projecting; the lateral portions
very narrow; clypeus broad; occiput moderately turgid; eyes
high; cheeks moderately broad.

Scutellum convex, with four bristles.

Wings: Marginal and submarginal cells comparatively broad; the
second section of the fourth longitudinal vein remarkably sinnate,
with the convexity encroaching upon the discal cell, so that the
latter appears much narrower before the small crossvein than behind
it; the last section of the fourth longitudinal vein is parallel to the
third vein or very slightly diverging; posterior angle of the anal
cell rounded.

A large number of closely resembling species belong to this
genus; the picture of the wings of most of them is nearly the
same, so that this picture alone helps to recognize the species
belonging here; it consists of four brown or blackish-brown
crossbands; the first starts from the root of the wing and is the
most oblique of all and the shortest; the second, somewhat
longer and less oblique, runs over the small crossvein; the third,
which covers the posterior crossvein, is perpendicular and reaches
from the anterior to the posterior margin of the wing; the fourth
starts from the anterior margin, near the origin of the third hand,
and forms a border along the apex of the wing. The North
American fauna seems to abound in these species. The apparently total absence of plastic differences between them and the,
as it seems, not unimportant variation in the coloring of some of
them, render their separation very difficult, especially when there
are only single specimens for comparison. I hope not to have
gone amiss in the definition of those which I know. Whether
I was mistaken or not, those may judge who have the opportunity
of observing these species in life.

Among the species described below, *Rivellia conjuncta* is the only one which does not belong to the difficult group just characterized; it is distinguished from it not only by a different picture of the wings, but also by some easily tangible plastic differences.

1st Group.   *Crossbands contiguous near the posterior margin.*

1. R. conjuncta n. sp.   ♀.—(Tab. VIII, f. 3.) Nigro-viridis, pedibus praeter tarsorum basim nigris, tribus primis alarum fasciis postice cohaerentibus.

Blackish-green; the feet, with the exception of the root of the tarsi, black; the first three crossbands of the wings contiguous posteriorly. Long. corp. 0.16; long. al. 0.14.

Blackish-green, shining. Front moderately broad, dusky ferruginous-brown, almost black, laterally with a rather broad border, pollinose with white. Antennæ reaching almost down to the edge of the mouth, brick-red, except the third joint which turns brownish or blackish towards its tip. Face and clypeus metallic-black. Feet black; the basis of the tarsi brick-red or dirty reddish-yellow to a considerable extent. Halteres black. Wings hyaline; the four crossbands much broader than in the following species, especially the first; the second coalesces with the first in the discal cell and the third unites with the first near the posterior margin of the wing; the band which forms a border along the end of the anterior margin and the apex is connected in the usual way with the third, at the anterior margin. The small crossvein is but little beyond the middle of the discal cell; the second section of the fourth longitudinal vein is strongly arcuated, and the posterior crossvein is bisinuate.

Hab. Maryland (Osten-Sacken).

2d Group.   *Crossbands separated near the posterior margin.*

2. R. viridulans R. Desv.   ♂ ♀.—(Tab. VIII, f. 4.) Nigro-viridis, interdum chalybraceus, pedibus praeter tarsorum basim nigris, primis tribus alarum fasciis separatis.

Blackish-green, sometimes more steel-blue; feet, with the exception of the root of the tarsi, black; the first three crossbands of the wings isolated from each other. Long. corp. 0.16—0.21; long. al. 0.15—0.2.

Syn. *Rivellia viridulans* R. Desv. Myod. p. 729, 2.
Trypeta quadrifasciata Harris, Cat. Ins. Mass.

Ortalis Ortanda WALK. List, IV, p. 992.
Ortalis quadrifasciata WALK. List, IV, p. 993.
Herina rufitarsis MACQ. Dipt. Exot. Suppl. V, p. 123, 7.
Tephritis melliginis FITCH, First Rep. 45.

Blackish-green, shining; the upper side of the thorax sometimes
less so; recently excluded specimens acquire a somewhat steel-
blue tinge after drying. Front reddish-brown, often very dark,
of the usual breadth, with a very narrow border of white pollen
on each side. Face and clypeus metallic black; the narrow
lateral portions of the face, bordering on the eyes, brownish-red,
more seldom dark-brown. Antennæ reaching to the edge of the
mouth, brick-red or yellowish-red; the third joint gradually
turning black towards the tip. Ovipositor and feet black; the
tips of the four anterior tibiæ usually brownish brick-red; the
first joint of the two front tarsi and the first two joints of the
four posterior tarsi pale brick-red. Crossbands of the wings
black, rather narrow; the first three, which are entirely separated from each other, reach from the anterior margin to the
fifth longitudinal vein; the fourth band, bordering the end of the
anterior margin and the apex, is often connected with the third
only by a rather narrow black border of the anterior margin; the
portion of the costal cell between the first and the second crossbands has a dingy, somewhat yellowish appearance. The small
crossvein is far beyond the middle of the discal cell and the
second section of the fourth longitudinal vein is very much arcuated. Halteres black.

Hab. New York; Georgia; Distr. Columbia (Osten-Sacken).

Observation 1.—The attentive reader of Walker's description
of *Ortalis Ortoeda* will easily notice that, before the end of the
fourth line, previous to the comma, several words have been
accidentally omitted, so that the end of the sentence does not
refer, as it should, to the second, but to the third crossband.
What Mr. Walker meant to say results sufficiently from the next
description, that of *O. quadrifasciata*, which reproduces again
the present, apparently very common, species. The fact that the
measurements of *O. Ortoeda* and *quadrifasciata* are different in
Walker does not prevent me from considering them as one and
the same species. Under the former name Walker describes a
male; under the latter, a female; hence, the greater size of the
latter has nothing surprising. Instead of the length of the single

wing, Walker gives the breadth of the wings from apex to apex,
a datum which is to be obtained only by approximation. This
breadth in *O. Ortorda* is said to be three, in *O. quadrifasciata*
four lines, a difference which is somewhat considerable, but,
owing to its uncertain nature, not to be relied upon exclusively
for separating the two species, as the female of *R. viridulans*
really has longer wings than the male. The quotation from
Harris's Catalogue has been introduced upon the authority of
Walker, who seems to have had original specimens of this
author; but as the species has never been described, the quotation might as well have been omitted. That *Herina rufitarsis*
Macq. belongs here is not doubtful. I have been able to compare a typical specimen of *Tephritis melliginis* Fitch.

Observation 2.—The following species agree so much with
R. viridulans in the breadth of the front, the shape and the
length of the antennae, and in the venation, that every statement
about these points would be useless. In speaking of the picture
of the wings, a statement about the points of difference will be
more useful towards discriminating the species than a detailed
description.

8. R. quadrifasciata Macq. ♂ .—(Tab. VIII, f. 5.) Thorace
viridi, capite praeter occiput, abdomine, pedibus, halteribusque luteis.

Thorax green; the head, with the exception of the occiput, the abdomen,
the feet, and the halteres, dark-yellow. Long. corp. 0.2; long. al. 0.19.

Syn. *Herina quadrifasciata* Macq. Suites, etc., II, p. 433, 8.

Head dark-yellow, the occiput metallic dark-green. Front
dusky red, with a narrow border of white pollen on each side.
Antennae dark yellowish-red; the third joint, with the exception
of the root, brown; blackish towards the tip. Palpi dark-yellow.
Thorax, including the scutellum, of a blackish-green, metallic
coloring, shining. Abdomen dark-yellow, more brownish-yellow
towards its end. Coxae and feet dark-yellow; hind tibiae yellowish-brown; the last four joints of the front tarsi, and the last
three, more seldom the last four, joints of the middle and hind
tarsi infuscated. Halteres dark-yellow. The crossbands on the
wings as narrow and nearly in the same position as in *R. viridulans*, but less dark; the first band is narrower and crosses the
fourth longitudinal vein but very little; the second reaches not

quite as for as the fifth longitudinal vein; the hyaline interval between them is broader and the intervening portion of the costal cell of a darker coloring than in *R. viridulans*; the costa itself, from the extreme basis as far as about the middle of the costal cell, is of a dirty-yellowish coloring.

Hab. Nebraska (?). [I possess a specimen from Washington, D. C., which agrees exactly with the above description. O. S.]

4. R. variabilis n. sp. ♂.—(Tab. VIII, f. 6.) Rufo-testacea, capite pectoreque piceis, abdomine nigro-piceo, basin versus plerumque dilutius piceo, pedibus luteis, tibiis posticis tarsorumque apice fuscis.

Brick-red; head and chest pitch-brown; abdomen pitch-black, towards the basis usually of a lighter pitch-brown; feet dark yellow; hind tibiæ and the tip of all the tarsi brown. Long. corp. 0.18—0.21; long. al. 0.18—0.2.

Brick-red. Head pitch-brown or reddish-brown. Front of an opaque dark-red coloring, on each side near the orbit with a very narrow border of white pollen. Antennæ reaching down to the mouth; the first two joints dark reddish-yellow; the third, with the exception of the basis, dark-brown, blackish towards the tip. Palpi dark-brown. The chest and the lower part of the pleuræ dark pitch-brown. Abdomen pitch-black, generally lighter pitch-brown near the basis. Coxæ and feet dark-yellow; the four anterior tibiæ but little infuscated; the hind tibiæ and the last three or four tarsal joints dark-brown. Halteres dark-brown. The picture of the wings almost entirely like that of *R. quadri-fasciata* in coloring and design, only the first two crossbands are a trifle longer and the first a little broader; the brown coloring in the anterior basal cell is a little less extended.

Hab. District Columbia (Osten-Sacken).

Observation.—I have a female, from the same locality, which I think belongs to the present species. It differs from the male, described above, in having the antennæ of an altogether dark-yellow coloring, except the slightly infuscated tip of their third joint; the color in the middle of the thoracic dorsum almost verges on blackish; the first crossband on the wings is a little longer, the front and middle tibiæ do not show any distinct infuscation and the tip of the tarsi is but little infuscated.

5. R. flavimana n. sp. ♂ ♀.—(Tab. VIII, f. 7.) Viridi-nigra, vel nigro-chalybea, pedibus anticis luteis, posterioribus semper ex parte, plerumque maxima ex parte, nigris vel fuscis.

Greenish-black, or more bluish-black; the front feet dark-yellow, the hind feet partly, and usually for the most part, black or bluish-brown. Long. corp. 0.16; long. al. 0.14.

Syn.? *Herina metallica* v. d. Wulp. Tijdschr. voor. Ent. 2, p. 154. Tab. V, f. 10.

Very like *R. viridulans*, but easily distinguished by its smaller size and the paler, although very variable, coloring of the feet. Metallic blackish-green or almost blackish-blue. Head shining black; occiput of a metallic greenish-black; front dusky reddish-brown, often blackish-brown, on each side near the orbit with a very narrow border of white pollen. The first two antennal joints brownish-red, the third blackish-brown or black. The coloring of the abdomen towards the tip, in the male, verges more on bronze-black; the only female which I can compare has no trace of this color. Fore coxæ and tibiæ yellowish; the upper side of the femora and the basis of the tibiæ very seldom show a trace of infuscation. The four posterior feet have the coxæ, femora, and tibiæ black or brownish-black, the tarsi yellow. The above-mentioned female has the tip of the middle femora and the middle tibiæ, with the exception of the dark-brown basal third, of a brownish-yellow color; the tips of the tarsi in this specimen are hardly infuscated at all, while the male specimens have the three or four terminal joints of the front tarsi and the last three or four joints of the middle and hind feet somewhat dark-brownish. Halteres brownish-black. The picture of the wings recalls, in design and coloring, that of *R. viridulans*, only the crossbands are a little narrower; in general also the second, and especially the first, reach less near the fifth longitudinal vein; the black coloring, which is apparent on the root of the anterior basal cell of *R. viridulans*, is wanting in *R. flavimana*, and this affords a good character for distinguishing the latter species from those allied to it.

Hab. Nebraska (Dr. Hayden).

Observation 1.—I possess a male, the four posterior feet of which, with the exception of the hind tibiæ, are yellow; it is also distinguished by the color of the antennæ, which are reddish-yellow as far as beyond the middle of the third joint, and by the somewhat narrower crossbands. Nevertheless, I consider it only as a variety of *B. flavimana*, which seems to be very variable in the coloring of the feet.

Observation 2.—*Rivellia Boscii* R. Desv. cannot very well be identified with *B. flavimana*, as it is described as considerably larger than *R. viridulans*, whereas *R. flavimana* is distinctly smaller. I did not succeed in identifying this species of Rob. Desvoidy; his data concerning the coloring do not agree with *R. quadrifasciata* and *variabilis*, and *R. pallida* is still less to be taken into account.

Observation 3.—At first, while in possession of insufficient materials, I took *B. viridulans*, *quadrifasciata*, *variabilis*, and *flavimana* for varieties of the same species, and it is only later that more abundant materials convinced me that they are actually different, although closely allied, species. It is in conformity with my former view that I have identified with *R. viridulans* the *Herina metallica* described and figured by v. d. Wulp in the Tijdschrift voor Entomologie, x, p. 154, Tab. V, f. 10. If my present separation of these species be correct, the only ones which can be taken into consideration in interpreting Mr. v. d. Wulp's species are *R. Boscii*, *flavimana*, and perhaps *B. micans*. *R. Boscii* is so inaccurately described by R. Desvoidy that its identification is very difficult anyhow; but as this species is 8 lines long, that of v. d. Wulp only 1½, I consider their identity as not probable. The assumption that my *R. micans* is the *Herina metallica* of v. d. Wulp is contradicted by the very brilliant metallic-green coloring of the former. Moreover, v. d. Wulp's figure does not show, at the basis of the first basal cell, the dark coloring existing in *R. micans*, which coloring has the same extent, although not the same intensity, as in *R. viridulans*. If the correctness of the figure of the wing of *Herina metallica* could be implicitly relied upon, its specific diversity from *R. micans* would be a matter of certainty. But in this case I would have also to admit that *H. metallica* does not coincide with any of the species of *Rivellia* known to me, as the said figure differs from those species, especially in the broad interval between the first and second crossbands, which does not occur to that extent in any of them. We are forced to assume, therefore, that the figure of the wing is only of an average correctness, and to pay attention, in its interpretation, to the principal features

only. If the want of a dark coloring at the basis of the first
basal cell be singled out as a characteristic feature, the supposition
suggests itself that the species is identical with *H. flavimana*,
which also partakes of this character; the shortening of the first
two crossbands, as well as the data concerning the size and coloring of *H. metallica*, do not contradict such an assumption;
even the statement about the coloring of the feet could be applied
to unusually pale specimens of *R. flavimana*, although I have
never met with specimens of this degree of paleness. Hence,
it appears not improbable, although far from certain, that *Herina
metallica* is identical with *R. flavimana*.

6. R. micans n. sp. ♀.—Speciebus praecedentibus minor, laete aeneo-
viridis, nitida, pedibus omnibus luteis, fasciis alarum fusco-nigris.

Smaller than the preceding species, metallic-green, shining; all the feet
saturate-yellow; the crossbands on the wings brownish-black. Long.
corp. 0.13—0.18; long. al. 0.13.

Not reaching the size of *R. variabilis* and perceptibly smaller
than the other preceding species; of a metallic-green, bright
and shining coloring. The front, the lateral stripes on the face
and the lower part of the occiput of a reddish-yellow, seldom of
a brownish-red coloring; antennae, as far as the basal third or
the middle of the third joint, reddish-yellow; beyond that,
brown. The abdomen shows a diluted, half-pellucid, reddish
crossband at the place where the first and second segments are
soldered together; in some cases this band is wanting. Coxae
and feet saturate-yellow, the former sometimes more brownish-
yellow; the tarsi, towards their tips, are strongly infuscated.
The picture of the wings, in its design, is not unlike that of
R. viridulans, but is rather brownish-black than deep black; the
dark crossbands are a little narrower, especially the first and
second, so that the hyaline interval between them is comparatively broader, almost equal in breadth to the interval between
the second and third bands (in *R. viridulans* the first interval is
considerably narrower than the second); the first and second
crossbands stop about the middle of the interval between the
fourth and fifth longitudinal veins; however, single specimens
occur in which they are shorter; in other specimens they reach
very near the fifth vein; the third band, towards its end, is perceptibly narrowed. The second section of the fourth longitu-

dinal vein is less arcuated towards the small crossvein than in *R. viridulana.* The coxæ and feet are dark-yellow; the hind tibiæ, towards their end, grow gradually, but very slightly, more brownish-yellow; the tarsi, from about the basis of the third joint, dark brown.

Hab. Texas (Belfrage).

Observation.—The present species differs from all the proceeding ones by the more pure and brilliant metallic-green color. Varieties of *R. flavimana,* with very pale feet, are nearest to it; but such specimens have at least the hind tibiæ, with the exception of the extreme basis and the extreme tip, brown. Moreover, they differ from *R. micans* by the coloring of the first basal cell, which is hardly perceptibly tinged with gray at its extreme basis only, while in the latter species it is infuscated up to the last third of the second basal cell.

7. R. pallida n. sp.   ♂ ♀.— (Tab. VIII, f. 8.) Flavo-testacea, Rivellia micanti æqualis, reliquis speciebus minor, fasciis alarum nigro-fuscis.

Yellowish brick-red, of the size of R. micans, but smaller than the other species; the crossbands of the wings blackish-brown. Long. corp. 0.14—0.15; long. al. 0.13.

Yellowish brick-red. Head concolorous; front more ferruginous; on each side with a narrow border of white pollen. Antennæ of the same color with the remainder of the body, only the third joint a little blackish at the extreme tip. One of my specimens has the first two segments of the abdomen black at the basis; but this color seems to have originated after death, being produced by the contents of the abdomen. Ovipositor not darker, or but a little darker, than the rest of the abdomen. Feet dark-yellow; last two, at the utmost last three, joints of the tarsi brown. Knob of the halteres brown. The picture of the wings reminds of that of *R. flavimana,* but instead of black it is blackish-brown; the costal cell is tinged with brown at the spot only where the first crossband has its beginning, elsewhere it is of a dingy yellowish; the root of the first basal cell shows, as in *R. flavimana,* no dark coloring; the first and the second crossbands usually reach very near the fifth longitudinal vein. This species is easily recognized by its smaller size and lighter coloring.

Hab. Washington, D. C. (Osten-Sacken.)

Gen. IV. STENOPTERINA Macq.

Charact.—*Body* long and narrow.

Head almost like that of *Dacus*; *front* of a considerable and equal breadth, somewhat projecting in profile; *face* somewhat excavated in profile, perpendicular towards the somewhat upturned anterior edge of the mouth, or but little projecting; the shallow *antennal fovea* long and narrow, not distinctly separated from the convex middle portion of the face; the lateral portions of the face very narrow; *clypeus* very large; eyes large; cheeks not very broad; oculpst only moderately turgid.

Antenna : The first two joints short; the third narrow and very long, generally reaching a little below the anterior edge of the mouth; arista apparently bare, or with a pubescence which is so short as to be almost imperceptible.

Thorax long and narrow; the transverse suture runs across the whole dorsum in the shape of a shallow depression; viewed laterally, the thorax appears remarkably attenuated towards its anterior end, as the pectus is truncated obliquely in front; *scutellum* with four bristles.

Abdomen remarkably narrow; the first segment more or less prolonged in the male.

Feet slender; the fore coxa very long, inserted remarkably near the collum, and unusually movable at the point of insertion.

Wings rather narrow; stigma long and narrow; small crossvein oblique, inserted more or less beyond the middle of the long discal cell; second section of the fourth longitudinal vein straight; posterior angle of the anal cell rounded; the picture of the wings consists chiefly in a dark border of the costa, reaching from the basis of the stigma to the apex of the wing, and in the darker coloring of the entire anterior basal cell, to which, in most of the species, is added a brown cloud along the posterior crossvein.

The great uncertainty which seems to have hitherto prevailed concerning the characters of the genus *Stenopterina* has induced me to enter in more detail about them than about the other genera. If my limitation of this genus be correct, it will contain only species closely related in their plastic characters. Their venation alone shows some differences; some species have the third and fourth longitudinal veins convergent towards their ends, the second longitudinal vein perceptibly shorter, more distant from the costa, and meeting it at a less acute angle; other species show the opposite of all these characters. As far as I can judge at present, the species of the former group seem to belong principally to the old world.

Æ *ænea* Wied. and *brevipes* F. may be considered as the types of the genus.

1. S. cæruiescens n. sp. ♂.—Viridi-chalybea, humeris concoloribus, thoracis dorso magis violaceo, halteribus nigris, alarum hyalinarum limbo costali inde a vena auxiliaris apice usque ad venam quartam pertinente, cellulâ basali primâ et venæ transversalis posterioris limbo fumo-nigris.

Greenish-steelblue, with concolorous humeri and the thoracic dorsum more violet; halteres black; wings hyaline, a costal border, reaching from the end of the auxiliary to the end of the fourth longitudinal vein, the first basal cell and a border along the posterior crossvein brownish-black. Long. corp. 0.32—0.39; long. al. 0.28—0.31.

Of a greenish-steelblue coloring, which on the abdomen has a somewhat stronger admixture of green and verges on violet on the thoracic dorsum; the humeral callosities and the pleura have the same greenish-blue color. Head dark-yellow, almost brownish-yellow; clypeus and palpi of the same color; front strongly infuscated anteriorly, this coloring having more or less extent; at the bottom of each of the foveæ a distinct brownish-black longitudinal streak; first and second antennal joints, as well as the root of the third, to a greater or lesser extent, dark-yellow; the third joint, towards its end, becomes more and more brown, even brownish-black. The last abdominal segment is only a little shorter than the penultimate. The hairs on thorax and abdomen are whitish, with the exception of the few and comparatively short bristles on the posterior end of the thoracic dorsum and of the four bristles of the scutellum. The coloring of the coxæ and feet is very variable, as that of the front and of the antennæ; the palest specimens in my possession have brownish-yellow coxæ, more yellowish feet, with a dark metallic streak, reflecting greenish-blue, upon the anterior side of the hind femora, and with tarsi which are dark-brown towards the tip; the darkest specimens in my collection have metallic-black coxæ, the femora almost black, with a bright metallic bluish-green lustre, excepting the tips of all the femora, which are brownish-red, and of the brownish-red basis of the middle ones; tibiæ and tarsi dark brownish-red; the latter, towards their end, colored with brownish-black to a considerable extent. Halteres black, only the basis of their stem a little paler. Wings hyaline;

7

their brownish-black picture consists of a narrow border along the anterior margin, which reaches from the end of the auxiliary vein to that of the fourth longitudinal vein, in the darker coloring of the first basal cell, which even crosses a little the small cross-vein and in a narrow border along the posterior crossvein.

Hab. Texas (Belfrage).

Observation 1.—The South American *S. brevipes* Fab. is distinguished from the present species by the ochre-yellow color of the humeri and the ferruginous-yellowish color of the halteres.

Observation 2.—*Herina metallica* Macq. (Dipt. Exot. II, 3, p. 208), from Mexico, is evidently no *Herina* at all, but a *Stenopterina.* It would seem possible, therefore, that *Stenopterina cærulescens* is that very species. Many of the statements in Macquart's description agree with *S. cærulescens.* It must be borne in mind, however, that these statements refer for the most part to characters which a whole series of *Stenopterinæ* have in common. The statement that the wings are yellowish is not applicable to *S. cærulescens*, and none of the varieties of this species which are in my possession have the black feet mentioned in Macquart's description of *H. metallica.* Nevertheless, I would not have doubted this synonymy if I had nothing but Macquart's description to consult. The figure of the wing, however, which Macquart gives (l. c. Tab. XXIX, f. 2) sets this supposition entirely aside, by showing an unusually broad dark border along the anterior margin, by which Macquart's species differs conspicuously from *S. cærulescens* and similar species with the ordinary narrow border of the anterior margin.

Gen. V. MISCHOGASTER Macq.

Charact.—Front of a considerable, rather equal, breadth; the anterior ocellus rather distant from the two others.

Face excavated in profile, hardly projecting below.

Antennæ rather long; arista with a distinct pubescence.

Wings narrowed towards the basis; auxiliary and first longitudinal veins closely approximated; posterior angle of the anal cell rounded.

Abdomen narrow, still more attenuated towards the basis; first segment basal with strong bristles; ovipositor rather conical.

The characters, as given here, are very incomplete, and require an entire revision. Unfortunately, I had no specimen at band for comparison, and was obliged to write from memory. The bristles on the first abdominal segment, the distance intervening between the anterior ocellus and the posterior ones, and even the shape of the oripositor remind very much of some genera in the group of *Richardina*, from which, however, *Mischogaster* is easily distinguished by the distinct bristles on the first longitudinal vein and the unarmed femora.

The typical species of the genus is the *Cephalia femoralis* Wied. No species from North America are as yet known.

Gen. VI. MYRMECOMYIA R. Desv.

Charact.—Body slender, not unlike that of an ant.

Head comparatively large; occiput conspicuously stout behind the vertex.

Front of a uniform, considerable breadth, very long and steep, so that the antennæ are below the middle of the head; the very large lateral stripes of the front have wrinkle-shaped cross impressions.

Antennæ reaching a little below the anterior edge of the mouth; arista with a rather short pubescence.

Front convex, not excavated in profile, but descending in an inclined plane; clypeus of a moderate transverse diameter; cheeks rather broad.

Thorax somewhat narrowed anteriorly; scutellum small, with two bristles.

Abdomen very much attenuated at the basis; the narrow first segment without bristles; about its middle it is so coarctate that its anterior portion assumes the shape of a knot.

Feet very slender.

Tegulæ wanting; *wings* narrow, running into a point towards the basis, so that the posterior angle of the wing and the alulæ are wanting; auxillary and first longitudinal veins closely approximated; the two posterior basal cells small; the posterior angle of the anal cell rather sharp.

The very peculiar structure of the head, the approximated ocelli, the absence of bristles on the first abdominal segment and its peculiar coarctation, sufficiently distinguish this genus from *Mischogaster*. The species upon which it was founded by R. Desvoidy are unfortunately unknown to me, so that I cannot affirm with certainty whether the characters as based by me upon the species described below would in all particulars apply to them. Judging by his statements, however, it seems very probable that the discrepancies are not important.

Myrmecomyia is not only very like *Cephalia* in appearance, but closely allied to it in reality. However, they may be distinguished by the presence, in *Cephalia*, of a mesothoracic bristle, and by the absence of the coarctation of the first abdominal segment, peculiar to *Myrmecomyia*. The alulæ and tegulæ in *Cephalia*, although small, are not wanting; the posterior angle of the wing, although very shallow, is likewise apparent.

M. myrmecoides Losw.   ♂ ♀.—(Tab. VIII, f. 9.)   Nigra, alarum hyalinarum imâ basi et apice extremo nigris.

Black; wings hyaline, extreme root and apex black.   Long. corp. 0.25—0.27; long. al. 0.31.

Syn. *Cephalia myrmecoides* Losw, Wien. Ent. Monatschr. IV, p. 83.

Black, glossy.   Head shining black, face and cheeks usually brown.   The very broad and long front, descending in a steep slope, has a very narrow middle stripe of velvet black, which does not reach much beyond the middle of the front, but is connected by a furrow with the frontal fissure; the latter is not in the shape of an arc, but of an angle.   Ocelli approximated to each other.   The vertex bears two strong bristles, and on both sides of them two shorter ones; moreover, far back of the ocelli there are two small erect bristlets, while there are none in the immediate vicinity of the ocelli.   The conspicuously large lateral parts of the front have irregular, wrinkle-like, transverse impressions, and along the orbits a very narrow border of white pollen.   Antennæ long and narrow, reaching to the anterior edge of the mouth; the first two joints brownish-red, the third black; arista with a very short pubescence.   Face convex, descending obliquely in profile, but not excavated; the anterior edge of the mouth not drawn upwards; antennal foveæ indistinct; the very narrow lateral parts of the face with a thin white pollen.   Eyes higher than broad.   Cheeks rather broad.   Clypeus projecting over the anterior edge of the mouth, however its longitudinal diameter does not equal its moderate transverse diameter; the rather broad palpi blackish-brown.   Thorax rather long and narrow, broader in the region of the wings than before and behind.   Scutellum very small, convex, with two bristles.   The metathorax descends in an inclined plane, and is conspicuously long; the pectus rises obliquely from the middle coxæ towards the front coxæ. Thoracic dorsum with a thin gray bloom, the impressions indicating the lateral beginnings of the transverse suture are more densely pollinose; the pleuræ, above the middle coxæ, are clothed with a very dense white pollen. The shining black abdomen is much narrower at its basis; its first segment is longer than each of the following ones; about its middle it is so attenuated that its smaller anterior portion is knot-shaped, the larger posterior portion funnel-shaped; the last abdominal segment is somewhat shorter than each of the two preceding ones. The comparatively large hypopygium is usually pitch-brownish, seldom blackish; the first segment of the black ovipositor is flat and rather broad. Feet very slender; anterior coxæ yellow; the four posterior coxæ yellowish-red or chestnut-brownish; all are clothed with white pollen. Front feet brownish-yellow, with pitch-brown femora; the tarsi, from the tip of the first joint, are blackish-brown; the four posterior feet are brownish-black; the knees, the extreme tip of the tibiæ and the root of the tarsi brownish brick-red; in very pale-colored specimens the light coloring of the tarsi is much more extensive. Halteres black. No tegula. Wings hyaline, with delicate black veins; the wings, towards the basis, are very much attenuated, without any posterior angle and without alula; auxiliary vein short, very much approximated to the first longitudinal vein; the latter rather stout, very gradually merging into the costa, so that the stigma is narrow, linear; second longitudinal vein very long and straight; the last section of the third longitudinal vein gently inflected backwards, so that it strongly diverges from the second longitudinal vein and ends in the extreme apex; small crossvein perpendicular, inserted but little beyond the middle of the long discal cell; the last section of the fourth longitudinal vein rather straight, only very little convergent towards the third; posterior crossvein straight; the two posterior basal cells comparatively small; the posterior angle of the anal cell rather acute, but not pointed; the sixth longitudinal vein rather short, but reaching distinctly to the margin. The picture of the wings consists in an obscuration of the extreme root and the extreme tip; the first extends in the costal cell a little beyond the humeral crossvein; behind the first longitudinal vein, however, it reaches as far as the posterior basal cell; the obscuration of the apex has its greatest breadth at the end of the first posterior cell; it hardly crosses the fourth longitudinal vein posteriorly; anteriorly it extends as a rapidly contracting border along the costa as far as the end of the second longitudinal vein, so that it has rather the shape of an apical spot than of an apical border.

Hab. Washington, D. C. (Osten-Sacken.)

Third Section : CEPHALINA.

Gen. I. TRITOXA nov. gen.

Charact.—Body slender ; abdomen narrow at the basis; feet rather long, front tibia before the end of the upper side with a stronger bristlet. Hairs and bristles rather short; thoracic dorsum with bristles along the sides and upon its posterior margin only.

Antennæ long and narrow ; the second joint short; arista with short hairs. Face almost shield-shaped, with rather indistinct antennal foveæ.

Palpi very broad; proboscis rather stout, mentum but little inflated. *Wings* cuneiform towards the basis, with a very narrow alula ; second longitudinal vein not conspicuously arcuated ; third and fourth irregular in their course, which causes the anterior basal cell to expand before its end; first longitudinal vein beset with bristles upon the greater portion of its course ; crossveins approximated to each other.

This genus contains reddish-brown and black species, with dark wings, marked with three hyaline, oblique, more or less arcuated crossbands.

1. T. flexa Wied. ♂ ♀.—(Tab. VIII, f. 10.) Nigra, capito thoraceque interdum fuscis ; alæ nigræ, fasciis hyalinis valde angustis arcuatis et tertia arcuatis, hac ab alæ apico lato remotâ, venâ transversâ posteriore subnormali.

Black, head and thorax sometimes brown ; the wings black, with three very narrow hyaline bands, the second and third of which are arcuated ; the latter is rather remote from the apex of the wing; posterior crossvein almost perpendicular.   Long. corp. 0.24—0.29 ; long. al. 0.21—0.23.

Syn. *Trypeta flexa* Wiedemann, Auss. Zweifl. II, p. 483, 11.
Trypeta arcuata Walker, Ins. Saunders, p. 383.   Tab. VIII, f. 3.

Fully colored specimens are altogether deep black; in very pale specimens, on the contrary, the whole head, the thorax, and the feet, the latter usually with the exception of the upper side of the femora, are often brown ; vestiges of this color frequently occur in a greater or lesser measure on specimens the prevailing color of which is black. Most specimens have the greater part of the front brown, some reddish-brown; the usual coloring of the antennæ, also, is more brown than black, especially towards the basis. The pubescence of the arista is short, but distinct. The front has on both sides a very narrow, the face a broader, border of white pollen; the face, also, is slightly hoary with white, which is not equally distinct in all specimens, nor from all points of view; it is most perceptible around the antennæ. The rather indistinct pollen on the thoracic dorsum forms two rather broad parallel lines. The first segment of the flattened ovipositor resembles in its nature the preceding abdominal segments, to which it is closely applied; it is clothed, like those segments, with short, black hairs. The wings are strongly cuneiform towards their basis, and towards their tip they are rounded in such a manner that the extreme apex is much nearer the posterior than the anterior margin; the second longitudinal vein is slightly wavy upon the first two-thirds of its course; its strongest curvature is just above the small crossvein; the latter is rather oblique; the posterior crossvein, on the contrary, is steep, almost perpendicular, slightly biainnated in the shape of an S. The color of the wings is black; only very immature or faded specimens have it brownish-black; the three usual crossbands have an almost whitish tinge, and are very narrow; the first among them is so oblique that it almost assumes the appearance of a longitudinal stripe; it starts at the basis of the third posterior cell, diverges greatly and moderately from the fifth longitudinal vein, becomes more and more attenuated and pointed, and ends already some distance from the posterior margin; the second pale crossband, which likewise has a very oblique position, begins at the tip of the costal cell, just before the end of the auxiliary vein, and runs to the posterior angle of the discal cell; it is perceptibly more arcuated on its anterior than on its posterior portion; the third crossband, running from the anterior to the posterior margin, likewise has a very oblique position, although less so than the second; between the posterior margin and the third longitudinal vein its course is straight; from there to the anterior margin it is more and more arcuated; the distance between the third crossband and the apex of the wing is very large, as it almost equals one-third of the length of the wing. In the immediate vicinity of the small crossvein the coloring of the wing is more ferruginous-brown than black, which is especially perceptible by transmitted light; specimens also occur which have other pale streaks in one or the other of the cells.

Hab. Northern Wisconsin River (Kennicott); Illinois (H. Shimer).[1]

Observation.—Wiedemann probably prepared his description of *Trypeta flexa* from a very imperfectly colored specimen. A drawing of the wing, which I prepared some twenty years ago after an original specimen in the Berlin Museum, proves conclusively that *Trypeta flexa* is distinct from *Tritoxa incurva* and *cuneata.* The former is proved by the dark coloring at the tip of the wing having a much greater extent than in *T. incurva*, and by the course of the third crossband in *T. flexa*, which is not arcuated towards its end, but almost straight; in *T. cuneata* the different shape of the wing and the entirely distinct delineation of the crossbands altogether exclude the possibility of its synonymy with *T. flexa.* The figure of the wing drawn by me and above alluded to agrees with the present species so well that I consider my opinion about the identification of this species as well founded. Should this not be the case, then *T. flexa* Wied. is a species which I do not possess. The statement of Wiedemann, that the ovipositor of the female is two-jointed, rests upon an error, which is easily explained away by the resemblance of the first joint with the preceding abdominal segment. That Walker's *Trypeta arcuata* is synonymous with the present species is not in the least doubtful, although in the figure of the head the arista is made too short and its pubescence too long.

2. T. incurva n. sp. ♂ ♀.—(Tab. VIII, f. 12.) Radiis, abdomine nigro; alis fuscis, fasciis hyalinis modice angustis, secundâ et tertiâ arcuatis, bac ab alis apice minus late quam in speciebus reliquis remotâ, venâ transversâ posteriore obliquâ.

Reddish chestnut-brown, with a black abdomen; the wings brown, with

---

[1] Mr. H. Shimer, from Mt. Carroll, Ill., informed me, in 1865, that this fly is very injurious to onion-plants, the larva occurring in the bulb. This fact has, since then, been mentioned in the Practical Entomologist, 1, p. 4; II, p. 64 (with figures of larva and imago); American Entomologist, II, p. 110. Specimens of *Tritoxa incurva* were found by Mr. Shimer, together with *T. flexa*, and taken for a mere variety of that species.

O. S.

only moderately narrow hyaline bands, the second and third of which
are arcuated; the latter is less remote from the apex of the wing than
in the other species; posterior crossvein oblique. Long. corp. 0.25—
0.3; long. al. 0.22—0.26.

Reddish, chestnut-brown, with a black abdomen. Front
opaque, with the exception of the edge of the vertex and of the
small callosities descending from it, and bearing the bristles;
along the orbits the front has a narrow border of white pollen,
which also extends over the face, but is much broader here. The
remainder of the face has a very thin, somewhat yellowish
pollen upon it, which is most perceptible in the proximity of the
antennæ. Antennæ reddish-brown; third joint darker brown
towards its end; pubescence of the arista short, but distinct.
The thoracic dorsum has a broad shining border upon its sides,
otherwise it is opaque. Its thin whitish pollen is a little more
perceptible than in T. flexa, and forms, as in that species, two
broad, parallel longitudinal stripes, the position of which corresponds to that of the intervals between the ordinary thoracic
stripes; upon the intermediate stripe between them the pollen
has a somewhat yellowish tinge, and is much more dense upon
the longitudinal line, which divides this stripe in two; well-
preserved specimens show the white pollen on the sides of the
thoracic dorsum also, while in less good specimens this is not
visible, and often very little of the pollen is left on the whole
surface. Scutellum, metanotum, and pleuræ are shining, the
latter with a thin white bloom. Abdomen black or brownish-
black, with a black pubescence, sometimes chestnut-brown on the
sides of the first and second segments. The flattened first joint
of the ovipositor is of the same nature as the preceding segments of the abdomen; it is very broadly truncated at the tip.
The feet have the same coloring as the thorax, often, however,
not only the upper side of the fore femora, the middle femora
towards their basis, and the hind femora, with the exception of
their last quarter, are more strongly infuscated, but also the fore
tibiæ towards their tip, as well as the entire fore tarsi; the middle
tarsi, with the exception of their basis and the entire hind tibiæ
and hind tarsi, are dark brown. Halteres yellowish. Wings
narrowed towards the basis, although not quite as cuneiform as
in T. flexa, the portion lying beyond the sixth longitudinal vein
not being quite as narrow as in that species; the end of the wing

is rounded in such a manner that the apex is equidistant from
the anterior and the posterior margins; the second longitudinal
vein, the course of which is rather wavy, has its strongest sinuosity only little beyond the small crossvein; the anterior end of
the latter is nearer to the root of the wing than its posterior end,
so that its position is entirely oblique; the posterior crossvein
is oblique in the opposite direction, as its anterior end is nearer
to the apex of the wing than the posterior.   The coloring of the
surface of the wing is a brown of unequal intensity; the design
consists of the three hyaline bands usual in this genus; the portion of the surface of the wing beyond the third band is dark
brown, with a large yellowish-brown spot, which leaves in the
submarginal cell only a dark brown border along the margin of
the wing, and, so far as it extends in this cell, also somewhat
crosses the third longitudinal vein; the interval between the
second and third bands, which has the shape of a crossband, is
yellowish-brown, margined with dark brown on each side, and
also dark brown at the end; the interval between the second
and first crossbands is dark brown, with a large yellowish-brown
spot, which fills up the basis of the submarginal cell, and, to a
great extent, that of the first basal cell, so that in the former
almost nothing is left of the dark brown color, in the latter only
a border; the root of the wing is tinged with yellowish-brown
as far as a little beyond the humeral crossvein; towards the
place of insertion of the wing, however, the dark brown color
appears again; the posterior angle of the wing, lying behind
the first crossband, is only tinged with gray.   The hyaline
crossbands are distinctly broader than in T. flexa, and the last
of them is much nearer the apex, so that the dark coloring of
the latter assumes the shape of a broad crossband.   The first
hyaline crossband is so oblique that it almost assumes the
appearance of a longitudinal stripe; it starts, as in T. flexa,
from the basis of the third posterior cell, but is broader than in
that species, and does not diverge from the fifth vein; gradually
becoming more pointed, it ends some distance from the margin
of the wing, and differs but little in intensity of coloring from
the gray posterior angle of the wing; the second pale crossband,
which has a very oblique position and is only gently curved, runs
from the tip of the costal cell to the posterior corner of the discal
cell; however, the tip of the costal cell itself is hyaline to a

very small extent only, so that the crossband appears somewhat
abbreviated near the anterior margin of the wing; the third
hyaline crossband, which is almost as oblique as the second, is
more curved upon its posterior than upon its anterior portion.

Hab. Illinois (Dr. Schimer).[1]

3. T. cuneata n. sp.   ♂ ♀.—(Tab. VIII, f. 11.) Rufo-badia, abdomine nigro; alæ fuscæ, fasciarum hyalinarum secundā obliquā et levis-
sime arcuatā, tertiā subnormali et rectā.

Reddish chestnut-brown, with a black abdomen; wings brown, their
second hyaline crossband oblique and only gently curved; the third
almost perpendicular and straight. Long. corp. 0.23—0.25; long. al.
0.21—0.22.

Reddish chestnut-brown, with a black abdomen.   Front
opaque, however, with the exception of the edge of the vertex and
of the two callosities, descending from it, and bearing the strong
frontal bristles, of a rather reddish coloring; with a very narrow
border of white pollen near the orbit; this border also extends
over the face, but is not very perceptible here.   The remainder
of the face is covered with a very delicate whitish pollen, which
is more perceptible near the antenns only.   The third antennal
joint, with the exception of its basis, brown; arista with a very
short, yet distinctly perceptible, pubescence.   Thoracic dorsum
upon its sides with a broad shining border, otherwise opaque;
the rather whitish pollen which covers it is very distinct in well-
preserved specimens, but even in such specimens it does not form
any distinct longitudinal stripes.   Scutellum, metathorax, and
pleura shining, the latter with a white bloom.   Abdomen black
or brownish-black, with a black pubescence, usually reddish
chestnut-brown upon the sides of the first and second segments.
The feet are of the color of the thorax; the fore tarsi usually altogether dark brown; the middle and hind tarsi towards their end
dark-brown to a great extent.   Halteres yellowish-white.   Wings
comparatively narrower than in *T. incurva*, attenuated to a rather
cuneiform shape towards their basis; second longitudinal vein only
slightly wavy; the small crossvein very steep, almost perpendicular; the posterior crossvein oblique, its anterior end somewhat nearer the apex of the wing, so that the posterior angle of

[1] *Tritoxa incurva* occurs together with *T. flexa*, so that Dr. Schimer, who
sent me specimens of both, took it for a mere variety of his *onion-fly*.—O. S.

the discal cell is a little larger than a rectangle. The coloring of
the surface of the wing is an uneven brown; the design is formed
of the usual three hyaline crossbands, the first of which, however,
is but little apparent. The portion of the surface of the wing
lying beyond the last hyaline crossband is rather dark-brown,
more brownish-yellow towards the anterior, more grayish-brown
towards the posterior margin; the interval between the third
and second bands is dark-brown below the fourth longitudinal
vein, above it, yellowish-brown with dark-brown borders; the
latter are broader, even sometimes coalescent, within the submarginal cell; the interval between the second and the first
hyaline crossbands is dark-brown, its inner portion more yellowish-brown; the basis of the wing yellowish-brown; beyond the
fifth longitudinal vein the brown coloring still continues, but soon
verges on grayish. The first crossband has the same position as
in the preceding species; only it is broader, less attenuated, and
much shorter; its outline can be plainly visible only when the
surface of the wing is viewed in an oblique direction; the second
pale crossband, which is very oblique, begins below the tip of
the costal cell, in the marginal cell, and reaches as far as the
fifth longitudinal vein, which it touches already before the posterior corner of the discal cell; this band is but little curved; about
its middle, it is more or less expanded in the shape of an angle,
in consequence of its margin (the one nearest to the apex of the
wing), between the third and fourth longitudinal veins, not running in the direction of the band itself, but being more or less
perpendicular to the axis of the wing; the third hyaline band,
running at some distance from the apex of the wing, is very
steep, but by no means entirely perpendicular, and somewhat
broader anteriorly than posteriorly; it begins at the anterior
margin and completely or almost completely reaches the posterior
one.

Hab. Nebraska (Dr. Hayden).

Gen. II. CAMPTONEURA Macq.

Charact.—*Body* slender, feet rather long; the hairs very short every-
    where; the thorax with bristles on the lateral and posterior margins
    only.

    Antennæ long and narrow; the second joint short. Face almost shield-
    shaped, convex, with rather indistinct fovea.

Palpi very broad. Proboscis rather stout, with a but moderately turgid mentum.

Wings broad, first longitudinal vein provided, to a great extent, with bristles; second longitudinal vein arcuated in a very striking manner; anal cell rounded at the tip; the anterior margin of the wings, at the end of the auxiliary vein, has a shallow, but very striking excision.

1. C. picta Fabr. ♂ ♀.—(Tab. VIII, f. 13.) Badia, abdomine nigro; alis nigro-fuscis, maculis costalibus binis trigonis, binisque guttis discoidalibus, marginis denique postici maculá trigoná et strigá obliquá hyalinis, angulo postico et alulá obrrascentibus.

Chestnut-brownish with a black abdomen; the wings blackish-brown; two triangular spots on the anterior margin, two dots on the middle of the wing, a triangular spot and an oblique streak beginning at the posterior margin, hyaline; posterior corner and alula grayish. Long. corp. 0.25; cum terebrá 0.32—0.34; long. al. 0.22—0.25.

Syn. *Musca picta* Fabricius, Ent. Syst. IV. p. 355, 175.
Dictya picta Fabricius, Syst. Antl. p 330, 18.
Tephritis conica Fabricius, Syst. Antl. p. 318, 10.
Trypeta picta Wied. Auss. Zweifl. II, p. 489, 20.
Delphinia thoracica R. Desvoidy, Myod. p. 720, 1.
Camptoneura picta Macq. Dipt. Exot. II, 3, p. 201. Tab. XXVII, f. 4.
Trypeta picta Walk. List, IV, p. 1041.

Head and thorax chestnut-brownish or reddish chestnut-brown; thoracic dorsum sometimes darker brown; abdomen always black or brownish-black. Front opaque, usually more ferruginous-red than orange-red, sometimes darker, with a very narrow border of white pollen along the orbits; this border also extends over the face, but although broader here, it is less distinct, or at least more perceptible only a little distance below the antennæ. The remainder of the face is a little pollinose in the vicinity of the antennæ only. The third antennal joint is usually strongly infuscated, with the exception of its basis. Thoracic dorsum with a grayish-white pollen, which does not form any distinct stripes, while the ground color of the broad intermediate stripe is often darker than its surroundings, so that it becomes distinctly visible. Feet yellowish-brown, tarsi strongly infuscated towards their tip. Halteres whitish-yellow. Wings comparatively large and broad with a rather strongly projecting posterior angle, and a rather narrow alula; at the anterior margin there is an excision, which is very conspicuous, although it forms only an obtuse angle; it is

canned by considerable sinuous expansion of the costal cell ; the
second longitudinal vein is very conspicuously arcuated ; the two
crossveins are rather approximated and perpendicular, the posterior one somewhat curved ; the posterior angle of the discal cell
is acute.   The coloring of the wings is blackish-brown, more
yellowish-brown near the root, grayish in the posterior angle ; on
the anterior margin there are two triangular hyaline spots, which
attain the third longitudinal vein more or less completely with
their very sharp points ; the first of these spots covers, near its
anterior end, the tip of the costal cell and the basis of the stigma,
while the second is immediately beyond the stigma ; the dark
crossband between these two spots is tinged with brownish-yellow inside of the marginal cell, with the exception of a brown
border, which becomes narrower towards the first longitudinal
vein.   The stigma, towards its end, gradually assumes the same
brownish-yellow coloring, so that the first hyaline spot has no
well-defined limit within it.   Upon the middle of the wing there
are two hyaline drops, elongated in a direction perpendicular to
the axis of the wing; the one is in the discal cell, somewhat this
side of the small crossvein, the other in the first posterior cell,
over the posterior crossvein.   On the posterior margin of the
wing, in the second posterior cell, there is a triangular spot, concave towards the apex of the wing, convex on the other side,
which is near the posterior crossvein and separated by a narrow,
brownish border from it.   The sharp point of this spot is directed
towards the dot in the first posterior cell, and is often connected
with it, while, in other specimens, it does not even reach the
fourth posterior vein.   Near the basis of the wing there is a
narrow, oblique, hyaline streak, beginning in the first basal cell,
crossing the end of the second basal cell and entering the third
posterior cell ; here it runs along the sixth longitudinal vein and
thus reaches the margin of the wing, where it becomes a little
grayish.

Hab. United States, common.

Observation.—The description which Fabricius gives of his
Musca picta in the *Entomologia Systematica* might suggest doubts
as to its identity with the above described species, doubts, however, which I hold to be without foundation.   First of all, it is
certain that Wiedemann's *Trypeta picta* is identical with our
species; his description, as well as the types of his collection,

proves it conclusively. Not less certain, according to my opinion, is the fact that Wiedemann's *Trypeta picta* and the *Tephritis conica* of Fabricius's Systema Antliatorum are synonyms. What Wiedemann says about the feet of his *Trypeta picta* clearly proves that he had examined the type in Fabricius's collection; moreover, Fabricius's description contains nothing to render this identification of *Tephritis conica* doubtful. In the preface to his first volume, Wiedemann gives a large number of synonymic and systematic emendations, the result of the examination of Fabricius's collection, undertaken by him; among them we find the statement that *Tephritis conica* and *Dictya picta* are the same species. But as *Dictya picta* of the Systema Antliatorum is nothing else but the *Musca picta* of the Entomologia Systematica, the synonymy of *Musca picta* F. with *Trypeta picta* Wied. and the above described *Camptoneura picta* seems to be sufficiently established. The correctness of this view seems confirmed by the fact, that *Musca picta* F. was described from a North American specimen, and that hitherto, besides *Camptoneura picta*, which has a wide range and is a common species, no other North American species is known which might come in conflict with it.

Gen. III. DIACRITA Gerst.

Charact.—*Body* rather robust. Pubescence everywhere very short; thorax with some bristles upon the posterior and lateral margins only.

Antenna of medium length; the oval third joint longer than the only moderately sized second joint. The face, retreating above between the rather short antennal foveæ, and obtusely carinate; below, it is again projecting and convex.

Palpi rather large, mentum swollen.

Wings narrow and long, the first longitudinal vein bristly at its end only; the third and fourth longitudinal veins converging towards the end; posterior angle of the anal cell drawn out to a very long point.

This genus contains brown or brownish-yellow species, rather opaque on account of the pollen which covers them; the thorax is usually spotted with black; the wings, on the anterior margin and the apex, have a broad black border.

1. D. costalis Gerst. ♂.—(Tab. VIII, f. 14.) Fusca, polline obscure asperna, thoracis maculis nigris ante antaram sex, pone antaram duabus, binisque minutissimis utrinque adjectis.

Almost chocolate-brown, with a grayish pollen; thoracic dorsum with six
black spots before the suture and with two beyond it, to which are
added on each side two very small dots. Long. corp. 0.82; long. al.
0.37.

818. *Diorrita australis* GERST. Stett. Ent. Zeitschr. xxi, p. 197. Tab. II.

Almost chocolate-brown, covered with a whitish-gray pollen
and opaque. Head dark-yellow, the upper part of the occiput
generally brownish-yellow; the broad front, in the vicinity of the
ocelli and in front of these, more reddish-yellow; on both sides,
near the orbit, there is a rather large, shallow impression, covered
with white pollen; on the anterior end of the front there is a
small triangular spot, covered with snow-white pollen. Immediately below each of these spots, upon the face, there is a velvet-
black round spot, contiguous with the orbit, and immediately
below the latter a spot covered with snow-white pollen. The
upper part of the face, which is carinate and retreating, has, on
each side, a transverse spot, clothed with white pollen. In the
same way, the posterior orbit of the eyes has a pollinose white
border, which also extends over the cheeks in the shape of a
stripe. The antennae are almost ochre-yellow, their third joint
elongated-oval; the basal joint of the arista is so short as to be
almost imperceptible; the second joint is comparatively long, both
dark ochre-yellow; the third joint is blackish, with the exception
of its extreme basis; in the vicinity of the basis, it is as stout as
the first two joints, more attenuated afterwards, and clothed with
an extremely short pubescence. The humeral callosities are
brownish-yellow, and rather shining; thoracic dorsum marked
with moderately large, rounded-oval, brownish-black spots; before
the region of the transverse suture there are six of them, arranged
in two regular transverse rows; beyond this region there are
two approximated spots, the interval of which is equal to that
between the spots of the first two rows; moreover, behind the
region of the suture, on each side, may be noticed two very small,
almost punctiform dots, placed one behind the other; of these,
the anterior one is situated before, the posterior one at an equal
distance behind the last two of the larger spots. The coloring
of the convex scutellum, which is beset with four, not very long
bristles, approaches the chestnut-red. The feet are concolorous
with the remainder of the body; an admixture of yellow is perceptible on the first joint of the tarsi only. Halteres whitish-

yellow. Wings comparatively long and narrow, of a very equal
breadth, in the middle only a little broader than at the basis and
at the apex; stigma strikingly long; the third longitudinal vein
gently curved backwards towards the tip, and hence, the submarginal cell very much expanded towards its end; the crossveins
very distant from each other; the fourth longitudinal vein,
towards its end, gently bent forward, and hence, the first posterior cell narrowed towards its end; the posterior angle of the
anal cell is drawn out in a narrow lobe, which is considerably
longer than the cell itself. The surface of the wing is bright,
shining, hyaline, upon its posterior half only with a weak trace
of a grayish-brown tinge. The design on the wing consists of a
broad, black, or blackish-brown border of the costal margin and
of the apex; the posterior limit of this border runs, at the basis
of the wing, along the fifth longitudinal vein; at the basis of the
discal cell, it suddenly turns towards the fourth longitudinal
vein, and, after running alongside of it for a short distance, it
turns suddenly towards the third longitudinal vein, alongside of
which it runs as far as a little beyond the small crossvein, here,
just opposite the end of the first longitudinal vein, it abruptly
turns towards the second longitudinal vein, leaves open a small
segment of a circle just above it, returns towards the second vein,
follows it for some distance, and, abruptly turning again, crosses
the submarginal and first posterior cells, turning towards the
apex in the vicinity of the fourth vein, alongside of which it
reaches the margin. This border is perceptibly broader at the
tip than along the anterior margin, and can therefore also be
described as a large spot, entirely confluent with the border along
the anterior margin. Inside of the dark anterior border, there
are three small, almost hyaline spots; the first lies at the end of
the second basal cell, the second, almost cuneiform, is in the
marginal cell, before the origin of the third longitudinal vein, the
third at the extreme tip of the costal cell; in the marginal cell,
beyond the end of the first longitudinal vein, between the small
hyaline spot in the shape of a segment of a circle and the costa,
there is a spot, tinged with yellowish-brown; the broad black
border along the apex is sometimes a little dilated in its middle.

Hab. Mexico (Germar).

Observation.—In the register of the second part of Wiedemann's Aussereur. Zweifl. Insecten, there is a *Platystoma castelia,*

8

which is not described in the work itself. Wiedemann's collection proves that this species is identical with the present one.

2. D. æmula n. sp.   ♀.—(Tab. VIII, f. 15.)   Lutea, thoracis dorso fusco, maculis nigris ante suturam quatuor, pone suturam nullis.

Clay-yellow, dorsum of the thorax brown, with four brown spots before the transverse sutura and none beyond it.   Long. corp. 0.25 ; cum terebra 0.3d ; long. al. 0.31.

Very like the preceding in all plastic characters. Almost more ochre-yellow than clay-yellow, the thoracic dorsum alone strongly infuscated. The front, as in *D. costalis*, has on each side, near the orbit, a shallow impression, clothed with white pollen ; below it is a round, velvet-black spot, and immediately below the latter again a spot of snow-white pollen, only the black spot is smaller than in the preceding species ; also the two snow-white transverse spots on the upper part of the face are apparent, as in *D. costalis*. On the thoracic dorsum there are not six, but only four rounded oval velvet-black spots before the transverse suture, which correspond to the outward ones of the preceding species ; there is no trace of black spots on the other side of the suture. The scutellum is convex and has four bristles ; the large first segment of the flattened ovipositor is brownish-yellow, long. only moderately attenuated towards its end. Feet of the same coloring with the remainder of the body ; the tarsi only moderately infuscated towards their end. Halteres whitish-yellow. Wings of the same shape as in *D. costalis*, only less long, especially their second half less elongate, so that the small crossvein is somewhat nearer the tip of the wing than in *D. costalis*, and that the last section of the longitudinal veins, ending in the apex of the wing, is shorter ; otherwise the venation almost entirely agrees with that of *D. costalis*. The surface of the wing is hyaline ; its posterior half strongly tinged with a smoky-brownish. The brownish-black design resembles that of the preceding species, differs, however, from it by the dark border along the apex being much narrower ; the posterior limit of the border along the costa is also similar to that in the preceding species, but not quite identical ; especially where, in *D. costalis*, this limit crosses the second longitudinal vein and leaves on the other side a hyaline segment of a circle ; instead of the latter there is here only an indistinct paler dot and between this and the costa no spot of a paler coloring ; the three byaline dots, contained within the black border of the costa, are much less clear in the present species, especially the first and the third among them.

Hab. California (Agassiz).

Charact.—Body robust. Hairs very short everywhere; thorax with bristles on its posterior and lateral borders only.

Antennæ of medium size; third joint oval, but little longer than the rather large second joint. Face obtusely carinate between the very long antennal fovea.

Palpi of moderate size; the mentum moderately turgid.

Wings narrow and very long; first longitudinal vein towards its end provided with bristles to a considerable extent; third and fourth longitudinal veins converging towards their end; anal cell not drawn out in the shape of a lobe.

This genus contains conspicuous pollinose species; their thorax is marked with distinct black stripes and the abdomen banded with black, the design of the wings not unlike the genus *Pteropoecila*, while the general shape of the body reminds of the true species of *Ortalis*.

1. 1. marginata Say. ♀.—(Tab. VIII, f. 16.) Ala colore fusco-nigro et luteo pulchre variegata, imâ cellulâ marginalis basi, tricnte apicali cellulæ basalis primæ, cellulisque posterioribus duabus primis præter venarum limbos pure hyalinis, angulo postico et cellulâ posteriore tertiâ fere totâ cinereo-hyalinis.

The wings with a handsome brownish-black and brownish-yellow picture; the extreme basis of the marginal cell, the last third of the first basal cell, as well as the first two posterior cells, pure hyaline, with the exception of the borders of the veins, including them; the posterior angle and the greater part of the third posterior cell grayish hyaline. Long. corp. 0.34; oum terebrâ 0.45; long. al. 0.46 lin.

Syn. *Ortalis marginata* Say, Journ. Acad. Phila. VI, p. 183, 2.

Head reddish-yellow. Front orange-yellow, opaque, with the exception of the immediate proximity of the ocelli and of the two little callosities, descending from the vertex and bearing the frontal bristles; the sides more orange-red, usually infuscated above the antennæ; on each side a rather narrow border of yellowish pollen. Antennæ of medium length; the first two joints of the coloring of the head; the second rather large; the third almost orange-yellow, of an oval shape, and but little longer than

the second; arista of medium length, with a short, but distinct
pubescence. The vertical diameter of the eyes more than twice
the length of the horizontal one. Face with very deep and long
antennal foveæ, which run down in a perpendicular direction;
their bottom is tinged with brownish-black. The face, between
the foveæ, is strongly, the lower part sharply carinate, and that
in such a manner that in profile the face runs down perpendicularly and in a straight line. Cheeks broad; at the lower corner
of the eye with an infuscated spot. Oral opening rather large,
somewhat drawn up above, so that the strongly developed,
although transversely narrow, clypeus, projects a great deal
beyond the peristomium. The reddish-yellow palpi rather large,
broader towards the end; the brown proboscis of medium stoutness and the reddish-yellow chin only moderately swollen. The
whole occiput is strongly and evenly convex. Thorax comparatively stout, but not strongly convex, distinctly narrowed anteriorly. Thoracic dorsum with a very dense, almost ochre-yellow
dust, and with well-defined black longitudinal stripes; lateral
border, and usually also the anterior one, chestnut-brownish or
more chestnut-red; the intermediate stripe, running at an equal
breadth from the anterior to the posterior border, is divided in
two halves by a stripe-shaped intermediate line, which is of the
same breadth with both halves of the intermediate stripe itself;
the lateral stripes, which are but very little abbreviated anteriorly
and posteriorly, are crossed by the yellowish-pollinose transverse
suture; their posterior part moreover has alongside of it a black
longitudinal stripe, which is not distinctly separated from the
anterior part of the lateral stripe. Pleuræ chestnut-brownish,
about their middle with a broad longitudinal stripe, which is
clothed with pale ochre-yellowish pollen and gradually disappears
posteriorly. Scutellum brownish-yellow. Abdomen black, but
little shining, more or less chestnut-reddish at the extreme basis
and on the sides of the first two segments; the second and each
of the following segments have a crossband, of a dingy ochre-yellow, very thickly laid dust, occupying almost the whole of their
anterior half, and narrowed on each side. The first segment of
the ovipositor is black, flat, broad, nevertheless strongly attenuated
towards its end. Feet brownish-yellow, tarsi strongly, but
gradually infuscated towards the end. Halteres yellowish. The
wings strikingly elongated, of a comparatively small and rather

equal breadth ; stigma rather long but not broad ; the crossveins
far distant from each other ; the posterior crossvein rather oblique,
its anterior end nearer the apex of the wing than the posterior
end ; fourth longitudinal vein strongly bent forward towards the
end ; the first posterior cell considerably narrowed in consequence
towards the apex ; posterior angle of the anal cell pointed, but
not drawn out in the shape of a lobe. The picture of the wings
consists, as to color, of brownish-black and brownish-yellow and
some hyaline cells of a peculiar shape. The root of the wings is
yellow, as far as the origin of the third longitudinal vein ; the
extreme basis, however, is strongly infuscated ; there is a rather
dark-brown crossband in the region of the humeral crossvein, and
the basis of the marginal cell is hyaline. A dark-brown color
follows next, the first portion of which forms a curved crossband,
reaching backwards as far as the posterior basal crossvein ; anteriorly it is prolonged in the marginal cell, as far as the end of the
first longitudinal vein, where it stops short abruptly. After some
interruption, the brownish-black color forms a broad border of the
anterior margin, beginning somewhat above the posterior crossvein, which does not only occupy the whole breadth of the marginal cell, but also encroaches on the submarginal cell, follows the
apex of the wing and the fourth longitudinal vein as far as the
small crossvein and also covers the latter ; posteriorly, it not only
runs along the posterior crossvein and extends over the end of
the discal cell, but follows also some distance along the end of the
fifth longitudinal vein, upon its posterior side ; the third longitudinal vein is bordered with brownish-black upon its whole length.
The portions of the marginal, submarginal and discal cells, free
from the brownish-black color, are tinged with brownish-yellow ;
the first basal cell, as well as the first two posterior cells, are
hyaline. The alula, as well as the anal angle of the wing and the
adjoining portion of the third posterior cell, is grayish-hyaline,
with a tinge of yellow ; the posterior side of the fifth longitudinal
vein has a brownish-yellow border, the middle of the third posterior cell is rather pure hyaline, only more grayish towards the
posterior margin of the wing.

Hab. Virginia, Pennsylvania (Osten-Sacken).

Fourth Section: ORTALINA.

Gen. I. **AUTOMOLA** gen. nov.

Charact.—Front broad, very much narrowed anteriorly. Eyes rather large, slightly protruding, irregularly rounded. Face in profile somewhat concave, obtusely carinate between the distinct antennal fovea. The anterior edge of the mouth very much drawn upwards, so that the rather strongly developed clypeus projects considerably beyond it. Cheeks broad.

Antenna reaching beyond the middle of the face; the first two joints short; the narrow third joint more than twice as long as the first two taken together, rounded at the end; antennal arista thin, slightly stronger at the basis only, with a very short pubescence.

Thoracic dorsum not bristly on its middle, before the region of the transverse suture. The tibia, before the end of their upper side, with a preapical bristle.

The first longitudinal vein bristly before its end; the auxiliary vein very much approximated to it; the costa more or less incrassated beyond the end of the first longitudinal vein; the third and fourth longitudinal veins parallel towards their end; the crossveins not approximated; the second basal cell and the anal cell comparatively rather small, the latter rounded at the end; the sixth longitudinal vein complete, but remarkably short, and hence, the anal angle of the wing very small; alula comparatively large.

The genus *Automola* contains unmetallic species. The picture of their wings generally consists in black spots upon the root of the wings and three black crossbands, the first of which is only at a short distance from the basis, while the second runs over the posterior crossvein and the third lies between the second and the apex of the wing; these bands being more or less incomplete, or the second and third expanding or even coalescing into one large spot, give rise to different modifications of the design of the wings.

Ortalis atomaria Wied. and *trifasciata* Wied. from Brazil, may be considered as the types of the genus. North American species have not been discovered yet.

I have already had occasion to mention in the Introduction that *Automola*, on account of the preapical bristles on the tibia, which distinguish it from the other genera, is not very well placed in the family of *Ortalidæ*.

Gen. II. **TETANOPS** Fall.

Charact.—*Front of a considerable and uniform breadth. Eyes rounded-oval, or oval. Face strongly projecting in profile, more or less retreating below. Clypeus small, but projecting beyond the edge of the mouth. Oral opening comparatively small; proboscis but little increased.*

The hairs and bristles on the body remarkably short, especially the bristles of the prothorax much smaller than in any other genus among the Ortalina; thoracic dorsum upon its middle only posteriorly with a few bristles.

Antennæ short, sometimes strikingly short; third joint oval, longer than the second.

First longitudinal vein bristly towards its end only; the crossveins rather distant; the second and third longitudinal veins parallel towards their end, or only gently convergent; posterior angle of the anal cell pointed, but not prolonged in the shape of a lobe.

The North American species of *Tetanops* are distinguished from the European ones by the more distinct and sharper anterior edge of the mouth, while in the latter the anterior end of the oral opening hardly shows a distinct margin. As one of the American species, known to me, has, moreover, the vertical diameter of the eyes considerably larger than the European species, I was for some time in doubt, whether it would not be better to separate generically the North American from the European species. Nevertheless, they possess enough characters in common, to render such a separation, at least for the present, unnecessary. Besides the stout head, with the very broad front, the striking bareness of the whole body and the great shortness of the prothoracic bristle, the absence of any picture on the wings, except some very faint spots along the costa, easily distinguishes the species of *Tetanops*.

1. T. luridipennis n. sp. ♂ ♀.—(Tab. VIII, f. 17.) *Fronte præter vittam mediam punctata; alæ sordide luteescentes, ad costam obsoletissime lurido-maculatæ.*

Front, with the exception of a median stripe, punctate; wings of a dingy clay-yellow, with very indistinct brownish-clay-yellow spots along the costa. Long. corp. ♂, 0.21; ♀ cum terebrâ 0.28—0.39; long. al. 0.18.

Head reddish-yellow. The very broad front more red; it has a small median stripe, which is not pollinose, and has, on each side, a brown border; the latter sometimes becomes indistinct above, and, on the anterior part of the front, is somewhat turned sideways, generally also more expanded and darker. The sides of the front, each of which is nearly double the breadth of the median stripe, are covered with white pollen, rendered cribrose by a dense punctation of pollenless dots, so that of the pollinose surface, nothing but a network is left. The face, in profile, projects very much in front of the eyes, and retreats very considerably below; its intermediate portion is, as in all the species of *Trianops*, comparatively narrow. The antennal fovea are deep and sharply defined, shining-black, except on their upper portion. Eyes rounded-oval; cheeks very broad. The upper part of the occiput is clothed with white pollen; in the vicinity of the orbits and of the edge of the vertex this pollen is likewise interrupted by punctiform pollenless dots. Antennæ yellowish-red, the third joint, with the exception of the basal third, more or less infuscated. Although the ground color of the thorax is shining-black or brownish-black, it is, with the exception of the humeri, concealed by a thick grayish-white pollen, sometimes yellowish on the thoracic dorsum; numerous punctiform, pollenless dots interrupt this pollen and give it a cribrose appearance; the region of the prothoracic spiracle alone is free from these dots. The pollen covering the scutellum is similar in coloring to that of the thorax, but it is, to a considerable extent, much less thick upon its sides. The abdomen has the same color and the same pollinose surface, interrupted by punctiform, pollenless dots, as the thorax, but the pollen is a little less thick and the punctiform dots a little larger, so that, here and there, they coalesce and the ground color becomes more apparent. The first segment of the flattened ovipositor is shining black, very broad, rather strongly attenuated, however, towards its end. Femora blackish-brown, the tip of the front ones yellowish-red to a small, the tip of the hindmost ones to a greater extent. Front tibiæ blackish-brown, with a yellowish-red basis; middle tibiæ usually entirely yellowish-red or but little infuscated towards their end; hind tibiæ blackish brown, with a yellowish-red basis and generally also the extreme tip of the same color. Tarsi yellowish-red at the basis, the front ones from about the tip of the first joint, the posterior ones from about the tip of the second or third joint, blackish-brown. Wings of a dingy clay-yellow, almost brownish in fully colored specimens, without any distinct picture; however,

Indistinct traces of three somewhat darker clouds are apparent; the first in the marginal cell, above the origin of the submarginal cell, the second at the end of the stigma, and the third, which sometimes is wanting, fills up the end of the marginal cell; all three are so little apparent that they can easily be overlooked.

Hab. Nebraska (Dr. Hayden).

2. T. Integra n. sp. ♀.—(Tab. VII, f. 16.) Frons tota punctata; alæ cinereæ, immaculatæ.

The whole front is punctate; wings gray, without any picture. Long. corp. cum terebra 0.28—0.31 ; long. al. 0.17.

Head brownish-black, rather dusky brownish-red upon the greater part of the front, the cheeks, and near the anterior edge of the mouth. The front has no median stripe, and is altogether covered with grayish-white pollen, rendered cribrose by numerous small and very dense pollenless dots; a fine network, covering the whole front, is all that remains pollinose. The pollen extends, from the front over the very broad lateral portions of the face, as far as the cheeks; the pollenless dots, however, do not reach beyond the middle of the face. The face in profile is less projecting in front of the eyes, and less retreating below, than in *T. luridipennis.* The antennal foveæ, on their outside slope, are covered, to a considerable extent, by a white pollen; at the bottom they are shining black. The flattened ridge of the carina, separating them, has also a whitish pollen. The vertical diameter of the eyes is larger than in the preceding species or in any of the species of *Tetanops* to me known. The cheeks are very broad, although somewhat narrower than in *T. luridipennis.* The upper half of the occiput is clothed with a whitish pollen, extending upon the hind side of the cheeks as far as the edge of the mouth; in the vicinity of the posterior orbit and of the edge of the mouth, this pollen is interrupted by pollenless punctiform dots. Antennæ brownish-red, the third joint for the most part blackish-brown. The ground color of the thorax is glossy, almost shining-black, but altogether covered by a whitish-gray or more yellowish-gray pollen, interrupted by countless dots, which are, however, much smaller and less sharply defined than in the preceding species. Quite in front, the thoracic dorsum shows an indistinct beginning of a median stripe, in the shape of two dark longitudinal lines, which are rather distant from each other,

Upon the pleura the pollen is perceptibly less dense than upon
the thoracic dorsum, so that they appear shining. Upon the
sides of the scutellum the pollen is thick and not interrupted,
while that upon its disk somewhat resembles the pollen on the
surface of the thoracic dorsum, only it is a little thinner and
has no distinct polleuless dots. The abdomen is shining black,
covered, towards the basis, with a gradually increasing, uninterrupted, but not very thick ash-gray pollen. The first joint of the
flattened ovipositor is shining black, very broad, but little
narrowed towards its end, with somewhat convex sides and comparatively shorter than that of *T. luridipennis*. Feet black or
brownish-black; the extreme tip of the femora, the basis and
extreme tip of the tibiae, as well as the tarsi, yellowish-red;
however, the last three or four joints of the fore tarsi and the
last two joints of the hind tarsi, brownish-black. Wings rather
hyaline, gray, with a delicate tinge of brownish-clay-yellow,
without any picture.

Hab. Illinois (Osten-Sacken).

Gen. III. TEPHRONOTA Loew.

Charact.—*Head* high and short. Front of a moderate and equal breadth,
    comparatively long. Face rather sharply carinate, only little pro-
    truding in front of the eyes in profile; almost vertical. The
    vertical diameter of the eyes almost double the size of the hori-
    zontal one. Anterior edge of the mouth not drawn upwards.
    Cheeks very narrow.
  Antennae of a medium length; the first two joints short; the third
    ending at a sharp angle, although not reaching above.
  Thorax upon its middle with bristles on the hind part only; covered
    with a gray dust.
  The first *longitudinal vein* with bristles upon its end only; the end of
    the fourth longitudinal vein not curved forward; the posterior
    angle of the anal cell, although sharp, is not extended in the shape
    of a lobe.

This genus contains only small-sized species, which, in their
whole organization, approach the species of *Pteropaectria*; this
is still more the case with the European species, than with the
only American one which I know. The latter, however, agrees
in so many characters with the European *Tephronota*, that it
can be placed, without any hesitation, in that genus. Its antennae
are a little shorter and their third joint somewhat broader; the

pollen on the body is thicker and more extended than in the European species; the crossbands of its wings are incomplete.

1. T. hummilis Loew. ♂ ♀.—(Tab. VIII, f. 24.) Nigricans, cinereopollinosa, capite flavo, pedibus lateis, alis albido-hyalinis, fasciis tribus nigris, intermediâ integrâ, reliquis postice abbreviatis.

Rather black, covered with gray pollen; with a yellow head, and rather clay-yellow feet; wings whitish-hyaline, with three black crossbands, the medial of which is entire; the two others are abbreviated. Long. corp. ♂ 0.12—0.14; cum terebrâ 0.11—0.16; long. al. 0.1—0.13.

Syn. *Herina ruficeps* v. d. Wulp, Tijdschrift voor Entomol., Jaarg. IX, p. 150.

Head yellow. Front brighter yellow, almost orange-red upon its anterior end; on each side with a conspicuous border of white pollen, which, becoming broader, extends below over the face as far as the cheeks. The occiput becomes blackish above, but is rather evenly covered with a rather thick whitish pollen. The ground color of the thorax is rather black, more brownish on the humeri and upon the lateral border, as well as below the root of the wings; this color, in well-preserved specimens, is covered by a grayish-white pollen; upon the thoracic dorsum there are two longitudinal stripes, of a somewhat darker color, very little apparent and abbreviated posteriorly. The color of the scutellum, which is likewise covered with gray pollen, verges more on dingy brownish, and on clay-yellow along the edges; in less fully colored specimens the whole scutellum is clay-yellow. The color of the abdomen is likewise rather black, sometimes only brown at the basis. In the male, this color appears distinctly as black or brownish-black upon the last segment and on the hypopygium, both of which are pollenless, while on the preceding segments this color is concealed under a rather thick pollen, which on the anterior portion of the segment has a light whitish-gray, on the posterior half a brown coloring. The female has the last abdominal segment likewise pollinose, the pollen being generally light white-grayish, or verging on brownish about the middle of the abdomen only; the pollen on the preceding segments is the same as in the male. The first segment of the altogether flattened ovipositor is not very long, but very broad and very broadly truncate at its end; its pollen is very little perceptible, so that it is glossy-black, more brownish-black in

immature specimens. Feet of a dirty clay-yellow, femora in the
middle and tarsi towards the tip, somewhat infuscated. Halteres
whitish-yellow. Wings whitish-hyaline, with three broad, perpendicular, more grayish-black than black crossbands. The first of
these bands covers, near the anterior margin, the latter half of the
costal cell, and reaches, without becoming more narrow, the fourth
or fifth longitudinal vein; in the first case it becomes perceptibly
paler between the third and fourth, in the second case between
the fourth and fifth longitudinal veins. The second band covers,
near the anterior margin, the apical half of the stigma and reaches
there, in most specimens, even a little beyond the end of the first
longitudinal vein; without attenuating, it runs over the small
crossveins as far as the fourth longitudinal vein, forms a very
broad border along the section of the fourth vein lying between
the two crossveins, and runs, afterwards, along the posterior
crossvein towards the fifth longitudinal vein; its breadth is not
the same in all specimens; when narrower, this crossband shows
a distinct knee-shaped bend, depending upon its passage from the
small to the posterior crossvein (this is the case with the specimen
figured by Mr. v. d. Wulp); when broader, this crossband
extends, in the shape of a blackish-gray shadow, as far as the
third posterior cell, so that of the knee-shaped bend only a trace
is left, which is due to a diluted spot upon the inner side of the
crossband, near the posterior margin of the discal cell (as represented in my figure). The third band covers, on the anterior
margin, the end of the marginal cell to a considerable extent,
becomes gradually more narrow posteriorly and reaches more or
less completely the fourth longitudinal vein, where it suddenly is
interrupted. The root of the wing is tinged with blackish-gray
as far as a little beyond the humeral crossvein. The second and
third longitudinal veins are strongly divergent towards their
end; the last section of the fourth longitudinal vein slightly converges towards the third vein and is not quite so straight as usual
in the species of *Tephronota*, but, at the same time, not so much
curved forward by far as in the case of the species of *Anacampta*,
Holodasia, and *Apyrrhacmica*. The crossveins are very much
approximated, as the distance between them is not much larger
than the length of the small crossvein, but smaller than the
posterior crossvein. The posterior angle of the anal cell is short
and sharp, and not prolonged in the shape of a lobe. The sixth

longitudinal vein is weak and indistinct soon after its middle, so
that it appears interrupted a long distance before the margin of
the wing.

Hab. New York (Osten-Sacken); Virginia; Texas (Belfrage).

Observation.—The description of *Herina ruficeps* by v. d.
Wulp, contains only one datum which might render its identification with *T. humilis* doubtful. He says that the third antennal
joint is four times as long as the second, while in all my specimens it hardly reaches three times its length. As, in other
respects, the agreement of the very good description is perfect,
I have not the slightest doubt that this difference arises from a
different mode of viewing or measuring the antennæ. Unfortunately, the name given by Mr. v. d. Wulp cannot be preserved,
as it has been preoccupied by Fabricius.

Gen. IV. CEROXYS Macq.

Charact.—*Head* rather roundish. Front very broad, somewhat narrowed
above, without stripe. The perpendicular diameter of the eyes is
much larger than the horizontal one. Cheeks of medium breadth.
Third antennal joint upon its upper side distinctly emoteed, very much
pointed at the tip. Arista distinctly pubescent.
Thorax, upon its middle, with bristles as far as its anterior portion.
First longitudinal vein with bristles upon its end only; the fourth
longitudinal vein not curved forward. The posterior angle of the
anal cell acute, but not prolonged in the shape of a lobe.

The genus *Ceroxys* contains species which are very much
alike; the thorax and abdomen are thickly covered with yellowish or grayish dust; the head is yellow. The picture of the
wings, consisting of comparatively large blackish-brown or black
spots, is the same in all the species; it consists of seven spots,
the first of which lies on the base of the submarginal cell, the
second upon the end of the stigmatical (third costal) cell; the
third covers the small and the fourth the posterior crossvein; the
last three spots lie on the ends of the second, third, and fourth
longitudinal veins; the last two generally coalesce completely,
while the one placed at the end of the second vein is generally
less completely united with them.

The species are easily distinguished by the shape and color of
the third antennal joint, by the presence or absence of a dark
crossband on the posterior margin of the abdominal segments, by

the greater or smaller extent of the spots on the wings, especially by the relative position of the stigmatical spot to the one covering the small crossvein, and by the separation or coalescence of both.

1. C. obscuricornis n. sp.   ♂ ♀.—(Tab. VIII, f. 20.) Polline ex cinereo lutescente veutino, tertio antennarum articulo fusco-nigro, pedibus luteis, alarum macula stigmaticali et limbo venæ transversalis mediæ fasciolam arcuatam efficientibus.

Covered with a grayish-clay-yellow pollen; third antennal joint brownish-black, feet clay-yellow; the spot at the end of the stigmatical cell and the one covering the small crossvein form a curved crossband. Long. corp. ♂ 0.21; ♀ cum terebra 0.25; long. al. 0.2—0.31.

The first two antennal joints brownish-ferruginous-yellow, or brownish-yellow; third joint brownish-black, of medium breadth; arista black. Scutellum upon its edge only indistinctly yellowish-brown. Abdomen without any trace of dark crossbands, except that the pollen, towards the posterior portion of the segments, becomes more brownish-gray in a hardly perceptible degree. The first joint of the flattened ovipositor is only moderately long, very broad; its truncature very broad also; the coloring and the pollen are the same as those of the abdomen. Feet clay-yellow; tarsi, with the exception of the basis, more or less strongly infuscated; the only male in my possession has the front femora very much infuscated upon the greater part of the posterior side; it is not probable, however, that this is a constant sexual character. The first spot on the wings extends from the first to a little beyond the fourth vein; the spot lying upon the end of the stigmatical cell is more or less completely coalescent with the one covering the small crossvein, and forms with it a rather oblique, distinctly arcuated crossband; the other spots have nothing peculiar about them.

Hab. Nebraska (Dr. Hayden).

2. C. ochricornis n. sp.   ♀.—(Tab. VIII, f. 21.) Polline ex cinereo lutescente veutino, segmentis abdominalibus postice anguste fusco-limbatis, antennis ex-ferrugineo ochraceis, pedibus luteis, alarum macula stigmaticali et limbo venæ transversalis mediæ in fasciolam rectam conjunctis.

Covered with a grayish-clay-colored pollen; the segments of the abdomen with narrow brown borders posteriorly; antennæ ochre-brownish, the feet clay-yellow; the spot upon the end of the stigmatical cell and the one covering the small crossvein, in coalescing, form a straight crossband. Long. corp. cum terebrâ 0.25; long. al. 0.21.

Antennæ altogether ochre-brownish; third joint distinctly broader than in *C. obscuricornis*; arista brownish-black. Scutellum generally yellowish, with the exception of its middle. Abdominal segments, with the exception of the last one, with very narrow, but very sharply limited and conspicuous brown posterior margins. The first segment of the very flattened ovipositor is only moderately long, very broad, and very broadly truncate at the end; its coloring and its pollen are similar to those of the abdomen. Feet clay-yellow; tarsi strongly infuscated, generally paler towards the basis. The first spot upon the wings reaches from the first to the fourth longitudinal vein; the spot upon the end of the stigmatical cell is more or less completely connected with the spot covering the small crossvein, forming a straight, almost perpendicular half-crossband; the other spots have the ordinary appearance.

Hab. Northern Wisconsin River (Kennicott).

3. **C. similis** n. sp. ♀.—(Tab. VIII, f. 23.) Polline intescente vestita, segmentis abdominalibus postice nigro-limbatis, alarum maculâ subbasali in fasciam dilatata, maculâ stigmaticali et limbo vena transversalis media in fasciolam conjunctis.

Covered with clay-yellow pollen: the abdominal segments margined with black posteriorly; the spot near the basis of the wing is extended in the shape of a crossband; the one at the end of the stigmatical cell forms a half-crossband with the spot covering the small crossvein. Long. corp. ♂ 0.22; ♀ cum terebrâ 0.27—0.28, long. al. 0.21—0.22.

First two antennal joints yellow; the third joint is unfortunately lost in all the three specimens which I have before me, but is probably of the same color. Scutellum yellow, or grayish upon its middle only. The segments of the abdomen have all, without exception, a brownish-black, narrow, well-defined border, upon their posterior side. The first segment of the flattened ovipositor is only moderately long, very broad, very broadly truncate at the end; its coloring and the pollen upon it, are of the same color as on the abdomen. Feet clay-yellow; tarsi, especially towards their tip, rather strongly infuscated. The first spot on the wings expands into a crossband, reaching anteriorly as far as the costa,

posteriorly it extends, although somewhat paler, along the sixth
longitudinal vein, which it finally crosses, as far as the posterior
margin of the wing, on the fifth longitudinal vein It forms an
obtuse angle, at which place, on the sides of the fifth longitudinal
vein, it is very faint, sometimes almost interrupted; the spot at
the end of the stigmatical cell coalesces with the one covering
the small crossvein, forming a steep, somewhat curved half-crossband; the spot covering the posterior crossvein is rather large;
the three other spots are of the usual shape.

Hab. Connecticut (Osten-Sacken).

Observation.—The name which I give to this species is intended
to call to mind its extraordinary resemblance to *C. crassipennis* Fab., occurring in Europe. This resemblance is so great,
that I would doubt the specific distinctness of the two species, if
the femora of the American one were not altogether yellow, while
those of *C. crassipennis* are blackish-brown from the basis as far
as the middle. In order to overlook this difference and to maintain the identity of the two species, the proof of a perfect agreement in all, even the minutest, plastical characters would be
required. The three specimens of *C. similis* in my possession
are not well preserved enough to enable me to undertake such a
comparison.

4. **C. camus** Loew. ♂ ♀.—(Tab. VIII, f. 22.) Pollino es lutescente
cinereo vel albido-cinereo vestitus, tertio antennarum articulo pedibusque fuscis, alarum maculá stigmaticali et limbo venae transversalis
medie separatis.

Covered with a yellowish-gray or grayish-white pollen; third joint of the
antenna and the feet brown; the spot on the stigmatical cell entirely
separated from the one which covers the small crossvein. Long. corp.
♂ 0.16; ♀ cum terebra 0.23; long. al. 0.16—0.18.

Syn. *Ortalis casa* Loew, Berl. Entom. Zeitschr. II, p. 374.

Smaller than the preceding species, with a grayish or whitish-
gray pollen, verging less on yellow. The first two antennal joints
brownish-yellow or yellowish-brown; the third joint of medium
breadth and rather blackish-brown. Antennal arista black. The
scutellum at most indistinctly yellowish-brown along the edges
only. Abdominal segments without any trace of darker borders.
The first joint of the flattened ovipositor distinctly longer than in
the three previous species and somewhat less broadly truncate at

the end; its coloring and the pollen upon it are the same as
those on the abdomen. Coxæ and feet blackish-brown; the
second coxal joint, the tip of the femur, the basis of the tibiæ and
the extreme tip of the middle tibiæ are yellowish-red. In the
European specimens this yellowish-red coloring has often a much
greater extent and also occurs at the basis of the tarsi; it is probable that the same is the case with some American specimens.
The surface of the wings is much more whitish than in the other
species; the first spot is small, although it reaches from the first
to the fourth vein; the spot at the end of the stigmatical cell is
also comparatively small, does not quite reach the second longitudinal vein, and remains quite separated from the spot covering
the small cross-vein; the spot covering the posterior cross-vein is
of a moderate breadth; the spots upon the ends of the longitudinal veins are of the ordinary size.

Hab. Yukon River, Alaska (Kennicott); Nebraska (Dr.
Hayden).

Observation.—Of this species I possess only a male from
Nebraska and a female from Hudson's Bay Territory. The most
careful comparison with specimens of *Cerarys canus* from the
southern part of middle Europe and from southern Europe has
not revealed any character indicative of a specific distinctness of
the European and the American specimens.

Gen. V. ANACAMPTA Loew.

Charact.—*Head* hemispherical, rather than round; front broad, somewhat
narrower above; the vertical diameter of the eye much larger than
the horizontal one; cheeks broad.

Third antennal joint distinctly cut out upon its upper side; pointed
at the end.

Thorax upon its middle provided with bristles near the posterior
margin only.

First longitudinal vein with bristles upon its end only; the end of the
fourth longitudinal vein curved forward in a striking manner;
posterior angle of the anal cell sharp, but not prolonged in the
shape of a lobe.

The genus *Anacampta* contains species of large size, which
resemble *Cerarys* in their general appearance, as well as in the
picture of the wings. They differ, however, sufficiently in the
black color of the body, in the thoracic dorsum not being provided
with bristles as far as its anterior part and in the conspicuous

9

curvature of the end of the fourth longitudinal vein. The black
coloring of the body they have in common with the species of
Holodasia and *Apospasmica*, which they approach in the whole
structure of their body. They differ from *Holodasia* in the fact
that the first longitudinal vein is not provided with bristles upon
its whole course, but at its end only. From *Apospasmica* they
differ in the shape of the anal cell, the posterior angle being only
acute here, while in *Apospasmica* it is drawn out in a long lobe;
moreover, in the latter genus, the end of the fourth longitudinal
vein is not curved forward; in *Anacampta* the picture of the
wings consists rather of spots, or bands consisting of spots,
while in *Apospasmica* there are complete crossbands. The
structure of the third antennal joint of *Anacampta* affords a
character for the distinction of it from all the other genera of
Ortalina, which renders any further developments superfluous.

1. A. latiuscula n. sp. ♂ ♀.—(Tab. VIII, f. 19.) Nigra, thorace
abdomineque fasciis duabus cinereo-pollinosis, capite ex rufo luteo,
pedibus rufis, alis nigro-maculatis.

Black, thorax and two crossbands on the abdomen covered with gray
pollen; head reddish-yellow; feet red; wings spotted with black. Long.
corp. ♂ 0.31, ♀ cum terebra 0.33—0.34; long. al. 0.28.

One of the largest species of the genus, and broader in shape
than most of them. Head reddish-yellow, opaque, covered with
a very thin, and hence not easily perceptible greenish-white
pollen; occiput more thickly pollinose with white. Front broad,
somewhat narrower above; the not very distinct frontal stripe
very much narrowed above, of a purer yellowish color and almost
pollenless; the comparatively thick pubescence of the broad
lateral portions of the front is inserted in very small, but distinct
brownish dots. Antennæ ochreous-brown, the color of the first
two joints more yellowish, that of the third joint more brownish.
Ground color of the thorax, with the exception of the brick-red
humeral callosities, black, but altogether covered with an ashy-gray
pollen, which is not quite so thick on the pleuræ as on the
thoracic dorsum. The hairs and bristles of the thoracic dorsum
are inserted on small, but distinct black dots. Scutellum black,
with a broad brick-red border, pollinose with ashy-gray. Abdomen shining-black, with black hairs and two broad crossbands
of whitish-gray pollen, situate on the anterior portion of the

second and third segments; they gradually become indistinct on the sides and finally disappear near the lateral margin. The fifth segment of the female abdomen is very much shortened. The first joint of the ovipositor is shining-black, with black hairs, about as long as the penultimate segment of the abdomen, not very broad, and, towards its end, rather narrowed. Feet brick-red; tarsi infuscated towards their end, the front ones much more than the four posterior ones; the front tibiæ also show sometimes a browner coloring. Wings grayish-hyaline, quite gray towards the posterior border, not very transparent; more yellow towards the basis, especially in the costal cell; stigma ochre-yellow, with a somewhat infuscated end. The picture of the wings is brownish-black; it comprises: 1, a spot upon the humeral crossvein, reaching as far as the fourth longitudinal vein; 2, a perpendicular crossband, covering the end of the costal cell near the anterior border, and reaching posteriorly as far as the sixth longitudinal vein; between the fifth and the sixth longitudinal veins it is much paler and disappears gradually in the gray coloring of the surface of the wing; 3, a perpendicular half-crossband, beginning near the anterior margin, immediately beyond the end of the first longitudinal vein, running over the small crossvein and reaching a little beyond its posterior end; 4, a spot, broadly covering the posterior crossvein in the shape of a half-crossband; 5, a spot occupying the end of the marginal cell and, with the end nearer to the root of the wing, reaching into the submarginal almost in the shape of a hook, without touching the third vein; 6, a spot near the apex of the wing, the limit of which runs almost perpendicularly from the end of the second longitudinal vein to the fourth longitudinal, beyond which it occupies only a small space at the extreme end of the second posterior cell.

Hab. California (Alex. Agassiz).

Gen. VI. APOSPASMICA nov. gen.

Charact.—Front of equal breadth. Face rather strongly carinate; rather perpendicular and straight in profile; the vertical diameter of the eyes very much larger than the horizontal one.

Third antennal joint, on its upper side, gently but distinctly excised, very pointed at the end; arista very bare.

Thorax along the middle with bristles on its hind part only.

First longitudinal vein with bristles towards its end only; the end of the fourth longitudinal vein not curved forward; the posterior angle of the anal cell drawn out in a narrow, exceedingly long lobe.

Robust, black species, of the same general appearance as *Holodasia* and *Anaramina*; the structure of the head more like that of *Pteropaectria*; the thorax generally shows longitudinal lines of a paler-colored dust, answering to the intervals of the ordinary thoracic stripes. The wings have complete crossbands.

The typical species is the *Ortalis fasciata* of Wiedemann, from Chile, which is identical with the *Tephritis quinquefasciata* Macq. Dipt. Exot. Suppl. IV, 291.

The shape of the anal cell reminds very much of *Diacrita*; nevertheless, there are no other points of relationship between the two genera.

Observation.—Should an American species be found which does not well fit in any of the above-described six genera, the characters of the European genera should be compared; they have been given in the part treating of the systematic distribution of the *Ortalidæ* in general.

Fifth Section: PTEROCALLINA.

Gen. I. PTEROCALLA Rond.

Charact.—General appearance: Trypeta-like.

Wings very narrow, in comparison to their length, of a rather striking shape on account of their equal breadth, very broadly rounded at the root and at the tip; auxiliary vein much shorter than the first longitudinal vein, so that the distance between the ends of both is strikingly large; first basal and discal cells very long; posterior crossvein very oblique, its anterior end being much nearer the apex of the wing than its posterior end; the posterior angle of the anal cell drawn out in a moderately long lobe.

The peculiarities in the outline of the wings and in the venation of the species belonging to this genus are so striking, that no doubt can possibly arise about the location of any of them. In some other respects, these species differ considerably from each other, so that, should their number increase, it would be necessary to break up the genus *Pterocalla* into smaller genera. The name *Pterocalla* would, in this case, remain to the genus which contains *P. ocellata* Fab., as Mr. Rondani established the genus for this species.

1. P. strigula n. sp. ♀.—(Tab. VIII, f. 30.) Albide-pollinosa, punctis maculisque deformibus fusco-nigris asperea; ala fusco-nigra, disco dilutins fusco, punctis maculisque fusco-nigris variegato, margi- nibus antice maculatum hyalinarum serie, postico limbo latiusculo hyalino ornata, venis longitudinalibus non undulatis.

Clothed with white pollen, marked with brownish-black dots and irregular spots; wings brownish-black, of a paler brown upon their middle, and with brownish-black spots and dots; the anterior margin with a row of hyaline spots and the posterior margin with a rather broad hyaline border; longitudinal veins not undulated. Long. corp. 0.12—0.13 Long. al. 0.17—0.18.

In the structure of the head and of its parts, the coloring and picture of the whole body, this species resembles *Myennis vau* very much, but it differs considerably in the narrow wings with almost parallel sides, with a different venation and a different picture. The ground color of the body is an opaque brownish-black, for the most part covered with a thick white dust; the latter's surface on the upper side is broken through by brownish-black dots and a number of rather regularly arranged, but very irregularly shaped, brownish-black spots; the face does not show any such broken through places; the upper, larger half of the pleura shows numerous brownish-black dots, which almost coalesce above into a stripe; a little below the middle of the pleura there is a brownish-black longitudinal stripe and immediately below it a narrower stripe, formed by a white pollen; the pectus is brownish-black. Femora and tibiæ brownish-black (the intermediate femora in the described specimen are paler perhaps in consequence of immaturity); all the femora have, upon their last third, a more or less complete ring of white pollen; their extreme tip, as well as the basis of the tibiæ, are tinged with yellowish-white; each tibia shows, upon its middle, a very conspicuous white ring and a very sharply limited white tip. The yellowish-white feet are somewhat infuscated towards the end. Wings strikingly long and narrow, of an unusually equal breadth; very obtuse at the end, like in other species of *Pterocalla*; the auxiliary vein is remarkably short, so that the distance between its end and the end of the first longitudinal vein is remarkably large; the second longitudinal vein is rather long; the third ends not far from the apex of the wing, and has, like the others, a very straight and not at all undulated course; the ends of the third and fourth veins hardly show a vestige of convergency; the crossveins are rather

closely approximated; the posterior crossvein, with its anterior
end, is nearer to the apex than with its posterior end; the posterior angle of the anal cell is drawn out in a very long and pointed
lobe (the figure makes it too short and heavy). The extended
and entirely uninterrupted picture of the wings leaves near the
anterior margin an irregular row of hyaline spots and on the
posterior margin a broader hyaline border, with an irregularly
undulated outline; the coloring of the picture is brownish-black;
its inner part is paler brown, with numerous brownish-black dots
and spots.

Hab. Georgia (Berlin Museum).

Gen. II. STICTOCEPHALA nov. gen.

Charact.—General appearance: Trypeta-like.

Front very broad, with punctures; cheeks comparatively broad;
clypeus somewhat projecting over the edge of the mouth.

Wings of the usual shape; the ends of the auxiliary and of the first
longitudinal veins are far distant from each other; posterior crossvein steep; posterior angle of the anal cell acute; the third and
fourth longitudinal veins, towards their end, at least with a trace
of a convergency.

All the species belonging here are opaque in their coloring;
thorax and abdomen are punctate in all of them; moreover, they
are generally marked with other pictures.

The species which I know of may be separated in two groups,
on account of the different size of the hairs on the front. *Stictocephala cribrum* and *cribellum*, would belong to the first group.
S. corticalis and *rau* to the second. In the two latter species,
the two uppermost of the short hairs, inserted on the lateral
border of the front, assume the appearance of bristles, so that in
this respect these species are like the *Trypetina*, while this is not
the case with the two preceding species.

1. **S. cribellum** n. sp. ♂ ♀.—(Tab. VIII, f. 26.) Cinerea, frontis
parte antica, antennis, facie, genis, proboscide, palpis pedibusque luteis;
alis hyalinis, fasciis quatuor, præter secundam, postice abbreviatis,
macula apicali et vena transversalis posterioris limbo fuscis.

Gray; the anterior part of the front, antennæ, face, cheeks, proboscis,
palpi, and feet clay-yellow. Wings hyaline, with four bands, which are
abbreviated posteriorly, except the second; a spot at the apex and a
border along the posterior crossvein, brown. Long. corp. 0.13—0.15;
long. al. 0.14—0.15.

Light gray, front somewhat yellowish towards its anterior margin, covered with rather coarse punctures; the uppermost hairs near the lateral margin of the front are not longer and stronger than usual. Antennæ clay-yellow, third joint rounded-ovate, sometimes rather brownish-yellow. Ground color of face and cheeks clay-yellowish, covered with a whitish pollen. Proboreis and palpi clay-yellowish. Thoracic dorsum with somewhat scattered blackish-brown dots, which sometimes coalesce in lines upon its posterior portion; moreover with four brownish-black spots in a row corresponding to the transverse suture. Scutellum with four bristles, turgid, pale-gray, with two conspicuously large shining-black spots at the end. Metathorax black, pruinose with whitish-gray. Pleuræ dotted with brownish-black above. Abdomen with similar dots, usually with a more clay-yellow ground color at the basis; this color is sometimes more extended and gives the abdomen a more yellowish-gray tinge, while the thorax is whitish-gray. Coxæ and feet clay-yellow; posterior coxæ at the basis and the tarsi towards their tip, somewhat infuscated. Wings hyaline with four perpendicular, not very dark, brown bands, a broad brown border on the posterior crossvein and a brown apex; the first band begins near the anterior margin immediately beyond the humeral crossvein, and is not distinctly perceptible beyond the sixth longitudinal vein; the anal cell is just filled out by it; the second band begins at the anterior margin quite near the end of the auxiliary vein, and ends upon the end of the sixth longitudinal vein; the third band begins immediately before the end of the first longitudinal vein and runs across the small crossvein, at the end of which it is interrupted; the fourth band generally reaches from the anterior margin not quite as far as the third longitudinal vein, or is continued a little beyond it in the shape of a faint shadow.

Hab. Nebraska (Dr. Hayden).

2. S. cribrum n. sp. ♀.—(Tab. VIII, f. 25.) Præcedenti simillima, sed major, alarum pictura simili, sed saturatiore, fascia tertia et vena transversalis posterioris limbo in fasciam integram confluentibus, tibiarum omnium apice, posticarumque annulo medio, apice denique tarsorum nigris.

Very like the preceding, but larger; the same picture of the wings, but darker; the third band and the infuscation along the posterior crossvein

coalesce into an incomplete crossband. The tip of all the tibia, a ring
on the middle of the hind ones and the tip of all the tarsi, black. Long.
corp. 0.21 ; long. al. 0.20.

Unfortunately, I possess only a single, badly preserved specimen of this insect. The resemblance to the preceding species
is so great, that only the observation of the living insect or
the comparison of a large number of specimens, will enable one
ultimately to decide about their specific diversity. The considerably larger size, the darker coloring of the picture of the
wings, the coalescence of the third crossband of the wings with
the infuscation on the posterior crossvein into a complete band,
the difference in the coloring of the feet (in *S. cribellum* the
tibiæ show only a weak trace of a darker coloring at the tips, and
there is no trace whatever of a ring on the hind tibiæ, the tarsi
are but slightly infuscated towards the end)—all these differences
render a specific distinctness probable, although, on the other
hand, the great resemblance of all the other characters tends to
diminish this probability.

Hab. Middle States (Osten-Sacken).

Observation.—In case the specific identity of *S. cribellum* and
cribrum is proved, the latter name should be retained for the
species, as representing the more fully colored, and hence, normal
specimens, while *S. cribellum* would then be regarded as a
smaller and paler variety.

3. S. corticalis Fitch in litt. ♂ ♀.—(Tab. VIII, f. 28.) Fusco-nigra,
polline albo-cinereo aspersa, punctis, maculisque fusco-nigris variegata ;
alis albido-hyalinis, venis omnibus, maculisque numerosis nigris.

Brownish-black, covered with a whitish-gray pollen and with brownish-
black spots and dots ; wings whitish-hyaline, with black veins and
numerous black spots. Long. corp. ♂ 0.16 ; ♀, 0.19. Long. al. 0.17.

The ground color of the body is an opaque brownish-black.
Head of the same coloring, only the front, towards its anterior
margin, seems to have a more or less reddish-brown or brownish-
red ground color ; the pollen on the whole head is whitish-gray ;
on the extreme lateral margin of the front it is more dense and
almost white ; upon the middle of the front and at a considerable
distance from its sides, there are two oval, oblique, opaque,
brownish-black spots ; a spot of the same coloring surrounds the
ocelli, and has, upon each side a smaller spot, upon which the

Inner vertical bristle is inserted. The two superior hairs upon
the sides of the front are prolonged and incrassated to the size of
distinct bristles; above the two spots upon its middle, the front
has no hairs, besides these bristles; below the spots, however, the
front is beset with erect black hairs, inserted upon hardly perceptible dark dots. Antennæ ferruginous-brown, more distinctly
ferruginous on their inner side towards the basis; the third joint
round, black towards the end. Arista slightly incrassated at the
basis and blackish-brown upon the incrassation, then pale yellowish and again darker towards the end. Thorax covered with
a white-grayish pollen and with a brownish-black punctation and
picture; the latter consists of ten regularly arranged spots upon
its disk, and of a longitudinal stripe on each side, which begins
at the anterior end and reaches up to the root of the wings; the
picture of the pleuræ consists of two irregular longitudinal stripes;
the pectus is neither punctate nor pictured, and the pollen upon
it is not equally distinct when viewed from different sides. The
rather turgid scutellum has a brownish-black picture, the whitish-
gray pollen remaining visible on the lateral corners and at the
end only. The abdomen agrees with the thorax in its coloring
and has, besides the punctation, a regular and elegant brownish-
black picture, which is more fully developed in the female than
in the male; it consists of two small, approximated longitudinal
stripes in the middle of the abdomen, which begin at the
posterior end of the second segment and end at the posterior
end of the fourth segment; on both sides of these stripes, between
them and the lateral margin, there is a row of conspicuous
spots, placed near the anterior margin of the segments and not
reaching the posterior one. The first segment of the ovipositor
is very broad and broadly truncate at the end; brownish-black,
like the rest of the body; its basis is marked with two very large
brownish-black spots, reaching as far as the middle and which
have only a narrow stripe between them; the latter, as well as
the posterior half are covered with a thin, whitish-gray pollen,
and punctate with brownish-black. Feet brownish-black; knees,
a rather broad ring upon the middle of the tibiæ and basis of the
tarsi yellowish. Halteres blackish-brown, the stem, with the
exception of its basis, of a dirty whitish. Wings hyaline, viewed
obliquely strikingly whitish; all the veins black upon their whole
extent. The picture consists of rather numerous black spots,

which seem to be rather constant in their position, but less constant in their extent; the figure is drawn from a female specimen, which has them less extended; usually, the inside of these spots is distinctly paler, but this varies in different specimens; very characteristic is the part of the picture surrounding the small crossvein, which does not seem to be subjected to any important variation.

Hab. New York (A. Fitch).

Observation.—The described specimens, a male and a female, were obtained by Baron Osten-Sacken from Dr. Fitch under the name of *Trypeta corticalis.*

4. **S. vau Say.** ♀.—(Tab. VIII, f. 29.) Fusco-nigra, pollinc albo-cinereo asperus, punctis maculisque fusco-nigris variegata; alis hyalinis, maculis octo nigris, quatuor costalibus, unicâ apicali, unicâ margini postico contiguâ reliquis majore et venam transversalem posteriorem includente, duabus denique minoribus venæ longitudinali sextæ appositis; præterea macula ovata luteocum permagna, a maculâ costali secundâ usque ad secundam venæ sextæ maculam pertinens conspicitur et macula costæ tertia eodem colore luteo cum maculâ marginis postici conjungitur, ita ut fascia integra, in mediâ alâ multo dilutior, appareat.

Brownish-black, powdered with whitish-gray, marked with brownish-black dots and spots; wings hyaline, with eight black spots, four on the costa, one at the apex, one, larger than the others, near the posterior margin, covering the posterior crossvein, two smaller spots upon the sixth longitudinal vein; besides, there is a very large ovate, brownish-yellow spot, extending from the second second spot on the anterior margin to the second of the two smaller spots on the sixth longitudinal vein; the third spot on the anterior margin is connected by the same coloring with the spot upon the posterior crossvein, thus forming a complete crossband, which is much paler in the middle of the wing. Long. corp. 0.16—0.19; cum terebrâ 0.18—0.24; long. al. 0.14—0.16.

Syn. *Ortalis vau Say,* Journ. Acad. Phil. VI, 184, 4.

Ground color opaque brownish-black. Head of the same color, but the anterior portion of the front and the face of a reddish-brown or dirty brick-red coloring, which sometimes also extends to the middle line of the front. The two superior hairs upon the lateral margin of the front are bristle-like. The front, from the anterior margin nearly as far as the ocelli, is clothed with black hairs, inserted upon impressed punctures; there is no definite picture upon it. The thorax is covered with a white pollen and punctate with brownish-black. The picture on the thoracic dorsum consists of ten small spots, the inner ones among which are sometimes dissolved into dots, and moreover, on each side, of a row of spots, almost coalescent into an irregular longitudinal stripe, closely approximated to the exterior margin; upon the pleuræ there are two irregular longitudinal stripes; the pectus itself is brownish-black without any paler pollen or paler picture. Abdomen with a whitish-gray pollen, with brownish-black dots and with four longitudinal rows of brownish-black spots, placed upon the anterior portion of the segments; between them, upon the middle of the third and fourth segments, there are two still smaller spots upon the posterior portion of these segments. The first segment of the ovipositor is brownish-black, opaque, without any whitish-gray pollen and without picture. Feet brownish-black, sometimes only dark-brown in not fully colored specimens; knees, a ring in the middle of the tibiæ and the tarsi clay-yellow; usually the last three joints of the front tarsi and the last two on the posterior tarsi, are more or less infuscated. Halteres yellowish-white. Wings hyaline, rather whitish when viewed obliquely, their picture consisting partly of a black, partly of a clay-yellow or brownish-yellow coloring; there are four deep-black spots upon the costa; the first is composed of the incrassated humeral crossvein, and a short line, immediately beyond it, between the costa and the auxiliary vein, so that it has the shape of a fork, or almost of a ring; below the humeral crossvein, as well as below the small arcuate crossband, there are small black dots (one under each); the second deep-black spot on the anterior margin lies in the costal cell, but little beyond the end of the small basal cells; it is circular; between it and the third spot on the anterior margin, there is a small deep-black dot, placed at the end of the auxiliary vein; the third, likewise deep-black spot on the anterior margin, lies on the end of the subcostal cell and reaches the second longitudinal vein; the fourth spot on the anterior margin lies before the end of the marginal cell; inside of this cell it is deep-black, but turns beyond it into brown and further into yellowish-brown; it ends in the middle between the third and fourth longitudinal veins, thus assuming the shape of a perpendicular crossband, which is broader at its anterior end. At the apex of the wing there is another black spot, which begins immediately beyond the termination of the second longitudinal vein and extends but little beyond the end of the fourth longitudinal vein. The posterior crossvein is covered by a brownish-black spot, which is especially expanded near the posterior margin and the anterior end of which is connected by an ochre-yellowish or somewhat brownish-yellow coloring with the third spot of the anterior margin, thus forming a complete crossband, somewhat expanded posteriorly and tinged with yellowish in the middle. Sometimes, however, the brown spot upon the posterior crossvein is somewhat more isolated from the yellowish coloring and extends in the direction of the half-crossband, formed by the fourth spot on the anterior margin. This less common variety is the one described by Say, l. c.; the ordinary picture is represented on Tab. VIII, f. 29, of the present volume. On the anterior side of the sixth longitudinal vein there are two black spots of only moderate size and rounded shape. Of them, the second only crosses that vein, gradually to fade away. Between the second costal spot and the second of the two spots of the sixth vein, there is a very large oval ochre-yellowish or more brownish-ochreous spot; it reaches on one side as far as the posterior basal cell, and assumes within the marginal cell a rather dark-brown coloring. The veins of the wing are black or brownish-black inside of the picture, clay-yellow elsewhere. The third and fourth longitudinal veins converge towards their end a little more than in the preceding species.

Hab. United States.

Observation.—I possess six female specimens and no male, but have seen the latter in other collections. It does not show any perceptible difference from the female, except in the sexual marks.

Gen. III. CALLOPISTRIA nov. gen.

Charact.—*General appearance almost Trypeta-like.*

Front exceedingly broad, with impressed punctures: cheeks comparatively broad; clypeus somewhat projecting over the edge of the mouth, sometimes withdrawn inside of the oral opening.

Wings with an unusually convex posterior margin; posterior crossvein very oblique, its anterior end much more approximated to the apex of the wing, than the posterior end ; the posterior angle of the anal cell is drawn out in a very long, acute lobe.

The species upon which this genus is based, cannot well be placed in the genus *Stictocephala* on account of the remarkable difference in the outline of the wings as well as in the venation.

In other respects this species agrees with the preceding genus in
the structure of the body; with *S. corticalis* and *vau* it even
agrees in the coloring and the picture of the body, as well as in
the bristle-like nature of the upper hairs on the sides of the front.

1. **C. annulipes** MACQ. ♂ ♀.—(Tab. VIII, f. 27.) Fusco-nigra,
albido-pollinosa, et punctis maculisque fusco-nigris variegata, tibiis
tarsisque pallide infuscentibus, illis nigro-triannulatis, his apicem versus
infuscatis; alæ hyalinæ, maculis punctisque nigris confertim asperæ.
Brownish-black, with a whitish pollen, pictured with brownish-black spots
and dots; tibiæ and tarsi pale-yellowish, the former with three black
rings, the latter brown towards their end. Wings hyaline, densely
covered with black spots and dots. Long. corp. ♂ 0.14—0.16; ♀ 0.17;
long. al. 0.16—0.18.

Syn. *Platystoma annulipes* MACQUART, Dipt. Exot. Suppl. V, p. 121.

The ground color of the body is brownish-black and opaque;
the pollen, covering it, is whitish-gray. Head of the same color,
covered everywhere with brownish-black spots, moreover, dotted
with brownish-black upon the front and the cheeks; upon the
posterior orbit especially there is a conspicuous short row of
brownish-black spots. Front very broad, perceptibly narrower
anteriorly, where it is yellowish or yellowish-red. Eyes rather
strongly projecting. Antennæ brown, the first two joints and the
larger part of the inner side of the third joint yellowish-brown,
sometimes much paler. Thoracic dorsum with brownish-black
dots, which coalesce into ill-defined, although regularly arranged,
spots. Scutellum somewhat swollen, with four bristles, two
brownish-black longitudinal stripes and two blackish-brown dots,
upon which the lateral bristles are inserted. Pleuræ likewise with
brownish-black dots and spots; the latter form two irregular and
incomplete longitudinal stripes. Pectus brownish-black, with a
brown, but little perceptible, pollen. Abdomen with brownish-
black dots and regularly arranged spots; the first segment of the
ovipositor is for the most part covered with a whitish-gray pollen
and punctate with brownish-black. Femora brownish-black, with
a more or less distinct, broad, irregular ring, covered with gray
pollen, and with black dots; the tip is pale-yellowish. Tibiæ
pale-yellowish with three regular brownish-black rings; the first
near the basis, the last before the apex; tarsi of the same color
as the tibiæ, infuscated towards the tip. Halteres pale-yellowish.

Wings of an unusual shape, on account of the great convexity
of the posterior margin, hyaline, with black veins and numerous,
partly only punctiform, partly rather large black spots of an
irregular shape; the punctiform dots prevail in the middle, while
the borders of the wing are principally occupied by larger spots,
among which those along the posterior margin do not entirely
reach the latter. The peculiarities of the venation are indicated
above, among the generic characters.

Hab. United States; very common.

Observation.—I do not entertain the slightest doubt that
Macquart's *Platystoma annulipes* is the above-described species.
His description agrees perfectly well, with the exception of the
words: "face blanche, une petite tâche ronde d'un noir luisant de
chaque côté." All my specimens have, on the sides of the face,
or rather on the cheeks, nothing but brownish-black, opaque,
irregular spots.

Gen. IV. MYENNIS R. Desv.

Charact.—General appearance: Trypeta-like.

Third antennal joint oval; cheeks broad, clypeus small, projecting
over the edge of the mouth.

Wings narrow in comparison to their length, a little more attenuated
towards the apex; the first longitudinal vein beset with bristles
upon the portion only, which forms the limit of the very long
stigma; before this spot the first longitudinal vein appears almost
bare, the pubescence being very short and delicate; the two posterior basal cells are comparatively large; the posterior angle of the
anal cell is pointed; the posterior end of both crossveins is nearer
the apex of the wing than their anterior end, so that their position
is a very oblique one.

The genus *Myennis* was established by Rob. Desvoidy for
Scatophaga fasciata Fab. As *Trypeta scutellaris* Wied. agrees
with that species in the above-enumerated characters, we can, for
the present, unhesitatingly refer it to *Myennis*. The peculiarity,
however, of the *Pterocallina*, of showing considerable plastic differences almost from species to species, appears again in the two
above-named species. In *P. scutellaris* Wied. the eyes are less
round, the cheeks broader, the scutellum less swollen, the crossveins less approximated, the longitudinal veins, instead of straight,
somewhat undulated, and the third and fourth longitudinal veins,
towards their end, not distinctly convergent, but parallel.

1. M. scutellaris Wied. ♂ ♀.—Cinerea, antennis flavis, pedibus ex fusco testaceis, thoracis margine laterali atro-maculato, scutello tumido; alis angustis, hyalinis, fasciola basali, fasciis duabus discoidalibus antice connexis, plagaque apicali ex nigro fuscis picta, præterea in cellulis marginali et submarginali maculis aliquot fuscis variegatis.

Var. ♂ fascia discoidali secunda inter venas transversales late interrupta.

Cinereous, with yellow antennæ and brownish-yellow feet; the lateral margin of the thorax with black spots; the scutellum swollen; the narrow wings are hyaline; a small crossband at the basis, two cross-bands, connected anteriorly, upon the middle of the wing and a large spot upon the apex, brownish-black; moreover several brown spots in the marginal and submarginal cells.

Var. ♂ the second of the two bands upon the middle of the wing, is broadly interrupted in the middle.

Long. corp. 0.17—0.18; long. al. 0.17—0.18.

Syn. *Trypeta scutellaris* Wiedemann, Auss. Zweifl. II, p. 484.
Trypeta? scutellaris Loew, Monogr. of N. A. Dipt. I, p. 92. Tab. II, f. 26, 27.

Very like a *Trypeta* in its general appearance. Head comparatively high. The under side of the occiput rather tumid. Front yellow, of a medium breadth, long, its anterior margin rather projecting. Face somewhat retreating, a little excavated, infuscated inferiorly, covered with a pale-colored dust; antennal fovea hardly indicated. Eyes oval. Cheeks brown, very broad. Proboscis not perceptibly incrassated. Palpi short, but broad, of a dusky reddish-yellow; clypeus small and narrow. Antennæ ochre-yellow; the third joint oval, altogether rounded at the end; arista rather long and bare; it is thin at the end, but gradually stouter towards the basis. The upper part of the thorax dark-gray from a thick dust; the ground color of the humeri more or less ferruginous-yellow. Upon the lateral border of the thorax there is an irregular row of, for the most part contiguous, black spots; the largest among them is near the posterior corner; one is higher upon the upper part of the thorax than the others and near the transverse suture. The hairs and bristles are also placed upon very small, and but little perceptible, black dots. Scutellum with four bristles, rather turgid, of a shining dark-brown, with a clay-yellow median stripe; sometimes the clay-yellow color is more extended. Pleuræ blackish-brown, the posterior part yellowish-brown. Abdomen of the male cinereous; the penultimate segment shining-black, more thickly dusted towards the posterior

margin, and hence gray and opaque; the last segment is similar
to the penultimate, only the dust on the posterior margin is less
extended. The female has a blackish-gray abdomen (its coloring, however, seems to have been unnaturally modified in the
four specimens which I had for examination); at the basis of the
last three segments a darker coloring is perceptible, but it is not
shining. The flattened, broad, yellowish-brown ovipositor is but
very little attenuated towards its end. Feet brownish-yellow,
the front femora at the basis, the four posterior ones near the
apex, brown. The more maturely colored male has the greater
part of the femora dark-brown, the first half of the tibiæ and a
faded ring upon the middle of their second half, yellowish-brown.
Wings comparatively long and narrow; the first longitudinal vein
reaches far beyond the middle of the anterior margin and is beset
with bristles along the side of the very long stigma only; the
longitudinal veins have a very irregular undulated course; both
crossveins have their anterior end nearer to the root of the wing,
than the posterior end; their position is consequently a distinctly
oblique one and both are slightly bisinuated; the third longitudinal vein is not beset with bristles. Both small basal cells are
rather large in size; the posterior angle of the anal cell is strongly
pointed; the third and fourth longitudinal veins are parallel
towards their end. The stigma is brownish-black; a brownish-
black picture is contiguous to it, which has almost the shape
of an inverted V; it is formed by two crossbands which are
coalescent in front; the first is broader and runs from the basis
of the stigma over the basis of the discal and of the third posterior cells rather perpendicularly, almost reaching the posterior
margin of the wing, while the narrower second band takes an
oblique course over both crossveins, as far as the posterior
margin; a short, but rather broad brownish-black crossband runs
from the humeral crossvein as far as the basis of the anal cell;
upon the apex there is a very large blackish-brown spot, beginning at the end of the marginal cell and extending to the tip of
the second posterior cell; in the submarginal cell, between this
large spot and the preceding crossband, there is a brownish-black
spot of a considerable size, which, however, is very variable in
different specimens; the portion of the marginal cell situated
between the stigma and the apical spot has blackish-brown,
brownish and almost hyaline spots; a small spot of a much darker

tinge lies near the anterior side of the second longitudinal vein, below the point of the stigma. The picture of the wings seems to be rather variable, the end of the exterior costal cell being sometimes blackish-brown, sometimes hyaline; the other dark spots are sometimes faded upon their middle, sometimes also less extended. In a male in the Berlin Museum, the only specimen of that sex which I have seen, the crossband covering both cross-veins is broadly interrupted between them (compare the figure in Monographs, etc., Vol. I, Tab. II, f. 26). At first, I supposed this difference to be a sexual one, but I doubt this now, since I have had an opportunity of ascertaining the great inconstancy of the picture of the wings of the female.

Hab. Mexico.

Observation.—The figures given in the Monographs, etc., Vol. I, Tab. II, f. 26, 27, are sufficiently correct as far as the picture of the wing is concerned, but the outline of the wing is not well rendered; they are represented as too broad in proportion to their length.

SECOND DIVISION.

ORTALIDÆ HAVING THE FIRST LONGITUDINAL VEIN BARE.

First Section: ULIDINA.

GEN. I. DASYMETOPA Loew.

Charact.—Front broad, narrower anteriorly, abundantly hairy on the whole surface, the hairs on its sides not longer.

Antennæ rather short, third joint elongated-oval, with a thin, bare arista.

Face not excavated, descending vertically; *clypeus projecting over the border of the mouth; opening of the mouth not large; proboscis* but little thickened.

Thorax bristly on its hind part only; *scutellum* with a rather even surface and with four bristles.

Wings broader than those of the related genera; stigma of a very conspicuous size; posterior cross-vein oblique, its anterior end being much nearer the apex of the wing than the posterior; the last section of the fourth longitudinal vein is strongly bent forward; the posterior angle of the anal cell is drawn out in a point.

The general appearance of the species of this genus is very much like that of *Trypeta;* the coloring of the species at present

10

known is not metallic. The peculiar venation distinguishes these species from all the others of the present group. The typical species is *D. lutulenta* Loew (Berl. Entom. Zeitschr. XI, 285; Tab. II, fig. 1), from Surinam.

No *Dasymetopæ* from North America are as yet known.

Gen. II. OEDOPA Loew.

Charact.—*Head* conspicuously large; *front* unusually broad; ocelli on the edge of the vertex, very closely approximated.

Antennæ very short and very distant from each other; third joint rounded, with a thin, bare arista; frontal fissure running in an almost straight line from antenna to antenna; no frontal lunule.

Face broad, somewhat convex, with a small excavation under each antenna; its lateral portions conspicuously broad, distinctly separated from the middle portion.

Eyes rather round, but somewhat broader than high, comparatively small, hardly reaching the middle of the height of the head; hence, the cheeks unusually broad.

Clypeus not horseshoe-shaped and thus surrounding the proboscis, but lobiform, connate with the anterior edge of the comparatively small oral opening; *proboscis* small.

Thorax with bristles on its hind part only; *scutellum* flat, with four bristles.

Wings: the last section of the fourth longitudinal vein, towards its tip, is somewhat curved forward and thus convergent towards the third vein; posterior cross-vein curved in the shape of an *S*; posterior angle of the anal cell drawn out in an elongated point.

The body appears very bare on account of the sparseness and shortness of the hairs, as well as of the shortness of the bristles. The structure of the head resembles somewhat that of some South Asiatic *Ortalidæ*, while similar American forms have, before now, not been known.

1. **O. capito** Loew. ♂ ♀.—(Tab. IX, f. 1–3.) Albicans, fascia frontis tenui, thoracisque vittis nigris, in supero faciei margine maculis atris tribus, lateralibus ovatis, media didyma.

Whitish; front with a black transverse band, thorax with black longitudinal stripes; the upper margin of the face with three deep black spots; the lateral ones oval, the middle one double. Long. corp. 0.18—0.25; long. al. 0.15—0.22.

Syn. *Oedopa capito* Loew, Berl. Ent. Zeitschr. XI, p. 287, Tab. II, f. 2.

Head yellowish-white, only the middle of the occiput somewhat blackish; the ocelli are placed upon a punctiform black dot; the very broad front has, somewhat below its middle, a narrow, gently curved, blackish crossband, above which the single, rather sparse hairs are inserted in small, somewhat darker colored pits; this is not the case below the crossband; no stripes run from the vertex down along the orbits of the eyes. Antennæ yellow, the place of insertion of the arista infuscated or blackened; between the eye and the antenna there is, on each side, a transversely-oval, velvet-black spot; between the antennæ and next to the frontal fissure is another velvet-black transverse spot; which consists of two small semi-oval transverse dots. The face, including the clypeus and the very broad cheeks, is more whitish than the front; the cheeks with a very delicate, easily rubbed off, whitish down. Eyes during life with two narrow crossbands, which are sometimes perceptible even in dry specimens. Palpi yellow, with delicate, pale hairs. Thorax and scutellum whitish-yellow; the dorsum of the thorax with six parallel, blackish longitudinal stripes; the two intermediate ones extend also over the flat scutellum. Pleuræ with three blackish longitudinal stripes, the upper one of which occupies the border between the dorsum and the pleura; quite downwards, moreover, there is a stripe-shaped black spot, which, however, seems to be produced by the rubbing off of the dust on the upper part of the pectus. Abdomen flat and rather narrow, whitish in consequence of the very dense dust which covers it; the ground color, however, is blackish, except the posterior part of the last segment in the female; the short, black hairs are inserted on small black dots, which are so closely approximated in the vicinity of the lateral border that they appear confluent, as irregular longitudinal spots; the last segment of the abdomen of the male is very much elongated; the first segment of the female ovipositor is attenuated towards its end, otherwise it looks like the remainder of the abdomen; its punctuation, however, is much closer and finer; its adaptation to the abdomen is so close, that it might easily be taken for the last abdominal segment, especially when, as often happens, the black second and the yellowish third joint of the ovipositor are altogether withdrawn into it. Feet yellowish with whitish dust; the posterior femora generally with a blackish spot, on the under side before the tip; all the tibiæ with two black rings, the upper one of which is narrower and usually interrupted on the upper side of the tibia; fore tarsi blackened beyond the

tip of the first joint; the other tarsi blackened to a smaller extent.
Halteres yellowish-white.   Wings rather hyaline, of a dirty
whitish tinge; the second and the next following longitudinal
veins, as well as the crossveins which connect them, are black;
the other veins yellowish; stigma small, of the same coloring as
the rest of the wing; the picture of the wing consists of five brown
spots with somewhat paler nuclei; three of them are in the
marginal cell, near the anterior margin: the first, which like the
second is oblique, is placed at the tip of the first longitudinal
vein; the last is at the end of the marginal cell; beyond this is
the fourth, a transverse spot in the submarginal cell, immediately
under the tip of the second longitudinal vein; and again under
the latter is the last spot, which is rounded and placed in the
first posterior cell.   The last three spots have the appearance of
a narrow, very much shortened transverse band, which appearance
is more distinct in those specimens, in which these spots are
somewhat larger than usual.   The small crossvein is beyond the
middle of the discal cell, but before the tip of the first longitudinal
vein.

Hab. Nebraska (Dr. Hayden).

Gen. III. NOTOGRAMMA Loew.

Charact.—Front of an equal, rather considerable breadth, scrobiculate.

Antennæ rather long; third joint elongated, with a thin, bare arista.

Face very short, the anterior edge of the mouth very much drawn
upwards; clypeus considerably projecting over it.

Thorax with bristles on its hind portion only; scutellum flat, with
sharp edges.

Wings: posterior angle of the anal cell drawn out in a point; second
half of the last section of the fourth longitudinal vein very much
bent forward; posterior crossvein perpendicular; auxiliary vein
unusually short, and hence, the narrow stigma very long.

1. N. stigma Fab. ♀.—(Tab. IX. f. 3.)   Nigro-chalybea, thorace
lineis alternantibus nigris et late virescentibus variegato, alarum limbo
costali maculisque parvis nigris.

Blackish-steelblue, thorax with lines, showing alternately a blackish and
a pale-green reflection; wings with the anterior margin bordered with
black, and with small black spots.   Long. corp. 0.11—0.16; long. al. 0.1.

Syn. *Musca stigma* Fabricius, Ent. Syst. Suppl. p. 563, 72.

Musca stigma Fabricius. Syst. Antl. p. 303, 96.

Dacus setarius Fabricius, Syst. Antl. p. 278, 30.

Ulidia signata WIEDEMANN, Auss. Zweifl. II, p. 505, 1.
Notogramma cimiciformis LOEW, Berl. Entom. Zeitschr. XI, p. 289, Tab.
    II, fig. 3.

Head rather disciform. Front reddish-brown, scrobiculate,
remarkably hairy; the rather conspicuous stripes, descending
from the vertex along the orbits of the eyes, and the elongated
ocellar triangle are steel-bluish, shining; the ocelli are placed
near the edge of the vertex, and are approximated to each other.
The first two antennal joints brownish-black; the elongated third
joint brownish-brickred, brown towards the tip. Face and
clypeus metallic blackish-green, but little tinged with blue. The
dorsum of the thorax has numerous black longitudinal stripes,
which are separated by finer lines, having a metallic, light-green
reflection and traced as if with a trembling hand. Pleuræ
metallic blackish-steelblue, strongly tinged with greenish; above
the fore coxæ with a large spot, covered with white pollen;
from this place to the suture which runs down from the root of
the wings, the pleuræ are covered with deep-black, punctiform
dots, upon which single hairs are inserted. Scutellum rather
large, flat, sharp-edged, metallic greenish-black, but rather dusky.
Abdomen shining, blackish-steelblue; the first segment of the flattened ovipositor is of the same color, and attenuated towards its
end. Feet black; tarsi brick-red, the foremost ones from the tip
of the first joint, the four posterior ones from the tip of the second
joint, brownish-black; the hind tibiæ somewhat compressed.
Halteres dirty-yellow. Wings comparatively short, rather hyaline, with conspicuous, black veins; the costal and marginal cells
have an altogether black coloring, which forms a border along the
apex of the wing, extending from the tip of the marginal cell
across that of the submarginal and of the first posterior cells; it
becomes less intense here; in the submarginal cell, above the
small crossvein, there is a black dot and farther towards the apex
a small, triangular black spot; between the two again a black longitudinal line, which extends as far as the triangular spot; the
picture in the first posterior cell is a similar one, only the first
black dot is wanting and the two other black spots are somewhat
more approximated to the apex of the wing; in the discal cell
there are also two black spots, the smaller one before, the larger
one beyond its middle; the second posterior cell is marked in the

middle with a punctiform black dot;[1] finally, in the third cell, not
far beyond the fifth longitudinal vein, there are two successive
punctiform blackish spots; the small crossvein is in the middle
of the discal cell; the posterior crossvein is straight.

Hab. Cuba (Gundlach).

Observation.—The accurate knowledge which Wiedemann had
of Fabricius's collection enables us to admit his authority as to
the synonymy of *Dacus obtusus* Fab. with *Musca stigma* Fab.
Wiedemann had a large number of specimens of *Musca stigma*
(which he placed in the genus *Ulidia*) for comparison, and it is
upon the ground of this comparison that he affirmed that the
presence or absence of a pale spot upon the black border of the
costa does not constitute a specific character. We can therefore
safely accept the synonymy of *Musca stigma* Fab. with *Notogramma cimiciformis* Loew, the latter being the variety in which
the pale spot is wanting.

Gen. IV. EUPHARA Loew.

Charact.—*Front* of an equal, moderate breadth; scrobiculate, coarsely
  hairy.

Antenna almost more than of medium length; third joint elongated,
  with a thin, bare arista.

Face excavated; *clypeus* projecting.

Thorax with bristles on its hind part only; *scutellum* convex, with four
  bristles.

Wings: Posterior angle of the anal cell drawn out in a point; the last
  section of the fourth longitudinal vein parallel to the third; the
  small crossvein rather approximate to the posterior crossvein; the
  latter perpendicular.

The principal characters which distinguish this genus from the
following one, to which it stands nearest, are the shorter and not
attenuated stigma and the parallelism of the third and fourth
longitudinal veins. Moreover, all the species of this genus seem
to have black crossbands on the wings, while in those of the next
following genus only the costal cell, the stigma, and the apex of
the wing are blackened. The typical species is *Cerozys coerulea*
Macq. (Dipt. Exot. Suppl. III, p. 62, Tab. VII, f. 6), from
Brazil, again described by me as *Euphara coerulea* (Berl. Ent.

_____

[1] It is inadvertently omitted in the figure; the spots in the next cell
likewise are but very feebly marked.

Zeitschr. XI, p. 291, Tab. II, f. 4; the figure of the wing is reproduced in the present volume, Tab. IX, f. 4).

I have not seen any North American *Euphara* yet.

Gen. V. ACROSTICTA Loew.

Charact.—*Front* of an equal, moderate breadth, scrobiculate, rather
coarsely hairy.

Antennæ rather short; the third joint elongate-ovate, with a thin,
bare arista.

Face excavated, *clypeus* projecting.

Thorax with bristles on its hind part only; *scutellum* convex, with four
bristles.

Wings: posterior angle of the anal cell drawn out in a point; the last
section of the fourth longitudinal vein converges towards the third
longitudinal vein; posterior cross-vein perpendicular; stigma narrow
and very long.

The difference between this genus and the preceding has been
mentioned under the head of the latter. The characters which
distinguish *Acrosticta* from *Euxesta* are: the elongated shape of
the third antennal joint, the front, which is marked with pits, the
stouter proboscis and the very long, narrow stigma. The picture
of the wings resembles that of the species of *Seoptera*, except
that the somewhat turgid front of the latter shows no vestige
of pits and the face is not transversely excavated, but carinate.
As typical species may be considered either *A. scrobiculata* Loew
(Berl. Ent. Zeitschr. XI, p. 293, Tab. II, f. 5) or *A. foveolata*
Loew (ibid. p. 294), both from Brazil.

No North American species is as yet known.

Gen. VI. SEOPTERA Kirby.

Charact.—*Front* of equal breadth, somewhat elevated, with very short
hairs.

Antennæ rather long, the broad third joint elongate-oval, with a thin,
bare arista.

Face carinate, *clypeus* projecting.

Thorax with bristles on its hind part only; *scutellum* convex, with four
bristles.

Wings comparatively long; the posterior angle of the anal cell pointed;
the very long last section of the fourth longitudinal vein converges
towards the third vein.

Feet somewhat longer and more slender than those of the related
genera.

Kirby called this genus *Scioptera*. Following the usual rule of latinization, I modified the name to *Scoptera*. Later, Rob. Desvoidy called this genus *Myadina*; this name, however, cannot supersede the older one of Kirby, which, moreover, characterizes very well the peculiar habit of the species belonging here.

1. S. colon Loew. ♂ ♀.—(Tab. IX, f. 6.) Nigra, nitida, fronte rufa, antennis et facie ex rufo flavis, alarum maculā apicali triangulā et cellulis costalis basi nigris, stigmate subfusco.

Shining black, front red, antennæ and face reddish-yellow; a triangular spot on the apex of the wing and the basis of the costal cell black; stigma brownish. Long. corp. 0.19—0.21; long. al. 0.19—0.22.

Syn. *Scoptera colon* Loew, Berl. Ent. Zeitschr. XI, p. 296, Tab. II, f. 6.

Of a shining black, somewhat bluish-black color; the abdomen more glossy than shining. Front of a fiery red, opaque, along the orbit of the eyes with a delicate line, powdered with white pollen. Antennæ yellowish-red; the third, elongate-oval joint is rather broad. Face and clypeus brilliant reddish-yellow, the latter often, the former seldom, tinged with chestnut-brownish. On the dorsum of the thorax there are two narrow lines of whitish pollen, which extend beyond its middle; they are easily overlooked, although very distinct in well-preserved specimens. Feet black, the tips of the femora and tibiæ and the basis of the hind tarsi have a reddish-brown tinge, even in specimens of the darkest coloring; in lighter specimens this coloring is brownish-brickred, and extends not only over the greater part of the tibiæ and the hind tarsi, but is also perceptible at the root of the fore tarsi. Halteres pale-yellowish. Wings hyaline; costa, auxiliary vein, and first longitudinal vein black; the other veins much paler, generally yellowish when seen in a reflected light. The costal cell blackened as far as the humeral crossvein; the stigma, as well as the whole subcostal cell, at the end of which it is placed, brownish; at the apex of the wing there is a triangular black spot, which covers the extreme tip of the marginal cell as well as the tip of the submarginal cell, and crosses a little beyond the third longitudinal vein. The small crossvein is nearly under the middle of the stigma, but beyond the middle of the discal cell; the last section of the fourth longitudinal vein is particularly long, straight, gradually converging towards the third; the anal cell is broad and has a sharp posterior angle, although it is hardly drawn out in a point.

Hab. New York (Osten-Sacken); Illinois (Kennicott).

Observation 1.—This species, as far as I know, is undescribed, although not absolutely new, because Wiedemann, as his collection shows, received it from Say under the name of *Ortalis colon*. Harris, in his Catalogue of the Insects of Massachusetts, also has *O. colon*, which is undoubtedly the same species. I preserved the name which Say gave it, although I do not find it described in his works.

Observation 2.—*Scoptera colon* is so exceedingly like the European *S. vibrans* Lin., that as long as I had only indifferently preserved specimens of it, I took it for the latter species. Although the differences are only slight, they are so constant that the specific distinctness of the two species cannot be called in doubt. The front of *S. colon* is somewhat broader than that of *S. vibrans*; the two whitish stripes of the thorax in *S colon*, although but little apparent, can easily be traced beyond the middle of the dorsum, while in *S. vibrans* it is not without difficulty that their anterior end alone can be perceived. The abdomen of *S. colon* is always less shining, and its blackish color more bluish, while *S. vibrans* has it more blackish-green. The costal cell of *S. colon* is blackish as far and even a little beyond the humeral crossvein; in *S. vibrans* this cell is entirely hyaline as far as its extreme basis; the stigma of *S. colon* is brownish, that of *S. vibrans* black or brownish-black; finally the black spot at the tip of the wings is somewhat different in both species; that portion of it which crosses the third longitudinal vein is of more equal breadth in *S. colon*, whereas it becomes more narrow towards the margin of the wing in *S. vibrans*.

Gen. VII. EUXESTA Loew.

Charact.—Front of equal, medium breadth, even, rather coarsely hairy.

Antennæ short, the third joint almost round or rounded-oval, with a thin, bare arista.

Face more or less excavated, *clypeus* projecting.

Thorax with bristles on the hind part only; *scutellum* convex.

Wings: posterior angle of the anal cell drawn out in a point; the last section of the fourth longitudinal vein converges towards the third; posterior crossvein perpendicular.

The general appearance of the species belonging here is not unlike *Trypeta*. Legs short. The coloring is metallic; the black picture of the wings consists either of some large spots along the anterior margin or of crossbands. The plastic characters of the species do not afford any features for their satisfactory distribution into groups; for this reason the following three groups are merely based upon the picture of the wings.

1st Group. *Wings with spots along the anterior margin.*

1. E. spoliata Loew.—(Tab. IX, f. 7.) Viridis, capite pedibusque flavis, extremo femorum apice fusco, tibiis anticis fere totis, reliquarum apice tarsisque inde ab articuli primi apice nigris, alarum stigmate nigro, macula subapicali nigricante.

Green, head and feet yellow, the extreme tip of the femora brown, fore tibiae almost entirely, the tips of the four posterior tibiae and the tarsi, from the tip of the first joint, black; wings with a black stigma and with a blackish spot immediately before the tip. Long. corp. 0.12; long. al. 0.12—0.13.

Syn. *Eurosta spoliata* Loew, Berl. Ent. Zeitschr. XI, p. 298, Tab. II, f. 7.

Metallic-green, shining; the color of the scutellum and of the anterior segments of the abdomen is somewhat more bluish-green. Head yellow; the upper part of the occiput is blackish-green; front ferruginous-yellow; the swellings descending from the vertex along the orbit of the eyes and the immediate vicinity of the ocelli is metallic greenish-blue. Antennae of a dark ferruginous-yellow; third joint round. Face shorter than in most of the other species. Clypeus yellow, protruding considerably beyond the anterior border of the mouth, although projecting but little in profile. Feet yellow; all the femora distinctly infuscated at the extreme tip; fore tibiae rather stout, brownish-black, before the middle with an incomplete yellow ring; the intermediate tibiae are blackened at the extreme tip only, the hind tibiae also at the tip, but to a greater extent; the first joint of the hind tarsi is yellow, except the tip; the following joints are black (the intermediate and hind tarsi are wanting in the described specimen). Halteres yellowish. Wings pure hyaline with pale clay-yellow veins; extreme root of wings pale yellowish; the last section of the fourth longitudinal vein is but very slightly arcuated, but converges in its whole length towards the third vein, its tip thus approaching very near this vein; stigma blackened;

Immediately before the tip of the wing there is a blackish spot, which reaches from the anterior margin to the third longitudinal vein and covers the extreme end of the marginal cell; the extreme end of the submarginal cell is not covered by it. It may be that, in more fully colored individuals, this spot is darker.

Hab. Cuba (Riehl).

2. E. pusio Loew; ♀.—(Tab. IX, f. 8.) Viridis vel ex chalybeo viridis, thoracis dorso albido-pollinoso, pedibus piceo-nigris, genibus, tibiarum apice tarsisque totis luteis, alarum stigmate et macula subapicali nigris.

Green or bluish-green; dorsum of the thorax covered with a white pollen; feet piceous-black; knees, tips of the tibiæ and the whole of the tarsi of a dirty-yellow; wings with a black stigma and a black spot immediately before the apex. Long. corp. 0.12; long. al. 0.13.

Syn. *Euxesta pusio* Loew, Berl. Ent. Zeitschr. XI, p. 299, Tab. II, f. 8.

Metallic bluish-green; thorax and scutellum rather opaque, in consequence of a comparatively dense white pollen; abdomen shining; its first segment of a dirty-yellow towards its sides. The very broad first segment of the flattened ovipositor is almost as long as two-thirds of the abdomen. Head of a reddish-brick color; the sides of the front, the frontal lunule, the face, including the clypeus and the cheeks, are covered with a rather dense, white pollen. The black hairs on the front are not conspicuous. Antennæ brownish-ferruginous, or rusty-brown; third joint round. Face rather short, considerably excavated; clypeus but little projecting beyond the opening of the mouth. Occiput apparently altogether metallic-black, but the ground color is very much concealed by a thick whitish pollen. Feet piceous black; the second joint of the coxæ, the knees, almost the whole latter half of the tibiæ and the whole tarsi dirty-yellow or brick-red. Halteres whitish-yellow. Wings somewhat whitish hyaline, the veins pale; stigma of a blackish color, which, on its first half, extends as far as the middle of the marginal cell; immediately before the apex of the wing there is a black spot, extending from the anterior border as far as a little beyond the third longitudinal vein, the tip of the marginal cell is also covered by it, that of the submarginal cell, however, is not; the last section of the fourth longitudinal vein in its whole course, converges towards the third and comes very near it at its tip; it is not perceptibly arcuate.

Hab. Cuba (Gundlach).

3. E. metata Wied. ♂ ♀.—(Tab. IX, fig. 9.) Chalybeo-nigra, abdomine feminæ fasciâ apicali flavâ ornato, pedibus nigris, genibus, tarsorumque basi rufis, alarum maculis duabus nigris, alterâ costali minutâ, alterâ apicali trigonâ, cellulæ costalis basi et stigmate cinereis.

Bluish-black, abdomen of the female with a yellow crossband at the tip, feet black, knees and the root of all the tarsi red; wings with a small black dot in the middle of the costa and with a larger triangular spot at the tip; basis of the costal cell and stigma gray. Long. corp. 0.15—0.16; long. al. 0.15.

Syn. *Ortalis metata* Wied. Auss. Zweifl. II, p. 462, 9.
    Eurasta metata Loew, Berl. Ent. Zeitschr. II, p. 300, Tab. II, f. 9.

Of a blackish-steelblue, generally verging on green-blue, often with a violet hue on the middle of the abdomen; rather shining. Front of a saturate yellowish-red, sometimes almost yellowish-brown; with a whitish pollen along the lateral orbit of the eyes; the black hairs are scattered and not conspicuous; the swellings running from the vertex downwards, along the borders of the eyes, generally also the immediate vicinity of the ocelli are shining bluish-black or black. Antennæ brown, ferruginous-red at the basis, which color is more extended on the inner side; third joint rounded. The very considerably excavated face, together with the rather projecting clypeus are bluish-black, very shining; the upper portion rather densely pollinose, and hence opaque, the ground color not being distinctly visible; the lateral swellings of the face are tinged with brownish-red and thinly whitish pollinose. The female has the latter part of the last abdominal segment, as well as the basis of the ovipositor of a saturate yellow color; in the male, I have never observed any trace of this yellow coloring. The first segment of the very much flattened ovipositor is of a very moderate breadth, brownish-black, but with a more or less distinct coppery-red reflection. Feet black, femora in part metallic-black or bluish-black; knees and the root of all the tarsi brick-red, on the front tarsi this red generally reaches only as far as the middle of the first joint, on the hind tarsi as far as the tip, on the intermediate ones as far as the basis of the next joint. Knob of halteres yellowish; stem generally infuscated. Wings hyaline with rather dark veins; at the tip of the costal cell there is a small black dot, which extends posteriorly as far as the second longitudinal vein; at the apex of the wing there is a larger triangular black spot, occupying the end of the sub-

marginal cell and crossing to a small extent the third longitudinal
vein, but being exactly limited by this vein near the apex of the
wing; the costal cell is tinged with brownish-gray as far as a
little beyond the humeral crossvein; the stigma has the same
color, but this is sometimes more blackened, especially towards
its end; the last section of the fourth longitudinal vein converges
in its whole course towards the third vein and approaches it considerably towards its end; shows, however, hardly any perceptible
curvature; the fifth longitudinal vein does not quite reach the
margin of the wing.

Hab. District of Columbia, New York, Illinois, Connecticut
(Osten-Sacken).[1]

Observation.—Wiedemann gives a description of the male of
this species which might easily lead to the conclusion that he had
before him a species different from the one I have just described.
According to his statement, the male has, on the posterior margin
of the penultimate abdominal segment, a saturate yellow crossband. But as Wiedemann's collection contains as *Ortalis notata*
the very species which I described under this name and as, among
a considerable number of males which I have before me, not a
single one is provided with such a crossband, I am compelled to
come to the conclusion that Wiedemann mistook the sex of the
specimen from which he drew his description; he may have had
before him a female the ovipositor of which was bent under the
abdomen.

4. E. nitidiventris n. sp. ♀.—Nigro-viridis, nitida, abdomine
feminæ toto æneo-viridi et nitidissimo, pedibus gilvis, tibiis anticis totis
posterioribusque adversus apicem infuscatis, tarsis adversus apicem
fusco-nigris, alarum macula duabus nigris, alterâ costali minutâ, alterâ
apicali trigonâ, cellulæ costalis basi luteâ, stigmate ex luteo cinereo.

Shining black-green, the entire abdomen of the female metallic-green, very
shining. Feet saturate yellow, the entire fore tibiæ and the posterior
ones towards their tip, infuscated; tarsi brownish-black towards the
tip; wings with a small black dot on the middle of the costa and with
a larger triangular spot at the apex of the wing; basis of the costal cell
clay-yellow; stigma yellowish-gray. Long. corp. 0.14—0.15; long. al.
0.14—0.15.

_____

[1] Mr. Riley gave me a male specimen of *E. notata* which he bred from
the pulp of an osage-orange (*Maclura*).—O. S.

Dark-green, shining, the abdomen altogether of a vivid metallic
green, very shining. The femora of a saturate dark-yellow; this
coloring changes into brownish on the fore tibiæ from the very
basis, on the posterior tibiæ farther down; the fore tarsi are
saturate yellow at the basis as far as the tip of the first joint, the
posterior tarsi nearly as far as the end of the second joint, beyond
this the tarsi are brownish-black. The basis of the costal cell is
clay-yellow, or pale ferruginous-yellow, as far as a little beyond
the humeral crossvein; the stigma is yellowish-gray. In all
other respects this species is so very like *E. notata*, that one
would be inclined to take it for a mere variety of coloring, unless
the much lighter coloring of the feet, combined with the darker
coloring of the much more shining abdomen, proved the contrary.

Hab. Texas (Belfrage).

5. **E. costalis** Fab. ♀.—(Tab. IX, f. 10.) Nigro-chalybea, pedibus
nigris, genibus tarsorumque basi rufis, alarum maculis duabus magnis,
altera costali, altera apicali, nigris.

Blackish-steelblue, feet black, knees and roots of the tarsi red; wings
with two large black spots, the first in the middle of the costa, the
second at the apex of the wing. Long. corp. 0.15; long. al. 0.15.

Syn. *Musca costalis* Fab. Ent. Syst. IV, p. 360, 196.
   Dacus costalis Fab. Ent. Syst. Antl. p. 278, 29.
   Dacus oculatus Fab. Syst. Antl. p. 276, 14.
   Ortalis costalis Wied. Auss. Zweifl. II, p. 464, 13.
   Eurina costalis Loew, Berl. Ent. Zeitschr. XI, p. 301, Tab. II, f. 10.

Very like both preceding species, but easily distinguished by
the narrower front, the absence of a yellow crossband at the end
of the abdomen of the female, the perceptibly larger size of the
black spot on the middle of the anterior margin of the wings, the
altogether black stigma and the course of the fifth longitudinal
vein, which reaches the margin of the wing. Blackish-blue,
shining; the head brick-red or of a rusty-red; front anteriorly
of a more saturate coloring, narrow, somewhat whitish pollinose
on the orbit of the eye; the hairs upon it are rather sparse and
not at all conspicuous; the stripes, descending from the vertex
along the orbits of the eyes and the immediate surroundings of
the ocelli are steel-blue, shining. Occiput blackish, its lower
portion and a spot back of the region of the ocelli, brick-red.
Antennæ brick-red or more yellowish-red; third joint rounded-

oval, generally somewhat infuscated on the outer side, towards
the tip. The larger portion of the rather excavated face shows
a steel-blue, shining color, which is but little concealed by the
whitish pollen; the projecting clypeus also has a steel-blue
reflection. The first joint of the flattened, black ovipositor is of
moderate breadth. Feet pitch-black, femora almost bluish-black,
knees and basis of all the tarsi brick-red. Halteres of a dirty-
whitish or yellowish color. Wings hyaline, almost grayish, with
very dark veins; the root of the wings up to the humeral crossvein and a little beyond, blackish; the whole stigma, as well as
the tip of the costal cell and a spot connected with the latter
and reaching as far as the fourth vein, are black; at the apex of
the wing there is a large, triangular black spot, covering the tip
of the marginal and the end of the submarginal cell, and, moreover, crossing to a considerable extent the third longitudinal
vein, so that its posterior limit is not far from the fourth longitudinal vein and runs parallel to it. The last section of the fourth
longitudinal vein is only very gently curved and converges
towards the third in its whole course, approaching the latter
considerably towards its end.

Hab. West Indies (coll. Wied.).

6. E. quaternaria Loew. ♀.—(Tab. IX, f. 11.) Nigro-violacea,
dimidio apicali abdominis flavo, alarum maculis costalibus quatuor
nigris.

Blackish-violet, second half of the abdomen yellow; wings with four spots
along the anterior margin. Long. corp. 0.12—0.14; long. al. 0.13—0.14.

Syn. *Euxesta quaternaria* Loew, Berl. Ent. Zeitschr. XI, 302, Tab. II, f. 11.

Blackish-violet, the middle of the thoracic dorsum, a large
portion of the pleura and the sides of the abdomen often more
blackish-blue. Front rather narrow, ferruginous, along the orbits
of the eyes with a very delicate border of white pollen and with
coarse black hairs; the little stripes, running from the vertex
down the sides of the front are blackish, but hardly shining.
Antennæ ferruginous-brown, more reddish at the basis, sometimes
of a lighter coloring; the third joint is rounded. Face, including
the but little projecting clypeus and the cheeks brownish-red, less
excavated than in most of the other species. Occiput for the
most part black. Thoracic dorsum with a thin covering of
whitish-gray pollen, and hence but little shining; more so on its

sides; the pleura likewise are rather shining. The anterior part
of the abdomen of a metallic dark-violet hue; the apical half
yellow, sometimes with a dark stripe in the middle. The first
segment of the very much flattened ovipositor rather broad and
long, black, usually with a bronze reflection. Feet black, only
the extreme tip of the femora reddish-brown and the basis of all
the tarsi brick-red. Halteres yellowish, the stem usually infuscated. Wings hyaline, with four black spots on the anterior
margin; the first among these spots, placed on and immediately
beyond the humeral crossvein, extends as far as the basis of the
anal cell, so that the extreme root of the wing itself is hyaline;
the second spot, covering the tip of the costal cell and the very
short stigma, with the exception of its extreme end, runs perpendicularly and preserves the same breadth, as far down as the
fourth longitudinal vein, beyond which it is still perceptible as
a blackish-gray shadow; the third black spot lies opposite the
posterior crossvein, is of an elongated triangular shape, and
reaches with its tip as far as midway between the third and
fourth longitudinal veins, the fourth spot has an irregularly
rounded shape and lies quite near the apex of the wing; it
covers the extreme end of the marginal cell and the end of the
submarginal with the exception of its extreme tip; on its posterior side (that is the side which is nearer the basis of the wing)
it crosses the third longitudinal vein; the last section of the
fourth longitudinal vein, which is distinctly, although not strongly,
curved, converges in its whole course towards the third longitudinal vein, without approaching it more, however, than in the
several preceding species.

Hab. Cuba (Gundlach).

2d Group. *Wings with two, very much abbreviated, crossbands.*

7. **E. bimotata** Loew. ♂.—(Tab. IX, f. 12.) Nigro-chalybea, capite,
lateribus segmentorum abdominalium primi et secundi femoribusque
luteis, tibiis tarsisque fusco-nigris, alarum fasciis duabus postice valde
abbreviatis nigris.

Dark steel-blue, the head, the sides of the first two abdominal segments
and the femora yellow; the tibiæ and tarsi brownish-black; wings with
two very much abbreviated black bands. Long. corp. 0.12; long. al.
0.13.

Syn. *Eurosta bimotata* Loew, Berl. Ent. Zeitschr. XI, p. 304, Tab. II, f. 12.

Head dark-yellow; front rather broad, with a very narrow border of white pollen; the hairs upon the front are not conspicuous. The stripes descending from the vertex along the sides of the front and the immediate surroundings of the ocelli are steel-bluish, somewhat shining. Antennæ dark-yellow; their third joint rather round. Face rather excavated, with a white pollen which is less dense in the vicinity of the anterior border of the mouth, and from under which a faint steel-blue reflection is still visible. Clypeus but moderately projecting over the anterior edge of the mouth, generally of a dark-yellow color, seldom with a faint trace of a steel-blue reflection. The upper portion of the occiput, with the exception of a large spot behind the vertex, is steel-blue, with a whitish pollen. Thorax steel-bloish, with a rather whitish pollon and hence but moderately shining. Scutellum, metathorax and abdomen bright, shining, almost metallic black; the sides of the first and second segments of the abdomen have a yellow coloring, which, however, usually does not reach the posterior margin of these segments and sometimes is more expanded in the middle. Front coxæ and femora dark-yellow; tibiæ, with the exception of the extreme basis, and the tarsi brownish-black. Halteres whitish with a dirty-brownish stem. Wings hyaline; immediately beyond the humeral cross-vein there is a small black spot, which extends, in the shape of a crossband, as far as the root of the anal cell; the rather long stigma is black; from its basis a black crossband extends in a somewhat oblique direction as far as the middle of the discal cell; immediately before the apex of the wing, another black perpendicular crossband is situated; anteriorly it is somewhat widened, posteriorly it crosses the fourth longitudinal vein, the last section of the fourth longitudinal vein is moderately but distinctly curved, and converges with the third longitudinal more in its latter half than in its first. The intervals between the black crossbands of the wings of this species, as in most of the others, by transmitted light assume a rather indistinct white coloring. In a similar light, however, the apex of the wings of this species assumes a very striking whitish coloring.

Hab. Cuba (Gundlach).

11

3d Group.   *Wings with four crossbands.*

6. E. annosa Fab. ♂ ♀.—(Tab. IX, t. 13.) Nigro-chalybea, facile alarum nigris quatuor, secundi postice abbreviata et reliquis paulo latiori.

Dark steel-blue; wings with four black bands, the second of which is abbreviated posteriorly and is somewhat broader than the others. Long. corp. 0.14—0.15; long. al. 0.14—0.15.

Syn. *Musca annosa* Fab. Ent. Syst. 358, 189.
   Tephritis annosa Fab. Syst. Antl. IV, p. 320, 19.
   Ortalis annosa Wied. Ausg. Zweifl. II, p. 463, 11.
   Urophora quadrivittata Macq. Suites, II, p. 456, 5.
   Euxesta annosa Loew, Berl. Ent. Zeitschr. XI, p. 306, Tab. II, f. 13.

Head brick-red; the little stripes running down from the vertex and the region of the ocelli steel-blue, rather shining; the larger portion of the occiput blackish, with a grayish-white pollen. The front is of only moderate breadth; the hairs upon it are strikingly coarse, more dense upon the pollinose lateral borders, scarce upon the remainder of the surface. Antennæ brick-red, third joint rounded-oval, towards its end brownish and more so on its outer than on its inner side. The face is very moderately excavated; the clypeus moderately projecting, both with a steel-blue reflection and a white pollen. Thorax of a very dark color, verging sometimes on green, sometimes more on steel-blue or violet, and always covered with a rather dense whitish pollen. The scutellum is of a still more dark violet-black color, and less pollinose. The abdomen is of a metallic, but very dark bluish-black or violet-black color. The first segment of the flattened ovipositor is generally still darker. Fore coxæ, with the exception of their basis and the tip of the hind coxæ, brownish-brickred, the former with a white pollen. Femora black; the first pair, and generally also the last, more metallic-black; all are brownish-brickred at the tip; tibiæ blackish-brown; dark brick-red at the tip and often also at the extreme root; tarsi brick-red at the basis, blackish-brown towards the tip. Halteres clay-yellow. Wings hyaline, with four black crossbands. The first lies upon and a little beyond the humeral crossvein and reaches the basis of the anal cell; the second begins at the anterior margin with the but moderately long, black stigma and the blackened extreme tip of the costal cell; it is perpendicular and reaches beyond the fifth

longitudinal vein, without, however, reaching the margin of the
wing; the small crossvein lies exactly upon its external limit;
the internal one is always sinuate in the vicinity of the fifth
longitudinal vein; the third and fourth bands are connected at
the anterior margin in such a manner, that the hyaline space
between them reaches either exactly as far as the second longitudinal vein, or goes very little beyond this vein; the third band,
which is nearly straight and rather perpendicular, runs over the
posterior crossvein and almost reaches the posterior margin of the
wing; the fourth crossband is of considerable breadth, reaches
as far as the fourth longitudinal vein and is continued even
beyond it, in the shape of a gray shadow; the second half of
the last section of the fourth longitudinal vein is very gently
curved anteriorly, so that it converges towards the third longitudinal vein, without approaching it, however, to any considerable
extent.

Hab. Cuba (Gundlach).

9. E. Thomæ Loew. ♂ ♀.—(Tab. IX, f. 14.) Læte chalybea, niti-
dissima, alarum fasciis nigris quatuor subintegris, ultimis tribus latis.

Bright steel-blue, very shining; wings with four black crossbands, the
last three of which are broad. Long. corp. 0.14—0.15; long. al. 0.14
—0.15.

Syn. *E. Thomæ* Loew, Berl. Ent. Zeitschr. XI, p. 306, Tab. II, f. 14.

Very like the preceding species, although very probably a
distinct one, notwithstanding the great resemblance in all the
plastic characters. The differences are the following: the whole
coloring of the body is of a lighter and more brilliant steel-blue,
which often verges on violet in the middle of the abdomen. The
thoracic dorsum is much less pollinose. The second crossband
of the wings is broader, approaches more the posterior margin
of the wings, and is not sinuate on its inner side in the vicinity
of the fifth longitudinal vein. The third crossband is much
broader than in *E. annonæ*, especially its anterior portion; the
fourth band crosses the fourth longitudinal vein a little, or else
the gray shadow beyond the end of this vein is somewhat darker.

Hab. St. Thomas (Westermann).

10. E. abdominalis Loew. ♂ ♀.—(Tab. IX, f. 15.) Chalybeo-
nigra, abdominis basi sordide lutea, alarum fasciis nigris quatuor
integris, ultimis duabus ad costam anguste cohærentibus.

Bluish-black, with a dirty-yellow basis of the abdomen; wings with four complete black crossbands, the last two of which are connected by a narrow stripe at the costa. Long. corp. 0.12—0.14; long. al. 0.12—0.14.

Syn. *Exreta abdominalis* Loew, Berl. Ent. Zeitschr. XI, p. 307, Tab. II, f. 13.

Head brick-red or brownish-brickred; the small stripes running down from the vertex along the orbits of the eyes and the surroundings of the ocelli, are steel-blue, shining; almost the whole occiput is black, with a grayish-white bloom. Front rather narrow; rather dense and conspicuously coarse hairs upon the lateral borders, which are covered with white pollen; the hairs upon the remainder of the surface are very scarce. Antennæ brownish-brickred, or brick-red; in the latter case the rounded-oval last joint is more or less infuscated towards its end. The face is moderately excavated, usually for the most part with a shining steel-blue reflection; its white bloom is very thin along the edge of the mouth. Clypeus only moderately projecting, with a more or less distinct steel-blue reflection on the sides. Thorax of a shining, blackish-steelblue color, which usually verges somewhat on green upon its dorsum. Scutellum and metathorax still darker greenish-black, not pollinose. Abdomen more greenish-black than bluish-, or metallic-black, at the basis always dirty clay-yellow. The coloring of the first segment of the flattened ovipositor is the same as that of the abdomen, or a more purely black one. Fore coxæ, at the tip at least, brownish-brickred, with white pollen; femora black, more or less metalescent, with a brownish-brickred tip; tibiæ blackish-brown, only the extreme tip reddish-brown; tarsi reddish-brown at the root, otherwise blackish-brown. Halteres whitish or yellowish. Wings with four not abbreviated black crossbands. The first is broader than in the two preceding species, but is likewise placed upon and immediately beyond the humeral crossvein, and extends as far as the basis of the anal cell. The second band begins at the anterior margin with the black tip of the costal cell and the black stigma; it is rather broad and gradually expands in approaching the posterior margin so that, at this place, its breadth exceeds considerably that of the other bands; the small crossvein lies exactly upon its outer margin. The third band likewise, which runs over the posterior crossvein, has a considerable breadth and a very perpendicular position. The fourth band runs along the apex of the wing; it is also rather broad and reaches beyond the fourth longitudinal vein; its connection with the third band near the costa is rather narrow, so that the hyaline space, inclosed between them, almost reaches the costa anteriorly. The last section of the fourth longitudinal vein is gently arcuate and slightly converges in its latter half towards the third longitudinal vein (the figure does not give this quite correctly).

Hab. Cuba (Gundlach).

Observation.—The Museum at Vienna contains a couple of specimens taken in Cuba by Pöppig, which differ, however, by their distinctly smaller size, as well as by a somewhat different picture on the wings; all the four black bands are dissolved into oval black spots, covering the veins, the portions of the bands lying inside of the cells are crossed in the middle by gray stripes. A closer examination, however, proves conclusively that these specimens are incompletely colored ones of *E. abdominalis.* The small size is probably due to the greater contraction in drying of these unripe specimens.

11. E. altermans Loew. ♂.—(Tab. IX, f. 16.) Obscure chalybea, alarum fasciis nigris quatuor integris, omnibus separatis, tertiâ reliquis multo angustiore.

Dark steel-blue, wings with four complete black crossbands, entirely separate from each other; the third much narrower than the others. Long. corp. 0.13; long. al. 0.13.

Syn. *Euxesta alternans* Loew, Berl. Ent. Zeitschr. XI, p. 308, Tab. II, f. 16.

Head brick-red or brownish-brickred; the little stripes running down from the vertex along the orbits of the eyes, as well as the surroundings of the ocelli, of a shining steel-blue; the whole occiput blackish, with a whitish pollen. Front rather narrow, with coarse hairs which are more dense on the somewhat whitish, pollinose, lateral borders and more sparse on the remaining surface. Antennæ brick-red or yellowish-red, the third joint oval. Face very much excavated; with the exception of its lower, considerably projecting, portion, it has a steel-blue reflection, but is so thickly covered with a white pollen, that the bluish ground-color is but little apparent. Clypeus rather strongly projecting, brownish-brickred, sometimes with a steel-blue reflection on the sides. Thorax and scutellum of a rather dark, steel-blue color, which turns somewhat to greenish-blue on the thoracic

dorsum; the latter is but little pollinose. Abdomen darker
steel-blue, shining, especially on the sides. Feet black; the
knees and the first joint of the intermediate tarsi brick-red, the
first joint of the hind tarsi brown or reddish-brown towards
the basis. Halteres yellowish-white. Wings with four black
unconnected bands. The first of them lies, as in the preceding
species, on and immediately beyond the humeral crossvein and
reaches the basis of the anal cell. The second band begins at
the black stigma and runs, expanding somewhat, as far as the
posterior margin, in the vicinity of which it gradually becomes
fainter; the third band is narrow, perpendicular, and covers the
posterior crossvein; the fourth runs along the apex of the wing,
is even broader than the second and completely isolated from the
third; beyond the fourth longitudinal vein, it becomes very faint.
The last section of the fourth vein is rather strongly curved and
its latter portion converges towards the third vein.

Hab. Brazil? Cuba! (Vienna Museum).

Observation.—The description is drawn from a male specimen
in the Vienna Museum, labelled: Mann, Toscana 1846. As I
have seen the same species, in other collections, marked as
Brazilian, I take the designation of the Vienna Museum to be
erroneous. I am confirmed in this supposition by the fact that
next to the above-mentioned specimen is placed another, a
female, pinned on the same kind of pin and labelled in the
same manner, which, however, is a specimen of *E. stigmatias*,
received hitherto from Cuba and Brazil only. Thus it appears
evident that both specimens were sent by the same collector, probably from the same country; and as *E. stigmatias* is a common
species in Cuba, the conclusion is not too far fetched that both
specimens came from that island. This is the reason why I did
not like to omit *E. alternans* in this volume.

12. E. stigmatias Loew. ♂ ♀.—(Tab. IX, f. 17.) Nigro-viridis,
macula atra inter antennas alti insignis, alarum fascia nigra quatuor,
ultimis duabus ad costam conjunctis.

Blackish-green, conspicuous by a deep black spot between the antennæ,
wings with four black bands, the last two of which are connected near
the costa. Long. corp. 0.13—0.15; long. al. 0.14—0.16.

Syn. *Eutreta stigmatias* Loew, Berl. Ent. Zeitschr. XI, p. 310, Tab. II, f. 18.

Head dark metallic-green or almost steel-blue. Front of a
dusky-red; the little stripes running down from the vertex along

the orbits of the eyes, as well as the well-defined ocellar triangle, shining steel-blue. The lateral border of the front shining and generally with a rather distinct steel-blue reflection; immediately above each antenna, a trace of a small swelling is discernible. The hairs on the front are not conspicuous, moderately dense on the sides, very scarce on the remaining surface. The first two joints of the antennæ brownish-black, the rounded-oval third joint reddish-yellow from the basis as far as the arista, more brownish beyond it. Face very much excavated, shining steel-blue, with a whitish pollen on its upper part only; above this, just between the antennæ, is a conspicuous, velvet-black spot. Clypeus very much projecting, shining, steel blue, pollinose on the margins only. The rather broad orbital circles of the eyes brick-red below, at the lower corner of the eyes. Thorax dark metallic-green, somewhat verging on steel-blue; the dorsum with a very thin gray pollen. Scutellum blackish-green. Abdomen of the same color as the thorax, but darker, often with a stronger steel-blue reflection; the last abdominal segments of the male sometimes more bronze-colored. The first segment of the flattened ovipositor metallic-black. Feet black; the tips of the knees and the basis of all the tarsi brownish-brickred. Halteres white-yellowish. Wings with four black crossbands. The first lies, as in several other species, on and immediately beyond the humeral crossvein and extends as far as the basis of the anal cell. The second band, which is rather broad, begins at the costa with the blackish end of the costal cell and the black stigma; it is generally very much fainter beyond the fourth longitudinal vein and disappears entirely between the fifth vein and the posterior margin of the wing; the small crossvein lies almost exactly upon the outer margin of this band. The third band, which is perpendicular, runs over the posterior crossvein and reaches the posterior margin of the wing almost completely; it is broader anteriorly than posteriorly, and is connected with the fourth band on the inside of the marginal cell, so that the hyaline interval between these bands extends exactly as far as the second longitudinal vein. The fourth band, lying along the apex of the wing, is also rather broad and extends as far as the fourth longitudinal vein. The last section of the fourth vein is distinctly curved and in its second half converges towards the third longitudinal vein.

Hab. Cuba (Gundlach); Brazil (coll. Winthem).

18. E. eluta Loew. ♂ ♀.—(Tab. IX, f. 18.) Nigro-viridis, sub-
chalybaeoecens, macula atra inter antennas sita insignis, alarum fasciis
nigris quatuor, secunda latissima sed maxima ex parte valde eluta,
tertia et quarta in cellula costali per maculam hyalinam separatis.

Blackish-green, verging on steel-blue, conspicuous by a deep black spot
lying between the antennae; wings with four black bands, the second
of which is the broadest, but, for the most part, very pale; the third
and fourth are separated by a hyaline spot, lying in the costal cell.
Long. corp. 0.14 – 0.15; long. al. 0.14—0.15.

Syn. *Eurosta eluta* Loew, Berl. Ent. Zeitschr. XI, p. 312, Tab. II, f. 19.

Front red or brownish-red; the little stripes, descending from
the vertex along the orbits of the eyes and the well-defined ocellar
triangle, are shining steel-blue; the hairs on the front are not
striking, moderately dense on the but slightly pollinose lateral
borders; otherwise very scarce. Occiput blackish-steel-blue, with
a grayish-white bloom. Antennae ferruginous-brown or reddish-
brown, more brick-red at the basis of the third joint; sometimes
the second joint has the same coloring. Face rather excavated,
generally steel-blue, or at least reddish along the anterior edge
of the mouth only; in some rare cases it has a light steel-blue
reflection on its upper part, the remainder brick-red; exactly between the antennae is a conspicuous velvety-black spot; clypeus
but little projecting beyond the edge of the mouth, reddish-brown,
with a steel-blue reflection; the orbits of the eyes brick-red or
brownish-red near the lower corner of the eye. Thorax dark
metallic-green; in less mature specimens greenish steel-blue.
Thoracic dorsum only slightly pollinose. Scutellum more blackish-green or blackish-blue. The color of the abdomen is not
unlike that of the thorax, but is darker and verges on bluish;
its middle sometimes almost violet; the last segments of the
male abdomen sometimes bronze-colored. Front coxae, except
the root, brick-red, with white pollen. Feet black, the tips of
the knees and the root of all the tarsi brick-red; the tip of the
middle tibiae likewise is generally brick-red; sometimes the
extreme tip of the front tibiae shows a brick-red coloring. Halteres yellowish-white. Wings with four black crossbands. The
first lies upon and immediately beyond the humeral crossvein
and extends to the extreme basis of the anal cell; it is rather
narrow and often pallid. The second crossband is of considerable breadth, begins near the costa with the infuscated tip
of the costal cell and the black stigma; but beyond the third,

or the fourth longitudinal vein It is so very faint that it extends to the posterior margin of the wing in the shape of a gray shadow ; the small crossvein lies, when the band is not too pale, almost exactly upon its external margin. The third band passes over the posterior crossvein, is narrow and generally rather pale, except in the vicinity of the anterior margin ; towards the posterior end of the crossvein it almost disappears ; from the fourth band it is separated by a rather large, whitish-hyaline spot in the marginal cell ; behind the second longitudinal vein fully colored specimens have, on the outer side of this third band a rather distinct gray shadow, between which and the fourth band only a narrow, whitish hyaline interval remains, from which, however, the above-mentioned hyaline spot near the costa is completely isolated. The fourth band, which lies along the apex of the wing, extends as far as the fourth longitudinal vein, or else it crosses it in the shape of a gray shadow. The last section of the fourth longitudinal vein is rather strongly curved and convergent towards the third vein.

Hab. Cuba (Guadlach).

Gen. VIII. CHÆTOPSIS Loew.

Charact.—Front of medium breadth, somewhat narrower towards the vertex, with a row of bristly hairs on the lateral border ; the remaining surface not hairy.

Antennæ rather short ; third joint very little excised on the upper side, with a sharp anterior corner and a thin, bare arista.

Face but moderately excavated ; clypeus but little projecting over the anterior border of the mouth.

Thorax with bristles on its posterior part only ; clypeus convex, with four bristles.

Wings: posterior angle of the anal cell drawn out in a point ; last section of the fourth longitudinal vein, towards its end, but very little convergent with the third vein ; posterior crossvein perpendicular.

The species known to me are conspicuous for the striking length of the bristles, inserted on the posterior part of the thorax and on the scutellum. Their coloring is metallic ; the wings are adorned with well-defined black crossbands. They cannot well be confounded with the species of the preceding genus, on account of their greater slenderness, and more especially, on account of the different shape of the third antennal joint and of the front, which is hairy on its lateral borders only. From the two next following

genera, which likewise have the third antennal joint with a sharp
anterior angle, the species of the present genus are sufficiently
distinguished by their less slender shape and the different
structure of the anal cell, not to mention other characters.

1. C. aenea Wied. ♂ ♀.—(Tab. IX, f. 19.) Viridis, antennis fusco-
nigris, basi tamen articuli tertii lutea, alis trifasciatis.

Metallic-green; antennæ brownish-black, the basis of the third joint yellow; wings with three bands. Long. corp. 0.16—0.18; long. al. 0.17
—0.19.

Syn. *Ortalis aenea* Wied. Auss. Zweifl. II, p. 472, 8.
   Ortalis trifasciata Say, Journ. Acad. Phil. VI, p. 184, 8.
   Urophora falcifrons Macq. Dipt. Exot. Suppl. V, p. 125, Tab. VI, f. 9.
   Chrtopsis aenea Loew, Berl. Ent. Zeitschr. II, p. 315, Tab. II, f. 21.
   Trypeta (Aciura) aenea v. d. Walp, Tijdschr. voor Ent. 1867, p. 137,
      Tab. V, f. 12—14.

Front red, on each side with a broad band, which is covered
with white pollen. The ocelli rather far distant from the edge
of the vertex; the region of the ocelli, as well as the little stripes
descending from the vertex along the orbits of the eyes are
blackish-green, only very little shining. Frontal lunule with
white pollen. Antennæ rather short; the first two joints brown,
the second sometimes in part brownish-yellow; the third joint
rather broad, very little excised on the upper side, always with
a sharp anterior angle, brownish-black, reddish-yellow at the
basis. Face only little excavated, steel-bluish, but rather opaque
on account of a whitish pollen; the edge of the mouth usually
brick-red. The clypeus has but a small transverse diameter and
is but little projecting over the anterior edge of the mouth.
Thorax and scutellum shining metallic-green, upon the dorsum
with a trace of a white bloom. Abdomen of the same color, or
somewhat more bronze-green, the last joints of the male abdomen
generally blackish-green. With less mature individuals the
coloring of thorax and abdomen is more bluish-green, and at the
basis of the latter an unmetallic, dirty-yellow coloring may be
seen. The coloring of the feet is variable; in some specimens
they are altogether pale-yellow, only a little darker at the tip of
the tarsi; as this occurs in those specimens which have the basis
of the abdomen yellow, one might almost be led to the conclusion
that they form a distinct species; however, the absolute similarity
of all the other characters renders this conclusion very improba-

ble; darker specimens have the color of the feet more brownish-
yellow, the root of the front coxæ and the tip of the tarsi dark-
brown; the femora of such specimens often show conspicuous
black, metallic-green longitudinal stripes; the darkest specimens
have the whole basal half of the femora, and even more, of this
black coloring, while the tibiæ also are partly infuscated.
Halteres yellowish-white. Wings with three brownish-black
bands; the veins are black upon these bands, but ochre-yellow
elsewhere, which gives the whole basal part of the wing an
ochre-yellowish tinge. The first band begins at the costa with a
short black stigma, is perpendicular and rather dark, as far as the
fourth longitudinal vein and even beyond; the remainder of the
band, as far as the posterior margin of the wing, is usually very
faint; the small crossvein is a little beyond the margin of this
band; the second band runs over the posterior crossvein and is
perpendicular and rather broad; its posterior end is very pale;
with the third band it is generally connected only by a dark
border along the costa; sometimes, however, this border becomes
broader and extends in some specimens as far as the second
longitudinal vein. The third band, running along the apex, is
likewise rather broad, extends as far as the fourth longitudinal
vein, and even beyond it, in the shape of a gray shadow. The
last section of the fourth longitudinal vein, beyond its middle,
converges towards the third; near its tip, however, this convergency becomes again much less.

Hab. United States, rather common (Osten-Sacken); Louisiana
(Schaum) Cuba (Gundlach).

Observation 1.—The comparison of the types in Wiedemann's
collection do not allow any doubt about the determination of this
species; they belong to the variety of a paler, but not of the
palest, coloring. Say's good description of *Ortalis trifasciata*
refers to the variety with dark feet. That Macquart's *Urophora
fulcifrons* belongs here seems certain; that he placed the species
in the genus *Urophora* is no objection, because he did the same
with several *Ortalidæ;* the figure of the wing, which he gives, is
incorrect, as the comparison of the description shows; the latter
proves conclusively that the second crossvein on the middle of the
wing is an arbitrary addition; it seems that Macquart drew the
small crossvein correctly on the extreme limit of the first crossband; later, however, in finishing his figure, he noticed that in

consequence of the very exaggerated breadth of the interval between the first and second bands, the position of the small crossvein with regard to the posterior one had become altogether disturbed, and in order to correct this, he may have drawn the small crossvein a second time, at a correct distance from the large one. Mr. Van der Wulp has erroneously taken *Chætopsis ænea* for a *Trypeta* and, supposing it a new species, accidentally described it under the same specific name.

Observation 2.—The *Urophora ænea* Macq. (Suites, etc., Dipt. II, p. 458, 18), may be a synonym of the present species, although I do not consider this as certain. The figure of the wing, as given in Dipt. Exot. II, 3, Tab. XXX, f. 7, shows at the basis of the wing an extensive and very conspicuous black spot, of which there is no vestige in *C. ænea*. It seems certain that *Urophora ænea* Macq. is a species belonging to the present group of *Ortalidæ*.

2. C. debilis Loew. ♀.—(Tab. IX, f. 20.) Viridi-chalybea, antennis totis pedibusque flavis, alis trifasciatis.

Greenish-blue; the entire antennæ and the feet yellow; wings with three bands. Long. corp. 0.12; long. al. 0.11.

Syn. *Chætopsis debilis* Loew. Berl. Ent. Zeitschr. XI, p. 316, Tab. II, f. 22.

Very like the preceding species, but smaller; the white bloom forming a border on both sides of the front is comparatively a little broader; it has a single row of four bristles upon it, whereas in the preceding species these hairs are much more numerous. The antennæ are altogether yellow and their third joint upon its upper side is somewhat more excised. The stigma is comparatively smaller; the three bands have the same position, but are less pale towards the posterior margin; the last two are entirely separated from each other, which is very seldom the case with *Chætopsis ænea;* the last section of the fourth vein is much more straight and shows only a vestige of a slight convergency towards the third longitudinal vein. The coloring of the described specimen is not green, but greenish steel-blue; of a dirty-yellowish at the basis of the abdomen; but as it is a rather immature specimen, these differences cannot have much weight. The first segment of the flattened ovipositor is comparatively long.

Hab. Cuba (Gundlach)

Gen. IX. HYPOECTA Loew.

Charact.—Front of an equal, rather considerable breadth, somewhat projecting when viewed in profile; delicately hairy on the sides only.
Antennæ short; third joint very much excised on the upper side, with
a very sharp anterior corner and with a thin, bare arista.

Face not excavated, somewhat retreating on the under side; clypeus
rudimentary, not projecting over the edge of the mouth, of a very
small transverse diameter.

Thorax with bristles on its hind part only; scutellum convex, with
four bristles.

Wings: posterior angle of the anal cell pointed, open; the last
section of the fourth longitudinal vein converges somewhat towards
the third; the posterior crossvein perpendicular.

The species of this genus are considerably more slender than
the species of *Chætopsis* and their shape is somewhat more like
that of *Eumetopia*. The third antennal joint, the shape of which
reminds one of *Cerurys*, the not excavated face, the rudimentary
clypeus and the open anal cell, are easy to recognize. The
ovipositor is conspicuously broad, and so closely joined to the
abdomen that it may be easily mistaken for its last segment.
The typical species is *H. longula* Loew, Berl. Ent. Zeitschr. XI,
p. 319, Tab. II, f. 23, from Santos (in Brazil).

No North American species are as yet known.

Gen. X. STENOMYIA Loew.

Charact.—Front of equal breadth, somewhat projecting in profile, hairy
on the sides; upon the remaining surface with two longer hairs
only.

Antennæ rather short, third joint hardly excised upon the upper side,
but with a sharp anterior angle; arista thin and bare.

Face not excavated, somewhat retreating, with a slight depression
under each antenna; gently convex between these depressions;
clypeus of moderate transverse diameter, somewhat projecting over
the border of the mouth.

Thorax with bristles on its posterior part only.

Wings comparatively long; posterior angle of the anal cell sharp, but
not pointed, last section of the fourth longitudinal vein about double
the length of the preceding section, gently converging towards the
third longitudinal vein; posterior crossvein rather perpendicular.

The striking slenderness of the narrow body and the metallic
coloring, are points of resemblance between the species of this
genus and those of *Eumetopia;* the picture of the wings is like-

wise a similar one. The former are at once distinguished, however, by the front, which is not conically projecting. They
are characterized also by the shape of the wings and the venation, which it will be easier to understand from the figure than
from a description.

1. S. tenuis Loew.   ♂.—(Tab. IX, f. 21.)   Chalybeo-viridis, pedibus
nigris, basi tarsorum rufa; alis cinereis, stigmate et plagâ permagnâ
apicali nigris.

Greenish-steelblue, the feet black, the root of the tarsi red; the grayish
wings have a black stigma and a large black spot at the apex.   Long.
corp. 0.14; long. al. 0.13.

Syn. *Stenomyia tenuis* Loew, Berl. Ent. Zeitschr. XI, p. 321, Tab. II, f. 24.

Front brown, almost black above, rather hairy along the orbits
of the eyes, upon the remaining surface only with two more
elongated hairs; the little stripes running down from the vertex
along the orbits of the eyes and the ocellar triangle are dark
bluish-green, shining.   Antennae black; the second joint at its
upper corner to a certain extent dirty-whitish; third joint rather
broad, upon the upper side hardly excised, but with a sharp
anterior corner.   Face somewhat retreating, with a distinct
depression under each antenna, longitudinally convex along its
middle, dark steel-blue, shining, but on its upper half with a thin,
whitish bloom.   Clypeus of a very moderate transverse diameter,
but distinctly projecting over the upper border of the mouth, deep
steel-blue and shining.   Palpi black.   Eyes large and rather
round, their horizontal diameter, however, is a little larger than
the vertical one.   Cheeks narrow.   Thorax dusky blue-green,
rather shining, scutellum greenish-black, but little shining, with
an entirely even upper side.   The narrow and long abdomen has
the same coloring as the thorax; however, towards its extremity
it gradually becomes more black and opaque.   Feet black;
femora and tibia with metallic, dark bluish-green reflections; the
extreme tips of the tibia and the root of the tarsi are dark brick-
red, the remainder of the feet brownish-black.   Halteres whitish.
Wings long and narrow, grayish, the root and a rather large spot
immediately behind the stigma lighter; the rather small, narrow
stigma is of a black color, which extends below it as far as the
second longitudinal vein; the last third of the wings, beginning
at the costa as far as the fourth longitudinal vein, is tinged with

blackish; this color, at its inner border, between the third and
fourth longitudinal veins, is very pale, and extends sometimes as
a gray shadow even beyond the fourth vein; the first, second,
third, and fifth longitudinal veins are conspicuous for their stoutness and black color; the basis of the second vein and the portion
of it lying in the clear spot beyond the stigma, are of a paler color
and less stout. The small crossvein is immediately below or but
little beyond the end of the stigma; but always beyond the
middle of the discal cell; the posterior crossvein is perpendicular;
the last section of the fourth longitudinal vein is conspicuous for
its great length and converges gently towards the third; anal cell
with a sharp angle, which is not, however, drawn out in a point.
Hab. Georgia.

Gen. XI. EUMETOPIA Macq.

Charact.—*Front* very much projecting anteriorly, so that the head, seen
in profile, appears conical; upon its sides and its anterior part it is
sparsely beset with short, not erect, hairs.

Antennæ of middle size; third joint oval, with a bare arista.

Face unusually retreating, almost horizontal, below each antenna
distinctly excavated and with a small ridge between these impressions; *clypeus* small, but distinctly projecting over the anterior
edge of the mouth.

Wings narrow and rather long; stigma very narrow, posterior angle
of the anal cell acute; the last section of the fourth vein somewhat
converging towards the third near the tip.

The species of this genus are always bare, very slender and
have a metallic coloring; moreover, they are easily distinguished
by the extraordinary projection of their foreheads and the conical
profile of their heads; the picture of their wings only consists in
a more or less extended black spot on the apex.

1. **E. rufipes** Macq. ♂.—(Tab. IX, f. 22.) Viridis, pedibus luteis;
alarum apice nigro.

Green, feet dark-yellow; wings with a blackish apex. Long. corp. 0.2;
long. al. 0.13.

Syn. *Eumetopia rufipes* Macq. Dipt. Exot. Suppl. II, p. 68, Tab. VI, f. 2.
Eumetopia rufipes Loew. Berl. Ent. Zeitschr. XI, p. 323, Tab. II, f. 25.

Front reddish-brown, often very dark, the projecting portion
on both sides of a lighter coloring; moreover, both sides of the
front have a white, pollinose margin; the sides and the anterior

portion bear some scattered, short, neither numerous nor erect
hairs; the little stripes running down from the vertex along the
orbits of the eyes and ocellar triangle are of a shining metallic-
green; the latter is somewhat distant from the vertex. Antennæ
rather deep black; face and clypeus moderately shining, bluish-
black; the lower orbit, however, reddish-brown, with a narrow
white border. Palpi and proboscis dark-yellow. The thorax,
the moderately convex scutellum, and the abdomen shining
metallic-green; the latter, however, becomes more opaque and
darker towards its end. The fore coxæ altogether, the second
joint of the posterior ones and the feet of a rather dark, saturate
yellow coloring, but by no means red; the front tarsi altogether
and the tip of the posterior ones brownish-black. Wings narrow,
somewhat grayish-hyaline; the veins are tinged with yellow at
the basis and in the proximity of the anterior margin, as far as
the black spot on the apex; this gives to those parts of the wings
a yellowish coloring; the other veins are blackish; a large
brownish-black spot on the apex of the wing occupies almost one-
quarter of the length of the wing and extends beyond the fourth
longitudinal vein. The small and narrow stigma is yellowish.
The small crossvein generally lies only a little beyond the end of
the stigma and very little beyond the middle of the discal cell;
the last section of the fourth longitudinal vein is perceptibly
longer than the interval between both crossveins, and gently converges near its end towards the third vein; the posterior crossvein is always perpendicular; the posterior angle of the anal cell
acute.

Hab. United States, not rare (Osten-Sacken).

2. E. varipes Loew.   ♀.—(Tab. IX, f. 23.) Viridis, femoribus nigris,
genibus tibiisque luteis, alarum apice nigro.

Green, femora black, knees and tibiæ yellow; wings with a blackish apex.
Long. corp. 0.25 ; long. al. 0.12.

Syn. *Eumetopia varipes* Loew, Berl. Ent. Zeitschr. IX, p. 191.
    Eumetopia varipes Loew, Berl. Ent. Zeitschr. XI, p. 323, Tab. II, f. 28.

Very like *E. rufipes*, but easily distinguished on account of
the different coloring of the feet. Front almost black. The palpi
of the only specimen in my possession seem to be yellowish-
brown. Scutellum more flattened than that of *E. rufipes.*
Coxæ and femora black with a bluish-green metallic reflection;

the tip of the femora and the tibiæ clay-yellow, the latter sometimes brownish-yellow; tarsi brown, the posterior ones paler at
the basis. The first segment of the flattened ovipositor black.
The wings of the same outline as those of *E. rufipes*, but the
veins at the basis and in the vicinity of the anterior margin less
yellow; the small crossvein is far beyond the middle of the discal
cell, and hence it is less distant from the posterior crossvein; the
fifth longitudinal vein is interrupted at a somewhat greater
distance from the posterior margin of the wing and the last
section of the fourth vein converges a little more towards the
third; the blackish spot at the apex of the wing is perceptibly
larger, so that it occupies more than one-fourth of the length of
the wing. All the rest as in *E. rufipes*.

Hab. Cuba (Gundlach).

Second Section: RICHARDINA.

Gen. I. CONICEPS nov. gen.

Charact.—*Head* in shape like a long, somewhat flattened cone; *Front*
rather broad, eyes rather distant from the posterior edge of the
head; their horizontal diameter somewhat longer than the vertical
one.

The first two *antennal joints* short, the third elongated and of equal
breadth, *arista* bare.

The *mesothoracic bristle* indicated only by a hardly perceptible little
hair; prothoracic bristle not extant.

Scutellum with two bristles.

Abdomen slender and elongated.

Femora not incrassated, unarmed; the under side of the hind ones
with some rather stiff bristles.

Wings: posterior angle of the anal cell abbreviated; crossveins not
approximated; the smaller one in the middle of the discal cell;
the third and fourth longitudinal veins parallel.

The present genus is very like *Eumetopia* on account of its
narrow, elongated shape and its strongly projecting front. I
place it here in order to bring it as near as possible to *Eumetopia*,
although I am far from considering it as a typical genus of the
group *Richardina*. It is distinguished from *Eumetopia* not only
by the abbreviated angle of the anal cell, but also by the still
more projecting forehead, by the somewhat turgid, cushion-
shaped occiput, and by the comparatively shorter, but broader
wings.

12

1. C. niger n. sp. ♂ ♀.—Modice nitens, niger, halteribus concoloribus, coxis pedibusque luteis, alis cinereis, adversus costam et apicem nigris.

Moderately shining, black, with the halteres of the same color; coxæ and feet dark-yellow; wings gray, tinged with black along the anterior margin and towards the apex. Long. corp. ♂ 0.18; ♀ cum terebra 0.21; long. al. ♂ 0.11; ♀ 0.12.

Black, moderately shining, beset with short, unconspicuous, black hairs. The bristles on the sides of the vertex of medium length. Antennæ deep black; third joint comparatively long, of equal breadth, rounded at the end; the bare arista of medium length, perceptibly stouter towards the basis; the parts of the mouth comparatively small and rather hidden. Abdomen long and narrow, of almost equal breadth. The first segment of the ovipositor, at the basis, has the same breadth as the posterior margin of the last abdominal segment; it is but little narrowed towards its end; it is clothed with a black pubescence which, although by no means long, is nevertheless rather conspicuous; in some specimens its sides are turned upwards, so that it appears narrower towards its end than it really is; the second and third joints of the ovipositor are generally retracted within the first, which might produce the impression that the species is a new form of *Micropezidæ*; when they are projecting, both prove to be comparatively rather broad and the third ends in a short, but sharp point. Coxæ and feet are of a dark yellow color; the tarsi are infuscated towards the tip; the hind femora with some stiff bristles of moderate length on their under side, which, however, do not resemble spines. Halteres blackish. Wings gray with black veins; the apex of the wings blackened and the costa with a black border, beginning at the tip of the costal cell.

Hab. Texas (Belfrage).

Gen. 11. RICHARDIA Rob. Desv.

Charact.—*Front* of most species rather broad; ocelli not far from the edge of the vertex; the anterior one more distant from the posterior ones than these from each other; in the males of several species the head is very much expanded transversely, as in the species of *Achias*.

Arista pubescent, or short-feathery.

Mesothoracic and *prothoracic bristles* present, although weak.

Scutellum with four bristles; *metathorax* steep.

Abdomen narrow, still more narrowed towards the basis.

Front femora only moderately incrassated; the intermediate ones not at all; the hind femora very much incrassated, beset with spines on the under side.

Wings: the crossveins approximated to each other; the third longitudinal vein towards its tip is more or less curved backwards; the third and fourth veins, for this reason, appear convergent; posterior angle of the anal cell obtuse.

The characters distinguishing this genus, which is peculiar to America, are as follows: the rather equally narrow abdomen; the unarmed front and middle femora; the very much incrassated hind femora, the under side of which is beset with spines; finally, the crossveins being approximated to each other.

The rather coarse hairs upon the feet of most species of *Richardia* look somewhat like spines at the further end of the under side of the front and middle femora; although I have not observed any real spines upon the under side of the four anterior femora in any of the species which I have examined.

The mention of the presence of the prothoracic and mesothoracic bristle has been introduced among the characters of this and of the following genera, wherever I was able to do so. But, as in several cases I had only a single, perhaps not particularly well-preserved, specimen for comparison, or one in which this character could not very well be ascertained, the statement about the absence of one of these bristles is not to be taken too strictly until further confirmation.

The typical species is the well-known *Richardia podagrica* Fabr., from South America.

<h3>Gen. III. CYRTOMETOPA nov. gen.</h3>

Charact.—Front broad, very much projecting in profile.

  Arista pubescent.

  Femora strong, although not exactly incrassated; all are beset with spines.

  Wings: posterior angle of the anal cell obtuse; crossveins not approximated to each other; the end of the fourth longitudinal vein converges very much towards the tip of the third vein.

The typical species is the *Odontomera ferruginea* Macquart (Dipt. Exot. II, 3, p. 215), in which, with tolerable certainty, I recognize an American species.

The *Odontomera maculipennis* Macquart (Dipt. Exot. Suppl. I), from Colombia, probably belongs to the genus *Cœlometopia*.

I have drawn the characters of this genus, as far as it was

possible, from Macquart's statements. The characters which prevent me from uniting this genus with the following are: the front, very much projecting in profile, the much shorter and stronger femora, the wings, which are not attenuated towards their basis, and the strong convergency of the third and fourth longitudinal veins. If the auxiliary vein is really as far distant from the first longitudinal as Macquart's figure shows it, this would furnish one distinctive character more.

Gen. IV. STENOMACRA nov. gen.

Charact. — *General shape* almost like *Sepsis.*

Front rather broad, somewhat narrower anteriorly.

Ocelli closely approximated to each other, almost in the middle of the front.

Antennal arista with a very distinct pubescence.

No mesothoracic and, to all appearances, no prothoracic bristle.

Scutellum with two bristles; *metathorax* sloping.

Abdomen narrow, almost pedunculate.

Feet slender, femora not incrassated, the intermediate ones attenuated towards the end; the hind femora a little longer than the middle ones; all are beset with spines towards the tip.

Wings rather large, very much attenuated towards the basis; posterior angle rounded off; the auxiliary vein very much approximated to the first longitudinal, coalescing with it at the tip; the second longitudinal reaches the margin of the wing far from the apex; the small crossvein is far before the middle of the discal cell; the last section of the fourth longitudinal vein almost parallel to the third vein; posterior angle of the anal cell obtuse.

1. S. Guerini Bco. ♂ ♀.—(Tab. IX, f. 25., Rufescens, pleuris, scutello, metanoto abdominisque basi nigris; alis hyalinis, strigula subbasali et macula magnâ apicali nigris.

Reddish, pleuræ, scutellum, metathorax and the basis of the abdomen black; wings hyaline with a little black streak at the basis and a large black spot at the apex. Long. corp. 0.20; long. al. 0.20—0.22.

Syn. *Sepsis Guerini* Buot, De la Sagra, Hist. físico, etc., p. 822, Tab. XX, f. 9.

Ferruginous-red, rather shining, the upper part of the occiput, as well as the region of the vertex and the little stripes running down from it upon the front, sometimes shining black, almost metallic. Front rather broad, somewhat narrower anteriorly; the bristles of the vertex long; the bristle in front of them, inserted upon the little stripe, is likewise long, removed to almost the middle of the front. The ocelli, near which the ordinary two

bristles are placed, are likewise removed to about the middle of
the front and are close to each other. Antennæ descending
to the edge of the mouth; the first two joints yellow; the
third more or less infuscated; the arista with a very distinct,
somewhat rare, pubescence. Face of the *Dacus*-like shape,
peculiar among the *Richardina*; proboscis and palpi sometimes
of a dirty reddish-yellow, sometimes more brownish-ferruginous.
The thoracic dorsum somewhat ferruginous; only very dark
specimens bare it black; the hairs upon it are placed in four
distinct longitudinal rows, the intermediate ones being very
closely approximated. Scutellum convex, with two bristles, black
ferruginous on the sides in very pale-colored specimens only.
Pleuræ, with the exception of the humeral region, as well as the
whole metathorax, black. The basis of the abdomen is black to
a greater or less extent; in rare specimens only does this color
reach the posterior margin of the rather considerably elongated
first abdominal segment; in some specimens, however, this color
extends to the very end of the abdomen, or, at least, turns here
into blackish-brown. The ovipositor, which is longer than the
last three abdominal segments taken together, is usually black
or blackish-brown; its upper side is excavated (at least in dry
specimens), and its under side convex, and hence, it is less flattened than in the other genera of the *Richardina*. Coxæ pale-
yellow. Front feet pale-yellowish; the tibiæ towards the basis
and the tarsi, beginning from the second joint, infuscated; femora
not incrassated, beset with a few, but rather strong, spines on the
under side towards its end. The anterior half of the middle femora
dark-brown and somewhat incrassated; the posterior half thin and
dark-yellow; the greater part of the under side sparsely spinose;
middle tibiæ dark-brown, in most specimens, gradually becoming
yellow towards the tip; tarsi yellowish, brownish towards the
tip. Hind femora not incrassated, whitish, the last third brownish-yellow, brownish towards the tip; both shades separated by
an oblique brownish-black ring; hind tibiæ and tarsi as in the
intermediate pair of feet. Wings very much attenuated towards
the basis, hyaline; their anal angle not projecting at all; from
the tip of the costal cell a narrow black streak extends over the
incrassated point, where the third longitudinal vein originates
and over the crossveins, closing the little cells at the basis of the
wing; the apex of the wing is occupied by a large black spot,

which runs from the anterior to the posterior margin, but is very much dilated beyond the fourth longitudinal vein. The second longitudinal vein is gently curved forward and ends some distance from the tip; the small crossvein is before the middle of the discal cell; the last section of the fourth longitudinal vein is almost parallel to the third vein; the posterior angle of the anal cell is rounded.

Hab. Cuba (Gundlach).

Observation.—Through the kindness of Dr. Gundlach, who sent me the specimens, I have been informed of the identity of this species with the one described by Bigot. I have not succeeded yet in comparing De la Sagra's work, which contains the description, and I draw the attention of those, to whom this work is accessible, to the fact, that among the Cuban species described by me, one or the other may have been previously described by Mr. Bigot in that volume.

Gen. V. SYNTACES nov. gen.

Charact.—*Front* moderately broad, broader above (according to Macquart's statement, his figure, on the contrary, shows a front narrower above).

Antennal arista pubescent.

Feet slender; all the femora thin and all armed.

Wings: posterior angle of the anal cell rectangular; crossveins not approximated; the last section of the fourth longitudinal vein only moderately convergent with the third.

The typical species is *Setellia apicalis* from Brazil, described by Macquart (Dipt. Exot. II, 3, p. 249). As I have not seen this species, I have borrowed the generic characters from that author's description and figure, which gives these characters a somewhat uncertain basis. The close relationship to the next following genus is, in my opinion, evident; still, it does not seem advisable to unite them, as, in the present genus, the front femora are weaker and armed with less conspicuous spines; as the hind feet are much less elongated in comparison to the front feet; as the posterior angle of the anal cell is not obtuse, but rectangular, and as the second longitudinal vein has no stump of a vein upon it; nevertheless it is not impossible that the examination of a specimen would lead to a different conclusion from that which seems warranted by Macquart's description.

Gen. VI. EUOLENA nov. gen.

Charact.—*Front* very broad, very little narrowed anteriorly; the excavation of its upper part very shallow; the ocelli near the vertex and closely approximated to each other.

Antennal arista with a very short pubescence.

No mesothoracic bristle, and, as it seems to me, no prothoracic one.

Scutellum with four bristles; the lateral ones weak and small.

Feet: front femora rather strong, with conspicuously long and strong spines; the four posterior feet remarkably long and slender, their femora with small spines near the tip only, otherwise these femora are thin and very long, especially the intermediate ones.

Wings: posterior angle of the anal cell obtuse; the small crossvein a little beyond the last third of the discal cell; opposite this crossvein, the second longitudinal vein emits a little stump of a vein into the submarginal cell; the last section of the fourth longitudinal vein is nearly parallel to the third.

The typical species is *Michogaster egregius*, from Columbia, described by Gerstaecker (Stett. Ent. Z. XXI, p. 179). I possess the male only. The ovipositor of the female is called sugar-loaf shaped by the author; which would indicate that it is less compressed than in the other *Richardina:* it may be somewhat of the same shape as in *Stenomacra Guerini.*

Gen. VII. IDIOTYPA nov. gen.

Charact.—*Front* very broad, not narrowed anteriorly; ocelli rather approximated to the edge of the vertex, and placed close to each other.

Antennal arista with a short pubescence.

No mesothoracic bristle; a weak prothoracic one.

Scutellum with two bristles; *metathorax* sloping.

Abdomen slender and elongated, almost pedunculate at the basis.

All the *femora* strong and armed with spines.

Wings: posterior angle of the anal cell quite obtuse; the small crossvein beyond the last third of the discal cell; opposite this crossvein the second vein has a stump of a vein, inside of the submarginal cell, and a second one on the opposite side, in the marginal cell, nearer to the apex of the wing; the last section of the fourth longitudinal vein almost parallel to the third.

1. I. appendiculata n. sp.   ♂ ♀.—(Tab. IX, f. 25.) Rx ochraceo ferruginea, thorace flavo-vario, alarum dimidio anteriore ex ochraceo ferrugineo, posteriore subhyalino, dilute infuscato.

Yellowish-ferruginous, with the thorax marked with yellow; the anterior
half of the wings ochre-brownish, the posterior half almost hyaline, yellowish.   Long. corp. 0.44; ♀ cum terebrâ 0.52; long. al. 0.4—0.41.

Of this species I possess a very well preserved, and, as it seems,
particularly fully-colored female, and two much paler males, probably having faded through long exposure.   This difference in
coloring notwithstanding, I have not the least doubt that both
sexes belong to the same species.   The condition of the specimens
induces me, however, to begin with the description of the female
and to add afterwards those characters by which the male specimens differ from it.

Female.—Head rather dark-yellow, of the ordinary *Dacus*-like
shape; the front of considerable, and altogether equal, breadth;
occipital bristles rather strong; the lateral bristles in front of
them are wanting; likewise the bristles generally inserted near
the ocelli; the ocelli are approximated to the edge of the vertex
and close to each other; a black, biarcuate band runs from the
orbit of the eye on one side to that on the other, across the ocelli;
immediately above the antennæ there is another black band, not
reaching the orbits, the upper limit of which forms a less arcuate,
the lower limit a more arcuate curve.   In consequence of the very
approximated position of the antennæ, the frontal lunule is more
isolated from the face, than is the case in any other of the *Ortalidæ*
I am acquainted with.   Antennæ brownish ochraceous-yellow;
the third joint comparatively long; the arista with a short, but
very distinct, pubescence.   The lower corners of the central portion of the face rather blackish.   The short, but rather broad palpi
ochraceous-yellow, brownish-black at the basis.   The occiput
shows, not far from the edge of the vertex, a narrow, black crossband, not quite reaching the orbit of the eye.   The thorax shows
a very variegated picture; the very broad middle stripe, running
from end to end, is of a brownish-ferruginous color, which changes
into black towards its posterior third; this stripe is divided in
two by a blackish, rather indistinct longitudinal line; it is separated from the lateral stripes by a longitudinal line of ochraceous-
yellow pollen; the broad lateral stripes are crossed by the transverse suture, which is covered with pale ochraceous-yellowish
pollen; the anterior portion of the lateral stripes is black and
leaves exposed only the pale yellow humeral stripe; the posterior
portion of the lateral stripe is black on the side turned towards

the middle stripe, otherwise brownish-ferruginous. Scutellum short, with two bristles, pale-yellow. Pleura black; the humeral region, including the prothoracic stigma and a broad band, running from the root of the wing to the interval between the fore and middle coxæ, pale-yellow; the suture, lying in this band and running down from the root of the wing, is margined with brownish-black. Metathorax black, separated from the pleura by a broad yellow stripe. The first abdominal segment rather long, very slender, considerably increased, however, towards its end, so that here it equals in breadth the following segment; its first third is black, the second pale-yellow, the remainder, as well as the remaining portion of the abdomen, yellowish-ferruginous, almost ochre-brownish, and beset with a short pubescence of the same coloring. Ovipositor of the color of the abdomen; quite flat; the first segment not quite so long as the last three abdominal segments taken together; rather narrow towards its end. Coxæ brownish-black; the second joint of the front coxæ, the tip of the first joint and the second joint of the middle ones, yellow. All the femora beset with spines, not increased, but strong, black, yellow to a small extent at the basis only, yellowish-red to a considerable extent towards the end. Front tibiæ reddish-yellow; the four posterior ones of a purer yellow with reddish-yellow tips. All the tarsi yellowish-red; the front tarsi from the second joint and beyond dark-brown; the other tarsi infuscated at the tip only. The hairs on the feet are very short, and of the same color as the ground upon which they are inserted. Wings comparatively long and narrow, with ferruginous veins; the anterior half has a yellowish rusty-brownish tinge, which is more ferruginous-yellow towards the basis, and more brownish towards the apex; the posterior limit of this coloring is almost rectilinear and reaches the fourth longitudinal vein at its root and at its tip only. The whole posterior half of the wing has a decidedly yellowish tinge, but is rather transparent. The second longitudinal vein is rather straight, gently bent forward towards its end only; it reaches the margin not far from the apex of the wing; two conspicuous stumps of veins project from it not far from each other; both are perpendicular, but placed at the opposite sides of the principal vein; one is just opposite the small crossvein, the other somewhat nearer to the apex of the wing; the small crossvein itself is a little beyond the last third

of the discal cell; the last section of the fourth longitudinal vein
is almost parallel to the third vein; the posterior angle of the
anal cell is quite obtuse.

Males.—The two specimens which I have before me differ from
the females by the absence of the upper black crossband on the
front, of the black crossband of the occiput and of the spots on
the face which have a black coloring; all which in the female is
described as black or blackish-brown, is of a dingy rusty-brown
in the male. As, at the same time, the contrast between the
yellow and the ferruginous regions is less striking, this gives
these specimens a less variegated appearance than that of the
above-described female. The first abdominal segment is just as
narrow as in the female; but this is less apparent here, as the
posterior part of the abdomen is less broad.

Hab. Cuba (Gundlach).

Gen. VIII. STENERETMA nov. gen.

Charact.—Front very broad, not attenuated anteriorly; occiput very convex; cheeks broad; ocelli small and rather approximate to each other.

Arista thin and bare.

A strong mesothoracic bristle; no prothoracic one.

Scutellum with two bristles; metathorax sloping.

Abdomen slender and elongate, attenuate towards the basis.

Femora of medium strength, all unarmed.

Wings but little developed, short and exceedingly narrow, attenuate in the shape of a wedge towards the basis, so that their surface beyond the fifth longitudinal vein is nothing but a narrow, veinless strip; the auxiliary vein so closely approximated to the first longitudinal vein, that they can be distinctly told apart at their end only; the two ordinary crossveins approximate to each other; the small one lies but little beyond the middle of the wing; second basal cell very small and narrow; the anal cell and the sixth longitudinal vein are wanting, with the exception of a rudiment of the latter, which does not reach beyond the axillary incision.

As the group of the *Ulidina* contains the genera with a more
developed anal cell, the group of the *Richardina* on the contrary
those with a less developed one, there can be no doubt that the
present genus, in the incompletely developed wings of which the
anal cell is altogether wanting, belongs to the *Richardina;* and
that this is its true location is proved by its relationship to

Idiotypa, especially evident in the structure of the abdomen. Among the differences of these two genera I will only mention that the structure of the head of *Idiotypa* is not unlike that of *Dacus*, while the head of *Stenereima* resembles that of *Tritoxa*. As *Stenereima* and *Tritoxa* also agree in the presence of a mesothoracic bristle and in the absence of a prothoracic one, the former genus, if its first longitudinal vein showed a distinct pubescence, would have to be placed next to *Tritoxa*.

1. S. laticauda n. sp. ♀.—Lutea, segmentis abdominalibus singulis postice angustis et æqualiter fusco-marginatis, tarsis præter basim nigro-fuscis, alis lutæo cinereis, albido-bifasciatis.

Dark-yellow, the single abdominal segments on their posterior margin with a narrow infuscated border; the tarsi, with the exception of the basis, blackish-brown; wings yellowish-gray with two whitish cross-bands. Long. corp. 0.14; cum terebra 0.19; long. al. 0.11—0.12.

Of a dark-yellow color, shining. The broad, rather convex front bears, besides the long bristles on the vertex and in the region of the ocelli, a moderate quantity of rather long black hairs; the comparatively strong convexity of the occiput almost obliterates the usual edge between it and the vertex. The antennæ are of the same color as the rest of the body, and of more than half the length of the face; their third joint elongate, rounded at the tip; the thin and bare arista is very long. Clypeus, palpi, and proboscis likewise partake of the general coloring of the body. Thorax but little elevated and rather narrow in comparison to its length; its dorsum on the sides and on its posterior border with a few rather long black bristles; upon the remainder of its surface only with a short, black pubescence. Scutellum small, bare, with the exception of the two bristles upon its end. Pleuræ glabrous; besides the mesothoracic bristle they bear only a single bristle not far below the root of the wing. The abdomen is narrow and elongate, attenuate towards the basis, not so much, however, as in the females of *Idiotypa appendiculata*; its segments have, on the posterior margin, a narrow border of equal breadth and of a brown or reddish-brown color; upon the last segment this margin becomes indistinct, or it is altogether wanting. The blackish pubescence of the abdomen is every-where very short and not conspicuous. The ovipositor is of the same color as the remainder of the body and is strikingly

broad; its first joint is about as long as the last three abdominal
segments taken together; from its basis to the middle it is
exactly as broad as the abdomen itself; beyond the middle it is
but little attenuate, so that the truncature at the end has a considerable breadth; the second and third joints of the ovipositor
are also rather broad; the latter does not end in a sharp point,
but in a narrow truncature.   Feet bare, their structure ordinary;
femora unarmed; the tarsi blackish-brown from about the tip of
the first joint. The yellowish-gray wings have two perpendicular
whitish crossbands; the first passes between the two ordinary
crossveins from the anterior to the posterior margin of the wing;
the second lies between the first and the apex of the wing, but
much nearer the latter, is obliterated in the marginal cell and does
not entirely reach the posterior margin; besides these two whitish
crossbands there is, at the end of the second basal cell and in the
adjoining region of the first basal cell a small, whitish spot; the
coloring of the wing, on this side of the first crossband, towards
the root of the wing, changes gradually into clay-yellow, while
beyond the second crossband the color is almost blackish-gray;
the posterior crossvein shows the trace of a delicate blackish-gray
lining, while there is no such trace on the small crossvein.

Hab. Texas (Belfrage).

Gen. IX. COELOMETOPIA Macq.

Charact.—Front of moderate breadth, slightly narrowed anteriorly, some-
    what excavated; ocelli far removed from the edge of the vertex,
    placed close to each other on a more or less projecting hump.

Antennal arista with a very short pubescence.

No mesothoracic and one prothoracic bristle.

Scutellum with four bristles; metathorax somewhat sloping.

Femora not incrassate, nevertheless strong, the four posterior ones
    considerably longer than the front pair; all are provided with
    spines, the fore femora, however, with a few small ones towards the
    tip only.

Wings: posterior angle of the anal cell quite obtuse; the crossveins
    not approximate to each other; the last section of the fourth longi-
    tudinal vein converges towards the third.

With *Coelometopia* a series of genera begins which have a
comparatively short, oval abdomen, not very attenuate at the
basis.   The type of the genus is *C. trimaculata* Fab. = *C. ferruginea* Macq. from South America, which Wiedemann placed in
the genus *Trypeta.*

1. C. bimaculata n. sp. ♂.—(Tab. IX, f. 27.) Rufa, abdomine chalybeo vel violaceo, pedibus flavis; tibiis tamen tarsorumque apice fuscis; alis hyalinis, nigro-bimaculatis.

Ferruginous-reddish, the abdomen steel-blue or violet; feet yellow; tibiæ and tip of the tarsi brown; wings hyaline with two black spots. Long. corp. 0.22—0.26; long. al. 0.21—0.22.

Head and thorax ferruginous-red, rather shining; only the hind coxæ sometimes pitch-brown. Front of very moderate breadth; narrower anteriorly, somewhat excavated; the bristles on the vertex, the very much advanced lateral bristles and the two bristles near the ocelli black and rather strong. The ocelli are placed close to each other on a flattened elevation, almost in the middle of the front; the frontal lunule is rather isolated from the face, in consequence of the very approximate position of the antennæ. The third antennal joint is sometimes more brownish-red towards the tip; arista with a short pubescence. The short hairs on the thoracic dorsum are whitish, and hence easily perceptible; the ordinary bristles are black or brown, sometimes only brownish; a blackish line in the middle is only occasionally perceptible. Scutellum convex, with four brownish or brown bristles. Abdomen metallic steel-blue, shining, with more or less extensive and vivid violet reflections; sometimes ferruginous-brownish at the extreme basis; its almost whitish pubescence appears much darker, when looked at against the light. Femora yellowish, usually brownish at the tip; the foremost ones strong, with a few weak and small spines on the under side, near the tip only; the four posterior femora much longer, also strong, with spines on the under side. Tibiæ brown. Tarsi of a dirty-yellowish brown from about the tip of the second joint. Wings pure hyaline, with a rather sparse and coarse microscopic pubescence and with black veins; the black stigma is confluent with a moderately large, sharply limited spot, reaching as far as the third longitudinal vein; a larger, almost triangular black spot occupies the apex of the wing; it begins before the second longitudinal vein and ends midway between the third and fourth veins; moreover, in the environs of the humeral crossvein, there is a grayish-black spot, which is easily overlooked. The third longitudinal vein is very straight; the small crossvein lies in the middle of the comparatively short discal cell. The anterior basal cell is somewhat expanded at the expense of the discal cell, so

that the latter is much narrower before the small crossvein than
beyond it; posterior crossvein straight, somewhat oblique; the
last section of the fourth longitudinal vein strikingly long,
distinctly converging towards the third longitudinal vein; posterior angle of the anal cell very obtuse.

Hab. Cuba (Gundlach).

Gen. X. HEMIXANTHA nov. gen.

Charact.—*Front* of medium breadth, somewhat narrower anteriorly, not
excavated; the posterior ocelli not very far from the edge of the
vertex; the anterior one removed to about the middle of the front.
Antennal arista with a distinct pubescence.

A small prothoracic, and, as it seems, no mesothoracic bristle.

Scutellum with four bristles; *metathorax* perpendicular.

Femora not incrassate, but rather strong; the posterior ones longer
than the foremost ones; all are beset with spines; the spines of
the foremost ones are but very few.

Wings: posterior angle of the anal cell obtuse; crossveins conspicuously approximate; the last section of the fourth longitudinal vein
is parallel to the third.

The difference from *Cœlometopia* consists principally in the
peculiar position of the ocelli, the remarkably approximate crossveins and the parallelism of the third and fourth longitudinal
veins.

I do not know of any described species of this genus and for
this reason give the following :—

1. **H. spinipes** n. sp.   ♀.—(Tab. IX, f. 28.)   Lutea, metanoto
epimerisque metathoracis nigris, abdomine chalybeo, violaceo-splen-
dente; alis subhyalinis, apice fasciisque tribus fusco-nigris; harum
secunda postice, tertia antice, abbreviata.

Clay-yellow, metanotum and epimera of the metathorax black, abdomen
steel-blue, with a violet reflection; wings rather hyaline, the apex and
three crossbands brownish-black; the second of these abbreviated
posteriorly, the third anteriorly.   Long. corp. 0.24; long. al. 0.23.

Clay-yellow, thoracic dorsum more yellowish-red. Front of
medium breadth, but little narrower anteriorly, not excavated,
with but a small depression on the vertex; the two posterior
ocelli are placed upon a very small black spot, at a moderate
distance from the vertex and close to each other; the anterior
ocellus is quite unusually distant from them, and placed about

the middle of the front; the bristles on the vertex, the rather distant lateral bristles and the two ocellar bristles comparatively long and strong, black. Antennæ reaching down to the border of the mouth; the comparatively long third joint sometimes somewhat infuscated at the tip. Arista pubescent. The pubescence of the thoracic dorsum is pale-yellowish, the ordinary bristles black. Scutellum of a pure yellow, with four black bristles; its surface rather even. The middle portion of the mesonotum, the lower portion of its sides and the epimera of the metathorax brownish-black. The pubescence of the pleura yellowish. Abdomen elongate-oval, clay-yellow at the extreme basis, the remainder shining steel-blue with violet reflections, more greenish-blue at the posterior end. The first segment of the ovipositor large, shining black, concave above, somewhat convex below. Feet clay-yellow, the basis of the middle tibiæ and the hind tibiæ brown; the tip of the tarsi but little infuscated; femora not incrassate, although rather strong, the four posterior ones longer than the two foremost ones: the latter with a few small spines near the tip only, the former beset with spines on the whole second half of the under side. Wings almost hyaline, with a yellowish-gray tinge, which is more yellow towards the anterior border; costal cell yellowish-brown; a narrow brownish-black band runs from the humeral crossvein to the axillary incision; a second one, somewhat broader, runs from the anterior margin over the basis of the submarginal cell and over the end of the small basal cells nearly, but not quite, to the posterior margin of the wing; a third band, inclosing the two remarkably approximate crossveins, extends from the posterior margin to the middle of the submarginal cell; the apex of the wing bears a large elongate brownish-black spot, beginning before the second longitudinal vein and occupying the border of the wing as far as beyond the fourth vein. The last section of the fourth longitudinal vein is parallel to the third vein; the posterior angle of the anal cell is obtuse; the microscopic pubescence of the surface of the wing is remarkably coarse and sparse.

Hab. Brazil.

Gen. XI. MELANOLOMA nov. gen.

Charact.—Front rather broad, somewhat narrower anteriorly, not emarginated; the posterior ocelli not far removed from the edge of the vertex; the anterior one at a considerable distance from them. Antennal arista bare.

A strong mesothoracic bristle and a very weak prothoracic one.

Scutellum with four bristles; metathorax rather perpendicular.

Femora not incrassate, only the hindmost ones with spines near the tip.

Wings: posterior angle of the anal cell quite oblique; the crossveins not approximate; the last section of the fourth longitudinal vein parallel to the third.

The species of this genus are distinguished by their robust thorax and short oval abdomen; the surface of the latter is not smooth, but entirely covered by shallow scars, almost chagreened. The picture of the wings of the species known to me consists of a black border of the anterior margin of the wing and of the apex, and of a narrow black streak over the small crossvein.

The typical species is a Brazilian one, described by Wiedemann as *Trypeta cyanogaster*. As, in Wiedemann's description, the plastic characters are not sufficiently taken notice of, I will give the description of a species closely related to his.

1. **M. affinis** n. sp. ♂.—(Tab. IX, f. 29.) Rufa, tibiis concoloribus, posticis tamen basim versus infuscatis, abdomine ex violaceo chalybeo; alis hyalinis, costâ cum apice et venâ transversâ mediâ angustè nigro-limbatis.

Red, the tibiae of the same color, the hindmost ones infuscated towards the basis; abdomen violet steel-blue; wings hyaline, anterior margin and apex, as well as the small crossvein, with a narrow black border. Long. corp. 0.24; long. al. 0.24.

Ferruginous-red, shining; abdomen of a dark steel-blue color, somewhat verging on violet. Front rather broad, somewhat narrower anteriorly, sometimes tinged with yellow on the sides; the short and thin hairs upon it are inserted in small, very shallow, and hence hardly perceptible pits. The two superior ocelli are quite near the vertex; the anterior one is quite a distance from them, but still above the middle of the front; bristles of the vertex, the lateral ones and the two bristles near the ocelli, are present. Antennae reaching a little beyond the border of the mouth; the third joint long, sometimes more reddish-brown.

Arista thin and apparently bare. Thorax strongly built; the fallow-yellowish pubescence of its dorsum very short; the ordinary bristles black. Scutellum convex, with four bristles. The perpendicular mesonotum, the pleuræ and the pectus of the same color as the upper side of the thorax. The mesothoracic bristle strong, black, and hence very conspicuous; the prothoracic bristle thin and fallow-yellowish, and hence easily overlooked. The metallic-blue abdomen is of a rounded-oval shape and is covered with shallow scars, which diminish its lustre; its short pubescence is whitish on the first segment only, otherwise rather blackish. Feet of a yellowish-ferruginous color, only the distinctly arcuate hind tibiæ are gradually infuscated towards the basis; the tarsi, beyond the second joint, are more or less ferruginous-brownish. Femora not incrassate, only the hindmost ones with spines near the tip. Wings hyaline; the costal cell, the stigma, and a narrow border, running from it to the fourth longitudinal vein, along the margin of the wing, black; the small crossvein likewise with a narrow black cloud; a blackish spot lies between the extreme basis of the submarginal cell and the end of the costal cell. The second longitudinal vein reaches the anterior margin rather far from the apex of the wing; the third longitudinal vein is very straight; the small crossvein is a little beyond the middle of the discal cell, which is considerably narrower before this crossvein than after it; posterior crossvein straight, a little oblique; the last section of the fourth longitudinal vein rather long, parallel to the third vein; posterior angle of the anal cell quite obtuse. The microscopic pubescence of the surface of the wing is comparatively sparse and coarse.

Hab. Brazil.

Observation.—*M. cyanogaster* Wied. is not quite as large as the above-described species; its wings are comparatively smaller and the black border along the costa is somewhat broader at the apex of the wing; the lateral bristle of the front is somewhat more removed from the bristles on the vertex; the shallow pits on the front are not perceptible; the pubescence of the thoracic dorsum is considerably longer; the pleuræ and the tibiæ are blackish-brown.

18

Gen. XII. EPIPLATEA Loew.

Charact.—*Front* broad, narrower anteriorly; not projecting in profile; rather densely hairy upon the whole surface.

Antennæ of medium size; third joint oval, with a thin, bare arista.

Face vertical, with a depression under each antenna; longitudinally convex between these depressions; *clypeus* of a moderate transverse diameter, projecting considerably beyond the anterior edge of the mouth, which is drawn upwards; *proboscis* stout.

Thorax with bristles on its hind part only; *scutellum* convex, with four bristles.

Femora of moderate length, strong, but not incrassate; all unarmed. *Wings* comparatively short; submarginal and first posterior cells broad; third longitudinal vein bent backwards towards its end; the last section of the fourth longitudinal vein does not converge towards the third; posterior crossvein perpendicular; the posterior angle of the anal cell rather acute.

The species of this genus are rather stout, not metallic, except sometimes on the abdomen. The structure of the head recalls that of some *Sciomyzidæ*, and is very like that of the two well-known species, described by Wiedemann as *Ortalis trifasciata* and *atomaria;* in their general appearance, the species of *Epiplatea* are also not unlike the two latter species, but are easily distinguished by the first longitudinal vein being bare, by the posterior angle of the anal cell not being rounded as in those species and by the absence of the erect bristle before the end of the upper side of the tibiæ, a bristle which is always present in the latter species.

1. E. erosa Loew.   ♀.—(Tab. IX, f. 24.) Fusco-testaceo vel ex ferrugine fusca, pedibus concoloribus; abdomine nigro, alis hyalinis, fasciis duabus et puncto centrali nigris.

Brownish-yellow or ferruginous-brown, with the feet of the same color and a black abdomen; wings hyaline, with two brown crossbands and in the middle with a brown dot. Long. corp. 0.17; long. al. 0.16.

Syn. *Epiplatea erosa* Loew, Berl. Ent. Zeitschr. XI, p. 325, Tab. II, f. 25.

The coloring of the lighter shaded specimens is yellow-brownish, in darker specimens it becomes ferruginous-brown. Head of the same color. Front broad, considerably narrowed anteriorly, upon its whole surface uniformly and rather densely clothed with an erect, black pubescence; along the lateral margin with a narrow border of white pollen; the stripes running down from

the vertex along the sides of the front and the ocellar triangle
are of the same color as the front and hence indistinct.
Antennæ not reaching quite to the edge of the mouth; the first
two joints of the color of the head, or a little lighter; the oval
third joint dark-brown, often quite black; the arista thin and
bare. Face excavated under each antenna, longitudinally convex between these depressions; descending vertically in profile;
the anterior edge of the mouth is strongly drawn upwards, so
that the clypeus projects considerably above it. Proboscis stout;
palpi brown, generally paler towards the tip. The thoracic
dorsum generally has, on the posterior side, an almost silvery-
white transverse crossband, and before the transverse suture, on
each side, a large spot of a similar pollen; these pollinose spots
are very distinct, when seen by reflected light, but can easily
be overlooked in any other light. Upon the pleuræ likewise
there are two spots of white pollen; one of them lies over the
fore coxa, the other immediately under the longitudinal suture
of the pleuræ, where the color is generally darker-brown. The
front part of the coxæ is likewise covered with a white pollen,
which, however, sometimes is entirely invisible. Abdomen black,
somewhat glossy, generally brown at the basis, with a rather
coarse pubescence, which is longer and black on the posterior
margins of the segments. The flattened ovipositor is somewhat
attenuate, its first two segments black, the third orange-yellow.
Feet of the same color as the body; tibiæ and tarsi darker
brown, in fully colored individuals brownish-black. Halteres
yellowish. Wings of very moderate length, rather broad,
hyaline, with brown veins; the basis of the wings as far as the
humeral crossvein and the anal cell are brownish; a narrow
brownish-black band begins at the costa, where it is confluent
with the small black stigma and a black spot, lying at the end of
the costal cell; it runs over the bases of the submarginal, discal,
and third posterior cells, as far as the sixth longitudinal vein,
which its end alone crosses a little; before the apex of the wing
there is a broader crossband, which is sinuate on both sides,
weaker, however, on the inside than on the outside; posteriorly
it bifurcates in two short, obtuse branches, the inner one of
which reaches the margin of the wing and covers the perpendicular posterior crossvein; the outside one is shorter and ends
in the second posterior cell, some distance from the margin of

the wing; between these two crossbands is the black spot, formed by a cloud over the small crossvein; the stigma is small; the small crossvein is beyond the middle of the discal cell; the sub-marginal and first posterior cells are broad; the end of the third longitudinal vein is gently curved posteriorly and ends exactly in the apex of the wing; the last section of the fourth longitudinal vein does not converge towards the third; the anal cell is comparatively rather small; the crossvein, closing it, is a little arcuate, but forms nevertheless a rather acute posterior angle.

Hab. Cuba (Gundlach).

APPENDIX,

CONTAINING THE DESCRIPTIONS OF THE SPECIES PUBLISHED BY PREVIOUS
WRITERS, AND NOT IDENTIFIED BY THE AUTHOR.

---

1. *Say, Journ. Acad. Nat. Sciences Phil., Vol. VI, Part II.*

Page 83. **Ortalis ligata.**

Wings quadrifasciate with fuscous.

Inhabits Mexico.

Body blackish; *head* ferruginous, tinged with glaucous behind
and on the vertex; *thorax* blackish-plumbeous; *wings* white,
subopaque, with four fuscous bands; the first a little oblique,
across the neck of the wing; second from the tips of the medi-
astinal and post costal nervures, and proceeding a little obliquely,
so as to be bounded posteriorly by the middle cross-nervure;
third, perpendicular to the costal margin and covering the posterior cross-nervure; fourth, terminal, slightly connected on the
costal edge with the third; *poisers* white; *tergum* coppery-black;
feet black; *knees* and *tarsi* ferruginous. Length three-twentieths
of an inch.

[Belongs very probably to the genus *Rivellia*, but it will be
difficult to decide to which species, on account of the great
similitude between the species of that genus.—*Loew.*]

2. *Rob. Desvoidy, Myodaires.*

Page 715. **Mechelia philadelphica.**

Minor M. eleganti; pedes fulvi, tibiis nigricantibus; alæ
flavescentes, unicâ maculâ subfuscâ.

Plus petite que la Mechelia elegans; frontaux, antennes, face,
rouges; opliques d'un gris rougeâtre; corselet d'un brun-gris;

(197)

abdomen un peu moins gris et d'un noir plus luisant; cuisses
fauves; tibias mélangés de noir et de fauve; tarses noirs; ailes
flavescentes, n'offrant que l'apparence d'une seule macule.

Originaire de Philadelphie.

(Translation.)—Smaller than *Mecknia elegans*; frontal bristles, antennæ,
face, red; optical bristles of a reddish-gray; thorax brownish-gray;
abdomen a little less gray and of a more shining black; femora fulvous;
tibia mixed with black and fulvous; tarsi black; wings flavescent, with
the appearance of a single spot.

From Philadelphia.

[It seems hardly doubtful that this species belongs to the
Ortalina; it is probably either an *Anacampta* or a *Cerozys*, as
Rob. Devoidy's genus Meckella has the third antennal joint
excised on the upper side and ending in a very sharp angle.—
Loew.]

8. *Walker, Insecta Saundersiana.*

Page 373.   **Ortalis basalis,** Mas. et Fœm.

Nigro-cyanea, caput fulvum; antennæ luteæ; abdomen basi
ferrugineum, *fœm.* apice luteum attenuatum; pedes fulvi; alæ
hyalinæ, basi fulvæ, vitta antica interrupta fusca.

Cerozys? Blackish-blue: head tawny; face with a whitish
covering; epistoma prominent; mouth pitchy; feelers luteous;
third joint much deeper than the second and more than twice its
length; sixth black, hare, very slender, more than twice the
length of the third; abdomen longer than the chest, ferruginous
towards the base; abdomen of the female pale luteous towards
the tip, which is much attenuated; legs tawny; wings colorless,
slightly tawny at the base, adorned along the fore border with a
dark-brown interrupted stripe, which is widened at the tip; veins
black; fifth vein converging towards the tip of the fourth; sixth
not reaching the hind border; crossveins straight, almost upright;
poisers pitchy.   Length of the body 1½—2 lines; of the wings
2—3 lines.   United States.

[It is utterly improbable that this species should be a *Cerozys*,
as Mr. Walker supposes; his description rather suggests that it
belongs to the *Ulidina.—Loew.*]

4. *Macquart, Dipt. Exot. II*, 111, *Tab. XXIX. fig.* 8.

Page 308. Herina mexicana.

Viridi-cyanea. Alis limbo externo nervisque transversis fascia.
Long. 4 lin.—Face testacée. Front noir; vertex et derrière
de la tête testacés. Antennes brunes; style fauve. Thorax d'un
vert brillant, à reflets bleus. Abdomen manque. Pieds noirs.
Ailes jaunâtres jusqu'à l'extrémité; cellules basilaires brunes;
nervures transversales bordées de brun; première oblique.

Du Mexique.

(*Translation.*)—Length 4 lines. Face testaceous; front black; vertex
and occiput testaceous. Antennæ brown; arista fulvous. Thorax of a
brilliant green, with blue reflexions. Abdomen—(wanting). Feet black.
Wings yellowish, anterior margin brown from the stigmatical cell, inclu-
sively, as far as the apex; basal cells brown; crossveins bordered with
brown; the first of them oblique.

Mexico.

[Macquart very improperly placed this species in the genus
Herina: it is a perfectly normal species of his own genus *Stenopterina.—Loew.*]

5. *Walker, List of Dipt. Ins. IV.*

Page 992. Ortalis maseyla, n. sp., Fem.

Viridis, capite ferrugineo, abdominis segmento quinto purpureo
apice fulvo, palpis ferrugineis, antennis pedibusque nigris, tarsis
fulvis, alis albis fusco trifasciatis.

Body metallic-green, slender, clothed with short black hairs:
head and chest beset with black bristles: head ferruginous above
and along the borders of the eyes; epistoma ferruginous, prominent, eyes red; fore part slightly convex; its facets a little larger
than those elsewhere: sucker black, clothed with tawny hairs;
palpi ferruginous; beset with black bristles: feelers black, much
shorter than the face; third joint conical, ferruginous at the base,
much longer than the second; bristle bare, very slender, more
than thrice the length of the third joint; abdomen long-obconical,
much longer than the chest, tapering, flat, and with a vein on
each side towards the tip, which is tawny; fifth segment dark-
purple: legs black, clothed with short black hairs; knees ferruginous; feet and tips of shanks dull tawny: wings white, with

three dark-brown bands; the first extends nearly to the hind
border, and joins the side of the middle crossvein; the second
reaches the hind border and incloses the lower crossvein; it is
darkest on the fore border, and there unites with the third, which
widens along the fore border and occupies the whole of the tip
of the wing; wing-ribs, veins, and poisers tawny; veins pitchy
in the brown parts of the wings; lower crossvein nearly straight.
Length of the body 1½—2 lines; of the wings 3—4 lines.

North America.

[This seems to be an *Euresta.—Loew.*]

6. *Walker, List of Dipt. Ins. IV.*

Page 994. **Ortalis? diopsides**, BARROW'S MSS. Fem.

Nigra, obscura, capite antico fulvo, palpis antennis pedibusque
picco-ferruginels, alis subcinereis ad costam fusco bimaculatis.

Body dull-black, clothed with very short black hairs: head
beset with a few black bristles, tawny in front and beneath, where
it is covered with white bloom; sides of the face without bristles;
epistoma slightly prominent; eyes dark-red; facets of the fore
part a little larger than those elsewhere; sucker and palpi ferruginous, partly pitchy; sucker clothed with tawny hairs; palpi
beset with black bristles; feelers ferruginous, shorter than the
face; third joint pitchy above, nearly round, longer than the
second joint; bristle black, bare, slender, much more than twice
the length of the third joint; abdomen spindle-shaped, much
longer than the chest; last segment flat; legs pitchy, mostly
ferruginous beneath, clothed with very short black hairs; claws
black: wings slightly gray, with a narrow pitchy band at half
the length of the fore border, on which, near the tip, there is a
small brown spot; wing-ribs tawny; veins black, tawny at the
base; longitudinal veins straight; lower crossvein straight,
slightly oblique, nearly twice its length distant from the middle
crossvein; poisers pale tawny. Length of the body 2 lines; of
the wings 2½ lines.

St. Martin's Falls, Albany River, Hudson's Bay.

[This species seems likewise to belong to the *Ulidina*, a group
which is so abundantly represented in America.—*Loew.*]

7. *Walker, List of Dipt. Ins. IV.*

Page 995. **Ortalis? costalis, n. s., Fam.**

Nigra, abdomine nigro-æneo, pedibus nigris, alis limpidis ad costam fusco bimaculatis, stigmate nigro.

Head wanting: chest dull black, beset with a very few black bristles: abdomen sessile, brassy-black, shining, slightly spindle-shaped, much longer but hardly broader than the chest: legs black, clothed with very short black hairs: wings colorless, with a small brown spot just above the tip, and another at the base of the fore border, where the vein is thickened; a black band along the middle of the fore border; wing-ribs and veins black; third longitudinal vein straight, with the exception of a very slight angle at its junction with the lower crossvein, which has two very slight curves, the upper inward, the lower outward. Length of the body 1¼ line; of the wings 3½ lines.

St. Martin's Falls, Albany River, Hudson's Bay.

[In this description, after the words "third longitudinal vein straight," something seems to be wanting, as this vein does not at all meet the posterior crossvein. The species very likely also belongs to the *Ulidina.—Loew.*]

8. *Macquart, Dipt. Exot. Suppl. IV, Tab. XXVI, fig. 17.*

Page 289. **Urophora antillarum.**

Viridi-nigra. Fronte testacea, alis fasciis duabus, apiceque fuscis.

Long. 1½ lin. ♂.—Palpes noirs. Face d'un vert noirâtre luisant, à leger duvet blanc sur les côtés. Front testacé; une tache verte sur le vertex. Antennes noirs. Thorax et abdomen d'un vert luisant noirâtre. Pieds noires; premier article des tarses testacé. Ailes claires, à base jaunâtre; une première bande passant sur la première nervure transversale, et n'atteignant pas le bord intérieur; la deuxième entière, passant sur la deuxième transversale; extrémité à tache brune, liée à la deuxième bande par le bord extérieur également brun.

Des Antilles.

[Almost undoubtedly an *Ulidina.—Loew.*]

9. *Bigot, Ramon de la Sagra, Hist. fis. d. i. Isla da Cuba.*

Ulidia fulvifrons.

Nigro-piceo-nitens, hypostomate nigro; fronte, oculis, antennisque fulvis, occipite brunnea; thorace nigro-nitente; abdomine nigro-piceo; pedibus fulvis; anticis, cruribus antice brunnescentibus; tibiis tarsisque brunneis; intermediis posticisque, femoribus basi, brunneis; tibiis postice brunneis; alis hyalinis; costa brunnea, punctoque apicali nigro.—Long. 4 mill.

[This species may belong to the Ulidina, but it is not probable that it is a true *Ulidia.* The *Ulidia metallica* Bigot, described in the same place, is not an *Ortalida* at all, but belongs to the *Agromyzidæ*, perhaps to the genus *Agromyza.—Loew.*]

10. *Walker, Trans. of the Ent. Soc., Tom. V. 1861.*

Page 324.   Ortalis bipars.

Nigricante viridis, capite supra antennisque rufis, harum articulo tertio longo lineari, pedibus nigris, alis albis nigro-trifasciatis et apice maculatis, vittis secundá tertiáque postice obsoletis, primá incompletá, halteribus pallidis.

Blackish-green: head above and antennæ red; third joint of the antennæ long, linear; wings white, with three slight black bands and an apical spot, first band very incomplete; second and third obsolete hindward; discal transverse vein straight, upright, parted by one-fourth of its length from the border and by much more than its length from the brachial transverse vein; halteres pale.

Length of the body 2½ lines; of the wings 4 lines.
United States.

11. *Walker, Trans. of the Ent. Soc., Tom. V. 1861.*

Page 324.   Bricinnia.

Corpus longinsculum, sat angustum. Peristoma magnum. Antennarum articulus tertius longus, gracilis, linearis; arista simplex, gracilis. Thorax longus, lateribus compressus. Abdomen longum, subfusiforme, apice attenuatum. Pedes validi. Alæ sat angustæ, venis mediis.

Fœm. Oviductus vaginæ productæ, gracilis.

Body rather long and narrow. Epistoma rather prominent; mouth large; third joint of the antennæ long, slender, linear, extending to the epistoma; arista slender, simple, nearly twice the length of the third joint. Thorax long, compressed on each side. Abdomen long, subfusiform, attenuated towards the tip. Legs stout, moderately long. Wing rather narrow; veins straight.

Female. Abdomen attenuated at the tip. Vagina of the oviduct slender, produced.

Briclmnia Sexivitta Fœm.

Nigra, capite apud oculos albo, vittâ antieâ albidâ, antennis ferruginicis basi fulvis, thorace vittis tribus albidis, pectore purpureo-cyaneo, abdomine cupreo, femoribus posticis basi flavis, tarsis fulvis, alis subcinereis, costâ apiceque luridis, vittâ discali angulatâ nigrâ, venâ discali transversâ vix arcuata.

Female. Black: head white about the eyes and with a whitish facial stripe, which is dilated towards the epistoma; antennæ ferruginous, tawny towards the base; thorax with three whitish stripes; pectus blue, varied with purple; abdomen cupreous; vagina of the oviduct attenuated; hind femora yellow towards the base; tarsi tawny; wings grayish, lurid along the costa and at the tips, and with a blackish stripe which extends from the base to and along the discal transverse vein; the latter is upright and hardly curved, and is parted by four times its length from the border, and by a little less than its length from the præbrachial transverse vein, which is oblique.

Length of the body 5 lines; of the wings 10 lines.

Mexico.

INDEX OF THE ORTALIDÆ.

14

REVIEW

OF THE

NORTH AMERICAN TRYPETINA.

INTRODUCTION.

In 1860, at the time of the publication of my paper on the *Trypetidæ*, contained in the first volume of these Monographs, only twenty-three North American species of this family were known. Since then, this number has reached sixty-one. Among these additions there is a number of species of previous authors, concerning which I did not possess sufficient information at the time of my earlier essay. Moreover, a number of species published by Wiedemann became accessible to me in type specimens, through the kindness of the Berlin and Vienna Museums. Since that time, also, several other authors have published new species belonging to the same group. And, finally, the systematic distribution of the group *Trypetina* has obtained, for the European species, a more solid foundation.

It would seem to be time, therefore, to undertake an entirely new work on the *Trypetina* of North America; but as the plan of the present series does not well admit of it, I have adopted the form of a supplement to my previous paper. One of the principal aims of the present essay will be, the adaptation to the American fauna, as far as it is possible, of the systematic distribution introduced among the *Trypetina* of the old continent. While I was engaged on Monographs, etc., Part I, the number of the North American species with which I was acquainted, was, as yet, too insignificant for an attempt at a subdivision in smaller groups; besides, similar attempts, undertaken for the European species

by other authors (an account of them may be found in Monographs, etc., Part 1, p. 49–51), seemed to me so ill conceived,
that I did not feel inclined to adopt them as a basis for further
development. I perceived, on the contrary, that any attempt to
subdivide exotic Trypetidæ must be preceded by a rational
systematic distribution of the more abundant material of the
European species. In 1862, in my monograph of the European
Trypetidæ, I divided the Trypetina into twenty subgenera:
Platyparea, Euphranta, Aciura, Hemilea, Anomœa, Acidia,
Spilographa, Zonosema, Rhagoletis, Rhacochlæna, Trypeta, Ensina, Myopites, Urophora, Sphenella Carphotricha, Oxyphora,
Oxyna, Tephritis, and Urellia. The definitions of these groups
will be found in the above-quoted work. To these must be
added: Hypenidium (established by me since, in the Berliner
Entom. Zeitschr., VI, p. 87), Orellia (separated by Schiner, in
his Fauna Austriaca, from Oedaspis) and Chetostoma (established by Rondani, in his Prodromus, Vol. 1). Such is the present state of the classification of the European Trypetina, upon
which the distribution of the known North American species is
to be based. Considerable as the number of the latter is, it is
certain at the same time that this number does not reach one-
fifth, perhaps not one-tenth, of all the existing North American
Trypetina. Any attempt at a distribution, therefore, would
probably be modified by further discoveries. In this dilemma,
the course I adopted was, to append to the description of each
species the necessary remarks on its systematic position, and to
give a general survey of all the results thus obtained, at the end
of the volume.

Detailed descriptions of those species only are given here,
which are not described in Monographs, etc., Part 1, or the
descriptions of which were insufficient. The descriptions contained in that volume are indicated by references; the diagnoses,
however, even of those older species are reproduced here, with
the modifications rendered necessary by the addition of the new
species.

An important defect of the present publication is, that a considerable number of the new species are not represented on the
plates. The reason is, that the plates were prepared more than
four years ago, at a time when the number of the known North
American species was not sufficient to fill the required number

of figures. This was done by the addition of a number of South American species, described for the sake of comparison, but the figures of which I would have preferred now to replace by those species from North America, which I received after the plates were printed.

The critical examination of the species described by other authors, appended to the first volume, p. 57-61, required several corrections and additions. I have, therefore, reproduced it, thus amended, at the end of the present volume, as Appendix I. Appendix II contains descriptions, by other authors, of species not known by me and not contained in Part I.

The materials for the present publication, as far as the North American species are concerned, are principally, almost exclusively, derived from the communications of Baron Osten-Sacken. If I had had a similar support from more than one side, my work might, of course, have been more complete and more perfect. As it is, I have been compelled to draw the descriptions of several species from single, often badly preserved, specimens, and I am afraid that these descriptions, as well as the opinions expressed by me on the systematic position of some species, may sometimes betray the incompleteness of my materials. I trust that no equitable critic will bear these circumstances in mind in framing his appreciations.'

H. LOEW.

Grass, August, 1873.

LIST OF THE DESCRIBED SPECIES OF TRYPETA.[1]

[1] The species from South America, described for the sake of comparison with North American species, are printed in smaller type and not numbered in this list.

DESCRIPTION OF THE SPECIES.

1. T. exímia Wied. ♂ ♀.—Lutea, abdomine nigro-fasciato; scutellum magnum, planum, setis sex validis instructum; alarum pictura fusca inde a basi maculis irregularibus variegata ad ultimum usque trientem pertinet, ubi vittam costalem et fasciam a margine antico ad posticum oblique ductam emittit; praeterea in margine antico duo maculae tri-,gonae et hyalinae, in postico duo subovatae et subhyalinae conspicuntur, ad quas in speciminibus plerisque macula rotunda hyalina in cellula discoidalis basi sita accedit.

Clay-yellow, abdomen banded with black; scutellum large, flat, with six strong bristles; the brownish-black coloring of the wings reaches from the irregularly spotted basis to the last third of the wing, where it emits two bands, one of which forms a border along the costa, the other runs obliquely from the anterior to the posterior margin; moreover, the anterior margin shows two triangular hyaline spots, the posterior margin two almost oval and less hyaline spots; most specimens have, besides, a round hyaline spot on the basis of the discal cell. Long. corp. 0.20—0.26, ♀ cum terebra 0.29—0.30; long. al. 0.20—0.26.

Syn. *Trypeta eximia* Wied. Zweifl. Ins. II, p. 477, 2.
Tephritis fascïventris Macq. Dipt. Exot. Suppl. IV, p. 291. Tab. XXVII, f. 3.

Clay-yellow; head of a somewhat purer yellow, rather disci-form. Front narrow, still more narrowed anteriorly, with a small, but well-defined frontal lunule. Frontal and vertical bristles black, rather long and strong; the upper half of the posterior orbit of the eyes with a row of black and blackish-brown bristles. Antennae clay-yellowish, third joint elongated, rounded at the tip; arista very slender, with a hardly perceptible pubes-cence. Face perpendicular; the edge of the mouth not upturned; palpi yellowish, broad, reaching as far as the anterior edge of the mouth; their pubescence, as well as that of the mentum and of the occiput, is yellow. Thorax rather strongly built, compara-tively broad between the roots of the wings; the humeral callus and a longitudinal stripe between it and the root of the wing, are yellowish-white or sulphur-yellow; a longitudinal stripe of a similar color, which is generally but little visible in dried speci-

(216)

mens, runs from the posterior corner of the thoracic dorsum to the transverse suture; in some specimens the posterior border of the thoracic dorsum also shows a trace of a lighter coloring; the dense, but very short, pubescence of the thoracic dorsum is yellowish; the macrochætæ upon it are black; there are seven of them on each side, viz.: three on each side, in a row beginning at the humerus and ending before the root of the wings; three others a little farther from the lateral margin in a row beginning at the transverse suture and ending in the vicinity of the posterior corner; finally, a single bristle between the last one of this second row and the lateral corner of the scutellum; there are only two pairs of macrochætæ on the longitudinally middle portion of the thoracic dorsum, not far from the posterior margin; the bristles of the posterior pair are at a moderate distance from each other, the distance between those of the anterior pair is perhaps three times greater. All the bristles and bristle-like hairs upon the pleuræ and the pectus are black; the short pubescence upon the upper half of the pleuræ is blackish, on the lower half it is pale-yellow. Scutellum comparatively large, flat, with a short, yellowish pubescence on the upper side, and with six strong macrochætæ along the edge; in life, the scutellum is probably altogether whitish-yellow or sulphur-yellow, while in dry specimens, this coloring is perceptible along the borders only. The abdomen has brownish-black bands, which do not reach the posterior margin of the segments; these bands occur upon the second, third, and fourth segments; they are often less developed upon the anterior segments than upon the posterior ones, and here sometimes interrupted; upon the rather large last abdominal segment of the male the brownish-black crossband is especially broad and more or less emarginate on its posterior side; my only female specimen has on the first abdominal segment an incompletely developed brownish-black band, situate before the posterior margin. The pile upon the abdomen is black; pale-yellowish on the upper side of the first segment and sometimes also on the basis of the second; however, all the pile upon the abdomen assumes, in a reflected light, and especially in specimens of a lighter coloring, a brownish-yellow, almost a ferruginous-yellow tinge (with the exception of the stronger, bristle-like hairs). The hypopygium is brownish-black; the brown ovipositor is conical, not flattened at all, perceptibly longer than the last

two segments taken together, but shorter than the last three. Its
pile is brownish-yellow or brown, the color of the rather long
bristle-like hairs on the end of the first segment is dark-brown or
black. Feet clay-yellow; front femora on the upper side with
short, on the under side with more elongate black bristles; front
tibiæ not bristly; middle femora at the end of the posterior side
with a few bristles and, also, on the under side, with two longitudinal rows of short black bristles, which are more developed in
the male than in the female; middle tibiæ with a single row of
bristles; hind femora, at the end of the upper side with elongated
bristles, with shorter ones on the under side; hind tibiæ with
bristle-like cilia. Tegulæ more than usually developed. Wings
rather large and broad; the first longitudinal vein altogether
beset with bristles, the third far beyond the small crossvein, the
fifth upon the first and upon the beginning of its second section,
bristly; the second longitudinal vein ends in the costa at an
acute angle, and diverges very strongly from the third, the latter
is not bent anteriorly at its end; crossveins rather approximate,
the small one perpendicular and of a comparatively considerable
length; the posterior one very steep and somewhat curved towards
its posterior end; posterior angle of the anal cell drawn out in a
rather long lobe. The brownish-black, sometimes almost black
picture of the wings, is recognizable in Macquart's above-quoted
figure, although not correctly rendered; the round pale spot in
the discal cell should be much nearer to its basis; the pale indentation at the posterior margin, near the basis of the wing, should
be much narrower; the stigma should be placed entirely in the
dark portion of the coloring; the hyaline double spot near the anterior margin is seldom merely emarginate posteriorly; in most cases
it is divided in two approximate triangular spots; other differences in the picture likewise occur; the most common is, that in
the discal cell, a little beyond the small crossvein, there is a short,
pale streak, crossing the cell, and which in some cases becomes
a hyaline transverse spot. A male from Brazil in my collection
has, instead of the round pale spot in the discal cell, only a
somewhat paler place without any distinct outline; the agreement in the other characters being perfect, I take it for a rather
unusual variety of *T. eximia*.

Hab. Brazil, especially Bahia and St. Paulo; Surinam;
Mexico.

Observation 1.—Mr. Macquart, in the above quoted place, supposes that his *Tephritis fasciventris* may be only a variety of the *Tephritis major*, Dipt. Exot. Suppl. II, p. 98, Tab. VI, f. 6. However, this *Tephritis major* is identical with *Tephritis socialis* Wied., a species which is very distinct from *fasciventris* Macq. (syn. *eximia* Wied.).

Observation 2.—I have gone into more detail about the plastic characters of this species than was strictly necessary for its specific identification. I did so on account of the great resemblance in the plastic characters of *T. eximia* with *T. amabilis*, with *T. socialis* Wied., and with several other South American species. These species form a very well-defined group, for which I choose the name of *Hexachaeta*, and which deserves to be considered as a separate genus. The generic character may be derived from what has been said, in the above description of *Trypeta eximia*, concerning the shape of the head and of its parts, the shape of the thorax and of the scutellum, the number and position of their macrochaetae, the bristles on the feet, as well as concerning the bristles on the wing-veins. The body and the picture of the wings of all the species of *Hexachaeta* are strikingly uniform. I know of no other but American species of this group.

2. T. amabilis n. sp. ♀.—Lutea, thoracis dorsum sulphureo-vittatum, postice nigricans; pleuris fusco-nigra, sulfureo-vittata; scutellum magnum, planum, setis sex validis instructum, nigrum, late sulfureo-marginatum; abdomen fasciis tribus interruptis nigris ornatum; femora intermedia magnâ ex parte, postica fere tota nigra; alarum pictura fusco-nigra, praeter maculam ingentem, quae in medià alà lorum habet et totam ejus latitudinem explet, fasciam angustam subperpendicularem, quâ vena transversalis posterior includitur, et vittam costalem inde ab basi famâ usque ad summam alae apicem pertinentem ostendit.

Clay-yellowish, thoracic dorsum with sulphur-yellow longitudinal stripes, blackish along the posterior margin; pleura brownish-black with sulphur-yellow longitudinal stripes; scutellum large, flat, with six macrochaetae, black, with a broad yellow border; abdomen with three interrupted black crossbands; intermediate femora partly, hind femora almost entirely brownish-black; the brownish-black picture of the wings shows, besides an unusually large spot upon the middle of the wing, occupying its whole breadth, a narrow, almost perpendicular crossband, covering the posterior crossvein, and from which a border extends along the costa as far as the apex of the wings. Long. corp. 0.26; long. al. 0.26.

Of the size of *T. eximia* Wied., and so closely allied to it in all the plastic characters, that their detailed description would be superfluous. Head and all its parts of the same coloring and the same structure as in that species, only the frontal bristles are somewhat weaker. The thoracic dorsum shows a delicate middle line, gradually fading anteriorly and expanding posteriorly into a large spot, which does not entirely reach the posterior thoracic margin, and is surrounded laterally and posteriorly by a blackish coloring; beginning at the shoulder, a sulphur-yellow stripe runs, gradually expanding, to the root of the wing; it emits, near the humeral callus, an upper branch, running towards the transverse suture; between both branches, the color changes into brownish. Pleura brownish-black, with a sulphur-yellow longitudinal stripe across the middle; moreover, the sulphur-yellow stripe between the humerus and the root of the wings, is prolonged under the latter as far as the posterior end of the thorax. Scutellum entirely of the same structure as in *T. eximia*, sulphur-yellow, at the basis of the upper side with a large, semicircular brownish-black spot, the border of the upper side only remaining sulphur-yellow. Metathorax brownish-black, spotted with brown on the sides, and with a yellow spot on the middle of its upper side. The dense and very short pubescence of the thorax and the scutellum is more whitish-yellow than is usually the case in *T. eximia:* otherwise the hairs and bristles of both species are alike in their coloring; the number and position of the macrochaetae is the same in both. Abdomen with three very broad black cross-bands, which lie on the second, third, and fourth segments, and leave uncovered only the middle line and the posterior margin of these segments. The pile on the abdomen is black; on the upper side of the first segment and along the posterior border of the second, pale-yellowish. Hypopygium brownish-black. Coxae and feet yellow; the intermediate femora towards the basis, to a great, but variable extent, brownish-black; hind femora black, somewhat yellow towards the end, especially on the under side. The bristles on the femora and tibiae are almost as in *T. eximia.* The shape of the wings, the venation, and the position of the bristles are exactly as in that species; the pattern of the picture is likewise a somewhat similar one; however, it differs considerably in the details; the bulk of the dark coloring extends a little beyond the small crossvein and is gently

DESCRIPTION OF THE SPECIES. 221

rounded off, the curve formed by it striking the anterior margin
nearly at a right, the posterior margin at an acute aagle; the
latter margin, however, is not quite reached, as a narrow hyaline
space remains between it and the dark coloring; this curve would
have been a perfect one, were it not for a small projection before
the posterior crossvein and for a small excision immediately
beyond it; near the anterior margin, the dark-brown coloring,
immediately before its end, is interrupted by a triangular hyaline
indentation, the tip of which reaches the third longitudinal vein
immediately before the small crossvein; the distal side is concave, the proximal side is straight and perpendicular to the
costa. The brown coloring has no distinct limit towards the
base of the wing; it gradually dissolves into a system of irregular spots; the costal cell is hyaline, with the exception of a
brown infuscation along the costa between the humeral crossvein
and the auxiliary vein; likewise hyaline are the extreme basis
of the marginal cell and the entire second basal cell with the
exception of a very narrow brownish-black border along the
veins inclosing it; the first basal cell at its root, as far as the
humeral crossvein, is also rather hyaline; beyond this, for an
almost equal distance, it is yellowish; the anal cell is of a dirty
yellow, blackish-brown towards its end, which color also extends
over the basis of the third posterior cell; also, posterior angle
of the wing, and the portion of the third posterior cell lying alongside of it, are hyaline; moreover, in the third posterior cell, quite
near its basis, at the place where it is contiguous to the second
basal cell, there is an elliptical hyaline drop; in the first basal
cell, below the beginning of the third longitudinal vein, there is
a longitudinal spot of a dirty ferruginous color; a somewhat
larger spot of the same coloring is in the marginal cell, below the
place, where the auxiliary vein diverges from the first longitudinal. The hyaline apical portion of the wing shows a narrow
crossband, covering the posterior crossvein, almost perpendicular,
very gently curved, of a brownish-black color; its anterior end
turns towards the costa in the shape of a bow and follows it
afterwards as a narrow border, as far as the tip of the fourth
longitudinal vein.

Hab. Mexico (collection of Mr. v. Roeder).

3. T. suspensa Lw. ♀. (Tab. X, f. 5.)—Tota lutea, alarum rivulis fuscanis, cellula basali secunda et cellula discoidalis basi non hyalinis, apice venae longitudinalis quartae recurvo.

Altogether clay-yellow, rivulets of the wings infuscated; second basal cell and root of discal cell not hyaline, the tip of the fourth longitudinal vein curved forward. Long. corp. 0.21; long. al. 0.22—0.23.

Syn. *Trypeta suspensa* Loew, Monogr., etc., I, 69. Tab. II, f. 5.

The present species begins a group of very closely allied species, very much resembling one another. I have nothing to add to my above-quoted description of *T. suspensa*; I will only notice that the absence of pale yellow stripes on the thorax and of a pale yellow coloring of the scutellum cannot be considered as absolutely distinctive of this species, as these marks often disappear in other species in the process of drying. The readiest distinctive mark between *T. suspensa* and the very similar, but larger *T. fraterculus* is, that in the former, the second basal cell and the root of the discal cell have a yellowish color, while in the latter they are hyaline. I regret to have to notice here, that the engraver, in figuring *T. suspensa*, has committed an error in drawing the curvature of the tip of the fourth vein; this curvature is exactly similar to that in *T. fraterculus*, that is, running forward; and although this curved tip in *T. suspensa* is a little shorter, the difference is not at all such as the figure would lead one to suppose. The second basal cell and the basis of the discal cell should be somewhat paler in the figure, as they are not brown, but only yellow.

Hab. Cuba (Pocy).

4. T. fraterculus Wied. ♀. (Tab. X, f. 6.)—Lutea, thoracis vittis et scutello dilutius tinctis, ultimo abdominis segmento duobus praecedentibus simul sumtis paulo breviore, alarum rivulis infuscantibus, cellula basali secunda et cellula discoidalis basi hyalinis, apice venae longitudinalis quartae recurvo.

Clay-yellow, longitudinal stripes of thorax and scutellum paler yellow; last abdominal segment a little shorter than the two previous ones taken together; wings with rather clay-yellow rivulets; first basal cell and root of the discal cell hyaline; the end of the fourth longitudinal vein curved forward. Long. corp. 0.26; long. al. 0.27.

Syn. *Dacus fraterculus* Wiedemann, Auss. Zw. II, p. 524.
Trypeta unicolor Loew, Monogr., etc., I, p. 70. Tab. II, f. 6.

To my former description of this species, I have to add two observations. First, it contains a misprint, as the third line should read "bristle very thin," and not "bristle very short." Secondly, the examination of well-preserved specimens renders it doubtless, that the dark spots on the thoracic dorsum, mentioned in the description, were produced by the immersion of the specimens in spirits, and that the better preserved specimens do not show them.

When I described *T. unicolor*, I took it for distinct from *Dacus fraterculus* Wied., as Wiedemann describes the bristles and hairs on head and thorax as black, and says that the large triangular hyaline spot at the end of the posterior margin is connected with the S-shaped hyaline band. The comparison of Wiedemann's original specimen, however, showed that my *T. unicolor* is nothing else but *Dacus fraterculus* Wied. By the terms *hairs* and *bristles* Wiedemann understood only the stronger and weaker bristles; the remaining short pile on the head and the thorax of his specimen is entirely similar to the yellowish pubescence of *T. unicolor*. The connection between the posterior hyaline spot with the S-shaped hyaline band, which he mentions, is only an apparent one, as the rivulet separating both is not interrupted at the tip of the triangular hyaline spot, but only very much faded.

Hab. Brazil, Peru, New Granada, Cuba.

Observation.—The *Tephritis obliqua* Macq. Dipt. Exot. II, 3, p. 225, Tab. XXX, f. 11, undoubtedly belongs in the relationship of the two preceding species; it differs, however, in the picture of the wings too much to be identified with any of them.

5. **T. ludens** n. sp. ♀. (Tab. XI, f. 19.)—Lutea, thoracis vittis et scutello latius flavis, ultimo abdominis segmento duobus praecedentibus simul sumtis multo longiore, alarum rivulis interscentibus, cellula basali secunda et cellulae discoidalis basi hyalinis, apice venae longitudinalis quarta recurva.

Clay-yellow, longitudinal stripes of thorax and scutellum of a purer yellow; the last abdominal segment much longer than the two preceding ones taken together; wings with rather clay-yellow rivulets, the second basal cell and the root of the anal cell hyaline; the end of the fourth longitudinal vein curved forward. Long. corp. 0.30; long. al. 0.31—0.32.

Pale clay-yellow. Front of a somewhat more bright yellow,

of a very moderate breadth; the usual frontal bristles black, only
the upper ones rather long and strong. The yellow antennæ
almost as long as the face; arista long and slender, with a very
short and delicate pubescence. Oral opening rather large; oral
edge rather sharp. Proboscis and palpi yellow, the latter rather
broad; the suctorial flaps somewhat prolonged. The upper side
of the thorax of a light, bright clay-yellow; a sulphur-yellow
middle stripe, gradually vanishing anteriorly, expanding posteriorly in a cuneiform shape, and nowhere well defined; scutellum
sulphur-yellow; on each side, above the root of the wings, a
well-marked pale-yellow longitudinal stripe, which runs from the
transverse suture to the posterior margin of the thorax; quite
on the lateral margin an indistinct, but broader pale yellow stripe;
the humeral corner and a well-defined stripe on the upper part of
the pleuræ, reaching to the root of the wings, likewise of a bright
pale yellow. The very short pile on the thorax is yellowish; the
usual bristles are black or blackish-brown. Scutellum with four
black bristles. Metathorax clay-yellow. Abdomen with short
yellowish pile and with black bristles on its posterior end; the
last segment very much prolonged, much longer than the two
preceding ones taken together (this character serves easily to
distinguish this species from *T. fraterculus*, which is very much
like it). Feet yellow; under side of the front femora with several
blackish-brown bristles. Wings not very broad in comparison to
their considerable length; the rivulets upon them are pale
brownish-yellow with narrow, but little conspicuous, and not
always perceptible brown borders; near the posterior margin and
on the apex of the wing they are altogether brownish; the hyaline
spaces between the rivulets are as follows: 1. An oblique band,
interrupted upon the third longitudinal vein, the anterior part of
which forms, immediately beyond the stigma, a spot extending
from the costa to the third longitudinal vein, while the posterior
part of the band occupies the portion of the basal cell which lies
under the stigma, the basis of the discal cell and the second basal
cell; 2. A broad S-shaped band which begins at the posterior
margin, between the tips of the fifth and sixth longitudinal veins,
passes between the two crossveins, reaches the second longitudinal
vein, turns backwards and reaches the margin in the vicinity of
the end of the fourth longitudinal vein; 3. A large triangular
spot near the posterior margin, which fills a considerable part of

the second posterior cell, reaches with its tip considerably beyond the fourth longitudinal vein, and almost coalesces here with the S-shaped hyaline band. The external costal cell also is hyaline, with the exception of its basis, but has a more yellowish tinge than the other hyaline spaces. Stigma rather long, almost imperceptibly darker than its surroundings. Crossveins straight and steep; the third longitudinal vein distinctly bristly; the end of the fourth longitudinal vein turned forward; the posterior end of the anal cell drawn out in a very narrow, long lobe.

Hab. Mexico (coll. Winthem).

Observation.—The comparison of the description of *Trypeta fraterculus* and *T. ludens* shows the great resemblance of the two species and an entirely satisfactory distinctive character in the different length of the last abdominal segment. The females of these species, which unfortunately I have not seen, will probably be easy to distinguish, if attention is paid to the size, which is larger in *T. ludens*, to the somewhat broader cheeks, the longer last abdominal segment of this species, and to the course of the third and fourth longitudinal veins, which suddenly diverge here, while their divergency in *T. fraterculus* is much more gradual. In using the coloring for distinguishing the two species, a certain caution is necessary here, as well as in the other species of this group.

6. T. tricincta n. sp. ♂.—Lutea, scutelli basi tribusque abdominis fasciis nigris, alarum rivulis nigro-fuscis, apice vense longitudinalis quartæ recurva.

Clay-yellow; basis of the scutellum and three crossbands of the abdomen black; the end of the fourth longitudinal vein somewhat curved forward. Long. corp. 0.26; long. al. 0.26—0.27.

Clay-yellow, more yellowish-red on the thoracic dorsum. Head of the same color and shape as in the three preceding species. In the middle of the thoracic dorsum there is a longitudinal sulphur-yellow stripe, proceeding from the posterior margin; it is rather broad posteriorly, gradually becomes narrower anteriorly, and finally disappears near the anterior margin; moreover each posterior corner emits a conspicuous sulphur-yellow stripe to the transverse suture; the humeral callosity and a broad longitudinal stripe reaching from it to the root of the wing and then passing under the latter to the posterior part of the thorax,

15

are, likewise, sulphur-yellow. The very short pile on the thoracic dorsum is pale yellowish, towards the posterior corners only it assumes a blackish tinge or at least a blackish appearance. The black macrochætæ of the thoracic dorsum are similar, in number and position, to those of the three preceding species. Scutellum sulphur-yellow, with four macrochætæ on the margin. Meta-thorax brownish-black, with a clay-yellow longitudinal stripe in the middle of its superior margin. Abdomen on the 2d, 3d, and 4th segments with a transverse band near the anterior margin; that of the second segment is entire and occupies only one-half of its length; those of the third and fourth segments are narrowly interrupted in the middle and cover a little more than the anterior half of the segment; the fourth segment is hardly longer than the preceding two, taken together. Hypopygium clay-yellow. The pile on the abdomen is blackish, and yellowish only on the upper side of the first and on the pale-colored portions of the upper side of the second segment; in a reflected light, the pile on the whole abdomen assumes a paler hue; the rather weak bristles at the end of the last segment are black. Feet clay-yellowish; the pile and bristles are similar to those in the three preceding species. Wings hyaline, with a rather dark-brown picture; it is not quite as brownish-black as that of *T. serpentina* Wied. figured on Tab. XI, f. 25, but it is more like it than any other species to me known. In order to form an idea of the picture of the wings of *T. tricincta*, let us represent to ourselves that the whole outer costal cell in that figure is rather hyaline, that the regions figured in gray are yellow and those represented as black are dark brown; that the S-shaped rivulet, beginning at the basis of the third posterior cell, running towards the anterior margin, and ending at the apex of the wing, is, upon its latter half, at least one-half broader than represented; that the band beginning at the posterior margin and covering the posterior crossvein is also broader than represented in the figure, and this in such a manner, that its side, looking towards the root of the wing, is a little less concave; finally, add to this picture a little streak of a saturate brown, beginning at the posterior margin and reaching somewhat beyond the fourth longitudinal vein (at the very place where Tab. XI, fig. 22, shows a similar streak, reaching only as far as the fourth longitudinal vein).

Hab. Hayti (caught on shipboard, by Mr. P. R. Uhler, sixty miles northwest of St. Nicholas, Hayti).

Observation 1.—The *Trypeta* described by Wiedemann as *Dacus serpentinus*, differs from *T. tricincta* not only in the picture of the wings, but also in the coloring. Wiedemann's original specimen, compared by me, comes from Brazil; but I have received a number of specimens of the same species from Peru. The *Urophora vittithorax* Macq. Dipt. Exot. Suppl. IV, p. 280, Tab. XXVI, f. 11, is identical with *T. serpentina* Wied. The habitat "de l'Inde," given by Macquart, is certainly erroneous, if it means the East Indies; but the species may occur in the West Indies, just as *T. fraterculus* occurs in Peru, Brazil, and Cuba.

Observation 2.— *T. suspensa* Lw., *fraterculus* Wied., *ludens* n. sp., and *tricincta* n. sp., and a considerable number of other American species, among which *T. serpentina* Wied. and *obliqua* Macq., have already been mentioned above, form a well-defined group, which well deserves to be considered as a separate genus. The character which distinguishes it from all other *Trypetina*, is the course of the fourth longitudinal vein, which, towards its end, is curved forwards in a rather striking manner, and reaches the margin at a very acute angle, being prolonged beyond as the costal vein. With reference to this character I propose to call it *Acrotoxa*. The species of this group have, moreover, the following characters in common: In the structure of the head and of all its parts they resemble the species of *Hexachæta*: the thorax has a similar structure, but it is a little smaller in bulk, as compared to the rest of tho body, and a little narrower between the roots of the wings; the macrochætæ of the thoracic dorsum agree with those of *Hexachæta* both in their number and position. The scutellum is smaller than in the latter genus and not quite as flat, and bears not six, but four macrochætæ. Front femora on the upper side with shorter, on the under side with longer bristles and the front tibiæ without bristles, as in the species of *Hexachæta*. Middle femora without bristles; only the basis of the under side is sometimes provided with one or several bristle-like hairs; the two rows of bristles which, in *Hexachæta*, are found on the under side of the middle femora, are replaced here by two rows of hairs. Middle tibiæ without bristles. Hind femora towards the end of their upper side, more or less densely bristly, on the under side with somewhat longer pile and moreover from the basis to a little beyond the middle, with a rather sparse row of long, almost bristle-like hairs; hind tibiæ ciliated with rather weak bristlets. Tegulæ almost as much developed as in *Hexachæta*. Wings large, and, comparatively to their length, less broad than in *Hexachæta*; the venation, with the exception of the difference in the course of the fourth vein, already adverted to, is very like that of *Hexachæta*, only all the cells, and especially the stigma, are longer in comparison to their breadth; the posterior angle of the anal cell is drawn out in an equally long and pointed lobe; the whole of the first longitudinal vein and the third some distance beyond the small crossvein, are bristly. The very characteristic picture of the wings in *Acrotoxa* is sufficiently rendered by the figures 5 and 6 of Tab. X, and 19–27 of Tab. XI. The portions of this picture which could not well be called bands (*fasciæ*), or stripes (*vittæ*), I have called *rivulets* (following in this Meigen's example, who called them *rivuli* in latin, and *Bäche* in german). The same term may be applied to the species of *Aridia*. The species of *Acrotoxa* are often very much alike, and very difficult to distinguish in the male sex; the females are frequently easier to distinguish on account of the very different length of the ovipositor in different species.

Observation 3.—In view of the difficulty of this group and of the probable occurrence of species belonging to it in some portions of the North American continent and of the West Indies (besides *Trypeta fraterculus* Wied., already referred to), I deem it useful to enter into a more detailed examination of them. Most of the numerous *Acrotoxæ* occurring in the European museums come from Brazil, and pass rather indiscriminately for the *Dacus parallelus* Wied. I will give a description of this species, based upon the original specimens in the Wiedemann-Winthem and the Seckenberg collections, and of some of the species more closely allied to it, confining myself to those species only which are known in both sexes. Special mentions of coloring and picture will be omitted, as the former is clay-yellow in all the species, and the latter very probably is pretty much like that of *T. ludens*, as given above, at least in living specimens; in drying it becomes somewhat indistinct, and affords no trustworthy marks for discrimination.

a. T. parallela Wied. ♂ ♀. (Tab. XI, f. 20.)

Long. corp. 0.37, long. terebræ 0.20—0.21; long. al. 0.40.

Arista with a short pubescence, which is longer, however, than in the following species. The pile on the body in general is somewhat longer than in those species, which is especially perceptible on the abdomen of both sexes and on the ovipositor. Ovipositor slender, not quite as long as the thorax and the rounded abdomen of the female taken together. Wings comparatively broad and very blunt and rounded at the tip; their venation differs from the allied species in the distinct modulation of the second vein and the peculiar bend, which the last section of the third vein shows in the vicinity of the small crossvein; two characters of which there is an indication in T. consobrina only. Picture of the wings brownish-yellow, in some places brown, more intense than in the following species; the uninterrupted and even course of the first hyaline space from the basis of the second basal cell to the costa is especially characteristic. The picture of the wings varies sometimes in the fact that both the S-shaped and the V-shaped rivulet each emit, exactly upon the third longitudinal vein, a little pointed projection, almost forming a narrow bridge between them; sometimes the portion of the V-shaped rivulet, cut off by the fourth vein, is filled by a brownish-yellow coloring; I have observed this variety much more often in female than in male specimens.

Hab. Brazil.

b. T. hamata n. sp. ♂ ♀. (Tab. XI, f. 22.)

Long. corp. 0.39, long. terebræ 0.26; long. al. 0.41—0.42.

Abdomen short. The ovipositor slender, proportionally somewhat longer than in T. parallela. Wings comparatively narrower and less rounded towards the end; second longitudinal vein without any trace of an undulated course and the third longitudinal vein beyond the small crossvein without the curvature, so characteristic in T. parallela. Picture of the wings paler and more yellow than in the latter species; the branch of the V-shaped rivulet which is more distant from the tip of the wing is prolonged in front beyond the third vein, without diminution of its breadth, so that it coalesces with the S-shaped rivulet between the third and the second vein; the branch of the V-shaped rivulet which is nearer the apex of the wing is either altogether wanting, or its pale yellowish tip only is visible near the posterior margin, as it is represented on Tab. XI, f. 22. The hyaline band running from the basis of the second basal cell towards the costa forms (as it also does in T. consobrina and pseudoparallela), a row of three contiguous spots. Besides the different picture of the wings, T. hamata differs from T. consobrina and still more from T. pseudoparallela in the shape of the wings, which are comparatively narrower and a little less obtusely rounded at the tip. Moreover, the ovipositor of the female is a little shorter and more slender towards the tip than in T. consobrina; but it is very much longer than that of T. pseudoparallela.

Hab. Brazil.

c. T. integra n. sp. ♂ ♀. (Tab. XI, f. 23.)

Long. corp. 0.41, long. terebræ 0.36—0.37; long. al. 0.42.

The abdomen of this species is longer and narrower than in the other species. The picture of the wings is paler and yellower than that of *Trypeta parallela*, but otherwise resembles it more than any other, as in both, the first hyaline band is not divided in three contiguous spots. However, in the present species this band becomes narrower towards the costa and stops before reaching it, neither of which is the case in *T. parallela*. Moreover, its wings are much narrower and less obtusely rounded at the tip; likewise they show no trace of the wavy course of the second longitudinal vein and of the curvature of the third, which is so well marked in *T. parallela*. The ovipositor is remarkably long in comparison to the size of the body, longer than in all the other species described here. The design of the picture might give rise to the supposition that *T. integra* and *T. obliqua* Macq. are identical. The much smaller size of *T. obliqua* Macq. and the much shorter ovipositor, however, render this impossible. From *T. consobrina* and *pseudoparallela* this species is sufficiently distinguished by the different shape of the first hyaline band of the wings.

Hab. Brazil.

d. T. consobrina n. sp. ♂ ♀. (Tab. XI, f. 21.)

Long. corp. 0.31—0.32, long. terebræ 0.26—0.27; long. al. 0.38.

Abdomen short. The venation shows more analogy to that of *T. parallela* than to any other species mentioned here, as the third longitudinal vein is somewhat curved beyond the small crossvein; the second longitudinal likewise shows a vestige of a weak undulation (which is not rendered in the figure). The outline of the wings likewise resembles that of *T. parallela* especially in the obtuse rounding of the apex; but the wings are narrower in comparison to their length. The picture of the wings is considerably paler than in *T. parallela*, and resembles that of *T. pseudoparallela*, so that the males of both species may easily be taken for each other, unless attention is paid to the difference in the course of the third vein. The females of both are very easily distinguished, as the ovipositor of *T. consobrina* is considerably longer than that of *T. pseudoparallela*.

Hab. Brazil.

e. T. pseudoparallela. ♂ ♀. (Tab. XI, f. 24.)

Long. corp. 0.35, long. terebræ 0.13—0.14; long. al. 0.38—0.39.

The wings resemble those of *T. parallela* in outline very much, differ, however, in the fact that the second and third longitudinal veins do not show the peculiar course which they have in *T. parallela*. The picture of the wings is but little paler than in *T. parallela*, but differs from it considerably in the breaking up of the first hyaline band into three contignous spots. In speaking of *T. consobrina*, I have adverted to the difference between the males of the two species, which otherwise are closely alike. The female of this species cannot easily be mistaken for that of *T. consobrina* or any other of the species described here.

Hab. Brazil.

The great importance which the comparative length of the ovipositor has for determination of the closely resembling species of the present group, induces me to give here the following figures representing the average of several measurements. The relation of the length of the ovipositor to that of the rest of the body is in *pseudoparallela* 1 : 2.5; in *pumillela* 1 : 1.8—1.9; in *hamato* 1 : 1.5; in *consobrina* 1 : 1.2; in *integra* 1 : 1.1. Their relation to the length of the wing is in *pseudoparallela* 1 : 2.6; in *parallela* 1 : 2.1; in *hamata* 1 : 1.6; in *consobrina* 1 : 1.4; in *integra* 1 : 1.2.

Trypeta Ocrraia Walker (List, etc., IV, p. 1016), from Jamaica, is an *Acrotoxa*, closely allied to the species described by me. Whether *Trypeta Aciduea* Walker (Ibid., p. 1014) from Jamaica likewise belongs here is uncertain, as the author does not state whether the end of the third longitudinal vein is directed forwards or backwards; moreover there is no statement whatever concerning the shape of the scutellum and the number of its bristles. If this species is an *Acrotoxa*, it cannot possibly be identified with any of those described above, on account of the differences in the coloring. The same applies, in a greater measure still, to *Trypeta serpentina* Wiedemann, already alluded to above.

In order to bring together whatever I know concerning the *Trypetæ* belonging to the group *Acrotoxa*, I give on Tab. XI, f. 26, a copy of the figure of the wing of *Trypeta grandis* Macq. (Dipt. Exot. Suppl., I, p. 212. Tab. XVIII, f. 14), from New Granada, and on Tab. XI, f. 27, that of the wing of *Urophora bivittata* Macq. (Dipt. Exot., II, 8, p. 222. Tab. XXX, f. 7), of unknown *habitat*. Both wings show an outline somewhat different from the other *Acrotoxæ*, more oblique transverse veins, a more narrow first posterior cell, a weaker forward turn of the third vein, etc. I am inclined to believe that these differences do not, for the most part, exist in reality, but are only due to the usual inaccuracy in Macquart's figures; and for this reason I believe that both *T. grandis* Macq. and *Urophora bivittata* Macq. are *Acrotoxæ*. Should my supposition prove correct, then it becomes very probable that America is the *habitat* of the latter species.

7. T. vulnerata n. sp. ♂ ♀.—Fusco-nigra, infra fusca; caput ex-
albidum, fronte et facie ochraceo-vittatis, antennis, palpisque interceun-
tibus; scutellum subtumidum, setis quatuor præditum; pedes lutei,
femoribus tamen posterioribus fusco-nigris; alæ latiusculæ, cellulâ
stigmaticali brevissimâ, quadratâ, cellulâ marginali latâ et cellulâ posteriore primâ adversus apicem angustatâ instructæ, fasciis nigris inter
se cohærentibus similiter atque *Acinra lychnidis V.*, pictæ, colore tamen
nigro adversus alarum basim latius diffuso.

Blackish-brown, under side brown; head whitish, front and face with an
ochre-yellow longitudinal stripe, antennæ and palpi more clay-yellowish; scutellum rather tumid, with four bristles; feet clay-yellowish,
the posterior femora, however, brownish-black; wings rather broad,
with a short, square stigmatical cell, a broad marginal cell and a first
posterior cell, which is attenuated at the posterior end; the black, connected crossbands almost resemble those of *Acinra lychnidis* Fab., but
the black coloring is more extended towards the basis. Long. corp., ♂,
0.18, ♀, cum terebrâ 0.24; long. al. 0.18.

Coloring of a rather shining brownish-black; the humeral
region and the under side of thorax and abdomen brown. Head
whitish, front and face with a conspicuous ochre-yellow or almost
orange-yellow middle stripe. Antennæ clay-yellowish, descending below the middle of the perpendicular, very little concave,
face; the first two joints with short black pile; the third with an
almost sharp anterior corner; arista brownish-black with an
extremely short pubescence; oral opening of a medium size; the
broad palpi do not extend beyond its anterior edge, which is
slightly drawn upwards. Cheeks of a very moderate breadth; at
the lower corner of the eye, there is an ochre-brownish spot and
a black bristle. The usual frontal bristles black and of a considerable length; between the two black bristles inserted upon
the little stripes, coming down from the vertical margin, there is,
on each side, a short, white bristle; four similar bristles are
inserted upon the posterior vertical margin; the erect pile of the
occiput and the cilia of the upper posterior orbit of the eye are
white. Thoracic dorsum and pleuræ with a very scattered, almost
stubble-shaped white pile and black bristles. Scutellum very
convex, perceptibly swollen, with four long bristles. The intermediate abdominal segments have a more or less distinct pale
coloring on the posterior margin; all segments, with the exception of the posterior one, have some scattered whitish pile towards
the posterior margin and blackish pile on the lateral margins; the

last segment, towards its end, has several black bristles. Ovipositor flat, rather broadly truncate, hardly as long as the last three abdominal segments taken together, blackish-brown or black, with black pile. Front feet, as well as the entire fore-coxæ, clay-yellow; on the posterior feet the first joint of the coxæ and the femora are brownish-black, or dark brown, the second joint of the coxæ, the tip of the femora, and the entire tibiæ and tarsi are clay-yellow; the under side of the front femora bears a row of black bristles, while the under side of the posterior femora is without them. Halteres infuscated. Wings large, rather broad, with convex anterior and posterior margins; veins, with the exception of the first longitudinal, without bristles; the first longitudinal vein turns, not very far beyond the end of the auxiliary vein, in a sharp, rectangular fracture, perpendicularly towards the margin of the wing, which causes the stigmatical cell to assume a strikingly short and square shape; the second longitudinal vein is rather distant from the anterior margin of the wing and has a rather straight course, so that the marginal cell, although rather broad, is attenuated towards its end; the third longitudinal vein is turned backwards towards its end, so that the first posterior cell is somewhat attenuated at the end; the small crossvein is placed about the middle of the discal cell, which becomes considerably broader towards its end; the last section of the fourth longitudinal vein has a wavy course; the posterior crossvein is very steep and only very gently curved; the posterior angle of the anal cell is drawn out in a point in the usual way. The picture of the wings has somewhat the appearance of rivulets, and consists of conspicuous and rather well-defined brownish-black crossbands, which come in contact almost in the same way as in the European *Acidia lychnidis* Fab. (compare Loew, *Rohrfliegen*, Tab. III, f. 4); the picture of the present species differs, however, in the more considerable extent of the black coloring on the basis of the wings; the black bands leave two hyaline indentations on the anterior and three on the posterior margin; these hyaline spots have, in a certain light, a whitish reflection. The first of these spots on the anterior margin is a rectangular triangle, the hypothenuse of which begins on the costa a little before the end of the first longitudinal vein and runs as far as the anterior end of the small crossvein; the second hyaline spot, separated from the first by an almost perpendicular

dark band, runs from the costa over the middle of the penultimate
section of the fourth vein, as far as the middle breadth of the
discal cell. The first hyaline spot of the posterior margin begins
at the end of the last longitudinal vein and reaches as far as the
fourth vein; the second and third spots begin, as usual in the
species with this kind of picture, at the posterior end of the
second posterior cell; both are very pointed at their end, and
while the second spot reaches only to the fourth vein, the third
goes as far as the third vein. Besides these hyaline spots, there
is, at the basis, a small hyaline mark, connected with the whitish
tegulæ; in the anal angle of the wing, near the margin, there is a
diluted dot. The last of the dark bands is separated from the
costa, as far as the third vein, by a narrow, hyaline border; the
small crossvein has a similar, very narrow, hyaline border. A
peculiar mark of this species is, that the spot at which the second
and third longitudinal veins diverge, forms a knot-shaped, blood-
red swelling, like a drop of coagulated blood; the first longitudinal vein, near its basis, likewise shows a more or less distinct
blood-red coloring.

Hab. Massachusetts (Mr. Sanborn).

Observation.—*Trypeta vulnerata* cannot be well located in
any of the genera hitherto formed out of the old genus *Trypeta*.
The great resemblance of the picture of its wings to that of
Acidia lychnidis Fab. (= discoidea Meig.), naturally suggests
its location in the same genus. A closer examination, however,
proves that, although its relationship to the species of that genus
is rather close, it differs very much in the structure of the head,
the very much more swollen scutellum, the structure of the ovipositor, some details in the venation, and the almost stubble-
shaped pile. Thus we are compelled to establish a separate genus,
Stenopa, for it, which finds its place next to *Acidia*.

8. T. fratria Lw. ♀. (Tab. X, f. 4.)—Lutea, corpore brevi et latiusculo, scutello setas quatuor gerente; ala rivulis luteo-fuscanis, maculam ovatam hyalinam in apicali cellulæ discoidalis parte sitam includen-
tibus, apice venæ longitudinalis quartæ non recurva.

Clay-yellow, stature short and somewhat broad, with four bristles on the
scutellum; wings with yellowish-brown rivulets, which inclose an oval,
hyaline spot before the end of the discal cell; the end of the fourth
longitudinal vein is not curved forwards. Long. corp. 0.33; long. al.
0.33.

Syn. *Trypeta fratria* Loew, Monographs, etc., I, p. 67.　Tab. II, f. 4.
† *Trypeta liogaster* Thomas, Eng. Kem, p. 678, No. 251.

Hab. United States (Osten-Sacken).

Observation.—I have nothing to add to the description of this species as given in the first part of these Monographs.　Its close relationship to the European *T. heraclei* Lin. is a sufficient proof that this species is a true, typical *Acidia.*　I believe that *T. liogaster* Thoms. is this same species, although he describes the ovipositor as darker than I find it in my specimen.

9. T. suavis Lw.　♂.　(Tab. X, f. 10.)—Dilute lutea, corpore brevi, latiusculo, scutello setis quatuor instructo; ala rivulis latissimis fascia, in formam litera S confluentibus, picta, apice vena longitudinalis quarta non recurva.

Pale clay-yellowish, stature short and rather broad, scutellum with four bristles; wings with very broad brown rivulets, which coalesce in the shape of the letter S; the tip of the fourth vein is not curved forwards. Long. corp. 0.20; long. al. 0.21.

Syn. *Trypeta suavis* Loew, Monographs, etc., I, p. 75.　Tab. II, f. 10.

Hab. Middle States (Osten-Sacken).

I possess only one very badly preserved specimen, which I described in the Monographs, etc., Part I.　The species is easily distinguished on account of the peculiar picture of its wings.　Of all the genera hitherto established in the family *Trypetidæ*, the present species undoubtedly belongs to *Acidia;* and, as far as the imperfect preservation of my specimen allows an opinion, it agrees with the *Acidiæ* in all the important characters, except one; while all the European *Acidiæ* have the third longitudinal vein more or less bristly, I perceive no bristles, whatever, in *T. suavis,* and have no reason to suppose that they have been rubbed off.　Such an agreement of characters decides me to place *T. suavis* in the genus *Acidia;* at the same time, however, the bristles of the third longitudinal vein cannot any longer be considered as characteristic of the genus *Acidia.*

10. T. canadensis n. sp.　♀.—Dilute lutescens, segmentis abdominalibus tertio et quarto fusco-fasciatis, corpore brevi, latiusculo, terebri mediocri, lata et late truncata; alarum rivoli angusti, fusci, apex vena longitudinalis quarta non recurva.

Pale clay-yellowish, with a brown armband on the third and fourth abdominal segments, stature short and somewhat broad; ovipositor of

medium length, broad and broadly truncate; wings with narrow pale
brownish rivulets and with a fourth longitudinal vein which is not
curved forwards at the tip.   Long. corp. 0.18, caus terebra 0.23; long.
al. 0.20.

Pale clay-yellowish. The head resembles that of *T. fratria* in
shape, only the front is somewhat broader and the vertical diameter of the eyes is a little smaller; the anterior edge of the mouth
is more projecting. On the border of the front the described
specimen bears, on each side, three long, but rather weak black
bristles. Antennæ of a more saturate yellow, not reaching the
edge of the mouth; their third joint is rounded at the tip; arista
blackish, yellow towards the basis, with a very short pubescence.
Rostrum and palpi pale yellow, the latter not reaching beyond
the anterior edge of the oral opening. Thoracic dorsum with
a very thin, whitish bloom, only the double middle stripe and
the narrow lateral stripes not pollinose, rather shining and
somewhat darker than their surroundings. The posterior end
of the thoracic dorsum and the scutellum likewise without pollen, shining, very pale yellow; a not very broad yellowish stripe
runs from the humeral corner to the root of the wings. The
scutellum is convex and not very large; in my specimen it has
three bristles on one side and only two on the other, so that I
cannot say whether the normal number of the bristles of the
scutellum is six or four. The bristles of the thorax and of the
scutellum, as well as the short pile of the thoracic dorsum, are
black. Metathorax distinctly infuscated on its superior margin
and its middle line. Abdomen shining, with short black pile;
the third and fourth segments have, each at its basis, a chestnut
crossband, interrupted upon its middle, while upon the second
segment only a lateral beginning of such a stripe is indicated by
a chestnut-brown spot. The very broad ovipositor is flat, almost
as long as the last three abdominal segments taken together, very
broadly truncate and infuscated at the end. The front femora
are sparsely beset with bristles upon the upper and under side;
the middle femora are entirely without bristles; upon the hind
femora, likewise, there are only a few bristle-like hairs before the
end of the upper side; the upper side of the hind tibiæ is merely
beset with exceedingly short bristle-like hairs. Wings of the
usual shape, hyaline, with a pale-brown picture; it consists: 1.
In an oblique half crossband running from the humeral crossvein

to the basis of the second basal cell ; 2. Of a crossband parallel
to the first, abbreviated behind, which begins at the stigma, near
the anterior margin, and runs across the basis of the submarginal
cell, as well as across the crossveins, which close the second and
third basal cells, and thus reaches the sixth longitudinal vein ; 3.
Of a rivulet which begins above the posterior crossvein, near the
third longitudinal vein, runs from it across the posterior crossvein as far as the posterior margin, is continued along this margin inside of the third posterior cell, but, before reaching the sixth
longitudinal vein, is suddenly turned upwards, running parallel
to the band which begins at the stigma, crossing the small crossvein, and thus reaching the anterior margin, where, gradually
expanding, it forms a border ending a little beyond the tip of the
fourth crossvein. The two crossbands, as well as the rivulet, are
of moderate breadth only ; the latter has, in the described specimen, the following faded spots, which, in more fully colored specimens, are probably less apparent or altogether absent : 1. A
rounded spot in the marginal cell, above the origin of the rivulet ;
2. Upon the longitudinal axis of the submarginal cell an indentation in the inner margin of the section bordering the apex of the
wing ; 3. Upon the longitudinal axis of the first posterior cell
an interruption of the rivulet at its origin and an indentation in
the inner margin of the portion bordering the apex of the wing ;
4. Upon the longitudinal axis of the discal cell a narrow interruption of the section, running again towards the anterior margin ;
5. The spot upon the posterior margin connects the first, descending, portion, with the second, which rises again upwards. The
first and third longitudinal veins are bristly ; the third and fourth
are parallel towards their end, both very gently curved backwards ; the section of the fourth vein preceding the discal cell is
gently, but rather distinctly arcuated backwards, so that the shape
of the discal cell somewhat reminds of that of the species of
Rivellia ; the crossveins are comparatively rather long, moderately
approximated, their distance being about equal to the length of
the posterior crossvein ; the latter is rather steep, however, perceptibly approximated to the apex with its anterior end, more
than with the posterior ; the posterior corner of the anal cell is
very much drawn out in a point.

Hab. Canada (Mr. Provancher). [Norway, Maine; S. J. Smith
—seems to be a common species in those regions. O. S.]

Observation.—*Trypeta canadensis* resembles the species of
Acidia in its general habitus and, at first sight, seems to differ
only in the somewhat modified picture of the wings, which seems
to hold the middle between the rivulet and the crossband. A
closer examination shows, that in the structure of the head and
of its parts, as also in the bristles upon the feet, this species is
closely allied to *Acidia*, but that it also shows characters not
belonging to that genus; such is the structure of the ovipositor,
which is longer, quite flattened, and broadly truncate at the end;
also the very peculiar course of the section of the fourth longitudinal vein preceding the small crossvein. If the scutellum is
provided with six bristles in normal specimens, we would have
another important distinctive character from *Acidia*. Thus the
admission of *T. canadensis* in the genus *Acidia* would render the
limitation of this genus too indefinite, and it becomes necessary
to establish a new genus for it, which would be characterized by
a modified type of the picture, a peculiar course of the fourth
vein, and a different structure of the ovipositor. I will call this
genus *Epochra*.

11. T. longipennis WIED. ♂ ♀. (Tab. X, f. 2 ♂, 3 ♀.)—Lutea.
capite tumido, corpore elongato et angusto; alis longis et angustis,
maris adhuc longioris et angustioris quam feminæ, rivulis luteo-fuscanis
pictæ.

Clay-yellow; head tumid; body long and narrow; wings long and narrow, those of the male still longer and more narrow than in the female,
pictured with yellowish-brown rivulets. Long. corp. 0.17—0.26; long.
al. 0.22—0.30.

Syn. *Trypeta longipennis* WIEDEMANN, Ausw. Zweifl., II, 483, 12 (♂ ♀).
Straussia armata R. DESVOIDY, Myod. 719, 2 (♂).
Straussia inermis R. DESVOIDY, Myod. 718, 1 (♀).
Tryphritis trimaculata MACQUART, Dipt. Exot., II, 3, p. 226, 8. Tab.
XXXI, f. 8.
Trypeta cornigera WALKER, List Brit. Mus., IV, p. 1010.
Trypeta corniffera WALKER, List Brit. Mus., IV, p. 1011.
Trypeta longipennis LOEW, Monographs, etc., I, p. 65.

It cannot be doubted that *Trypeta longipennis* Wied. either
is a very variable species, or that North America possesses a
number of closely allied species, resembling it very much, and
which, as long as they are represented only by single, often
imperfectly preserved specimens, it is as difficult to distinguish

and to describe as, for instance, the majority of the European
Trophora. It is only by observations upon the insect in life,
that the question will probably have to be solved, whether we
have here different species or only varieties. In writing the first
part of these Monographs I surmised that I had specimens of a
single, but very variable species before me. In the mean time
my materials have increased considerably, and specimens have
been added to it, which differ so materially from the typical *T.
longipennis*, that my former conviction has been shaken, without,
however, having been superseded by the opposite one. I prefer
therefore to continue to treat these different forms as varieties
of the same species, but, at the same time, to define these
varieties with more precision than has been done in the first part
of the Monographs. In order to avoid useless repetitions, I will
notice in advance that in all the varieties the anterior end of the
middle stripe is colored black, and that in all of them, immediately above the root of the wing, there is a small, deep-black dot,
which is not visible when the wings are folded.

1. *Varietas perfecta*, ♂ ♀.—Of the four lateral bristles of the
front, the two upper ones, in the male, are very much incrassated
and truncated at the end. Thorax without black lateral stripes.
Scutellum unicolorous; metathorax without black picture. Picture
of the wings not very deep in its coloring, complete in both sexes;
the male as Tab. X, f. 2.

Of this variety I have compared rather numerous specimens.
Among those of my collection there is a male and two females,
caught at the same time.

2. *Varietas typica* ♂ ♀.—Of the four lateral bristles on the
front the two upper ones are very much incrassated in the male
and truncate at the end. Thorax without black lateral stripes;
scutellum upon each lateral corner with a well-defined black spot.
Metathorax without any black coloring. The picture of the
wings is of a rather dark shade, especially towards the tip; complete in the female, incomplete in the male, almost like Tab. X, f.
2, except that the rivulet covering the posterior crossvein does
not reach the margin of the wing, but gradually becomes more
attenuated and pointed and never reaches beyond the posterior
end of the posterior crossvein; the branch of this rivulet which
runs along the last section of the fourth vein is likewise very
narrow and always disappears at a considerable distance from

the margin of the wing; the hyaline interval between it and the
branch bordering the anterior margin of the wing is, in the male,
comparatively longer and conspicuously narrower than in var.
perfecta; the female shows the same difference, but very feebly.

Wiedemann's description is based upon specimens of this
variety, which is a very common one. The other synonyms,
quoted above, likewise belong here, with the only exception of
Trypeta cornigera Walker. I possess of this variety four perfectly well-preserved specimens (a male and three females), caught
at the same time by Mr. Auxer in Lancaster City, Penn.; the
three females have, at the posterior end of the two posterior
abdominal segments, longer, stronger, and somewhat more abundant pile than the females of other varieties.

3. *Varietas longitudinalis* ♂ ♀.—Of the four lateral bristles
of the front the two uppermost, in the male, are very much
increased and truncated at the end. Thorax without any black
lateral stripes; scutellum on each lateral corner with a black
spot; metathorax without black picture. The wings of the male
comparatively narrower than in all the other varieties; their
picture coalesces into a single broad longitudinal stripe, which,
from the root of the wing as far as nearly the end of the posterior basal cells, has a dirty clay-yellowish coloring; beyond this
point, it changes into dark-brownish. The interval between the
second and fourth longitudinal veins is completely filled by this
stripe, with the only exception of a small hyaline spot at the end
of the fourth longitudinal vein; moreover, the stripe encroaches
a little beyond the second and fourth veins in the shape of little
wavy expansions. The picture of the female hardly differs from
that of var. *typica*; only the spot in the costal cell, between the
stigma and the humeral crossvein, which is usually wanting in
var. *perfecta* and present in var. *typica*, is much darker than in
the latter species; this is also the case in the male.

These statements are taken from a very fine pair of specimens
from Sharon Springs, N. Y., collected by Baron Osten-Sacken.
He sent me at the same time a male from Connecticut (collected
by Mr. Bassett), which agrees with the former in the picture and
in the shape of the wings, except that the uniformly brown part
of the picture of the specimen from Sharon is clouded with yellowish-brown and dark-brown; moreover, in the latter specimen,
the spot placed between the humeral crossvein and the stigma is

very much faded. The description which Mr. Walker gives of
his *Trypeta cornigera* refers, if I understand it right, to this
variety. [The male specimen from Sharon was caught on the
same spot with the female; I possess, moreover, a couple from
Connecticut, stuck on one pin, as if caught *in copula.* Thus
there can hardly be a doubt as to the sexes belonging together,
the very different picture notwithstanding. O. S.]

4. *Varietas vittigera*, ♂ ♀.—Of the four lateral bristles of the
front, the two upper ones are very much incrassated and truncate
at the end. The thoracic dorsum shows, besides the anterior
end of the middle stripe, two well-marked black lateral stripes of
a moderate breadth, abbreviated in front, rather broadly interrupted at the transverse suture and pointed posteriorly. Scutellum, upon each lateral corner, with a black spot; metathorax
on each side with a deep black longitudinal spot. Wings of the
male somewhat less elongated than in the male of the var. *perfecta.* The picture of the wings in both sexes is complete, hardly
different from that of var. *perfecta.* Of this variety I possess
only a male and a female from Nebraska (Dr. Hayden).

5. *Varietas intermedia* ♂.—Of the four lateral bristles of the
front, the two superior ones, although strong, are not incrassated and not truncate at the tip, but end, as usual, in a point.
Thorax without black lateral stripes; scutellum upon each lateral
corner with a black spot; metathorax on each side with a deep
black longitudinal spot. Wings of the male less elongated, and
perceptibly less pointed than in the first two varieties; the
picture of the wings rather luteous in coloring, the design
resembling that of the female of the first variety; however, the
hyaline band passing between the two crossveins is rather conspicuously expanded at its posterior end. The last joint of all
the feet is rather conspicuously infuscated on the sides and at
its end. Of this variety I possess only a single male, without
indication of the precise locality.

6. *Varietas confluens*, ♂.—Of the four lateral bristles of the
front the two upper ones are rather strong, but not incrassated
and not truncate at the tip, but end, as usual, in a point. The
thoracic dorsum, besides the anterior end of the middle stripe,
shows two well-defined black lateral stripes of a moderate breadth,
which are abbreviated anteriorly, rather broadly interrupted at
the transverse suture, and pointed posteriorly. Scutellum upon

16

each lateral corner with a black spot. Metathorax on each side with a deep-black longitudinal spot. Wings of the male comparatively less elongated, and less attenuated towards the tip, consequently comparatively broader than in the first and second variety. The picture of the wings is complete, its coloring uniform, not very saturate, seldom here and there with a trace of darker margins; the oblique hyaline crossband passing between the crossveins is comparatively narrow, reaches, however, the anterior margin completely. The brownish-yellow rivulet rising across the posterior crossvein is of a considerable breadth in all its parts, so that the branch of it which borders the margin of the wing and that which runs along the last section of the fourth longitudinal vein, coalesce in their middle.

I possess a single male only (Connecticut; Mr. Norton); it is one of the smallest specimens of this species in my collection.

7. *Varietas arculata* ♂.—Of the four lateral bristles of the front, the two upper ones are not stronger than usual among the species of the same size; as usual, also, they end in a point. The thoracic dorsum shows, besides the anterior end of the middle stripe, two strongly marked black lateral stripes of moderate breadth, which are abbreviated anteriorly, rather broadly interrupted at the transverse suture, and end in a point posteriorly; scutellum with a black spot upon each lateral corner; metathorax on each side with a deep black longitudinal spot. The wings of the male are less attenuated towards the apex than in the males of the first and second varieties, but comparatively less broad than in the sixth variety. The picture of the wings has a rather uniform yellowish-brown coloring. It differs from that of all the other varieties in the fact that the oblique hyaline band, running between the two crossveins, does not reach the anterior margin, but suddenly ends between the second and the third longitudinal veins, so that the border of the anterior margin is not at all interrupted beyond the triangular hyaline spot near the stigma; at the same time, this hyaline band is connected with the hyaline streak in the latter portion of the first posterior cell, the rivulet crossing over the posterior crossvein being interrupted here. These modifications give the picture a very different appearance.

Of this variety I likewise possess but one specimen (Illinois; Mr. Brendel); it is but little larger than the male specimen of the sixth variety.

Observation.—*Trypeta longipennis* has no immediate relatives among the European *Trypetidæ*. From *Spilographa abrotani* Meig., and *macrochæta* Lw., which resemble it somewhat in the peculiar shape of the frontal bristles, it differs too much, in the stature of the body, the shape of the head, as well as in the outline, the venation, and the picture of the wings, to be placed in the same genus *Spilographa*. It must be considered, therefore, as the type of a separate genus. Mr. R. Desvoidy has given it the name of *Straussia*, which may be preserved, after being modified into the more correct form of *Straussia*. The principal characters of the genus Straussia are the following:—

Body long and narrow; head remarkably swollen, especially the occiput; eyes rounded and rather small for a *Trypeta*, so that in the profile the front advances much before the eyes and the cheeks are very broad. Lateral border of the front raised in the shape of a cushion, so that the whole front assumes the appearance of a basin. Antennæ short, reaching, perhaps, as far as the middle of the face; the last joint rounded at the tip. Face retreating inferiorly; oral opening small, without any sharp anterior edge; the rather broad palpi not reaching beyond this edge. Scutellum convex, with four bristles. Abdomen elongated and considerably narrower than the thorax. Ovipositor of the female not flattened. Wings comparatively long and only moderately broad, in the male narrower than in the female, especially towards their end; the picture consists of rivulets; first and third longitudinal veins distinctly bristly; the third and fourth veins towards their end somewhat divergent and rather strongly bent backwards; small crossvein placed about the beginning of the last third of the discal cell; the posterior angle of the anal cell is drawn out in a sharp point.

12. **T. elecia** Say. ♀. (Tab. X, f. 7.)—Lutea, vittis thoracis et scutello ex-albidis, angulis lateralibus hujus nigris; tibiæ posticæ setis nigris, proportione longis ciliatæ; alæ hyalinæ, fasciis duabus integris adversos marginem posticum convergentibus, strigulâ interjectâ a costâ ad venam longitudinalem tertiam ductâ, et costæ ipsius limbo inde a fasciâ secundâ usque ad apicem cellulæ posterioris secundæ pertinente, fuscis.

Clay-yellow, longitudinal stripes of the thorax and scutellum whitish; the latter with blackish lateral corners; posterior tibiæ cilisted with comparatively long black bristles; wings hyaline, with two complete

cromohands, converging towards the posterior margin, an incomplete
band beginning at the anterior margin and running as far as the third
longitudinal vein, and a border of the costa, beginning at the tip of the second
crossband and ending at the tip of the second posterior cell); the whole
of this picture being brown. Long. corp. 0.29; long. al. 0.29.

Syn. *Trypeta electa* Say, Journ. Acad. Phil., VI, p. 185, 1.
Trypeta electa Loew, Monographs, etc., 1, p. 71, 6. Tab. II, f. 7.

I have nothing to add to the description, given in the first part
of these Monographs, but I must observe that, deceived by Macquart's insufficient description of his *T. flavonotata*, I have taken
it to be merely a paler variety of *T. electa* Say, while a specimen
received since then has convinced me that it is a very closely
allied but distinct species.

Hab. Florida (Osten-Sacken).

Observation.—*Trypeta electa* belongs to the genus *Spilographa.*

13. T. flavonotata Macq. ♀.—Lutea, vittis thoracis et scutelli
unicolore pallidioribus, tibiis posticis setulis brevissimis pallidis subcil-
latae: alae hyalinae, fasciis duabus posticae paulo abbreviatis adversus
marginem posticum convergentibus, strigula interjecta a costa prope ad
venam longitudinalem tertiam ducta et costa ipsius limbo inde a fascia
secunda usque ad cellulae posterioris secundae apicem pertinente, fuscis.

Clay-yellow, longitudinal stripes of the thoracic dorsum and the unicolorous scutellum paler; hind tibiae somewhat ciliated with very short,
pale bristles; wings hyaline, with two crossbands, which are somewhat
convergent posteriorly and interrupted a little before the posterior margin, a little crossband between them, extending from the anterior margin almost to the third longitudinal vein, and a border of the costa,
running from the second crossband to the tip of the second posterior
cell; the whole picture being brown. Long. corp. 0.18; long. al. 0.21
—0.22.

Syn. *Tephritis flavonotata* Macq. Dipt. Exot. Suppl. V, p. 123. Tab.
VII, f. 9.

This species is very like *Trypeta electa* Say, differs, however,
from it as follows. It is smaller; the head is comparatively
smaller and has much narrower cheeks. The third antennal
joint ends at a much sharper angle. In what way the picture
of the thorax differs from that of *T. electa* cannot be well
ascertained in my specimen, in which it has become somewhat
indistinct, probably in the process of drying; the whitish stripe,
running from the humerus to the root of the wings, is very per-

ceptible; there is also a trace of the whitish stripe above the root of the wings; but this stripe shows no trace of the dark border on the inside, which it has in *T. electa;* nor do I see a whitish median line. Scutellum comparatively smaller and somewhat more convex, without black spot on the lateral corners. The upper border of the metathorax is marked, at each end, with a very small spot of a deep black color. The punctiform black lateral dots, which exist on the last abdominal segment of the female of *T. electa*, are not perceptible in the male of the present species. All the bristles of the body are less strong and of a paler color, especially upon the femora, and instead of the comparatively long black bristles with which the upper side of the hind tibiæ of *T. electa* is fringed, there are in the present species only very short pale yellow bristlets. The third longitudinal vein of the wings has, at its basis, several little bristles, but upon the remainder of its course, is entirely bare (while the bristles extend much farther in *T. electa*). The picture of the wings is very like that of *T. electa*, with the following differences: the two crossbands in the middle of the wings do not altogether reach the posterior margin and are also less approximated, that is, they do not form the figure V; the basal portion of the submarginal cell lying before the first of these bands is hyaline; the picture in the vicinity of the root of the wing is much less extended and much paler, so that its darker portions do not, as in *T. electa*, form a kind of crossband, running almost parallel to the following band.

Hab. Yukon River, Alaska (R. Kennicott).

Observation.—*T. flavonotata* is very closely allied to those European species, which I have placed in the genus *Zonosema* (in my Monograph of the European *Trypetidæ*), and should be placed in it, as long as it is separated from *Spilographa*. Should, however, *Zonosema* be united with *Spilographa*, which seems the best course to follow, owing to the intermediate forms, which occur among the exotic species, then, as a matter of course, *T. flavonotata* will have to be placed in the genus *Spilographa.*

14. T. tetanops n. sp. ♂. (Tab. XI, f. 15.)—M-riles, capite subinflato, mollis parvis; alæ hyalinæ, fasciis duabus adversus marginem posticum convergentibus, strigulâ interjectâ inde a costâ ad tertiam usque venam perducente, maculis duabus duabus partis, alterâ in venâ longitudinalis tertia, alterâ in quartæ apice altâ, fascia, his maculis limbo marginis tenuissimo fusco conjunctis.

Honey-yellow, with a rather tumid head and small eyes; wings hyaline, with a brown picture, which consists of two crossbands, converging towards the posterior margin, of a little band, between both, reaching from the costa to the third longitudinal vein and of two little spots upon the third and fourth longitudinal veins, which spots are connected by a narrow infuscation along the margin of the wing. Long. corp. 0.19—0.20; long. al. 0.17—0.18.

Honey-yellow, the head of a purer yellow, somewhat tumid. Front broad, with some scattered, short, very delicate blackish pile; its lateral bristles weak. Frontal lunule very small. Eyes small, elongated, with a rather projecting anterior corner. Face descending straight; edge of the mouth blunt, somewhat swollen; the conspicuously deepened antennal furrows become narrowed below and disappear in the lateral edges of the mouth; the part of the face between them forms an acute, level triangle; the cheeks are remarkably broad, beset with a few short black hairs; oral opening very small; clypeus unusually little developed; palpi short, but considerably broad, sparsely beset with short, black hairs. Proboscis rather short and stout; the stout sucto-rial flaps, although somewhat long, are not prolonged, nor folded backwards. The upper side of the thorax, with the exception of the posterior and lateral margins, which are shining, is covered with a thin ochre-yellow pollen, and hence opaque; the short pile upon it and the bristles are black; the number and position of the latter is the usual one; of the two pairs of bristles in front of the scutellum, the anterior one is inserted upon very small dots of a somewhat darker color; in the proximity of the suture there are two similar dots; moreover, the trace of a slender dark middle line is perceptible. Scutellum shining honey-yellow, rather convex, sparsely beset with little black hairs and bearing four strong black bristles. Pleurae of the same color with the scutellum, beset with black pile. Abdomen, likewise, shining honey-yellow, in the middle with a trace of an ochre-yellow dust, beset with black pile, but without longer bristles. The yellow feet have rather strong femora; the two front femora are beset with bristles upon the under and upper side. Wings hyaline, with a picture which is very like that of the two preceding species. The principal feature consists in two narrow brown transverse bands; the first, somewhat faded at its beginning, starts from the end of the stigma and runs perpendicularly over the small crossvein as far as the proximity of the posterior margin, while

the second begins at the tip of the second longitudinal vein and
runs in an oblique direction over the posterior crossvein to the
posterior margin; between these two bands there is a short,
brown one, extending from the anterior margin to the third
longitudinal vein; it follows the same direction as the second
band; the tips of the third and fourth longitudinal veins bear
each a small brown spot and these spots are connected by a narrow brown shade along the margin of the wing; a small brown
spot covers the end of the anal cell, which is drawn out in an
acute point; the inner costal cell, the beginning of the first basal
cell, as far as the origin of the third vein, the basis of the submarginal cell as far as the first brown crossband, the stigma and
the anal cell are tinged with yellow; a yellow coloring likewise
surrounds that crossvein, which divides the second basal cell from
the discal cell; the basis of the exterior costal cell is tinged with
yellowish-brown. The third longitudinal vein is, in the vicinity
of its origin, densely beset with bristles; more sparsely beyond
that point; the third and fourth longitudinal veins somewhat
diverge towards their end; the small crossvein is a little before
the middle of the discal cell; the posterior crossvein is straight
and steep.

Hab. Mexico (Deppe; Mus. Berol.).

Observation.—The principal difference between this species
and the typical *Spilographæ* consists in the structure of the head,
which has been described above; moreover, the wings are comparatively shorter and the third vein has, as far as its tip, an
entirely rectilinear course, while, in all the species of *Spilographa* (comp. Tab. X, f. 7), it is gently curved backwards.
Should a new genus be founded for this single species, the name
Œdicarena, alluding to the structure of its head, might be
adopted for it. It would seem preferable, however, until a
number of allied species becomes known, to let *T. tetanops*
remain in the genus *Spilographa*, with which it is undoubtedly
related on account of the great resemblance of the picture of its
wings with that of *T. electa* and still more of *T. flavonotata.*

15. T. sarcinata Lw. ♀. (Tab. XI, f. 16.)—Sordide lutea, dorso
thoracis cinerascente, punctisque aliquot majusculis atris picto, scutello
luteolo, bimaculato atro, alarum angulo axillari fasciisque quatuor
valde obliquis ex luteo fuscis, venis transversis obliquis et valde
approximatis, cellula discoidali adversus basim valde angustata.

Dingy clay-yellow, with several deep black dots upon the gray thoracic dorsum and with a tumid bituberculate black scutellum; wings with a yellowish-brown posterior angle and four very oblique yellowish-brown crossbands, with oblique and very approximate crossveins and with a discal cell which is gradually attenuated towards its basis. Long. corp. 0.28; long. al. 0.26—0.27.

Syn. ?*Tephritis quadrifasciata* Macquart, Dipt. Exot. II, 3, p. 228. Tab. XXX, f. 8.

Trypeta serrinata Loew, Berl. Entom. Zeitschr., VI, p. 218, and Dipt. Amer. Cent., I, 98.

Dark clay-yellow, almost brownish-yellow. The broad head is of a lighter color; front very broad, on the anterior part of the lateral margin with two bristles, and before them, near the orbit, with a small black dot. Antennæ yellowish, by far not reaching the edge of the mouth. Face somewhat excavated, but very little protruding towards the edge of the mouth, broad and with broad orbits along the eyes. Cheeks rather broad, with a small black spot near the lower corner of the eye. Oral opening transversely oval; proboscis and palpi yellowish, short, entirely withdrawn in the oral opening; the usual frontal bristles black; the pile on the cheeks, below the black dot which occurs upon them, blackish; the remaining pile on the head is whitish. The upper side of the thorax seems to have an almost black ground color, assumes, however, in consequence of the rather thick pollen which covers it, a gray, entirely opaque, appearance; upon the middle of the thorax, lengthways, there are three pairs of large, black, opaque dots, the largest, anterior pair being on the transverse suture, the posterior pair immediately in front of the scutellum; upon the lateral margin of the thoracic dorsum, the humeral callus, the callus in front of the root of the wings, and a rather large spot above the root of the wings are not clothed with pollen and rather shining black. The ordinary bristles are black; the bristles in pairs, along the thoracic dorsum, are inserted upon the black dots, described above, except upon the anterior pair (where they may have been rubbed off in the described specimen). Scutellum shining black, remarkably swollen, but with a strong coarctation along the longitudinal middle line, and thus appearing bituberculate; each of the tubercles bears a strong bristle, below which a second one, much weaker, seems to have existed. Metathorax and pleura clay-yellow; the immaculate, glabrous abdomen is of the same color. Ovipositor flat, pointed, somewhat longer

than the last four abdominal segments taken together, of the
same color with the abdomen, or somewhat more reddish-yellow,
black at the extreme tip only, with scattered, blackish pile. Feet
dark clay-yellow. Wings rather large; their picture consists,
besides the yellowish-brown posterior corner, of four oblique yellowish-brown crossbands, with dark-brown borders; the brown
coloring which fills the posterior corner is separated from the
first band on the posterior half of the wing only, and that by an
oblique hyaline half band, lying in the third posterior cell, but
which does not reach the root of this cell; a small, square hyaline
spot near the humeral crossvein indicates the separation of the
yellowish-brown coloring of the base of the wing from the first
crossband; the first and second crossbands are completely coalescent before the third longitudinal vein; beyond this vein, they
are separated by a hyaline, very oblique band, which begins
below the basis of the comparatively long stigma and ends at the
tip of the fifth vein; the second and third brown bands are
separated by a narrow hyaline band, which crosses the whole
breadth of the wing, but is almost interrupted upon the second
longitudinal vein; the third and fourth brown bands, the latter
of which runs along the apex of the wing, are entirely coalescent
upon their anterior portion; their posterior portion is separated
by a narrow, hyaline, half band, which does not reach the third
longitudinal vein; upon the last section of the anterior margin
the brown coloring is somewhat spotted and shows here and there
a very small pale drop. The venation shows the following peculiarities; stigma rather long, third and fourth longitudinal veins
curved backwards towards their end; the very approximate
crossveins are very oblique and have their posterior ends nearer
to the apex of the wing than the anterior ones; the discal cell is
very much contracted towards the basis, and very much dilated
towards the end; the posterior angle of the anal cell is drawn
out in a sharp point; the third vein has scattered bristles upon
nearly its whole extent.

Hab. South Carolina (Zimmerman; Mus. Berol.).

Observation 1.—In the synonymy, I have doubtfully quoted
Trypheta quadrifasciata Macq. from Georgia. It is true that
Trypeta sarcinata is not recognizable in Macquart's description;
and if Macquart's figures had the least claim to faithfulness, the
synonymy of these two species would be out of question. But

with the knowledge we have of the character of Macquart's publications, we cannot but suspect that his species is after all nothing
but the one we have described above. The position and direction
of the crossveins, as well as the general pattern of the picture of
the wings, distinctly show a certain analogy to *T. sarcinata.* The
synonymy cannot be assumed as certain, as Macquart, in his
description, does not mention either the black dots on the thoracic
dorsum, or the black coloring and the very striking shape of the
scutellum of *T. sarcinata;* moreover his figure of the wing shows
important discrepancies in outline, venation, and picture. By
all means, should even the identity of these species be confirmed,
Macquart's name would be lost for it, as it has been preoccupied
by Meigen.

Observation 2.—The great approximation of the crossveins and
their oblique position indicate the relationship of the present
species with *Œdaspis.* It differs, however, in the peculiar shape
of the scutellum, the greater length of the wings, and the shape
of the discal cell, which is more attenuated towards the basis.
The pattern of the picture of the wings differs from that of the
European and American species, as far as they are known. For
this reason, I do not think that it would be well placed in the
genus *Œdaspis,* and I propose for it the formation of a new genus,
Perosyna. The position and direction of the crossveins, as well
as the picture of the wings (the second crossband of which, as in
Œdaspis, incloses both crossveins), remind of *Trypeta obliqua*
Say and the species related to it; however, the structure of these
latter species has too little in common with *T. sarcinata* to allow
their juxtaposition in the same genus.

16. T. discolor Lw. ♀. (Tab. X, f. 1.)—Lutea, abdomine nigro,
alarum fascia quatuor obliquis fuscanis, prima et secunda antice, tertia
et quarta postice connexis, vena longitudinali tertia setosa, venisque
transversis valde approximatis.

Clay-yellow, with a black abdomen; wings with four oblique infuscated
bands, the first and second of which are connected anteriorly, the third
and fourth posteriorly; the third longitudinal vein is beset with bristles;
crossveins very much approximated. Long. corp. 0.13; long. al. 0.15.

Syn. *Trypeta discolor* Loew, Monogr., I, p. 64. Tab. II, f. 1.

Hab. Cuba.

This pretty species is so closely allied to *T. obliqua* Say, that

generically they cannot be separated; the systematic position of
these two species and of some South American ones, related to
them, will be discussed below (see the last observation to the
next following species).

17. T. obliqua SAY. ♂ ♀. (Tab. XI, f. 14.)—Flava, thoracis dorso
postice atro-bipunctato, abdomine maris utrinque punctis atris in seriem
dispositis quatuor, feminæ quinque notato, alis hyalinis, fasciis quatuor
obliquis flavis et fusco-marginatis variegatis.

Yellow, with two deep-black punctiform dots on the posterior end of the
thoracic dorsum, and on each side of the abdomen with rows of four
similar dots in the male, and of five in the female; wings hyaline with
four oblique, yellow crossbands, bordered with brown. Long. corp.
0.12—0.14; long. al. 0.13—0.14.

SYN. *Trypeta obliqua* SAY, Journ. Acad. Phil., VI, p. 188, 3.
Trypeta obliqua LOEW, Monogr., I, p. 99.

Say's description, with the additions given by Baron Osten-
Sacken in these Monographs, Vol. I, p. 100, is sufficient for the
identification of this pretty species. I would only add that in all
the specimens examined by me, the males had four, the females
five black dots on each side of the abdomen, and that all the
specimens showed three deep black dots on the posterior part of
the pleura; one immediately above the middle coxæ, the second
above the hind ones, the third crescent-shaped, surrounding the
basis of the stem of the halteres. Ovipositor about as long as
the last two abdominal segments taken together, of the same
coloring as the abdomen, very little infuscated at the end.

Hab. Indiana (Say); Pennsylvania (Osten-Sacken; on *Vernonia* in August); Texas (Belfrage).

Observation 1.—I am in doubt whether *Trypeta obliqua* also
occurs in Brazil. The specimens generally labelled with this name
in the collections, seem to belong to a different, although closely
resembling species. They are usually somewhat larger than the
North American specimens of *T. obliqua* Say; the pile on the
whole body as well as the bristles on the third vein are somewhat
longer; moreover, I notice on the sides of the abdomen of the
male only two, of the female only three black dots; not fully
colored specimens do not show any trace of the three black spots
on the posterior part of the pleura, as they occur in *T. obliqua*;
better colored specimens have a trace of the two posterior spots

only. In all other respects the agreement with *T. obliqua* is so
great, that I do not dare to decide whether this Brazilian *Trypeta*
is a distinct species or merely a variety of *T. obliqua*. It is not
to be confounded with another Brazilian species, which is considerably larger, and of which I possess only the female. I let
its description follow :—

T. biseriata n. sp. ♀.—Trypeta obliqua Say, quam magnitudine
superat, simillima, sed capite proportione majore, pilis totius corporis
longioribus, pleuris immaculatis, alis minus pure hyalinis et cellula
basali secunda non hyalina, sed lutea distincta.

Very like T. obliqua Say, but larger, with a comparatively larger head,
longer pile on the whole body and unspotted pleura; wings of a less
pure hyaline; second basal cell not colorless, but yellow. Long. corp.
0.17—0.16 ; long. al. 0.22—0.23.

Coloring and picture of the body similar to the female of *T. obliqua* Say,
especially the two black dots upon the posterior portion of the thoracic
dorsum and the five black dots upon each side of the abdomen; the black
dots which *T. obliqua* has on the posterior portion of the pleura are
entirely wanting here. The pile on the whole body is much longer, black
upon the abdomen and especially striking upon the posterior edge of its
first segment. The head is proportionally larger. The wings are comparatively somewhat broader and their surface, especially towards the
posterior margin, is a little more dusky ; the first and third longitudinal
veins are beset with much longer bristles; the venation agrees, in the
main, with that of *T. obliqua*; the picture of the wings also is very much
alike, only the dark portions of it are less brownish-black and more
diluted ; the last two yellow bands are much less extensive ; the second
basal cell, which in *T. obliqua* is always hyaline, is altogether tinged with
clay-yellow here. The ovipositor is about as long as the last two abdominal segments taken together, and is broadly truncate at the end.
     Hab. Brazil.

     Observation 2.—*Trypeta discolor* and *obliqua* Say, as well as
the *T. biseriata* described in the preceding observation, are three
very closely resembling species, agreeing in all the principal
characters. They have no immediate relatives in Europe, with
which they could be placed in the same group; however, they
are somewhat allied to *Œdaspis*, as they have the direction of the
crossveins and the course of the second crossband, covering the
crossvein, in common with that group ; in almost all the other
important characters they show striking differences. I propose,
therefore, the formation of a new genus for them, which I call *Pla-*

piotoma. The characters of this genus are as follows: In the structure of the head and of its parts and of the scutellum it resembles *Acidia* very much; the scutellum, provided with four bristles, is convex, without appearing swollen; the shape of the abdomen likewise reminds one of the species of *Acidia*; the ovipositor also has a similar structure, but is longer than in *Acidia*, rather broadly truncate at the end. Wings rather large, with a distinctly convex anterior margin; the first and third veins are distinctly bristly; the crossveins are very much approximated; their posterior end is nearer to the apex of the wing than the anterior one; the last section of the fourth vein forms a bow, the convex side of which is turned towards the anterior margin, so that it distinctly diverges at the end from the end of the third vein, which is much more straight; the posterior corner of the anal cell is drawn out in an acute point. The picture of the wings consists of four very oblique crossbands, the second of which runs over both crossveins; the last crossband forms a border along the apex of the wing.

18. T. palpata Lw. ♂. (Tab. I, f. 9.)—Lutea, abdomine punctorum nigrorum seriebus quatuor picto; alae hyalinae, fasciis tribus sordide luteis, prima et secunda perpendicularibus et parallelis, tertia marginali et inde a praecedente usque ad cellulae posterioris secundae apicem pertinente.

Clay-yellow, with four longitudinal rows of black dots on the abdomen; wings hyaline with three crossbands of a dingy clay-yellow, the first two of which are perpendicular and parallel; the third forms a border along the margin of the wing, reaching from the second band to the end of the second posterior cell. Long. corp. 0.26—0.27; long. al. 0.26.

Syn. *Trypeta palposa* Loew, Monogr. I, p. 74, 9. Tab. II, f. 9.

The quoted description, drawn from an indifferently preserved male, is sufficient for the identification of the species. I will only notice here that in the first line of that description, *Cederh.*, must be read, instead of *Cederli*, and that on page 75, line 4, the expression "the edge of the tip" means the third band, which forms a border along the last portion of the anterior margin and the apex of the wing.

Hab. Northern Wisconsin River (Kennicott).

Observation.—The present species is a type of the genus *Trypeta*, in the narrower sense, as defined in my Monograph of the European *Trypetina*. It belongs in the group of those species which are related to *Trypeta arctii* Deg. and are abundantly represented in the European fauna. The most salient features of *Trypeta* sensu strict. are also the shape of the head, as well as the size and position of the rather broad palpi, which reach beyond the somewhat projecting anterior edge of the mouth. As these characters are easier to perceive than to describe in a few words, the present species deserves to be studied as a type of *Trypeta* in the narrower sense.

19. T. florescentiæ Lin. ♂ ♀.—Ex flavo-virescens, thoracis disco nigricante, postice breviter bifido, maculis alarum hyalinarum quatuor nigris, intermediis fere contiguis, aut in fasciam perpendicularem confuentibus.

Yellowish-green; the blackish color of the thoracic dorsum which does not reach the lateral margin is slightly bifid posteriorly; the hyaline wings show four black spots, the two intermediate ones of which are almost contiguous, or confluent in a perpendicular crossband. Long. corp. ♂ 0.17, ♀ cum terebra 0.20—0.21; long. al. 0.16.

Syn. *Musca florescentiæ* Linné, Syst. Nat. X, p. 601, 99.
Musca rejiciunda Fabricius, Ent. Syst. IV, p. 353, 169.
Tephritis punctata Fallen, Act. Holm. 1814, p. 167, 12.
Trypeta florescentiæ Meigen, Syst. Beschr. V, p. 321. Tab. XLVIII, f. 3.
Trypeta florescentia Loew, Germar's Zeitschr. V, p. 338. Tab. I, f. 16.
Trypeta florescentia Loew, Europ. Bohrfl. 59, 11. Tab. IX, f. 2.

Pale yellowish-green. Front, third antennal joint, and palpi usually of a much more vivid yellow. Eyes very much rounded. Face short, excavated; the anterior edge of the mouth distinctly projecting. Antennæ rather short; the longer bristle upon the second antennal joint but little conspicuous. Palpi comparatively long, reaching beyond the anterior edge of the oral opening. Thoracic dorsum blackish, with the exception, however, of the lateral border and of a cuneiform beginning of a middle stripe, starting from the posterior end, and which renders the black coloring bifid posteriorly. Scutellum immaculate, except on the under side of the lateral angles, and provided with four bristles. Metathorax black. Pleuræ more or less infuscated, sometimes rather blackish-brown, with a yellowish-green longitudinal stripe upon their upper side and another across the middle. Abdomen with four rows of conspicuous black spots; its pile, in both sexes, is usually whitish; however, along the posterior margin of the single segments, some black hairs are usually inserted; the last

segment of the abdomen of the male is often clothed with altogether black pile. Ovipositor red or brownish-red; at its basis
two, sometimes confluent, black spots are visible; the extreme
tip also is usually black; in length, the ovipositor hardly exceeds
the last two abdominal segments; it is not very much attenuated
towards the end and is beset with black or blackish pile. Feet
altogether pale clay-yellow. Wings hyaline, with a black or
rather blackish picture; the outlines of this picture are surrounded, in immature specimens, with a purer hyaline, in riper
ones, with a more whitish-hyaline hue; beyond this pellucid
border, the former kind of specimens show an indistinct, the latter
ones a more pronounced gray shade; the picture of the wings
consists of four spots, very variable as to their size and the intensity of their coloring; the first spot covers the stigma and usually
reaches only as far as the second longitudinal vein; the second
begins near the anterior margin immediately above the posterior
crossvein, thus leaving the tip of the marginal cell uncovered; it
becomes narrower and more faint posteriorly, thus reaching
more or less completely the anterior end of the posterior crossvein; the third spot usually appears as a broad border along the
posterior crossvein and is more or less coalescent with the second,
forming a perpendicular crossband; the fourth spot lies upon the
apex of the wing and is more or less triangular, as its inner limit
runs perpendicularly from the tip of the second vein to the fourth
vein, which limits it posteriorly; around the small crossvein and
in the environs of the root of the third vein there is a more or
less apparent, sometimes very distinct infuscation.

Hab. Canada (Mr. Provancher); common also in all Europe,
where the larva inhabits the flower-heads of different species of
Cirsium.

Observation 1.—Europe possesses, besides the variety of this
species, discovered by Mr. Provancher in Canada, another form,
distinguished by considerably larger and darker spots on the
wings. Specimens of both varieties might easily be taken for
different species; nevertheless, passages from one form to the
other occur in the picture of the wings, and I am not able to
discover between both the slightest plastic difference. In Germar's Zeitschrift, Part V, Tab. I, f. 15, I have figured a wing of
the first variety. An extreme instance of the second variety is
figured in my Monograph: *die Europäischen Bohrfliegen*, Tab.

IX, f. 2. Meigen's figure (Syst. Beschr. V, Tab. XLVIII, f. 3) likewise represents the latter variety. It is probable that it will also be found in America.

Observation 2.—The present species, as well as the preceding, belongs to the genus *Trypeta* in the narrower sense.

20. T. polita Loew. ♀. (Tab. X, f. 12.)—Atra, nitida, scutello tumido concolore, capite praeter faciem exalbidam pedibusque intercontibus, alis albido-hyalinis, macula basali atra, fasciisque tribus latissimis fusco-nigris, venis transversis valde approximatis.

Deep black, shining; the tumid scutellum is concolorous; the head, with the exception of the whitish face, and the feet clay-yellowish; the whitish-hyaline wings have a deep black spot upon the basis and three very broad deep black crossbands; the crossveins are very much approximated. Long. corp. ♀ 0.17—0.18, cum terebra 0.22; long. al. 0.17—0.18.

Syn. *Trypeta polita* Loew, Monogr. Vol. I, p. 77. Tab. II, f. 12.

Hab. Mississippi (Schaum); Washington, D. C.; New York; Connecticut (O. S.).[1]

Observation.—I have nothing to add to the above-quoted description. The systematic position of this species will be discussed in the second remark to the following species.

21. T. atra Lw. ♂ ♀. (Tab. XI, f. 17.)—Atra, nitida, scutello tumido, concolore, capite praeter faciem albidam, femorum apice, tibiis tarsisque luteis; alis albido-hyalinis, macula basali atra, fasciisque tribus latis fusco-atris, venis transversis valde approximatis.

Deep black, shining; the tumid scutellum concolorous; the head, with the exception of the whitish face, the tip of the femora, the tibiae, and the tarsi clay-yellow; the whitish-hyaline wings have a deep black spot upon the basis and three broad, deep brownish-black crossbands; crossveins very approximate. Long. corp. ♂ 0.12—0.13, ♀ 0.13—0.14, cum terebra 0.17—0.18; long. al. 0.13—0.15.

Syn. *Trypeta atra* Loew, Berl. Entom. Zeitschr. VI, p. 219, *Trypeta atra* Loew, Dipt. Amer. Sept. Cent. II, No. 89.

Deep black, shining. Front rather broad, of a vivid reddish-yellow; the ocellar triangle, as well as the little stripes descending from the vertex and bearing the uppermost bristles of the vertex, black, with a whitish-gray pollen; anteriorly, on the lateral

---

[1] This species produces the galls on *Solidago*, described by me in the Trans. Amer. Entomol. Soc. Vol. II, p. 301.　　　　O. S.

margin of the front there are on each side two black bristles.
Antennæ yellow; the blackish arista distinctly incrassated at the
basis. Face whitish; the anterior oral margin not at all projecting. Cheeks whitish, under the eyes with a more or less
brownish-red spot. Oral opening rather round. Proboscis
short. Palpi short, but broad, pale yellowish, with some short,
whitish pile. The upper and middle part of the occiput for the
most part black. The ordinary frontal bristles and some of the
bristles on the cheeks are black; otherwise the pile upon the
head consists of very scattered, bristle-like, or stubble-shaped
whitish hairs, which easily drop off. The upper side of the thorax
is shining black, very convex; besides the usual black bristles, it
shows white, bristle-like hairs, which border the denuded stripes.
Metathorax with white pollen; its lower part shining black;
pleuræ shining black, with some rare, stiff, bristle-like white hairs.
Abdomen short, shining black, at the root of the single segments
only somewhat glossy, in consequence of a very thin grayish pollen.
The scattered, very rough pile on the abdomen is whitish; only
the posterior margin of the segments and partly also the middle
line of the abdomen, have black hairs. Ovipositor stout, conical,
not flattened, shining black, beset with black pile, somewhat
longer than the last three abdominal segments taken together.
Coxæ and femora shining black, only the front femora on the
under side with a few black bristles; the tip of the femora, the
tibiæ, and the tarsi brownish-yellow or more reddish-yellow.
Wings whitish-hyaline, short and rather broad, with very much
approximated and very perpendicular crossveins. The extreme
root of the wings is whitish; next follows a rather large and
almost deep black spot, reaching as far as the axillary excision,
and not much beyond the basis of the small basal cells; the first
two crossbands, which follow next, are connected near the anterior
margin and strongly diverge towards the posterior one; the first
of them is even a little broader than the second and altogether
black, while the inner part of the second is partly brown; the
third band is separated from the second, near the anterior margin,
only by a very narrow hyaline spot; it borders the apex of the
wing far beyond the tip of the fourth longitudinal vein, but actually touches the margin of the wing only beyond the tip of the
third vein; its inner portion is brown anteriorly.

Hab. Mexico (coll. Winth.); New York (Osten-Sacken).

17

Observation 1.—The appended figure of the wing is taken from a Mexican specimen. The specimens which I received from New York differ from the former in being a little larger and in the circumstance that the face is somewhat more uneven; perhaps only in consequence of a stronger desiccation. Moreover, the last section of the fourth vein is a little less curved, and the posterior end of the first crossband is prolonged further along the margin towards the posterior corner of the wing. In all other respects the agreement is such that I cannot believe *T. atra* to be a different species. From *T. polita* the present species is easily distinguished by the much greater divergency of the second and third crossbands on the wings, by the absence of the pale gray border of the crossbands, which is always perceptible in *T. polita*, and by the black coloring of the femora; moreover, the anterior part of the lateral border of the front bears only two bristles in *T. atra*, while there are three in *T. polita*. The Brazilian species *T. nigerrima* Loew is very much like *T. atra*, nevertheless they are easily distinguished. In order to facilitate the comparison, I let the description of this species follow.

T. nigerrima Loew. ♀. (Tab. XI, f. 18.)—Atra, nitida, scutello tumido concolore, thoracis maculis lateralibus utrinque binis velutinis, abdomine fasciis albido-pollinosis ornato, capite flavo, pedibus ex-ferrugineo luteis, femoribus tamen posterioribus anticorumque litura ex-fusco nigris; alis albido-hyalinis, macula basali atra, fasciisque tribus fusco-atris, prima latissima, reliquis minus latis, venis transversis valde approximatis.

Deep black, shining; the tumid scutellum concolorous; thorax denuded with two velvet black spots on each side; abdomen with crossbands of white pollen; head yellow; feet brownish-yellow, the posterior femora and a stripe on the front femora brownish-black; wings whitish-hyaline with a deep black spot on the base and with three black crossbands, the first of which is very broad, the two others less so; crossveins very much approximated. Long. corp. 0.12—0.13; long. al. 0.12—0.13.

Syn. *Trypeta nigerrima* Loew, Berl. Ent. Zeitschr. VI, p. 218.
Trypeta nigerrima Loew, Dipt. Amer. Sept. Cent. II, p. 69.

Shining black. Head whitish-yellow; the rather narrow and steep front much darker yellow; the frontal bristles black. Antennae dark yellow, rather large, especially the elongated third joint, which has a rather sharp anterior corner. Arista apparently bare, rather slender, not incrassated towards its root, of a pale color. Face but very little excavated, and very little retreating; the anterior edge of the mouth distinctly projecting in the profile. Eyes elongated. Cheeks somewhat broad, with an infuscated spot near the inferior corner of the eye, and with white pile. Oral opening small, rounded. The rather broad palpi yellowish, beset with whitish pile. The short and not geniculate proboscis dark brown. Thorax shining black, with a metallic lustre in the middle; upon its lateral border, on each side, there are two large, opaque, velvet black spots, separated by the origin of the transverse suture, which is tinged with yellow. The nasal bristles are black; the number of pairs which were inserted on the thoracic dorsum cannot well be ascertained. Moreover, the surface of the thoracic dorsum shows remains of stiff, yellowish hairs, which seem to have bordered the broad, bare stripes and to have also been inserted on the posterior part of the broad middle line. Scutellum turgid, shining black, with four bristles. The upper part of the metathorax is black, as in most of the allied species; the lower portion is covered with white pollen, which does not quite reach its lower margin. Femora with whitish pollen and white hairs; the humeral corner, as well as a little stripe behind it, near the upper margin, are velvet black. Abdomen shining black; a thin whitish pollen covers the whole anterior part of the first segment, forms, upon the first, second, and third segments, a band along their posterior margin which is perceptibly expanded and sharply emarginate in the middle; the posterior margin of the fourth segment has a similar, although narrower, band. The scattered pile on the abdomen is black, gray at its basis, in part yellowish-white upon the last segment. The flat, shining black ovipositor is about as long as the three last abdominal segments taken together, and is beset with delicate, black pile. Feet reddish-yellow, the middle and hind femora, with the exception of the extreme root and of the tip, brownish-black; the front femora have a brownish-black stripe upon their upper side. Wings broad, the apex but little rounded, hyaline, somewhat whitish; at their basis there is a large black spot, reaching into the basal cells; besides, there are three black crossbands, entirely coalescent at the anterior margin of the wing and diverging posteriorly; the first of them, which is by far the broadest and is rather perpendicular, runs from the stigma, over the basis of the discal and of the third posterior cells, towards the posterior margin of the wing; the second band is the narrowest, and runs from the stigma over both crossveins, and hence, obliquely, towards the posterior margin; the third band starts from the stigma and follows the anterior margin and the apex, as far as the tip of the fourth vein, but, nevertheless, remains separated from the costal vein by a narrow, irregular, hyaline interval, which extends almost to its very end; near the submarginal cell, this interval is a little expanded and includes a penciliform dot, placed near the third vein; the first and second longitudinal veins are a little more distant from the anterior margin than in most of the related species; both crossveins are very approximate; the third longitudinal vein is beset with short bristles.

Hab. Brazil (coll. Winthem).

Observation 2.—*T. polita* and *atra*, as well as *T. nigerrima* are closely related in their organization. Among the European *Trypetæ*, the species of the genus *Oedaspis* stand next to them, especially when this genus is confined to *Oedaspis multifasciata* Loew and its next congeners, at the exclusion of *Oed. Wiedemanni* Meig. and *trauxiana* Costa. The American species differ from the above-mentioned European ones (*multifasciata* Lw., *dichotoma* Lw., and *flava* Loew) in several characters, which they have in common; the most striking of these are: 1. The rather long, stubble-shaped pile; 2. The longer and more pointed ovipositor; 3. The different picture of the wings. The latter difference will be sufficiently apparent, when the figures which I give of the wings of *polita*, *atra*, and *nigerrima* are compared with the figures of the wing of *T. multifasciata*, produced in the *Europ. Bohrfliegen*, Tab. VI, f. 2. The pictures of *T. flava* and *dichotoma* agree, in their general features, with that of *multifasciata*. These differences of the three North American species are not of sufficient importance to require the establishment of a new genus for them, and I have not the slightest hesitation in placing them in the genus *Oedaspis*, in the narrower sense, defined above.

22. T. gibba n. sp. ♀.—Atra, nitida, scutello tumido, concolore, facie albicante, pedibus subbadiis; alæ albido-hyalinæ, macula basali atrâ fasciaque tribus latis ferro-atris, venis transversis valde approximatis, cellulâ marginali per venulam transversalem adventitiam divisotâ.

Deep black, shining; the turgid scutellum of the same color; face whitish; feet chestnut-brownish; wings whitish-hyaline, with a deep black spot at the basis, and with three brownish-black crossbands, very much approximated crossveins, and a supernumerary crossvein dividing the marginal cell. Long. corp. 0.13, cum terebrâ 0.17; long. al. 0.14 —0.15.

Very like the three preceding species and closely allied to them, nevertheless, distinguished in some peculiar plastic characters. Deep black, shining. Front conspicuously broad, of an opaque, dirty, brownish, more reddish-brown on the sides; the four bristles on the posterior part of the vertex, the bristles near the ocelli, the four bristles crowded together and inserted on the small stripes running from the vertex towards the front, finally two bristles on each side, near the lateral frontal border, are all black; the latter two are inserted, one very high up, the other very low

down, so that the distance between them is remarkably large.
Otherwise the head is beset with almost bristle-like white stubble-
shaped pile. The very large and sharply defined frontal lunule,
the face, including the cheeks, and the lower half of the occiput
are whitish; the upper part of the latter blackish, although
covered with whitish pollen. The perpendicular diameter of the
eyes has about double the length of the horizontal one; nevertheless, the cheeks are remarkably broad; a brownish stripe runs
from the lower corner of the eye perpendicularly towards the
edge of the mouth; the hairs, inserted upon its lower end, are
brownish-black or black. The first two antennal joints are clay-
yellowish; the third joint is dark brown, rather large, short-oval
in outline; arista bare, not incrassated at the basis, black. Oral
opening larger than in the preceding species; its transverse
diameter comparatively larger; proboscis and palpi short, brown.
The very convex thorax and the turgid scutellum are deep black,
shining, with a very weak metallic, violet reflection; the remarkably broad lateral stripes and the anterior end of the broad middle
stripe are bare. The lateral stripes are bordered with coarse,
yellowish, stubble-shaped pile, and the posterior two-thirds of the
middle stripe, besides being covered with white pollen, are
densely beset with similar hairs. The ordinary bristles of the
thoracic dorsum are black, and more numerous than usual, as
there are four pairs of them along the longitudinal middle line,
the anterior pair being inserted immediately in front of the
transverse suture. The shining black metathorax has, under the
swelling lying immediately under the scutellum, a crossband of
thick white pollen. The pleura show upon the greater part of
their upper half, a thin, whitish-gray pollen, and are everywhere
beset with stubble-like white hairs. The abdomen seems to be
covered everywhere with a thin gray dust, which is somewhat
more dense and more whitish-gray upon the posterior border of
the single segments; its rather long stubble-like pile is white.
The comparatively long and pointed ovipositor is deep black,
shining, and beset with short, fine, black pile. Feet chestnut-
brownish. Wings short, rather broad in proportion to their
length; the altogether black venation is very similar to that of
the immediately preceding species, except that the comparatively
broad marginal cell is divided in two halves by a perpendicular
crossvein, which touches the costa at a point perceptibly nearer

from the tip of the first than from that of the second vein. I take
this crossvein to be a constant character of the species, as it
exists on both wings of my specimen, and as several closely allied
Trypetidæ, for instance *Gonypl. Wiedemanni* and *Caprom. cæsu-
riana*, have it likewise, although incompletely developed. The
picture of the wings is not unlike that of *T. atra*, in its design
as well as in its coloring; the black spot upon the basis of the
wings does not cover their extreme root, and extends, on the
anterior margin, only very little beyond the humeral crossvein; it
hardly reaches beyond the first longitudinal vein, and dissolves in
several radiating points, which occupy the longitudinal middle of
the marginal and of the three basal cells and almost come in contact (except the hindmost), with similar rays, meeting them from
the opposite side and emitted by the first crossband; the first
black crossband has almost the same position as in the three preceding species, but it is much narrower, especially towards its
end, which reaches the posterior margin; its interior does not
show any brownish tinge. The second band runs over both crossveins, exactly as it does in those three species, and is connected
with the first on the anterior margin in the same manner as this
is the case in *T. atra*; the stigma, lying within this connecting
portion, is very short; the velus surrounding it have, on the
inner side, a very narrow hyaline border; the interior of the
second band is for the most part brownish. The last black band
begins in the marginal cell somewhat beyond the supernumerary
crossvein in this cell, and reaches some distance beyond the end
of the fourth vein; as far as this vein, it is separated from the
margin of the wing by a narrow hyaline border, which somewhat
projects on the inside on the second and third veins; beyond the
fourth vein the band comes in immediate contact with the margin
of the wing; the inside of this band is brownish upon the anterior two-thirds of its course.

Hab. Texas (Belfrage).

Observation. —The differences between the present species and
the three preceding ones are evident: they consist in an aberrant
arrangement of the bristles of the front and of the thoracic dorsum,
in the size and shape of the third antennal joint, and in the presence of the crossvein, dividing the marginal cell; nevertheless
the agreement between those species in most of the other plastic
characters, in the shape of the body and in the picture of the

wings, is convincing enough to remove all doubt as to its location in the genus *Œdaspis.*

23. T. cingulata Lw. ♂ ♀. (Tab. X, f. 11.)—Nigra, capite pedibusque luteis, thoracis margine laterali scutelloque præter margines
laterales et antennam diluto flavis, margine postico segmentorum abdominalium singulorum albido; alæ hyalinæ, macula parva apicis fus-
colisque quatuor fusco-nigris, harum duabus primis postice abbreviatis et
liberis, duabus ultimis integris et antice conjunctis.

Black, head and feet clay-yellow; lateral border of the thorax and the
scutellum, the latter with the exception of the anterior and lateral
border, light yellow; abdominal segments whitish on the posterior
border; wings hyaline; a small spot upon the apex and four crossbands
brownish-black; the first two bands abbreviated posteriorly and not
connected; the two posterior bands are entire and connected on the
anterior margin. Long. corp. 0.14—0.22; long. al. 0.15—0.20.

Syn. *Trypeta cingulata* Loew, Monogr. 1, 76. Tab. II, f. 11.

Hab. Middle States; Long Branch, N. J., in July (Osten-
Sacken).

· *Observation.*—The description given by me in the first part of
these Monographs will easily help to identify this species. I
have nothing to add to it, but must call attention to the great
variation in the size of different specimens. The smallest ones
which I possess, are without exception males. *T. cingulata* is
closely allied to the European species of *Rhagoletis,* especially to
R. flavicincta Loew; its systematic location is, therefore, not
doubtful.

24. T. tabellaria Fitch. ♀.—Atra, capite, trochanteribus, tibiis
tarsisque diluto luteis, thoracis margine laterali scutelloque præter
margines laterales albis; segmentorum abdominalium singulorum margine postico exalbido; alæ puro hyalinæ, fasciis quatuor latis nigris,
duabus primis postice, duabus ultimis antice cohærentibus.

Deep black; head, second joint of the coxæ, tibiæ, and tarsi yellow;
lateral border of the thorax and scutellum, with the exception of the
anterior and the lateral borders, white; the posterior borders of the
abdominal segments whitish; wings of a pure hyaline, with four broad,
black crossbands, of which the first two are connected at the posterior,
the last two at the anterior margin. Long. corp. 0.14—0.15; long. al.
0.14—0.15.

Syn. *Tephritis tabellaria* Fitch, First Report, p. 66.

Shining black; head yellowish; occiput black, with a pale yellow border; front broad, more bright yellow; only the spot upon which the ocelli are placed and the small, very narrow stripes, which run down from the vertex upon the front, are of a blackish color; the usual frontal bristles are black. Antenne of a vivid ochro-yellow; their last joint is elongated-oval, obtuse at the end; arista blackish, with a hardly perceptible pubescence. Oral opening rather large, somewhat longer than broad; its anterior edge drawn up, but not projecting in the profile. Proboscis and palpi short, brown, the latter more clay-yellow towards the tip. The thoracic dorsum shows two longitudinal stripes, rather distant from each other, somewhat abbreviated posteriorly and covered with a thin, white pollen; upon the anterior part of the thoracic dorsum a similar pollen covers not only the lateral between the stripes, but also extends beyond them. The whole of this pollen, however, is but little conspicuous and seems to be easily rubbed off. The humeral angle and a stripe running from it towards the root of the wings, are white. The flat scutellum, with the exception of its lateral border, has the same color. Metathorax without any pollen, altogether shining deep black. The usual bristles of the thorax and the four bristles of the scutellum are deep black. The other hairs on the thoracic dorsum are very short and delicate. Abdomen shining black; its first two segments are more opaque, being clothed with a brownish-black pollen. The first three segments, upon their posterior margin, have a crossband of a whitish pollen. The very short and soft hairs upon the abdomen are black; the paler crossbands upon the posterior border of the first three segments show some whitish hairs; the bristles upon the sides of the intermediate segments and upon the rather large last segment are black. Ovipositor shorter than the last abdominal segment, broad at the basis, much narrower at the end, shining black and with a black pubescence. Second coxal joint pale clay-yellowish. Femora black, only the extreme tip yellowish-brown; tibiæ and tarsi pale clay-yellowish; the former somewhat more brownish at the basis; the bristles upon the upper side of the hind tibiæ are remarkably short. Wings pure hyaline, almost whitish hyaline, with four entire black crossbands, the first of which of a medium breadth, the three others very broad. The first band is somewhat oblique and begins on the humeral crossvein; the second is perpendicular and begins on the stigma; both converge posteriorly and coalesce quite a distance from the posterior margin, so that the cuneiform hyaline space between them does not reach beyond the anterior angle of the basis of the third posterior cell. The third black band runs over the posterior crossvein and is parallel to the second band, so that between both there is a somewhat irregularly limited hyaline crossband, which is perceptibly dilated between the third longitudinal vein and the anterior margin; it reaches the latter immediately behind the stigma; the posterior end of the third band shows some inclination to coalesce with the second band near the posterior margin. The fourth band completely coalesces with the third between the costa and the second longitudinal vein, and follows the margin of the wing some distance beyond the end of the fourth longitudinal vein; between the tips of the second and fourth veins, however, there is a rather broad hyaline interval between it and the margin; beyond this point, it touches the margin completely.

Hab. New York (Dr. A. Fitch); Canada (Mr. Provancher).

Observation.—In the first volume of the Monographs I expressed the supposition that the *Tephritis tabellaria* of Fitch may not be a *Trypeta* at all, but an *Ortalida*; this supposition, however, proved to be erroneous; it is a *Trypetida*, belonging to the genus *Rhagoletis*.

25. T. pomonella WALSH. ♀.—Fusco-nigra, capite, trochanteribus, femorum apice, tibiis, tarsisque luteis, thoracis margine laterali, scutelloque praeter margines laterales et antiquum albis, abdominis colore in plorum vergente, segmentorum marginibus penticis confertim albidopollinosis, terebra latissima, sed brevi; alis hyalinae, fasciis quatuor nigris, prima subbasali, reliquis tribus integris, antice conjunctis, postice divergentibus.

Brownish-black; head, second joint of the coxa, tip of the femora, tibia, and tarsi clay-yellowish; lateral margin of the thorax and scutellum, the latter with the exception of its basis and of its lateral margins, white; abdomen more pitch-brown, with crossbands of white pollen on the posterior margins of the segments; ovipositor very broad, but short; wings hyaline, with four black crossbands, the first of which lies near the basis, the last three are connected near the anterior margin and divergent towards the posterior one. *Long. corp.* 0.17, *cum terebra* 0.19; *long. al.* 0.17.

Syn. *Trypeta pomonella* WALSH, First Rep. Illin. etc., p. 29–33, f. 2.

I possess but a single specimen of this species. Its coloring is not fully developed, although otherwise its preservation is perfect. It is black, with a distinct brownish tinge; its abdomen is more pitch-brown and rather shining. Head pale yellowish, with a narrow dark yellow front and more ochre-yellow antennæ; the third joint of the latter is narrow and rather long, rounded at the end; the slender arista is dark brown, with a short, although distinctly discernible pubescence. The usual frontal bristles are black; behind the ocelli, however, near the lateral margin, two shorter, whitish bristles are placed. Oral opening large, broader than long. Palpi and proboscis pale yellowish, with a pale pubescence; the former do not project beyond the anterior edge of the mouth, the flaps of the latter somewhat prolonged. The thoracic dorsum shows four rather narrow longitudinal stripes, formed by a whitish pollen; these stripes, arranged in pairs, are confluent anteriorly; the outside stripes are moderately abbreviated before the posterior margin of the thorax; the inside ones reach only as far as the anterior pair of bristles, inserted upon the longitudinal middle of the thorax; each of the bristles of this pair is placed between the end of the corresponding inside stripe and the outside one; the inside stripes are separated by a broad dark interval, which shows the shining brownish-black color of the remainder of the thorax. When the thorax is viewed from the front side, the light falling in from behind, the pollinose stripes appear somewhat more broad; the interval between the inside stripes appears somewhat narrower and a little more opaque; at the same time, this point of view discloses upon the outside stripes and upon the margin of the inside ones, alongside of them, some short, snow-white pile, while the remaining pile of the thoracic dorsum is black. The humeral callosity and a stripe running from it to the root of the wing, is white. The rather flat scutellum is white, blackish on the sides and at the base. The bristles of the thorax and the four bristles of the scutellum are black. The first four segments of the abdomen have each, on the posterior margin, a rather uniformly broad crossband, formed by whitish pollen; the last segment, which has no such band, is paler brown along the posterior margin. The comparatively scattered and not very short pile on the abdomen is black; it is white only on the pale crossband on the posterior part of the first segment. The bristles

on the sides of the middle and of the last segments are black.
Ovipositor very short, about once and a half the length of the
last abdominal segment, very conspicuously broad, not much
attenuated towards the end, very broadly truncate and somewhat
convex; its coloring is a shining brownish-black or black; the
pubescence is black. In agreement with the unusual breadth of
the ovipositor, the last abdominal segment is also very broad,
which causes the whole abdomen to have a peculiar shape. The
second coxal joint yellowish; posterior femora black with a clay-
yellow tip; front femora clay-yellow, with a large, broad, brownish-black stripe upon the hind side; tibiæ and tarsi clay-yellowish,
the tip of the latter dark brown. Hind tibiæ on the upper side
beset with rather long bristles.

Hab. Illinois (Walsh); the larva, originally feeding upon the
fruit of a *Cratægus*, is now frequently found upon the fruits of
the apple-tree, which it damages.

Observation.—The next relatives of *T. pomonella* are found in
a series of South American species, only a single one of which,
as far as I know, has been previously described; it is to be found
in Macquart's *Diptères Exotiques,* Suppl. IV, p. 288, Tab.
XXVI, f. 15, under the name of *Urophora scutellaris.* It is not
an *Urophora* however, and moreover, the name of *scutellaris*
cannot be maintained, as Wiedemann has previously used it for
another species. The species may, therefore, be called *Trypeta
Macquartii.* Macquart's figure shows, that this Brazilian species
differs in the picture of its wings from the species of *Rhagoletis*
previously described, and that, in this respect, it is more like the
species of *Acidia.* The structure of its body shows a corresponding approach to the species of this latter genus, while, on
the other hand, coloring and picture of the body are most strikingly like those of *Rhagoletis.* As this species is also very like
the North American *Rhagoletis* in the structure of its body, the
question arises whether it is better to place it in the genus *Acidia*
or in *Rhagoletis.* I prefer the latter course, because we thus
facilitate the generic determination of the allied species. *Trypeta
pomonella,* as has already been mentioned above, is among the
number of such species, the picture of its wings being very like
that of *T. Macquartii.* It is true that it differs not inconsiderably
from *T. Macquartii* in the greater length of the third antennal
joint, the considerable size and breadth of the oral opening, and

the strikingly large transverse diameter of the short ovipositor;
but, like *Trypeta Macquartii*, it agrees with the true species of
Rhagoletis in the coloring and in the picture of the body, so that
I prefer, for the present, to leave it in that genus. It may be
objected that, in this case, I lay a greater stress upon peculiarities of the coloring and mere differences of *habitus* than upon
plastic characters. In answer to this objection I may state that
I fully appreciate the value of plastic differences in matters of
generic grouping of species, but that the knowledge of the exotic
Trypetæ, as well as the existing descriptions of them, are not
sufficient for their generic distribution upon plastic characters
only. Most descriptions mention but very little about these
characters, the more so as in most cases they have to be drawn
from a few indifferently preserved specimens, which do not allow
a sufficiently clear view of such characters. And thus it happens
that peculiarities of coloring and other habitual characters become
in many cases very useful for the generic distribution of exotic
Trypetæ, especially in cases where the only available plastic
characters are of a very delicate nature and hence more difficult
to perceive. It is true that the exotic species thus treated are
merely *grouped*, and not systematized; but this grouping in itself
is a progress towards the determination of the species, and is one
of the usual steps towards a systematic distribution.

26. T. insecta Lw. ♀. (Tab. X, f. 8.)—Thorace nigro, capite,
abdomine pedibusque luteis, alarum nigrarum incisuris marginalibus,
guttulisque inter venarum longitudinalium tertiam et quartam tribus
vel quatuor pellucidis, venâ longitudinali tertiâ nudâ, setis scutelli
duabus.

Thorax black; head, abdomen, and feet clay-yellow; wings black, with
hyaline indentations along the margin and with three or four hyaline
drops between the third and fourth veins; the third vein not bristly;
scutellum with two bristles. Long. corp. 0.14; long. al. 0.14.

Syn. *Trypeta insecta* Loew, Monogr. I, p. 72. Tab. II, f. 8.

Hab. Cuba (Poey). [Hayti; P. R. Thier.—O. S.]

Observation 1.—*T. insecta* belongs to the typical species of
the genus *Aciura*, the scutellum of which bears only two bristles.
The picture of the wings of this genus is characteristic.

Observation 2.—Another *Trypeta* of the same genus occurs
in Brazil, which may be easily mistaken for *Trypeta insecta.* I
prefer, therefore, to describe it here :—

T. phœnicura n. sp. ♂ ♀. (Tab. XI, f. 12.)—Nigra, capite pedibusque ochraceis, alarum nigrarum incisuris marginalibus guttulisque inter venas longitudinales tertiam et quartam tribus pellucidis, venâ longitudinali tertiâ nudâ, setis scutelli duabus.

♂. Abdomen ex ferrugineo rufum, segmento ultimo nigro.
♀. Abdomen nigrum, basi ferrugineâ, terebrâ latâ late aurantiacâ.

Black, head and feet ochreous-yellow; wings black, with hyaline indentations along the margin and with three hyaline drops between the third and fourth longitudinal veins; the third longitudinal vein is not bristly; the scutellum has two bristles.

♂. Abdomen ferruginous, its last segment black.
♀. Abdomen black, ferruginous at the basis; the broad ovipositor is of a vivid orange-yellow. Long. corp. ♂ 0.14, ♀ 0.15—0.16; long. al. 0.14.

Black; head of an impure ochre-yellow; the occiput alone mostly blackish; front narrow, especially anteriorly; frontal bristles black. Eyes very large, cheeks very narrow. Face short, concave; nevertheless, the anterior oral edge not projecting in the profile. The antennæ reach down to the oral edge; their third joint is rounded at the tip; the blackish arista is long and slender, apparently bare. Oral opening of medium size, rounded; proboscis not geniculate. The thorax and the two-bristly scutellum are black, their short pile yellowish-white, their bristles rather black; the somewhat rounded abdomen of the male is of a dirty ferruginous color (in living specimens its color may be purer); its last segment is black. The extent of the black color is greater in the female abdomen, the first segment, the basis of the second, and the anterior corners of the third alone, being ferruginous. The short pile of the abdomen is paler, almost yellowish in the male, somewhat brown in the female; on the posterior border of the last segment of the abdomen of the female there are some black hairs. The flattened, comparatively broad ovipositor, attenuated towards its end, has a shining surface; its color is a very bright orange-yellow, the tip alone shows a narrow black border; its short pubescence is pale. Coxæ and feet ochreous-yellow; the extreme tip of the posterior femora is somewhat blackish. Wings comparatively long and narrow, towards the end somewhat less broad and less obtuse than those of T. insecta, black, with a hyaline picture; near the costa, anterior to the stigma, there are three small hyaline spots, the first anterior to the humeral crossvein, the two others in the costal cell; immediately beyond the stigma, which is altogether black, there are two conspicuous triangular hyaline spots, which, with their pointed end, do not quite reach the third longitudinal vein; on the posterior margin of the wing there are six hyaline indentations, the last of which alone ends in a point; the first two are connected with the almost hyaline posterior angle of the wing, reach as far as the fifth longitudinal vein, and are separated by a much broader black band than the other indentations; the two following indentations cross beyond the fifth vein, the first below the small crossvein, the second immediately before the end of the discal cell; the fifth indentation follows the outer side of the great crossvein (which runs obliquely backwards); the sixth, separated from the preceding by a black band of moderate breadth, is almost triangular; the three small hyaline dots between the third and fourth veins lie, the first under the stigma, the second between the two crossveins, near the fourth vein, the third above the last of the hyaline excisions along the posterior margin. *Hab.* Brazil.

The coloring of the abdomen of *T. inserta* and *phœnicura* seems to be somewhat variable, and hence not to be relied on as a specific character; the more marked are the differences in the outline and picture of the wings.

27. T. pœcilogastra n. sp. ♂.—Lutea, scutello setis sex instructo, abdomine nigro-variegato, alis latis fuscis, inæqualiter limpido-guttatis, venisque longitudinalibus primâ, tertiâ et quintâ coufertim nigro-setosis.

Clay-yellow, scutellum with six bristles, abdomen variegated with black; wings broad, blackish-brown, with unevenly distributed hyaline drops; the first, third, and fifth longitudinal veins densely beset with black bristles. Long. corp. 0.21; long. al. 0.24.

Clay-yellow; the color of head and antennæ more ochre-yellow; the last joint of the latter elongated, rounded at the tip; the long brown arista beset with a very short pubescence. The face is rather retreating nearly as far as the vicinity of the anterior edge of the mouth; the latter is somewhat turned upwards and abruptly projecting when seen in profile. The vertical diameter of the eyes has double the length of the horizontal one; hence, the cheeks are very narrow. Proboscis tumid; palpi rather broad and short, although they project a little beyond the anterior edge of the mouth. The usual frontal bristles are black. The two pairs of bristles on the middle line of the thoracic dorsum are weak and of a blackish-brown color, like the other thoracic bristles; the anterior pair is at an unusual distance behind the transverse suture. Scutellum rather flat, with six brown bristles. Metathorax with two brown longitudinal stripes. Abdomen with a complicated black picture, the only visible portions of the ground color being an uninterrupted middle line of almost trapezoidal spots, and on both sides of it, two rows of other spots; the spots of the outer row lie on the anterior angles of the single segments; those of the inner row on the anterior borders of the segments. Feet pale clay-yellowish. Wings broad, blackish-brown, with large and small hyaline dots, unequally distributed; the costal cell is pale brown between the extreme basis and a trifle beyond the humeral crossvein; next follows upon the costa a square brown spot, and then a square hyaline space, somewhat encroaching upon the stigmatical cell, so as to include the end of the auxiliary vein, which runs perpendicularly towards the margin of the wing; the stigmatical cell is otherwise tinged with blackish-brown and has, close to the anterior margin, two hyaline drops; immediately beyond the tip of the first longitudinal vein, near the anterior margin, there is a hyaline drop, reaching as far as the second longitudinal vein, the largest in the whole picture of the wing; in the vicinity of the apex of the wing the drops are larger than in the middle and more close together; so that a row of dots, reaching from the tip of the second vein to the posterior angle of the second posterior cell, and moreover four dots along the margin of the wing, may be discerned; among the latter, the first lies in the submarginal cell and is connected with a little drop behind the third vein; the second lies at the extreme tip of the wing; the last two in the second posterior cell; a second group of larger drops lies in the third posterior cell, immediately below the stigma; it consists of four drops, between which the black ground color is more or less faint, and of two other drops on the anterior side of the fifth vein; between this group of drops and the fifth longitudinal vein, there is, near the margin of the wing, a single larger drop; the posterior angle of the wing is brownish-gray, with several rather large limpid drops; the middle of the wing shows only small and isolated drops. The first, third, and fifth longitudinal veins are very closely beset with rather strong bristles; the second is strongly curved; the third and fourth diverge towards their end; the small crossvein is but little beyond the middle of the very broad discal cell, and the posterior crossvein has a very steep position; the anal cell is drawn out in a narrow and very long lobe.

Hab. Cuba (Gundlach).

Observation.—The six bristles upon the scutellum, as well as the dense bristles upon the first, third, and fifth longitudinal veins, distinguish *T. poecilogastra* from all the following species, provided with a reticulate picture of the wings. It is very

closely allied to the species of *Hexachæta*, in which, however, as
far as I know them, the fifth vein has bristles upon the basis only,
while in the present species the bristles almost reach to the tip.
For this reason, as well as on account of the different character
of the picture of the wings, I do not deem it convenient to place
it in the genus *Hexachæta*. Whether Mr. Saunders's genus
Dasyneura would better answer for it, I am unable to say, as I
have not been able to procure the publication which contains it.
For the present therefore I set this species up as the type of a
new genus, which I call *Blepharoneura*.

28. T. contudimen n. sp. (Tab. XI, f. 13.)—Ex luteo fusca, capite,
thoracis dorso, pedibusque luteis, terebra duobus ultimis abdominis
segmentis semel sumtis paulo longiore; alis valde dilatatis, e nigro
fusca, strigis duabus hyalinis inde a margine cellulæ posterioris
secundæ usque ad venam longitudinalem tertiam ascendentibus, primo
limbi costalis dimidio grosse nigro maculato, disco alarum guttulis
minutis pellucidis confertim asperso.

Yellowish-brown, head, thoracic dorsum, and feet clay-yellow; the ovipositor only a little longer than the last two abdominal segments taken
together; wings very broad, blackish-brown; two hyaline indentations
reach from the posterior side of the second posterior cell to the third
longitudinal vein; the anterior half of the region along the costa shows
a number of large, black spots; the central portion of the wing is
occupied by many small, hyaline drops. Long. corp. cum terebra 0.21;
long. al. 0.19.

A species very much resembling the *T. latipennis* Wied., but
differing in the smaller size and the less minute dots on the
central portion of the wing. The coloring of the body is yellowish-brown, but may be somewhat darker in fully colored specimens. The ground color of a great part of the upper side of
the thorax is blackish, but very much concealed under a thick
clay-yellow pollen. Front opaque, of a moderate breadth, still
narrower anteriorly; the usual frontal bristles are brown. Eyes
large, elongated; cheeks very narrow, with much pile; face short,
descending rather perpendicularly, but distinctly excavated under
the antennæ; the anterior edge of the mouth not projecting.
Antennæ ochre-yellow, of a medium length, but, owing to the
shortness of the face, reaching to the anterior edge of the mouth;
the third joint has a rather rounded anterior corner; the moderately long arista thin and bare. The middle of the thoracic

dorsum shows traces of a pair of bristles. Scutellum but little
convex, provided with four bristles. Metathorax blackish with
a grayish-yellow pollen. The color of the pleuræ, in the described
specimen, does not differ much from that of the remainder of the
body; it seems, nevertheless, that, in more fully colored specimens, a considerable portion of the pleuræ may be blackish; they
are thickly clothed with a clay-yellow pollen; the pile and the
bristles upon them, like those on thorax and scutellum, are yellowish-brown. The abdomen shows a trace of four dark longitudinal stripes, formed by very much faded blackish spots; the pile
upon it is somewhat shorter and rather blackish upon the anterior
half of the single segments; upon their posterior half, it is somewhat longer and almost whitish; yet the long bristles on the
posterior border of the last segment are blackish-brown. The
flat ovipositor, which in the allied *T. latipennis* Wied. equals
the last four abdominal segments in length, is but a little longer
here than the last two segments taken together; it is of the same
color with the abdomen, somewhat blackened at the root and tip,
and beset everywhere with short blackish pile. Feet brownish-
ochre yellow. Wings very broad, very like those of *T. latipennis*
in outline, venation, and picture; proportionally, however, they
are not quite as broad and not quite as convex on the anterior
margin; upon the apical third of the wing there are three crossbands, connected anteriorly and separated by narrow, hyaline
intervals, beginning at the posterior margin; the first band is
contiguous, on its outer side, to the posterior crossvein, and
expands across it near its posterior end; the second runs across
the middle of the second posterior cell, the third borders the apex
of the wing. The remaining portion of the surface of the wing,
beyond the second longitudinal vein, has a somewhat darker
brownish tinge, and is covered with a multitude of small hyaline
drops, which partly coalesce into longitudinal rows, and in some
places, as at both ends of the small crossvein and here and there
on the longitudinal veins, leave unbroken brown spots. Upon
the posterior margin, there is a broad brown border, bearing a
few larger, but not very well-defined drops, which are also less
hyaline than those of the centre of the wing; on the posterior
angle of the wing the border is somewhat faint. The brownish-
black stigma coalesces with a spot of the same color immediately
behind it, which spot crosses but little the second longitudinal

18

vein; two large spots of the same color lie in the exterior costal
cell and fill out a large portion of it; a double spot of the same
color is in the marginal cell immediately beyond the stigma;
finally, there are two large spots of the same kind on the second
longitudinal vein, the one upon its root, the other below the
double spot in the marginal cell. The basis of the exterior costal
cell is irregularly reticulate with very small drops. A small hyaline spot is situated between the double spot of the marginal cell
and the end of this cell, filled out by the common origin of the
three crossbands which occupy the apex of the wing. The third
longitudinal vein is distinctly bristly, gently curved forward before
its end and as gently backwards; posterior crossvein long, but
not as long as in *T. latipennis* Wied.

Hab. Cuba (Otto); in the Berlin Museum.

Observation.—The present species forms, with *T. latipennis*
Wied. and a group of related species from South America, an
easily recognizable genus, very well characterized by the breadth
of its large wings, their outline, which reminds of *Phasia*, and
their peculiar picture. These species also have the structure of
the head and the bristly third vein in common. I adopt for this
genus, apparently exclusively American, the name of *Acrotaenia*,
in allusion to the most striking peculiarity of the picture of the
wings.   •

29. T. sparsa Wied. ♂ ♀. (Tab. X, f. 13.)—Fusca, ala latissima,
subrotundata, nigra, albido-guttulata, apice albido-marginata ornata.

Brown; wings very broad, almost round, black, with whitish drops, and
the apex margined with white. Long. corp. ♂ 0.15—0.27; ♀ cum
terabra 0.19—0.30; long. al. 0.16—0.26.

Syn. *Trypeta sparsa* Wiedemann, Auss. Zweifl. II, p. 492.
Trypeta calliptera Say, Journ. Acad. Phil. VI, p. 187, 5.
Platystoma latipennis Macquart, Dipt. Exot. II, 3, p. 200. Tab. XXVI,
f. 8.
Acinia semiobscurans Fitch, First Report, 67.
Trypeta sparsa Loew, Monographs, etc., I, p. 78. Tab. II, f. 13.

Hab. Northern Wisconsin River (Kennicott); Texas (Bol-
frage).

Observation I.—*Trypeta sparsa* Wied. is either a very variable species, both in its size and in the shape of its wings, or else
several species are mixed up here, which, owing to the insuffi-

ciency of my materials, I am unable to distinguish. The
description given in the first volume of these Monographs refers
to the specimen from Northern Wisconsin River. Another specimen from the same locality, much smaller and paler and with
less broad wings, has been mentioned in a note, appended to the
same description. The mention concerning the size of the specimen, however, has been omitted there. The drops on the wings
of that specimen are larger and more rounded than in ordinary
specimens and show less tendency to form longitudinal rows; the
costal cell also contains such drops, while in the larger specimens
it shows at the utmost some pale drops along the auxillary vein.
Nevertheless, even now, I would not consider this specimen but
as a variety of *T. sparsa*.

Observation 2.—Wiedemann's collection contains at present,
under the name of *T. sparsa*, a pair of specimens, the communication of which I owe to the kindness of the Vienna Museum.
In the list of species sent to me, they were marked as coming
from Brazil. As Wiedemann prepared his description from a
single female of unknown origin, it seems hardly probable that the
female specimen now existing in his collection is the typical one.
It is more likely, on the contrary, that the couple of specimens
from Brazil now to be found in the collection was later added to
it by Wiedemann. Both sexes most closely resemble my Wisconsin specimens, except that the wings are still broader, which
is caused by the greater breadth of the costal and stigmatical
cells; their anterior margin is distinctly more convex. These
specimens seem therefore to belong to a South American species,
very closely allied to the North American one. However, my
conviction that such is the case has been somewhat shaken by a
number of specimens from Texas, collected by Mr. Belfrage.
The larger ones have the wings a little broader than the larger
specimens from Wisconsin, and the pellucid drops are less regularly distributed; the costal and stigmatical cells are not broader;
a small and incompletely colored specimen has much narrower
wings than the larger specimens; yet they are broader than the
wings of the above-mentioned smaller specimen from Wisconsin.
Whether the specimens from Wisconsin and Texas belong to the
same species, will have to be proved by further observation.

Observation 3.—The present species, together with *T. rotundipennis*, as well as the species represented by the above-

mentioned specimens from Brazil, now called *T. sparsa* in
Wiedemann's collection, form a separate genus, the characters of
which may be easily gathered from the descriptions of *T. sparsa*
and *rotundipennis* in the first volume. I call it *Eutreta*, in
allusion to the characteristic picture of the wings.

30. T. rotundipennis Lw. ♂. (Tab. X, f. 14.)—Fusca, alis latissima, rotundatis, nigris, albido-guttatis, in marginibus antico et apicali
maculas minutas albidas gerentibus.

Brown, wings very broad, rounded, black, dotted with white; the anterior
and apical margins are beset with small whitish spots. Long. corp.
0.28; long. al. 0.28.

Syn. *Trypeta rotundipennis* Loew, Monographs, etc., I, p. 79. Tab. II, f. 14.

Hab. Middle States (Osten-Sacken).

Observation.—Since the above-quoted description was drawn,
I have not received any addition to the single, imperfect specimen
in my collection, and have, therefore, nothing more to add about
it. The systematic position of this species has been discussed
above, in the third observation to *T. sparsa.*

31. T. culta Wied. ♂ ♀. (Tab. XI, f. 3.)—Ex rufo-lutea; caput
nigro-maculatum; alae luteae, in margine antico toto, in apice et in
marginis postici dimidio apicali eleganter radiata, in disco maculis
aliquot magnis fuscescentibus, macula minuta atra, guttisque aliquot
limpidis, fusco-circumscriptis, notatae, in angulo postico confertius lim-
pido-guttatae, vena longitudinali tertia nuda.

Reddish-yellow; head with black spots; wings clay-yellow, the anterior
margin, the apex, and the apical portion of the posterior margin are
handsomely adorned with ray-like streaks; upon the middle there are
some brownish spots, a small black dot, and a moderate number of
hyaline drops, margined with black; on the posterior angle numerous
hyaline drops; the third longitudinal vein not bristly. Long. corp. ♂
0.21, ♀ cum terebra 0.31; long. al. 0.29—0.32.

Syn. *Trypeta culta* Wiedemann, Auss. Zweifl. II, p. 496, 16.
Acinia fimbriata Macquart, Dipt. Exot. II, 3, p. 228, 5. Tab. XXXI, f. 5.
Trypeta culta Loew, Monogr. etc., I, p. 94. Tab. II, f. 29.

Reddish-yellow, opaque; the head somewhat paler yellow.
The front of moderate breadth, dark yellow; the two bristles
before the ocelli, directed forwards, and three strong bristles on
the lateral margin of the front, are black; the other frontal
bristles yellowish. The frontal lunule and the anterior part of

the lateral frontal border are shining; upon the first, almost
without exception, a very small, deep black longitudinal dot is
perceptible; near the antennæ, at the orbit of the eye, there is
a deep black dot and a black spot in the middle of the posterior
orbit The face is deeply excavated, shining and sometimes with a
distinct steel-blue reflection; upon its middle, below the antennæ,
there is a rounded black spot, on each side an elongated, larger one,
descending from the lower angle of the eye to the oral margin; the
oral opening is very large, somewhat drawn upwards anteriorly.
Palpi yellowish, broad, reaching to the anterior edge of the oral
opening, with black pile at the tip, and with yellowish hairs elsewhere. Proboscis brown, sometimes yellowish-brown, rather
stout, not geniculate. The thorax unicolorous, yellowish-red
or reddish clay-yellow, opaque; the usual bristles, of which there
are two pairs on the middle of the dorsum, are black, the short
pile is pale yellowish. Scutellum somewhat paler yellow and
rather shining, with erect yellowish bristle-like pile upon the
middle and with four black bristles; the two apical ones are
inserted upon black dots, while round the basis of the two anterior ones only a darker shade of the ground color is perceptible.
The abdomen has the same coloring as the thorax and no spots,
or only a trace of two longitudinal, contiguous rows of somewhat
darker spots; all the pile and bristles upon it are yellowish and
only a certain number of the bristles upon the posterior border
of the last segment are usually blackish. The flat ovipositor is
almost as long as the four posterior abdominal segments taken
together, red, blackish towards the tip. Feet, as well as the
bristles on the under side of the front femora, yellow; often,
however, some of the bristles are black; the front femora have, a
short distance before their end, on the outer side, a small black
dot; the posterior femora, on the under side, have two black
dots, the one before the middle, the other before the tip.   The
wings are rather long; their yellowish-red, almost gamboge-yel-
low color ends in rays along the anterior margin, the apex and
the posterior portion of the hind margin; these rays are separated
by hyaline intervals; between the humeral crossvein and the end
of the auxiliary vein there are three narrow rays, running perpendicularly from the auxiliary vein to the costa, the first of
which is less dark than the others; moreover, the extreme root
and the extreme tip of that cell are marked by a blackish-brown

crossline; the short stigmatical cell, which is somewhat yellowish, is divided in two halves by a narrow dark brown line and is marked at both ends by a ray; in the marginal cell, besides a ray at the end of the first longitudinal vein, which is incompletely formed and margined with brown on its outer side only, there are three yellow rays, margined with brown and running towards the anterior margin; the first two are attenuated towards the margin and much narrower, the third is much broader; the five following rays are again so narrow, that only the first among them preserves a trace of the yellow coloring of its inner side; they gradually grow longer and end: the first at the tip of the second longitudinal vein, the next two between this and the third vein, the fourth exactly upon the tip of the third, the last a little before the tip of the fourth vein; the hyaline intervals between the last of these rays show upon their middle a faded cloud. The rays upon the latter portion of the posterior margin gradually grow shorter, are rather broad and altogether brown, but not as dark as the narrow rays of the anterior margin or the dark borders of the broader rays which follow upon the latter; they are five in number, or six if the last of them, which is very short, is counted for one; the second and third are less completely separated from each other than the rest, and the fifth, which includes the tip of the fifth vein, is the broadest of all. Upon the middle of the wing the following hyaline drops are visible: 1. Between the second and third longitudinal veins a very small one (sometimes a second one beyond it) below the end of the auxiliary vein and a second, somewhat larger one below the second ray, which runs, in the marginal cell, towards the anterior margin; 2. Between the third and fourth veins, nearer to the latter, there are three drops in a row; the middle one is nearly opposite the middle of the discal cell, the first one beyond the anterior end of this cell, and the last one at an equal distance before its posterior end; 3. In the second posterior cell only a single drop almost in its inner corner; 4. In the discal cell four or five, two of which upon its longitudinal axis (one near the anterior, the other near the posterior end) and three inconstant ones on the posterior margin of the cell (the first sometimes wanting, the second being the largest); sometimes a very small drop in the posterior corner of the discal cell is added to them. All these drops are encircled with dark brown or almost black, in such a manner, that this

dark ring becomes paler round those drops which are more distant from the anterior margin The convex spot in the first
posterior cell is rather large; it contains a comparatively small
rounded-ovate deep black dot. Moreover, in the submarginal
cell, in the first and second posterior cells, and in the discal cell,
differently colored spots (one in each) may be noticed, which, at
an oblique view, assume a dark coloring. In the third posterior
cell, in the posterior angle of the wing, and on the alula, there is
a number of hyaline drops, among which only those placed
immediately behind the fifth vein show a trace of a brown border.
The double costal spine is strong and comparatively long, the
small crossvein is placed upon the last third of the discal cell;
the posterior crossvein is steep, but distinctly sinuate; the third
longitudinal vein is not bristly.

Hab. Savannah (Wiedemann); Carolina (Macquart); Texas
(Belfrage).

Observation.—*T. culta* is closely allied to the European *T.
pupillata* Fall. and *strigilata* Lw., and this relationship is sufficient to justify its location in the genus *Carpodricha*, formed by
me for the reception of these species, as well as of *T. guttularis*
Meig. However, in consequence of this addition, the definition
of the genus, as given by me in the Monograph of the European
Trypeta, will have to be somewhat modified. In *T. culta* the
scutellum is less convex, and, although smooth, it is not polished;
the tip of the abdomen is not shining. The nature of the pile
and the pattern of the picture of the wings, the structure of the
head, and the arrangement of the frontal bristles furnish sufficient
data for the modification alluded to.

82. T. solidaginis Frrck. ♂ ♀. (Tab. X, f. 16.)—Sordide ferruginea, capite pedibusque luteis; fronte latissima; scutelli valde convexi
vena dua; alae fusco-reticulata, apice fasciarisque tribus, una marginis
antici duabusque postici, hyalinis et parce fusco-maculatis.

Of a dingy ferruginous-red; head and feet clay-yellowish; front exceedingly broad; scutellum very convex, with two bristles; wings reticulate with brown; the tip and three indentations, one on the anterior
and two on the posterior margin, hyaline, sparsely dotted with brown.
Long. corp. ♂ 0.24—0.25, ♀ cum terebra 0.26—0.29; long. al. 0.23—
0.24.

Syn. *Tephritis asteris* Harris, Ins. Injur. to Veg., 3d Edit., p. 629.

Acinia solidaginis Fitch, First Report, 66.

Trypeta solidaginis Loew, Monographs, etc., I, p. 82.   Tab. II, f. 16.

Hab. New York (Fitch); Washington (Osten-Sacken); New England (Harris). [Canada.—O. S.]

Observation 1.—To the description of this species in the *Monographs*, Vol. I, I may add, by way of correction, that the costal spine of the wings is not altogether wanting, but that it is very short and weak, and hence, in some specimens, hardly visible. The words "the first longitudinal vein alone being hairy," in the observation to the above description, only meant that the bristles upon that vein were more like hairs, and not that this vein alone is provided with bristles; the third vein also, bears weak, hair-like bristles.

Observation 2.—Baron Osten-Sacken, having seen the original specimen of *Tephritis asteris* Harris in Mr. Harris's collection in the museum of natural history in Boston, has settled its identity with *Acinia solidaginis* Fitch.   Harris's name, although based upon an error in the name of the plant upon which this fly undergoes its transformations, would have to be retained, but for the circumstance that Mr. Haliday had previously used it for another European *Trypeta*.

Observation 3.—Among the genera established for the European *Trypetina*, *Oxyphora* is the only one in which *T. solidaginis* might, perhaps, be placed.   Among the European species *Oxyphora Schæfferi* Frnf. is nearest to it in its general appearance; the outline of the wings reminds somewhat of *O. Westermanni*.   The much heavier body, the strikingly broad front, and the much broader cheeks, as well as the peculiar shape of the wings, which are broadly rounded at the tip, the heavy, conical, not at all flattened ovipositor of the female, isolate this species sufficiently to justify the formation of a new genus, for which I propose the name of *Eurosta*.

38. T. comma Wied. ♀. (Tab. XI, f. 3.)—Sordide rufa aut fusca, capite magno, thoracis dorso, tibiis, tarsisque interscentibus; alae obtusae, ex fusco nigro, guttulis minutis candidis dilutioribus adspersae, macula costali trigona comma fuscam includente, limbo apicis angustissimo, guttulisque aliquot confertioribus prope venam longitudinalis sextam apicem, hyalinis; vena longitudinali tertia setosa; scutellum setis duabus instructum; terebra conica, non depressa.

Dingy red or brown, head large, thoracic dorsum, tibia, and tarsi clay-
yellowish ; wings obtuse, brownish-black, covered with small, moderately limpid drops; a triangular indentation on the costa contains a
brown comma; a narrow border along the apex and a dense cluster of
drops near the tip of the sixth vein, are hyaline; the third longitudinal
vein is bristly; scutellum with two bristles ; ovipositor conical, not
flattened. Long. corp. ♀ mm terebra 0.32—0.34 ; long. al. 0.30—0.31.

Syn. *Trypeta comma* Wiedemann, Auss. Zweifl. II, p. 478, 4.
Acinia comma Macquart, Dipt. Exot. II, 3, p. 229, 8.
Trypeta comma Loew, Monographs, etc., I, p. 93. Tab. II, f. 28.

This conspicuous species was described by Wiedemann from a
very pale-colored specimen, which I have had occasion to
examine. The coloring varies from a dingy brick-red almost to
dark brown; the abdomen especially is often dark. The large
head is yellow; the front is more than half as broad as the head,
usually of a darker yellow ; the usual bristles upon it are brown
or brownish, weak, and rather short. Antennæ clay-yellow, very
short, not even reaching to the middle of the face. Face perpendicular, very little excavated; oral opening of a very moderate
size, and the anterior edge of the mouth not projecting ; ocular
orbits very broad. Eyes elongated, but the cheeks of a considerable breadth, although by far not equalling those of the preceding
species; the pile upon them is brownish or brown, sometimes
paler ; proboscis short, not geniculate ; the clay-yellowish
palpi broad, reaching to the anterior edge of the oral opening.
The upper side of the thorax covered with a thick clay-yellowish
pollen and with short, dense clay-yellowish pile; the latter sometimes has a more ferruginous tinge ; the usual bristles of the
thoracic dorsum are brown and weak; upon its middle there are
only two pairs, the anterior one very much behind the transverse
suture; it is weaker and shorter than the posterior one. Scutellum dark brown, very convex, with only two bristles. Metathorax and pleuræ are sometimes brick-red, sometimes brown or
blackish-brown; the darker the pleuræ are, the darker the bristles
upon them. Abdomen unicolorous, brick-red, brown, or brownish-black, with rather delicate blackish or black pile. Ovipositor
not compressed, conical, about as long as the last two abdominal
segments taken together, with delicate black pile ; in paler specimens the ovipositor is red, the extreme tip only black ; in very
dark specimens it is black with a reddish crossband upon the
middle. Very dark specimens have blackish-brown femora; their

tip and the tibiae are yellowish-brown, the tarsi dirty yellowish;
in paler specimens tibiae and femora are not much darker than
the tarsi; front femora with black bristles; tarsi, especially their
first joint, somewhat longer than usual, especially in *T. solidaginis*. Knob of the halteres blackish or black. The wings broad
and very obtuse at the end, blackish-brown or black, including the
extreme root; upon their whole surface are a very variable
number of very small dots of but moderate transparency; upon
the anterior margin, immediately beyond the stigma, there is a
triangular hyaline spot, the tip of which does not quite reach the
third longitudinal vein and which includes a blackish-brown
crossline, extending from the costa to the second longitudinal
vein; the end of the sixth vein is surrounded by a cluster of small,
more or less coalescent drops, which extends especially on the
anterior side of this vein; the extreme tip of the wing has a very
narrow hyaline border, which begins a little before the tip of the
third longitudinal vein and ends beyond the tip of the fourth
vein; at the tip of these veins the border is very often interrupted;
on the posterior margin of the wing there are often two, sometimes three or four, in such a case larger, hyaline drops. The
third longitudinal vein is beset with scattered but distinct
bristles; at its end, it is strongly bent backwards so that its
divergency from the second vein is unusually large; the latter
ends rather far from the apex of the wing; the crossveins are but
little approximated, the small one is oblique, the posterior one
arcuated.

Hab. Kentucky (Wiedemann); Maryland (Osten-Sacken).

Observation 1.—This species is subject to remarkable variations in the coloring of the body, as well as in the shape of the
wings; the tip of the latter is sometimes more, sometimes less
distinctly obtuse; all these differences certainly do not constitute
specific distinctions. The figure which I have given in the first
volume of these Monographs was prepared from a specimen in
the Berlin Museum, and as it is based upon a rather hasty pencil
sketch, made many years previously, it lays no claim upon an
absolute fidelity. This figure shows some discrepancies however,
which raise a suspicion that this Berlin specimen is not *Trypeta
comma* at all, but a closely allied species.

Observation 2.—*Trypeta comma* differs from *T. solidaginis* in
its larger eyes, a less excavated face, and a smaller and much

narrower oral opening; the shape of the body, the striking breadth of the forehead, the distribution of the bristles upon it and upon the thoracic dorsum and scutellum, the shape of the ovipositor, the outline of the wings, and the pattern of the picture are remarkably analogous in both species, so as to preclude a generic separation.

84. T. latifrons Lw. ♀. (Tab. X, f. 22.)—Obscura, capite, tibiis tarsisque lutescentibus, fronte latissima, scutello convexo, alis duabus instructo, alis latinascule, colore fusco-nigro picta, in disco parcius et subaequaliter reticulata, in dimidii apicalis margine radiata.

Coloring dark; head, tibia, and tarsi clay-yellowish, front unusually large; the convex scutellum with two bristles only; wings rather broad, with a brownish-black picture, upon their middle somewhat sparsely and not very evenly marked with hyaline drops, their apical border radiate. Long. corp. ♀ cum terebrá 0.30; long. al. 0.27.

Syn. *Trypeta latifrons* Loew, Monographis, etc., I, p. 69, 22. Tab. II, f. 22.

Hab. Carolina (Zimmerman); Connecticut (Norton).

Observation.—A female from Connecticut, communicated to me by Baron Osten-Sacken, is not much better preserved than the female from South Carolina, from which my description in the Monogr. Vol. I was drawn, and for this reason I am not able to give a better one here. Of the two pairs of bristles upon the thoracic dorsum the anterior one has dropped off; it seems to have been inserted rather far behind the transverse suture. The structure of thorax and abdomen, the broad front, the bisetose scutellum, and the conical, not at all flattened, ovipositor, indicate a relationship between this species and the two preceding ones, from which, however, it differs in the shape of the wings and the pattern of the picture. In the latter two points it reminds one of *Trypeta platyptera* Lw., which differs again in the more narrow front, a four-bristled scutellum, and a flattened ovipositor. Such being the case, we will be better justified in connecting this species with *T. solidaginis* and *comma*, than with *T. platyptera* and its congeners.

85. T. melanura n. sp. ♀. (Tab. XI, f. 6.)—Lutea, metanoto, abdominis maculis in series quatuor dispositis et terebrá brevi, atris; capat laetius luteum, fronte latissimá, facie modice recedente, antennis longis et acutis; femora anteriora macula minutá nigrá notata; alarum pictura fusca, guttis majusculis hyalinis reticulatá, quarum in cellulá posteriore secundá tres, in tertiá quatuor conglobatae.

Clay-yellow; the metanotum, four rows of abdominal spots, and the short
ovipositor, deep black; head of a brighter clay-yellow; front very
broad, face moderately receding; antennæ long and acute; the anterior
femora with a little black spot; picture of the wings brown, reticulate
with rather large hyaline drops, among which three form a cluster in
the second posterior cell and four in the third. Long. corp. ♀ corm
terebra 0.13—0.14; long. al. 0.14.

Head almost ochreous-yellow, the rather level face, somewhat
retreating on the under side, the moderately broad cheeks, and
the lower portion of the occiput pale yellowish. Front more than
half as broad as the whole head. Frontal lunule very flat.
Third antennal joint unusually long, with a remarkably sharp
anterior corner; the thin, bare arista is incrassated at its basis
for a short distance only. Oral opening rather large, rounded,
but somewhat broader than long; its anterior edge is neither
drawn upwards, nor projecting in the profile. Proboscis and
palpi yellowish, withdrawn in the oral opening. The pile on the
head is ochreous-yellow; the ordinary frontal bristles are brownish or brown. The ground color of the thoracic dorsum is blackish,
with the exception of the pale yellow humeral callus, but very
much concealed under ochre-yellow pollen, and reddish ochre-yellow, coarse, and almost stubble-shaped pile. When the thorax is
viewed from behind, several opaque black, punctiform dots become
apparent, especially two on the transverse suture and two larger
ones between the first and the posterior border. The bristles of
the thoracic dorsum are partly pale yellow, partly brown; viewed
against the light, they appear dark. The scutellum, which, in the
described specimen, is much damaged, seems very convex; it is
smooth and for the most part yellow; among its four bristles, the
two apical ones are inserted on small black dots. The abdomen
is reddish-yellow or almost honey-yellow and somewhat shining;
upon the second segment there are four black dots in a row, the
lateral ones of which are small; upon each succeeding segment
the lateral spots become larger, and upon the fifth segment the
lateral spots completely coalesce with the middle ones, only a
median reddish line being left on the segment. The flat, shining
black ovipositor is hardly longer than the last abdominal segment.
Feet rather dark ochre-yellow; the front and intermediate
femora have, upon their hind side, beyond the middle, a little
black spot. The reticulate picture of the wings is brown, black-

ish-brown within the stigma; the hyaline drops, appearing in a
different light whitish, and which perforate the brown coloring,
are generally large, but not numerous; the stigma contains but
a single yellowish drop; its extreme basis also has a narrow hyaline border; the triangular cluster of larger drops which occurs
on the anterior margin, immediately beyond the stigma, consists
here of five drops, absolutely separated from each other; the end
of the marginal cell contains but a single small drop; a larger
drop occurs below the end of the second longitudinal vein and a
similar one under it, in the first posterior cell; between these two
drops and the apex of the wing there are four smaller drops,
forming a somewhat arcuated crossband; especially characteristic
for the species are three conspicuous drops in the second and four
similar ones in the third posterior cell, between which the brown
coloring is so pale or faded, that they appear almost coalescent;
(this is not well expressed in the figure, which is kept altogether
in too dark a shade); upon the middle of the discal cell there is
a large drop, occupying its whole breadth. The third longitudinal vein is distinctly bristly about as far as the small crossvein;
this crossvein corresponds to the last third of the discal cell; the
posterior crossvein is straight and very perpendicular.

Hab. Distr. Columbia (Osten-Sacken).

Observation.—In several respects this species resembles the
European species of *Carphotricha;* but, on account of the striking breadth of the forehead, the unusual length of the antennæ,
and the comparatively very even face, somewhat retreating below,
it cannot well be placed in that genus, especially when *T. culta*
Wied. is admitted in it, on account of its rather close relationship
to *Carpotricha pupillata* Fall. As I know of no other species
with which the present one could be generically united, I prefer
to establish a separate genus for it, which I call *Acidogona.*

36. T. alba Lw. ♂ ♀. (Tab. XI, f. 11.)—Albida, alis concoloribus
immaculata, capite, pleuris, scutello segmentorumque abdominalium
singulorum margine postico pallide sulphureis, antennis, terebra, pedibusque luteis.

Whitish, with whitish, altogether immaculate wings; head, pleura, scutellum, and the posterior margin of the single abdominal segments,
sulphur-yellow; antennæ, ovipositor, and feet clay-yellow. Long. corp.
♂ 0.13, ♀ cum terebra 0.17; long. al. 0.15—0.16.

Syn. *Trypeta alba* Loew, Berl. Entom. Zeitschr. V, p. 345, 72, Ib., Dipt.
   Amer. Cent. I, p. 39, 72.
   Trypeta alba Loew, Monographs, etc., I, p. 100, 18.

Hab. Pennsylvania (Osten-Sacken).

Observation 1.—I have only the following remarks to make
concerning this species, described in the above-quoted places and
easily recognizable. The antennæ are often not clay-yellow, but
more or less bright ochre-yellow, which is especially the case in
the best preserved and fully colored specimens; in such specimens the face is pale sulphur-yellow, while, on the contrary, the
front, probably in consequence of desiccation, shows, in other
specimens, a more dark yellow, often impure, hue.

Observation 2.—This and the next following species show a
striking agreement in all plastic characters, especially in the
structure of the head, and the characteristic outline of the wings,
so that they may be considered as the types of a new genus, distinguished from the related ones by the above-mentioned characters, and which may be called *Aspilota*.

37. T. albidipennis Lw. ♂ ♀. (Tab. XI, f. 10.)—Nigro-cinerea,
thoracis dorso albicante, capite, thoracis vitta laterali scutelloque sulphureis, alarum albidarum stigmate fusco, terebra feminæ atra.

Blackish-gray, thoracic dorsum whitish; head, a stripe on the lateral
margin of the thorax, and the scutellum sulphur-yellow; wings whitish
with a brown stigma; the ovipositor of the female black. Long. corp.
♂ 0.17, ♀ cum terebra 0.20; long. al. 0.18—0.19.

Syn. *Trypeta albidipennis* Loew, Berl. Entom. Zeitschr. V, p. 345, 73, and
   Dipt. Amer. Cent. I, p. 39, 73.
   Trypeta albidipennis Loew, Monographs, etc., I, p. 100, 19

Hab. Pennsylvania (Osten-Sacken).

Observation.—The antennæ are usually more ochre-yellow than
ferruginous-yellow. The generic location of this species has been
mentioned in the note to the preceding one.

38. T. Vernoniæ Lw. ♂ ♀. (Tab. XI, f. 8.)—Dilute lutea, capite,
thoracis vitta marginali in pleuras dilatata, scutelloque purius flavis,
thoracis dorso subhelvo, metanoto nigro; alarum dimidiata basali
impletum, apicale colore subfusco grosse reticulatum, guttis magnis confluentibus, iis ut fasciæ tres valde inæquales fuscæ conspiciantur; prima
incompleta et obsoletiore, secunda integra, tertia postice abbreviata.

Pale clay-yellowish; head, a lateral thoracic stripe, dilated upon the
pleura, and the scutellum of a purer yellow, thoracic dorsum more
Isabelle-yellow, metanotum black; the basal half of the wings is imma-

culate, the apical half shows a very coarse brownish reticulation, the large hyaline drops of which coalesce in such a manner, that three brown, irregular crossbands are formed; the first is only incompletely developed and rather faded, the second complete, the third abbreviated posteriorly. Long. corp. ♂ 0.18, ♀ cum terebrâ 0.22; long. al. 0.17 —0.18.

Syn. *Trypeta Vernoniæ* Loew, Berl. Entom. Zeitschr. V, p. 346, 74, and Dipt. Amer. Cent. I, p. 40, 74.

Trypeta Vernoniæ Loew, Monographs, etc., I, p. 101, 20.

Hab. Pennsylvania (Osten-Sacken); on the Iron-weed (*Vernonia*).

Observation.— T. *Vernoniæ* agrees in all the plastic characters, especially in the structure of the head and the shape of the wings, with the two preceding species in a very striking manner, and the presence of a picture on the wings alone is not a sufficient ground for a generic separation.

99. T serinta Lw. ♂. (Tab. X, f. 18.)—Lutea, alis concoloribus, latis æqualibus et obtusis, per maculas minutas fuscas seriatim dispositas reticulatis, adversus marginem præter trientem basalem nigricantibus, venâ longitudinali tertiâ setosâ.

Clay-yellow; wings of the same color, of a very equal breadth, obtuse at the end, reticulate with small brown spots arranged in rows; blackish along the margin, except on the proximal third of its extent; third longitudinal vein bristly. Long. corp. 0.24; long. al. 0.20—0.27.

Syn. *Trypeta seriata* Loew, Monographs, etc., I, p. 84. Tab. II, f. 18.

Hab. Illinois.

Observation.—Should T. *seriata* be placed in one of the genera established for the European *Trypetina*, it would of course be the genus *Oxyphora*, the most characteristic marks of which are the reticulate wings and the bristles on the third vein. And, indeed, this species reminds one very much of *Oxyphora Westermanni* Meig. in the very peculiar shape of the wings, and even in the coloring of the body and the pattern of the picture of the wings. But when we bear in mind that this European species occupies in the genus a very isolated, in fact an artificial position,[1] it will appear more natural to withdraw O. *Westermanni* from the genus and to form a new genus of it, together with the above described as well as the next following American species. This genus may be called *Icteria*.

———

[1] The European *Oxyphora Schæfferi* Egger shares this exceptional position, though for other reasons.

40. T. circinata n. sp. ♂ ♀.—Lutea, alis concoloribus, totis aequalibus et obtusis, per circulos fuscos inter se cohaerentes reticulatis, adversus marginem praeter dimidium basale nigrisantibus, vena longitudinali tertia setosa.

Clay-yellow, wings of the same color, of very equal breadth, obtuse at the end, reticulate with small, brown, contiguous circles; infuscated along the margin, except upon its first half; the third longitudinal vein bristly. Long. corp. ♂ 0.24, ♀ cum terebra 0.27; long. al. 0.24—0.27.

The resemblance of this species to *T. seriata* is so striking that one would almost be tempted to take it for a mere variety. However, the picture of the wings, perfectly identical in both sexes, shows such differences from that of *T. seriata*, as occur in closely allied species, but not in a variety of the same species. While the reticulation of *T. seriata* consists of small, angular brown spots, arranged in double rows between each pair of longitudinal veins on the middle of the wing, in the present species the spots are replaced by small brown ringlets, mostly closed, but some of them open, and connected with each other. The infuscated portion of the anterior margin in *T. seriata* begins before the end of the auxiliary vein and fills the stigmatical cell entirely, with the exception of a but little perceptible clay-yellow drop at the tip, and a similar, obsolete drop at the basis; between the ends of the first and second longitudinal veins there are, besides the somewhat hyaline spot immediately beyond the former, only two brownish-yellow drops near the anterior margin. In *T. circinata* the extreme tip of the auxiliary vein and the spot on the costa corresponding to it are black, but there is no trace of dark coloring in the costal cell before the tip of the auxiliary vein; the stigma is rather saturate yellow, and has upon its middle a considerable rectangular black spot; the pale spot which follows immediately upon the tip of the first longitudinal vein is more extensive, but less limpid, and the two drops which lie between it and the second longitudinal vein are much larger and more limpid, so that they entirely interrupt the black border along the anterior margin. A similar interruption is caused by a drop immediately beyond the tip of the second longitudinal vein, which is entirely wanting in *Trypeta seriata*. By these complete breaks in the black anterior border *Trypeta circinata* is very easily distinguished from *Trypeta seriata*, which has only one break of this kind immediately beyond the apex of the first longitudinal vein.

Hab. New York (Mr. Akhurst).

41. T. Lichtensteinii WIED. ♂. (Tab. XI, f. 9.)—Tota lutea; alis dilute cinereo-hyalinis, guttis majusculis albicantibus, maculisque tribus fusco-nigris variegata, prima harum reliquis minore et a stigmate obliqua decurrente, secundâ quadrangulâ et venam transversam posteriorem includente, tertiâ denique primis duabus majore et apicem ala cingente.

Altogether clay-yellow; wings grayish-hyaline, with rather large whitish drops and three brownish-black spots, the first among which is smaller than the others and descends from the stigma in an oblique direction, the second is square and includes the posterior crossvein, and the third is larger than the two preceding ones and forms a border along the apex. Long. corp. 0.23; long. al. 0.23.

Syn. *Trypeta Lichtensteinii* WIEDEMANN, Auss. Zweifl. II, p. 497, 31.
Trypeta Lichtensteinii LOEW, Monographs, etc., I, p. 92. Tab. II, f. 25.

Clay-yellow, the pile on head, thorax, and feet yellowish; the bristles yellow or yellowish-brown, according to the light in which they are seen; the pile on the abdomen yellowish at the basis only, black elsewhere. Front of a more vivid yellow, rather broad, with long bristles, the eyes rather large, oval; cheeks of a medium breadth. The face rather retreating, somewhat excavated under the antennæ; the anterior edge of the mouth not projecting in the profile. Antennæ yellow, of medium length; the third joint with a rounded anterior corner; the rather long arista is much incrassated at its extreme basis, otherwise very thin and bare. Oral opening rather large, rounded; palpi and proboscis not projecting beyond it; the latter not geniculated. The middle of the upper side of the thorax seems to bare borne only two pairs of bristles. The very moderately convex scutellum bears four bristles. Scutellum and abdomen are more shining than the thoracic dorsum, which is opaque in consequence of a yellowish pollen; abdomen without any picture. Wings rather long and of nearly equal breadth; the third longitudinal vein distinctly bristly for a considerable portion of its length; crossveins straight and steep; small crossvein a little beyond the middle of the discal cell. The picture of the wings is a very peculiar one; its principal feature consists of three very conspicuous brownish-black spots; the smallest among them has the shape of an oblique, somewhat irregular half-crossband; with its anterior end it covers the tip of the stigma, with its posterior end it covers the small crossvein and suddenly stops near the fourth vein; the second spot, which covers the posterior crossvein, has a square shape, is

19

higher than broad and reaches from the fourth vein to the posterior margin; the third spot forms a broad margin of the tip of
the wing, which begins not far beyond the first longitudinal vein
and, gradually increasing in breadth, reaches beyond the beginning of the second posterior cell. The outlines of these three
spots are irregular and sinuate. The remaining surface of the
wings is grayish-hyaline; held against the light this grayish
surface shows some round, whitish spots of a rather considerable
size, occurring especially within the sinuosities along the margins
of the dark spots, however, without following their outline exactly.
In some places the grayish tinge of the wings becomes infuscated,
thus forming several other, probably very variable, spots; the
typical specimen shows the following ones: a narrow little spot
in the middle of the anterior margin of the costal cell; a hook-
shaped spot, which begins at the anterior end of the third brown
spot and runs to the second vein; a small, thimble-shaped spot,
situated on the fourth vein, a little beyond the posterior crossvein
and directed forwards; a little spot upon the posterior margin,
in the middle between the second and third of the large brown
spots; a punctiform dot upon the middle of the discal cell; a
larger spot, behind the preceding one, within the third posterior
cell; finally, behind the latter, upon the posterior margin, another
small, faded, little spot. It is probable that, sometimes, the
greatest part of the grayish surface becomes brownish, and then
it may happen that, in some specimens, beyond the root of the
wing, but little pale colored portions remain, except the large
drops with a whitish reflection. The fact that the described
specimen does not seem to be a fully matured one, serves to
confirm this supposition.

Hab. Mexico (Wiedemann).

Observation 1.—Description and figure are prepared after the
same specimen in the Berlin Museum, which Wiedemann had
before him in drawing his description. In the figure, the
engraver has represented the large whitish drops somewhat more
vividly than they appear in nature. The relationship of *T.
Lichtensteinii* to the two preceding species, is close enough to
enable us to place it in the genus *Icterica*.

Observation 2.—Among the species described in the sequel,
Trypeta æqualis (Tab. X, f. 90) stands next to the species of
Icterica in the shape of the wings. But, besides the fact that

Its wings are neither as equally broad, nor as obtuse, as those of
the species united in the genus *Icterica*, that species differs also
in the absence of bristles upon the third vein.

42. T. humilis Lw. ♂ ♀. (Tab. X, f. 17.)—Luteo-cinerea, capite
pedibusque saturate flavis, femoribus tamen nigris adversus apicem in
mare late, in femina latissime flavis; peristomium valde productum,
proboscis geniculata, alis rare reticulatæ, stigmate atro, non guttato.

Yellowish-gray; head and feet saturate yellow; the femora black, a considerable portion at their tip in the male, a still more considerable one
in the female, yellow; edge of the mouth very much produced, proboscis
geniculated, wings sparsely reticulate, the black stigma without pale
drops. Long. corp. ♂ 0.09—0.1, ♀ cum terebra 0.11—0.12; long. al.
0.11—0.12.

Syn. *Acinia picciola* Bigot, B. de la Sagra, Hist. Fis. Vol. VII. Tab. XX,
f. 10.
Trypeta humilis Loew, Monogr. etc. I, p. 81. Tab. II, f. 17.

Hab. Cuba (Poey, Gundlach). [Key West; communicated by
Mr. Burgess. O. S.]

Observation 1.—The saturate yellow coloring of the apex of
the femora in the male has a rather considerable, but at the
same time variable, extent; in the female, the yellow sometimes
occupies so much space, that the blackish color remains visible
at the basis of the femora only. Females with the femora as pale
as that, mentioned by me in the first part of these Monographs,
seem to be rare, as among the numerous specimens of my collection that single one only is to be found.

Observation 2.—To recognize the present species in the *Acinia
picciola* Bigot is not possible. Nevertheless the synonymy is not
doubtful, as, through the kindness of Mr. Gundlach, I have been
put in possession of numerous typical specimens. It is to be
regretted that Mr. Bigot has given the species a name which
cannot possibly be admitted, unless names like *littlella, petitella,
kleinella* for any small species were likewise tolerated.

Observation 3.—The strongly produced oral edge and the
strikingly geniculated proboscis, with its very much prolonged
flaps, reaching backwards as far as the mentum, define this
species as an *Ensina*. As soon as exotic species are taken in
consideration, this genus cannot be maintained within exactly the
same limits which I defined for it in my Monograph of the European species. A part of the species, which I placed there under

the head of *Oxyna*, as for instance *Oxyna elongatula* Lw., and its congeners, will have to be admitted in the genus *Ensina*.

Observation 4.—A Brazilian species, not rare in collections, likewise belonging to *Ensina*, is so very like *humilis*, that I give here its description, in order to avoid a possible confusion.

T. peregrina n. sp. ♂ ♀. (Tab. X, f. 30.)—Luteo-cinerea, abdomine nigro-maculato, genis angustissimis, peristomio exímie producto, proboscidis geniculatae labellis longíssimis, alis elongatis et subaequaliter fusco-reticulatis ; pedes lutei, basali femorum posticorum dimidio piceo ; terebra foeminæ atra, tribus ultimis abdominis segmentis simul sumtis longiore.

Yellowish-gray, abdomen spotted with black ; the cheeks very narrow, the oral edge very much produced, the flaps of the geniculated proboscis very much prolonged ; wings comparatively long and rather uniformly reticulated with brown ; feet of a saturate yellow, basal half of the hind femora black ; ovipositor of the female black, larger than the last three abdominal segments taken together. Long. corp. ♂ 0.12—0.13; ♀ cum terebra 0.14—0.16; long. al. 0.13—0.14.

Resembles *T. marmula* Wied. from Teneriffe and the European *T. elongatula* Lw. very much, both in the structure of the body and in general appearance. In the female sex, it differs from the latter easily by its ovipositor, which is once and a half as long ; the male is easily distinguished by several features of the picture of the wings, which in other respects is very much the same: namely, the drop which lies at the tip of the submarginal cell is not present in *T. elongatula*; in the dark coloring at the extreme end of the discal cell there is only a single hyaline drop, while in *T. elongatula* there are several of them, usually three. From *T. humilis* it differs sufficiently in the scutellum, which is tinged with yellow at the tip, in the coloring of the feet and in the picture of the wings. Yellowish-gray ; the head, of the same structure as in the species just compared with it, rather saturate yellow, as well as antennae, palpi, and proboscis ; the occiput alone in part gray. Front long and not very broad ; along the orbit with a narrow, rather whitish border. Antennae rather broad, not quite descending to the anterior edge of the mouth, which is somewhat drawn upwards and remarkably projecting in the profile. Eyes rounded ; cheeks very narrow. Oral opening very much drawn out ; the very elongated flaps of the geniculated proboscis reach backwards to the mentum. The usual bristles of the front, the thorax, and the scutellum are black ; the latter is yellow at its tip only. The abdomen is of the same color as the thorax, and bears, like the latter, some short, pale yellowish pile, while the longer hairs on the posterior border of the last segments are black. The flattened and only moderately pointed ovipositor is shining black and a little longer than the last three abdominal segments taken together ; its short pubescence is almost without exception black.

Feet dark yellow, only the hind femora are brownish-black beyond their middle, and the other femora somewhat infuscated near the root and with a brown stripe on the under side. The wings are elongated, hyaline, with a grayish-brown, very loose, but not disconnected, reticulation; the root of the wings is not spotted up to the end of the small basal cells; beyond this, up to the stigma, there are only three inconspicuous grayish spots. The grayish-brown stigma contains a rather conspicuous hyaline drop (represented too small on the figure); a spot adjoining it, comparatively small and not much perforated, reaches beyond the second vein with two points only, and contains a little drop immediately before the second vein. The larger and less perforated spot before the end of the second longitudinal vein always contains a considerable hyaline drop near the anterior margin; between the second and third longitudinal veins, the same spot contains two or three small drops and is variously connected with the remaining reticulation. Between these two less perforated spots, there are, in the marginal cell two, in the submarginal three, large hyaline drops, which generally assume the shape of quadrangular spots, and are only separated by grayish-brown lines, running from one longitudinal vein to the other. Upon the remainder of the surface of the wing, the reticulation is formed by rather considerable rounded drops, and is more regular; only in the proximity of the posterior crossvein there are no drops.

Hab. Brazil.

43. **T. angustipennis** Lw. ♂ ♀.—Cinerea, capite pedibusque flavis, femoribus magna et parte nigris vel fuscis; proboscide non geniculata; ala subangustata, nigro-reticulata, in basi et limbo marginis postici subimmaculata, stigmate non guttato, maculis duabus ordinariis obscurioribus mediocribus, separatis, secunda gutalam unam, rarius duas includente; terebra foemina atra, duobus ultimis abdominis segmentis simul sumtis subaequalis.

Gray; head and feet yellow; femora for the most part black or brown; proboscis not geniculated; wings reticulate with black, almost without spots at the basis and in the vicinity of the posterior margin; the two ordinary dark spots only of middle size and separated from each other; in the second, one, rarely two, hyaline drops; ovipositor black, almost as long as the last two abdominal segments taken together. Long. corp. ♂ 0.13, ♀ 0.14—0.15; long. al. 0.14.

Syn. *Tephritis leontodontis* ZETTERSTEDT, Ins. Lapp. 745, 6. Var. a. (ex p.).
Trypeta angustipennis LOEW, Germ. Zeitschr. V, p. 362. Tab. II, f. 4.
Tephritis angustipennis ZETTERSTEDT, Dipt. Scand. VI, p. 2229, 35.
Tephritis angustipennis LOEW, Trypetidae. p. 113, No. 24.
Tephritis segregata FRAUENFELD, Verb. Zool. Bot. Ges. XIV, p. 147.

Gray; thorax without picture; the pile upon it is whitish; the bristles black. Abdomen blackish-gray, without spots; the pile whitish, only the bristles upon the posterior margin of the last segment are black. Ovipositor black, hardly as long as the last two segments taken together; with distinct whitish pile upon its anterior half. Feet yellow; the femora for the most part black or brown. The wings are comparatively a little longer and narrower than in most of the related species. The rather dark reticulation is loosely meshy and somewhat disconnected; it disappears almost entirely in the region of the posterior margin, with the exception of a few little spots, which distinguishes this species from the otherwise related ones; the black stigma does not include a hyaline dot; the two ordinary dark spots are of moderate size; the first is connected with the stigma and reaches from it directly backwards; the second usually contains, near the anterior margin, only a single hyaline drop, which lies immediately beyond the tip of the second longitudinal vein; this spot reaches as far as the fourth longitudinal vein; the two rays which, in the related species, run from this vein over the second posterior cell to the posterior margin, are incomplete or wanting; the posterior crossvein also has only a comparatively narrow dark border, which sometimes exists on its posterior half only; upon the posterior part of the crossvein, this border emits a short branch, characteristic for this species, and reaching into the discal cell; this branch sometimes coalesces with a second similar branch upon the posterior side of the fourth vein, so as to include a hyaline drop; otherwise the picture of the discal cell is limited to a small crossband, lying beyond its middle, or there is sometimes before it, near the anterior margin of the cell, another dark spot, which in some specimens becomes a second small crossband; upon the posterior side of the fifth vein generally two small, dark spots of variable size are observable, of which the one nearer the root of the wing is often wanting.

Hab. Yukon River (Kennicott).

Observation 1.—I cannot distinguish this species from the *T. angustipennis* occurring in Scandinavia; the typical pair after which I have described it in *Germar's Zeitschrift* has, it is true, the femora much less dark, but as the specimens seem to be immature, I do not consider this a specific difference. The figure given in *Germar's Zeitschrift* has not well succeeded in the engraving and gives only an approximate idea of the picture of the wings.

Observation 2.—Should we distribute the present and all the next following species among the subgenera which I have established for the European *Trypetidæ*, they would have to be referred to the genera *Oxyphora*, *Oxyna*, *Tephritis*, and *Urellia*. The genus *Urellia* is easily distinguished from the others by the picture of the wings: It consists in a conspicuous star-shaped black design near the apex, while the rest of the wing is altogether immaculate, or is marked with only a few isolated spots, at the utmost with a very pale reticulate picture. A part of the species described in the sequel, can undoubtedly be referred to *Urellia*. Among the remaining species, those would have to be located in the genus *Oxyphora*, which have the third longitudinal vein of the wings beset with bristles. This character is of a very easy application when a number of well-preserved specimens is at hand, but it becomes of much less value when applied only to single and indifferently preserved specimens. For this reason I am not quite sure whether in all the species in which I have not been able to discern the presence of bristles on the third vein, they are really wanting; and hence, with the materials I now possess, I am not able to refer with certainty to *Oxyphora* the North American species which may belong to it. Among the North American species with a distinctly bristly third longitudinal vein, *T. geminata* alone comes near the European species of *Oxyphora*, while *T. timida* is more related not to the former, but to the European *T. guttata* Fall., and to the American *T. tenuis*, *melanogastra*, and *mexicana*, in which I am unable to discern the bristles upon the third vein. Thus, the maintenance of the genus *Oxyphora* for those species only which have bristles upon the third vein, would separate from each other species most closely allied. In order, therefore, to make this genus applicable to the North American species, we should exclude from it all the species the picture of the wings of which ends in distinctly developed rays, in which case only *T. geminata* would remain in it. Theoretically there is no objection to such an arrangement; practically, however, there remains the difficulty of ascertaining positively the presence of bristles upon the third vein in all the specimens which I have at hand, and this difficulty compels me to drop entirely the genus *Oxyphora* for the present. Should we follow the suggestion already made above, of removing from the genus *Oxyna* those species which have remarkably prolonged

flaps of the proboscis, and placing them in the genus *Ensina*,
then the difference between *Oxyna* and *Tephritis* is rendered so
very subtle, as to become unavailable for my essay of a classification of North American *Trypetina*, based as it is upon very
insufficient materials. The question arises, therefore, whether it
would not be better, temporarily, to bring together all the species
to be described below (with the exception of the *Urellia*) under
the head of the genus *Tephritis*, or else to distribute those species
in genera on some other principle. The latter course seems to
me preferable, in rendering the determination of the species
easier. I would propose to call *Tephritis* those species, the
picture of the wings of which does not form at the apex distinctly
developed rays, and those which have such rays would form a
new genus *Euaresta*. Most species will then gain a position in
conformity to their true relationship, as well as to their habitual
affinities; and although it cannot be denied that the location of
some species will thus be rendered somewhat artificial, this dis-
advantage cannot well be avoided as long as the knowledge of
the American fauna is not more complete than it actually is.

That *Trypeta angustipennis* belongs to the genus *Tephritis*
results from the foregoing explanation.

44. T. similis Loew. ♂ ♀. (Tab. XI, f. 4.)—Cinerea, capite pedibusque luteis, proboscide non geniculata, alis nigro-reticulatis, fascia
obliqua inde a stigmate trans venas transversales ad posticum alæ marginem ducta, maculisque duabus alterā subapicali, costa contiguā et
alterā apicali non reticulatis, stigmate nigri tasi dilutissimo subflaves-
cente, venā longitudinali tertiā nudā.

Cinereous; head and feet clay-yellow; proboscis not geniculated; reticulation of the wings black; a crossband running from the stigma over
the crossveins, a spot near the anterior margin before the apex, and
another one on the apex, are not reticulate; the basis of the black
stigma is of a very faint yellow; the third longitudinal vein is not
bristly. Long. corp. ♂, 0.16; cum terebrā 0.24; long. al. 0.20—0.21.

Syn. *Trypeta similis* Loew, Dipt. Am. Cent. II, 78.

Cinereous, thorax and abdomen without any picture. Head,
antennæ, and palpi rather dark yellow, the larger part of the
occiput dark brown. The front is of a very moderate breadth;
its nasal bristles are black. The antennæ do not reach to the
anterior edge of the mouth; their second joint does not bear a
longer bristlet; the anterior corner of the third joint is rounded;

the arista is but little incrassated at the basis, its pubescence is
but very little perceptible. The upper side of the thorax bears
some short, yellowish-white pile and black bristles, two pairs of
which seem to have been inserted upon its middle. Scutellum,
at the basis, of the same color with the thorax, towards the tip
more or less yellowish; it bears four black bristles. The comparatively somewhat narrow abdomen is likewise of the same
color with the thorax, its last segment a little elongated; its short
pubescence is yellowish-white; the long bristles at the end of the
last segment are usually black. The flat ovipositor of the female
is somewhat longer than the last two abdominal segments taken
together, red, blackened at the root and at the extreme tip only;
its short and fine pile is of a very pale color. The wings are
comparatively long and narrow, coarsely reticulate with brownish-
black upon their whole surface; the root of the wing, up to a
little beyond the end of the small basal cells, shows but some
scattered spots; upon the rest of the surface the single drops are
large and hence rather close together, although but little coalescent; no drops at all, or almost none, are to be found on a
crossband running obliquely from the stigma over both crossveins
to the posterior margin of the wing, on a spot beginning at the
anterior margin near the apex of the wing, and on a smaller spot
upon the apex itself; the basis of the black stigma forms a large,
limpid drop, somewhat tinged with yellowish; the usual triangular
cluster of drops between the stigma and the unperforated crossband before the apex consists of six drops, three quadrangular
ones between the costa and the second longitudinal vein, a larger
quadrangular spot and a smaller rounded one between the second
and third longitudinal veins, finally a large round one beyond the
third vein. The latter vein has no bristles; the small crossvein
corresponds to the last third of the discal cell.

Hab. California (A. Agassiz); Texas (Belfrage).

Observation.—This species is a normal *Tephritis.*

45. T. clathrata Lw. ♀. (Tab. X, f. 15.)—Cana, capite pedibusque
flavis, femoribus litura nigricante signalis, abdomine bifariam nigro-
maculato; ala colore nigro rara maculato-reticulata, stigmate atro
guttam hyalinam includente, vena longitudinali tertia nuda; peristomium mollice productum et proboscis breviter geniculata; terebra aterrima, duobus ultimis abdominis segmentis simul sumtis aequalia.

Whitish-gray, head and feet yellow, femora with a black streak, abdomen
with two rows of black dots, wings with a sparse reticulation, almost
reduced to spots; the stigma includes a hyaline drop; third longitudinal vein not bristly; oral edge moderately produced, proboscis short,
geniculate; the deep black ovipositor is as long as the last two abdominal segments taken together. Long. corp. 0.12; long. al. 0.13.

Syn. *Trypeta clathrata* Loew, Monographs, etc., I, p. 80.   Tab. II, f. 15.

Hab. Middle States (Osten-Sacken).

Observation.—In accordance with what has been said in the
second observation to *T. angustipennis*, *T. clathrata* belongs
to the genus *Tephritis*. Should the distribution adopted by me
in my Monograph of the European *Trypetidæ* be strictly applied
to this species, it would, on account of the distinctly geniculate
proboscis with but moderately prolonged flaps, be referred to the
genus *Oxyna*; and it agrees very well with a number of European species, placed in that genus.

46. T. geminata Lw. ♀. (Tab. XI, f. 1.)—Ex luteo-cinerea, capite,
thoracis margine laterali, scutello, abdominis dimidio basali, femorum
apice, tibiis tarsisque flavis, pleuris, metanoto, abdominis maculis et
apice, terebrâ femoribusque ex nigro fuscis; alis præter basim fuscam,
limpido-guttatæ, guttulis disci minutis et raris, guttis margine postici
majoribus, anguli axillaris confertioribus, maculis denique duabus
costalibus trigonis limpidis, venâ longitudinali tertiâ setosâ.

Yellowish-gray; head, lateral margin of the thorax, scutellum, anterior
half of the abdomen, tip of the femora, tibiæ, and tarsi, yellow; pleuræ,
metanotum, spots and posterior part of the abdomen, ovipositor, and
femora blackish-brown; wings, with the exception of the basis, brown,
with pale drops, which are small and scattered in the middle, larger
upon the posterior margin, more dense upon the posterior angle; upon
the anterior margin there are two triangular hyaline spots; the third
longitudinal vein is bristly.   Long. corp. 0.17; long. al. 0.20.

Syn. *Trypeta geminata* Loew, Dipt. Am. Sept. Cent. II, 75.

Head pale yellow, only a large spot upon the occiput blackish-
brown; front rather broad; the ordinary bristles pale brownish
or almost yellowish.   Antennæ dark yellow; the short pile upon
the second antennal joint pale yellowish; a single more elongate
hair is black; the anterior corner of the third joint is rather
sharp.   Face rather concave and the anterior corner of the mouth
rather conspicuously projecting.   Cheeks narrow.   Oral opening
large, rounded; palpi and proboscis short, not reaching beyond

the anterior edge of the oral opening; proboscis not geniculated. The ground color of the upper side of the thorax is black, but, in consequence of its pulverulence and of its short, yellowish pile, it appears gray; upon its anterior margin, in the vicinity of the yellowish humeral callus, there are some blackish hairs; the ordinary bristles, of which I perceive only two pairs upon the middle of the dorsum, are brown. The lateral margin of the thoracic dorsum is yellow; scutellum yellow, with four bristles. Metanotum and pleurae blackish-brown; the latter rather shining; the bristles upon them for the most part black. The ground color of the abdomen is yellow; it has four rows of brownish-black spots, which begin to expand upon the third segment; upon the fourth and the following segments they coalesce in such a manner that the segments appear altogether blackish-brown. The pile upon the abdomen is generally whitish-yellow, but upon the black spots it is black; the bristles upon the posterior margin of the posterior segments are generally black. The rather broad ovipositor is of a shining blackish-brown, flattened, although somewhat swollen at the basis; its short and very delicate pile is not easily discernible; it seems to be brownish. Femora brownish-black, the anterior ones with long black bristles; the extreme root and the tip dark yellow. Tibiae and tarsi rather dark yellow; wings of the ordinary shape, blackish-brown, sparsely guttate; the root of the wings, almost as far as the tip of the small basal cells, is rather hyaline and almost altogether immaculate; the alula also, bears no spots and is without dark coloring; the brown coloring begins on the anterior margin about the middle of the costal cell, and includes before its end a rather large hyaline drop, close by the margin; a smaller hyaline drop is placed upon the tip of the brownish-black stigma; immediately beyond the stigma, on the anterior margin, there are two triangular, hyaline spots, separated only by a brown stripe; their end crosses the second longitudinal vein; the whole middle portion of the wing is perforated by a few isolated, very small hyaline drops; upon the second half of the posterior margin there are four large hyaline drops, two before and two after the end of the fifth longitudinal vein; a fifth, much smaller drop, is placed much nearer the tip of the fourth vein; the last portion of the sixth longitudinal vein is surrounded by a cluster of somewhat larger spots, which, in consequence of the more faded brown,

surrounding them, appear more coalescent; in the posterior angle
of the wing the pale drops are more numerous and somewhat
larger than upon the middle of the wing, and moreover, well
separated from each other; the apex of the wing shows between
the third and fourth veins a very narrow, hardly apparent hyaline
border.

Hab. Pennsylvania (collection v. Winthem).

Observation.—In accordance with the explanations given in
the second observation to *T. angustipennis* I leave *Trypeta
geminata*, in spite of its distinctly bristly third vein, in the genus
Tephritis, but I do this with the explicit understanding that this
position is an unnatural one. In the above-quoted place I have
already explained why one would feel tempted to place this
species in the genus *Oxyphora* on account of the pattern of its
picture, as well as of the bristles upon the third vein; but I must
again add that this location would not be natural. Its rather
stubble-shaped pile, the distribution of the bristles upon the front,
and the structure of the antennae indicate a rather close relationship to those European species which I have united in the genus
Carphotricha; nevertheless, in some other characters it differs
from those species in a measure which prevents its reception in
that genus. A number of South American species stand in the
same relation to the European *Carphotricha*, although they differ
among themselves in many very striking plastic characters. A
more complete study of these species will result in the breaking
up of the genus *Carphotricha*, based upon too insufficient material, and then only, in all probability, *T. geminata* will find its
true position.

47. T. fucata Fabr. ♂.—Lutea, capite pedibusque flavis; setis scutelli quatuor; alis guttis hyalinis majusculis subrarii reticulatis, retis
parte postica unicolore os cinereo-fusca, antice luteo et fusco varia, ita
ut guttulae luteae guttis hyalinis interjectae sint, margine antico strigulis
quinque os maculis subapicali fuscis notato, vena longitudinali tertia
setosa; prohumeris non goniculata.

Clay-yellow, head and feet of a purer yellow; scutellum with four bristles;
the reticulation of the wings, formed of rather large and moderately
numerous hyaline drops, is uniformly grayish-brown upon the posterior
part of the wings, yellow and brown upon the anterior portion, in such
a manner that yellowish drops are mixed among the hyaline ones; upon
the anterior margin, there are five small brown transverse streaks and

before its end there is a brown spot; the third longitudinal vein is beset with bristles; proboscis not geniculated. Long. corp. 0.17; long. al. 0.20.

Bes. *Musca fucata* Fabricius, Ent. Syst. IV, p. 359, 194.
  Tephritis fucata Fabricius, Syst. Antl. p. 321, 24.
  Trypeta fucata Wiedemann, Auss. Zweifl. II, p. 506, 44.

Clay-yellowish, almost ochre-yellow. Head rather pale yellow. Front and sides of the face with short, unusually dense yellowish pile. Front of a medium breadth; the bristles brownish-yellow, brown towards the tip. Antennæ pale yellow, of medium length, reaching almost to the anterior edge of the mouth, which is very much drawn upwards; the short pile on the second joint is yellowish; the third joint has an indistinctly rounded anterior corner; antennal arista apparently bare, but little incrassated at the basis. Face rather narrow, somewhat excavated, distinctly carinate between the antennal foveæ; in the profile, its lower part is produced in the shape of a short snout. Eyes large, oval; cheeks narrow, with yellow pile and bristles. Oral opening large, longer than broad; the rather broad palpi yellowish and with yellowish pile, reaching to the anterior edge of the oral opening; proboscis short, not geniculated. The whole thorax is so thickly covered with yellow pollen and short, yellow pile, that its ground color, which seems to be grayish-brown, is hardly visible; the ordinary bristles, two pairs of which are inserted upon the middle of the upper side, are brownish-yellow; their tip is dark brown. The ground color of the scutellum is pale yellow, which color is, however, but little apparent, on account of a short yellow pile, similar to that on the thorax; the scutellum has four bristles. Abdomen of the same coloring as the thorax; the short hairs and bristles are all yellow. Feet yellow, with yellow pile, the anterior femora have yellowish bristles. The reticulation of the wings consists of hyaline, almost whitish, rather large, and not very numerous drops; it does not reach the extreme root of the wings; upon the posterior margin and at the extreme apex of the wing the coloring is uniformly grayish-brown; elsewhere, it is clay-yellow, with a brown picture, which partly frames in the hyaline drops, partly includes little clay-yellowish drops, so that the coarser reticulation formed by the hyaline drops, in its turn appears reticulate. Upon the anterior margin itself there are five, in part almost punctiform, brownish-black transverse streaks; upon the

end of the marginal cell a brownish-black spot; the streaks are
upon the humeral crossvein, in the middle between the latter and
the basis of the stigma, upon the latter, on the end of the
stigma, and between that and the tip of the second longitudinal
vein. The small crossvein lies a little beyond the last third of
the discal cell. The third longitudinal vein is distinctly bristly.

Hab. The Antilles? (Fabricius); South America (Wiedemann); Buenos Ayres (collect. Wiedemann).

Observation 1.—Fabricius, the first describer of the species,
names Dr. Pflug as the discoverer, and the South American
islands as the *habitat*, which probably means the Antilles. Later,
the species was described by Wiedemann, who names South
America as the *habitat*. It is impossible to tell from the descriptions of both authors, whether they really meant the same species,
although the descriptions contain nothing positively contrary
to this assumption. As the species is easy to identify, and as
Wiedemann's identification was based upon the comparison of
Fabricius's specimens, it can be safely assumed that he has
described the same species. My description is based upon a
male, marked Buenos Ayres and communicated to me as a type
from Wiedemann's collection.

Observation 2.—This species may also remain in the genus
Tephritis, for the sake of facilitating identification, although its
third vein is distinctly bristly. This character, as well as the
not geniculated proboscis, recalls those species which, in my Monograph of the European Trypetidæ, I placed in the genus *Ory-
phora;* in fact I know of no other American species which stands
closer than *T. fucata* to the typical species of that genus, as, for
instance, to *T. corniculata* Zett., *biflexa* Lw., etc. I also call
attention to a peculiarity of most species of this group, that the
dark spots of the picture in the female are more extensive than
in the male; this may likewise be the case with *T. fucata.*

48. **T. albiceps** n. sp. ♂ ♀. (Tab. XI, f. 5.)—Ex luteo cinerea,
capite albicante, fronte, antennis, scutello pedibusque luteis, abdomine
bifariam nigro maculato: ala lutescente, præter imam basim tota colore
fusco-nigro guttato-reticulata, guttis valde inæqualibus, in apice et prope
venam transversam posteriorem quam in reliqua ala minus confertis,
stigmate nigro uniguttato, vena longitudinali tertia non setosa; terebra
feminæ aterrima, duobus ultimis abdominis segmentis simul æqualia
æqualis.

Yellowish-gray; head whitish; front, antennæ, scutellum, and feet yellow; the abdomen with two longitudinal rows of black spots; wings somewhat broad, and with the exception of the extreme basis, entirely covered with a guttate brownish-black reticulation; the drops are of a very unequal size and less numerous upon the apex and in the vicinity of the posterior crossvein; the black stigma has a hyaline drop; third longitudinal vein not bristly; ovipositor of the female deep black; as long as the last two abdominal segments taken together. Long. corp. ♂ 0.13, ♀ 0.16; long. al. 0.15—0.16.

Yellowish-gray; thorax and abdomen with whitish-yellow pile; the latter with two longitudinal rows of black or blackish dots. In well-preserved specimens the head is white, and it probably has the same color in living ones; in some of the dried specimens it has assumed a yellowish hue; the front, with the exception of its lateral margins, is yellowish; the usual bristles upon it are almost without exception black; the bristles upon the vertical margin are pale yellowish. Antennæ pale yellowish; the third joint has an almost sharp anterior angle. Oral opening large, somewhat longer than broad; the anterior edge of the mouth rather drawn upwards, somewhat projecting in the profile. Palpi pale yellowish. Proboscis yellowish, short geniculate, with but moderately prolonged, comparatively stout flaps. The upper half of the occiput is gray, with the exception of the margin along the orbit. The ground color of the humeral callosities is yellow, while upon the rest of the thorax it is blackish. The bristles of the thoracic dorsum are all black, those of the pleuræ are partly black, partly pale yellowish. Scutellum pale yellow; lateral angles and sometimes also the basis darker; with four black bristles. The bristles upon the posterior margin of the last abdominal segments have the same pale yellowish tinge as the pile upon the abdomen; only exceptionally a dark bristle is sometimes found among them. The ground color of the abdomen is not quite constant; as a rule, it is blackish; I possess specimens, however, in which, upon the posterior margin of the second and third segments, it is yellowish-red. The ovipositor is shining black, rather strongly contracted towards its end, as long as the last two abdominal segments taken together; their short pile is very delicate and hence somewhat difficult to discern; it seems to have the same coloring as the pile on the abdomen. Feet saturate yellow. The wings have an almost regularly elliptical shape and are somewhat broader in the female than in the male (the figure is made from a male specimen). The guttate reticulation, which leaves open the extreme basis only, has a brownish-black coloring, which assumes a paler hue wherever the drops are nearer together; upon the stigma, however, and upon the end of the marginal cell, it becomes nearly black; the stigma contains a rather conspicuous hyaline drop; the drops upon the remaining surface are in general large, upon the middle of the wing, however, numerous, much smaller drops are interspersed, which perforate the dark coloring between the larger drops; this also takes place between the six large drops which form the usual pyramid of drops, situated beyond the stigma; upon the portion of the wing beyond this pyramid there are generally but very few little drops, and those are usually in the proximity of the pyramid; some larger drops, rather distant from each other, are also to be found there, and among them a row of very rounded drops along the margin of the wing, sometimes a little remote from it; they are either of very unequal size (as in the figure), or of the same size; the proximity of the posterior crossvein shows a more considerable space, which is but little perforated. The third longitudinal vein is not bristly.

Hab. Canada (Couper); English River (Kennicott); Maine (Packard).

Observation.—In the distribution adopted by me for the American species, the present one would belong to the genus *Tephritis.* Should my distribution of the European *Trypetæ* be applied to it, the shape of its oral opening and of the proboscis would refer it to *Oxyna.*

49. T. euryptera n. sp.   ♀.—Ex luteo-cinerea, abdomine bifariam nigro-maculata, capite et apice scutelli flavicantibus, pedibus luteis; alis valde dilatatis, rotundato-ovalis, præter imam basim totis colore fusco-nigro guttato-reticulatis, guttis valde inæqualibus, in apice et prope stigma venamque transversam posteriorem minus confertis, stigmate uniguttato, vena longitudinali tertiâ non setosâ; terebrâ fæminæ aterrimâ, duobus ultimis abdominis segmentis simul sumtis æqualis.

Yellowish-gray; abdomen with two longitudinal rows of black spots; head and tip of the scutellum pale yellow; feet saturate yellow; wings very broad, rounded oval, with the exception of the extreme basis covered with a guttate, brownish-black reticulation, the drops of which are of a very unequal size and less numerous in the vicinity of the stigma, of the posterior crossvein, and on the apex of the wing; stigma with a hyaline drop; the third longitudinal vein not bristly; the ovipositor of the female deep black, as long as the last two abdominal segments taken together. Long. corp. exm terebrâ 0.18 ; long. al. 0.16.

Closely allied to *T. albiceps* and very like it, but easily distinguished by its very broad wings. Yellowish-gray ; thorax and abdomen with yellowish-red pile ; the abdomen with two longitudinal rows of black spots. Head yellowish ; front and antennæ more yellow ; the usual bristles on the front black, the bristles on the vertical margin bright reddish-yellow. The third antennal joint with an almost sharp anterior corner. The oral opening longer than broad, the upper oral edge somewhat drawn upwards, distinctly projecting in the profile. The rather broad palpi and the proboscis are yellowish ; the latter short geniculate, with but moderately prolonged, rather stout flaps ; the occiput, in the vicinity of the point of attachment, grayish. The ground color of the humeral callus is yellowish, that of the thorax blackish ; the bristles of the dorsum are black, the two pairs upon its middle are inserted upon very small black dots, easily overlooked. Scutellum yellow at the tip, with four black bristles. Ovipositor of the female shining black, about as long as the last two abdominal segments taken together (in the only specimen in my possession the shape of the ovipositor is not distinctly discernible, but it does not seem to differ from that of *T. albiceps*) ; its short pubescence is delicate, and hence somewhat difficult to perceive ; its coloring seems to be altogether reddish. Feet saturate yellow. The wings are very broad and have a rounded elliptical shape. The guttate reticulation shows the most striking likeness to that of *T. albiceps*, so that the description of the latter may be applied to this ; the only addition to be made would be, that the region immediately below the stigma is somewhat darker and a little less guttate. Thus the figure of the wing of *T. albiceps* gives quite a correct idea of the wing of the present species, except of its broader shape ; moreover, the three posterior drops of the usual pyramid are smaller, and separated by larger intervals, and the intervals of all the six drops are perforated by much more numerous small drops. The third longitudinal vein is likewise not beset with bristles in this species.

Hab. West Point, N. Y. (Osten-Sacken).

Observation.—The systematic position of this species is exactly the same as that of *T. albiceps.*

20

80. T. platyptera n. sp. ♀.—Cinerea, abdomine quadrifariam nigro-maculato, capite pedibusque luteis, femoribus tamen posterioribus nigro-maculatis, scutello nigro- et flavo-variegato; alis valde dilatatis, rotundato-ovalis, tota colore nigro guttato-reticulate, vena longitudinali tertia non setosa.

Gray, abdomen with four rows of black spots, head and feet yellow, the hind femora spotted with black; scutellum variegated with yellow and black; wings very broad, rounded-ovate, covered upon their whole surface with a reticulate black picture; third vein not bristly. Long. corp. cum terebra 0.21; long. al. 0.16.

Of this species I possess a single badly preserved specimen, and I would not have attempted to describe it, but for the circumstance that it is distinguished by a number of very peculiar characters, which render its recognition easy, even should the description be imperfect. Head yellowish; occiput immediately above the point of attachment somewhat blackish; on each side, near the basis of the antennæ, there is, on the border of the eye, a small, almost punctiform, blackish-brown transverse streak. The breadth of the front, which is distinctly narrowed anteriorly, is comparatively considerable, as it equals half the breadth of the head; the usual frontal bristles are black, those upon the vertical margin are yellowish-white. The third antennal joint is gently excised upon its upper side, and has a rather sharp anterior angle. Cheeks rather broad, with a black bristle, in front of which, along the lateral edge of the mouth, there is some black pile. Oral opening very wide; its anterior edge is but little drawn up, although rather projecting in the profile. Palpi very broad, reaching beyond the anterior edge of the mouth, beset with black and whitish-yellow hairs. Proboscis short geniculate, with moderately prolonged, stout flaps. The thorax of the specimen is greasy, and it is impossible to make any positive statement about its coloring and the pile upon it; the coloring upon the dorsum seems to have been more blackish; on the sides more brown; the pile seems to have been stubble-shaped, yellowish-white; all the bristles, upon the thoracic dorsum as well as upon the pleuræ, are black. The very convex, blackish scutellum has, upon the lateral margins and upon the tip, a broad yellowish border; the four blackish bristles of the scutellum are placed inside of this border upon blackish dots; the pair of those dots which is near the tip, although smaller, is connected with the black coloring of the scutellum. Abdomen gray, with four rows of black spots. The spots of both intermediate rows are comparatively large rectangular triangles, one cathetus of which lies along the posterior margin of the segment, the other is parallel to the longitudinal axis of the abdomen; thus between both rows of spots, only a narrow gray intermediate line remains visible; the spots of the outer rows lie upon the lateral margins and also occupy the whole length of the segments, forming broad, uninterrupted lateral stripes. The whitish pile upon the abdomen is rather stubble-shaped; the comparatively long and strong bristles upon the posterior margin of the last segment are black. Venter somewhat dirty brick-red, gradually becoming blackish towards the lateral margins. Ovipositor flattened, broadly truncate at the end, shining black on the surface; the under side bright yellowish-red, with a black tip. Feet of an impure yellowish, the posterior femora on the under side with two well-defined blackish spots, and near the tip with a faded blackish spot. Wings very broad, of the same rounded elliptical shape as in *T. euryptera*. The black, guttate reticulation covers the whole wing to the extreme basis; along the whole posterior margin as far as the apex, there is a row of hyaline drops of middle size, separated by considerable intervals; beyond the apex, along the anterior margin, these drops become larger, their intervals growing smaller; in the marginal and costal cells they coalesce with a little drop placed behind them, so that, in these cells, the reticulation emits something like little rays, running towards the anterior margin; the stigma, upon the extreme basis, has a whitish crossline and includes a hyaline drop at the end; upon the whole inner side of the surface of the wing the black color is rather sparsely perforated by drops of middle and of the very smallest size; the latter are more numerous upon the posterior than upon the anterior half of the wing. The cells of the wings are all of an unusual breadth, and the crossveins accordingly of an unusual length; the distance between them is but little shorter than the middle crossvein; the second and third longitudinal veins are considerably divergent towards the end; upon the third I do not perceive any bristles.

Hab. Connecticut (H. F. Bassett).

Observation.—I leave this species provisionally in the genus *Tephritis*; the description shows sufficiently that it is a stranger there, whose affinities point towards the genus *Eurosta*. To

found a special genus for this single form would be premature,
as there are several concurrent South American species, without
the knowledge of which it is difficult to choose the characters
upon which to establish the genus. To place the species in the
genus *Eurosta* is likewise unadvisable, as the absence of bristles
upon the third vein, and the not conical but flattened ovipositor
are in conflict with the chief characters of *Eurosta*.

51. **T. æqualis** Loew. ♂ ♀. (Tab. II, f. 20.)—Dilute lutea, terebrâ
concolore, tribus ultimis abdominis segmentis simul sumtis longiore,
pilis, setisque totius corporis exalbidis; alæ colore ex-fusco nigricante,
adversus costam et apicem in nigrum mutato, æqualiter guttato-reticulatis, guttis confertis plerisque majusculis, picturâ marginis anticæ
radiatâ, marginis apicalis subradiatâ; vena longitudinalis tertia non
pilosa.

Pale yellowish; ovipositor of the female likewise yellow, longer than the
last three abdominal segments taken together; pile and bristles of the
whole body whitish; wings with a brownish-black guttate reticulation,
black near the anterior margin and the apex; the drops are crowded
and the majority of them are of a considerable size; the pattern of the
picture consists of rays along the anterior border, which are less well-
marked along the apex; the third vein is not beset with bristles.
Long. corp. ♂ 0.22, ♀ cum terebrâ 0.23—0.26; long. al. 0.24—0.25.

Syn. *Trypeta æqualis* Loew, Monogr. etc., I, p. 86. Tab. II, f. 20.

Hab. Illinois (Kennicott). [Maryland, P. R. Uhler; Ohio,
H. F. Bassett.—O. S.]

Observation.—The present species shows such a peculiar
structure of the head and of the parts of the mouth, that I would
not have hesitated to establish a separate genus for it, if I had
had better preserved specimens for examination. The general
appearance reminds of the species which I have united in the
genus *Icterica*, but it differs in a smaller oral opening, a different
shape of the wings, and a third longitudinal vein which is not
beset with bristles. Not being able to assign a better position
for it at present, I had the choice of leaving it in the genus
Tephritis or of removing it to the genus *Eurosta*, proposed in
the second observation to *Tryp. angustipennis*. The choice is
not a very easy one, because, although the picture of the wings
is distinctly radiate along the anterior margin as far as the apex,
the apex itself and the space immediately behind it are more
guttate than radiate. By all means, the question is more about

an artificial than about a final location of the species, as the latter will have to depend upon the results of a future investigation. The circumstance that the pyramid of drops beyond the stigma, usually well developed in the species collected in the subgenus *Tephritis*, is not distinctly marked here, decides me to place the species in *Euaresta*, although its affinities to the types of this subgenus may be very slight.

52. T. festiva Loew. ♂ ♀. (Tab. X, f. 21.)—Lutea, unicolor, alis inaequaliter guttato-reticulatis, in margine antico et apice radiatis, pictura in basi et disco sordide intumescentis, prope marginem anticum et in apicali alarum trivate fusco-nigri; terebra faemina quatuor ultimis abdominis segmentis simul sumtis subaequalis, non depressa, adversus apicem valde angusta, superne nigra vel fusco-nigra, infra adversus basim rufa.

Clay-yellow, unicolorous, the reticulation of the wings unequally guttate, radiate along the anterior margin and on the apex, more dingy clay-yellow upon the basis and in the middle; brownish-black along the anterior margin of the wing and upon the apex; the ovipositor of the female is almost as long as the last four abdominal segments taken together, not flattened, very narrow at the tip, black or brown on the upper side, the under side red towards the basis. Long. corp. ♂, 0.17 —0.18 ; ♀ cum terebra 0.20—0.23 ; long. al. 0.22.

Syn. *Trypeta festiva* Loew, Monographs, etc., I, p. 56. Tab. II, f. 21.

Hab. Pennsylvania (Osten-Sacken) ; Connecticut (Norton). [New Jersey, Mr. Iung; Illinois, Dr. Brendel; Ohio, H. F. Bassett.—O. S.]

Observation 1.— *Trypeta festiva* may be considered as a typical form of the genus *Euaresta.* As the third longitudinal vein of the wings is beset with spines, this species would have to be placed in the genus *Oxyphora*, in the classification adopted by me for the European species.

Observation 2.—Brazil possesses a conspicuous species closely allied to the present one, but more approaching the next following ones in the pattern of the picture of the wings. I let its description follow :—

T. spectabilis n. sp. ♂ ♀. (Tab. X, f. 27.)—Tota luteola, terebra tamen obscure ferruginea, non depressa et quatuor ultimis abdominis segmentis subaequalis ; scutellum quadrisetosum : alarum pictura nigra, in apice pulchre, sed breviter radiata, adversus angulum posticum rarins, in disco radiatim-guttata, gutta cellulae posterioris primae unica; vena longitudinalis tertia setosa.

Altogether yellowish, except the ovipositor, which is dark ferruginous, not flattened, and nearly as long as the last four abdominal segments taken together. Scutellum with four bristles; the black picture of the wings shows, on the apex, handsome, although short, rays; it is sparsely guttate towards the posterior angle, very sparsely in the middle of the wing; the first posterior cell contains but a single drop; the third longitudinal vein is bristly. Long. corp. 0.24—0.27; long. al. 0.24.

A rather conspicuous species, of the same coloring as the European *T. valida* Lw. With the exception of the ovipositor, it is altogether yellowish, only the heels of the abdomen is sometimes brownish. Front of a middle breadth and somewhat convex; its brownish-yellow or reddish-yellow bristles are comparatively strong; the frontal lunula rather large. Antennæ short, by far not reaching the edge of the mouth; the second joint bears a conspicuous bristle; the anterior edge of the mouth considerably drawn up, but not very projecting in the profile. Eyes not very high; cheeks broad. Oral opening rounded, rather large; proboscis not geniculate; palpi rather broad, reaching abundantly as far as the anterior edge of the mouth. The short pile on the thorax is partly pale ferruginous, partly pale yellowish-red; the anal bristles are pale yellow or brownish-yellow. The somewhat convex scutellum has four bristles. Metathorax and pleuræ yellow, like the rest of the body. Abdomen likewise uniformly yellow, but there are specimens the abdomen of which is infuscated at the basis; the pile on the abdomen is like that on the thorax, only its coloring is more yellowish. The stout, conical ovipositor is not flattened at all, about as long as the last four abdominal segments taken together; in paler specimens it is reddish-brown with a black tip; in darker specimens it is rather brownish-black; it is broad, as far as the tip, with comparatively long pile, which assumes a more yellowish hue near the basis, a more brownish one near the tip; in darker specimens it is sometimes blackish-brown. Feet altogether yellow. Wings hyaline with a very much expanded and very little perforated black reticulation, which is radiated at the apex of the wing. The root of the wings is not spotted nearly as far as the end of the small basal cells; the costal cell contains a gray crossline near the humeral cross-vein, a brownish-black crossband upon its middle, and a crossline of the same color at its extreme end; the obliterate end of the auxiliary vein, running perpendicularly towards the margin of the wing, is rather hyaline; the stigma is altogether black and does not include any hyaline drop; immediately beyond the stigma near the anterior margin, there are two cuneiform hyaline spots, the first of which is a little broader than the second and crosses the second vein a little further; between these spots and the end of the second vein the brownish-black coloring is entirely unbroken; five short brownish-black rays of almost equal length run towards the apex; the first ends between the second and third longitudinal veins, the next two coincide with the ends of the third and fourth veins; the last two cross the second posterior cell; the last of all is connected with the remaining brownish-black coloring by a narrow brownish-black bridge and sometimes interrupted at the basis; upon the anterior side of the fourth vein there are only two hyaline drops, the one below the stigma, the other between both crossveins; in the third posterior cell there are six hyaline drops, the one of which is at its extreme basis and the others upon its latter half; some of the latter drops are sometimes confluent; in the posterior angle there are, moreover, four or five hyaline drops. The small crossvein is almost perpendicular and is nearly opposite the last third of the discal cell; the posterior crossvein likewise is rather perpendicular; the third longitudinal vein is distinctly bristly.

Hab. Brazil (collection v. Winthem).

53. T. bella Lw. ♂ ♀. (Tab. X, f. 23.)—Luteo-cinerea, capite, pedibus, abdomineque flavis, hoc apicem versus nigricante; setis scutelli quatuor; alarum pictura nigra, in margine antico et apice pulchre radiata, prope marginem posticum paulo confertius, in disco rarissime guttata, gutta cellulae posterioris primae plane nulla; vena longitudinalis tertia setosa.

Yellowish-gray; head, feet, and abdomen yellow; the latter blackish towards the end; the black picture of the wings handsomely radiate on the anterior margin and the apex; in the vicinity of the posterior margin with numerous drops, upon the middle of the wing with very few, in the first posterior cell with none; third longitudinal vein bristly. Long. corp. ♂ 0.12—0.13, ♀ cum terebra 0.13—0.15; long. al. 0.11—0.12.

Syn. *Trypeta bella* Loew, Monographs, etc., I, p. 88. Tab. II, f. 23.

Hab. New York (Fitch); Washington (Osten-Sacken); Wisconsin, etc. [Rather common everywhere in the U. S.—O. S.]

Observation.—Closely related to *T. festiva*, and, as to its systematic location, the remarks appended to that species are also applicable here.

54. T. humida Lw. ♂. (Tab. X, f. 25.)—Lutea, metanoto pleurisque ex-nigro fascia, capite pedibusque flavis; setis scutelli quatuor; alarum pictura nigra, in apice pulchre radiata, prope marginem posticum rare et in disco rarissime guttata; gutta cellulae posterioris primae unica; vena longitudinalis tertia setulis paucis brevissimis instructa.

Clay-yellow, metathorax and pleura blackish-brown; head and feet yellow; four bristles upon the scutellum; the black picture of the wings is prettily radiated at the tip, in the vicinity of the posterior margin sparsely, and upon the middle of the wing very sparsely guttate, in the first posterior cell with a single drop; the third longitudinal vein is

beset with extremely short and scarce bristles. Long. corp. 0.17; long.
al. 0.16.

Syn. *Trypeta timida* Loew, Dipt. Am. Cent. II, No. 78.

Clay-yellow; the coloring of the head is of a purer yellow, but
the middle of the occiput is grayish. Front comparatively narrow; its pale brownish bristles are strong and long. Antennæ
yellow, not reaching to the oral edge; anterior corner of the third
joint rounded; arista comparatively thin, its pubescence so short,
that, to the naked eye, the arista appears bare. Face excavated;
the anterior edge much drawn upwards, but little projecting in
the profile. Eyes elongated-rounded; cheeks very narrow.
Oral opening of a middle size, rather round; the yellowish proboscis not geniculate, short; palpi short, yellowish. The upper
side of the thorax is clothed with pale yellowish hairs; upon its
middle there is a weak trace of a very broad grayish stripe, which,
however, in less denuded specimens, may be hardly visible. The
bristles upon the upper side of the thorax are pale brownish;
upon its middle there are three pairs. The yellow scutellum
bears four bristles. The ground color of the metathorax is
blackish-brown, but assumes a grayish aspect from a thin covering of pollen. The pleuræ have a similar coloring, but towards the
upper margin, it becomes more yellow, and below the root of the
wings there also is a spot of dingy yellow. The clay-yellow abdomen shows, in the described specimen, upon the last two segments
brownish spots, which, however, seem to be the result of some
lesion. Feet yellow. Wings rather broad with a brownish black,
very sparsely reticulated picture, which is radiated on the apex;
the root of the wings is very sparsely spotted before the end of
the two small basal cells; the costal cell, near its basis, has a
blackish transverse line, a brownish-black one beyond its middle,
and another brownish-black one upon its extreme end; the
obliterate end of the auxiliary vein, which runs perpendicularly
towards the anterior margin, is rather hyaline; stigma brownish-
black with a yellow crossline in the vicinity of its end; immediately beyond the stigma there are two cuneiform hyaline indentations, which extend from the margin to the second longitudinal
vein; the latter is somewhat remote from the margin; between the
second of these indentations and almost the end of the second
vein, the brown color is not perforated; along the apex, the

brown color emits five brown rays of almost equal length. The
first of these rays ends a little before the middle of the distance
between the tips of the second and third veins; the two next ones,
which are a little expanded at the tip, lie on the ends of the third
and fourth veins, the last two in the second posterior cell; the
last of these rays, in the vicinity of its origin, is not quite well
separated from the remaining brownish-black picture. The hyaline drops are rather large, but few in number; there are two
between the third and fourth longitudinal veins, the first before
the small crossvein, the second less far beyond it; the discal cell
also contains but two drops, placed under the small crossvein and
nearer to the posterior side of the cell; the third posterior cell
has a drop at its extreme basis and five considerable ones in the
posterior angle of the wing, which, however, are less conspicuous,
because the dark coloring in that region is more faded. The
distance of the first and second longitudinal veins from the margin
is a little larger than usual; the second and third veins are
strongly diverging towards the end; a weaker divergency exists
between the third and fourth veins; the two crossveins are perpendicular and straight; the small crossvein is almost twice as
far from the proximal end of the discal cell as from the distal end.
In my first description of this species I said that the third vein
was not beset with bristles; a more attentive examination of the
specimen, however, revealed to me, on one of the wings, a few very
short bristles, which are either rubbed off on the other wing, or
else in a situation which does not allow their close scrutiny; the
first posterior cell does not contain a conspicuous concavity, like
that in *T. bella;* and the corresponding spot is not darker than
its surroundings.

Hab. Mexico (collect. v. Winthem).

Observation 1.—The systematic position of *T. timida* is exactly
the same as that of *T. festiva* and *bella.*

Observation 2.—The next relative of *T. timida* is a Brazilian
species, which can be very easily mistaken for it; and in order to
prevent this confusion, I let its description follow here:—

T. obscuriventris n. sp. ♀. (Tab. X, f. 26.)—Ex luteo cinerea,
capite prollbusque infrascentibus, abdomine ex pioeo nigro et nitido,
terebrâ concolore, tribus ultimis abdominis segmentis simol exemptis
aequali; seta aequalil quatuor; alarum pictura nigra, in apice pulchra

radiata, prope marginem posticum raro et in disco rarissime guttata,
gutta cellula posterioris prima unica; vena longitudinalis tertia setosa.

Yellowish-gray, head and feet yellow, abdomen shining brownish-black,
ovipositor concolorous, as long as the last three abdominal segments
taken together; scutellum with four bristles; the black picture of the
wings handsomely radiated on the apex, sparsely guttate in the vicinity
of the posterior margin, very sparsely in the middle of the wing; a
single drop in the first posterior cell; the third longitudinal vein basal
with bristles. Long. corp. cum terebrā 0.20; long. al. 0.16.

Head, including palpi, proboscis, and antennæ, yellow; only the occiput
for the most part grayish. Front comparatively narrow; its brown
bristles are long and strong. Antennæ not reaching to the edge of the
mouth; third joint rounded at the end; arista comparatively thin, appearing bare to the naked eye, as the pubescence is very short; face excavated;
the oral opening hardly of middle size, round; proboscis short, not geniculate. Palpi of middle size; the ground color of the thorax is altogether
black, including even the humeral callosities, but this color is so much
concealed under ochre-yellow pile and pulverulence, that it assumes a
yellowish-gray hue; upon the pleura and especially on the metanotum
the dark ground color is more apparent. The scutellum, bearing four
bristles, is yellow to a considerable extent at the tip; the abdomen is of
a shining brownish-black and shows weak traces of a yellowish-brown
pollen; the pile is short and scattered, of mixed yellow and black hairs;
the latter prevail or seem to do so, as many of the yellow hairs assume a
blackish hue when they do not reflect the light. The flat, not very
pointed ovipositor is pitch-black, shining, about as long as the last three
segments of the abdomen taken together, beset as far as the tip with a
brown pubescence, appearing black in some directions. Feet yellow. The
comparatively rather broad wings have a brownish-black, very sparsely
guttate picture, which is handsomely radiate at the tip; the root of the
wings, as far almost as the end of the small basal cells, is hardly spotted
at all; the costal cell, quite near the humeral crossvein, has a grayish
crossline, a brownish-black one upon the middle and one of the same color,
but narrower, at the end; the obliterate end of the auxiliary vein, running perpendicularly towards the anterior margin, is rather hyaline;
stigma altogether brownish or only with a trace of a very small yellowish
drop in the vicinity of its apex, near the anterior margin; immediately
beyond the stigma there are two hyaline indentations on the anterior
margin, the first of which alone reaches the rather distant second longitudinal vein; before the end of the second longitudinal vein near the
anterior margin, there always is a considerable hyaline drop, which *T.
timida* does not possess; five rays of almost equal length occupy the apex;
the first of these reaches the margin nearer to the end of the second than
of the third vein; the two following are somewhat expanded at the tip
and end upon the tips of the third and fourth veins; the last two rays

cross the second posterior cell, and the last of them is a little broader than the preceding one and generally connected in the vicinity of its root with the remaining brownish-black picture by a brownish-black bridge, which cuts off the end of the hyaline indented interval in the shape of a drop. The hyaline drops are of a considerable size, but not very numerous; two are placed between the third and fourth veins, the one before, the other less far behind the small crossvein; in the same way there are only two drops in the discal cell, placed upon its posterior side, below the small crossvein; the third posterior cell contains a drop near its extreme basis and five considerable drops upon its distal half; finally four drops are situated in the posterior corner of the wing, which, however, are less conspicuous on account of the less dark coloring surrounding them. The first and second longitudinal veins are somewhat more distant from the anterior margin than usual; the second and third are strongly divergent towards the end; a lesser divergency exists between the third and fourth; both crossveins are perpendicular and straight; the small one is twice as far from the basis as from the end of the discal cell; the third vein is distinctly bristly; there is no distinct concavity in the first posterior cell, and the spot where it occurs in some species is not darker than the surroundings.

Hab. Brazil (coll. v. Winthem).

55. **T. melanogastra** Lw. ♂ ♀.　(Tab. X, f. 24.)—Luteo-cinerea, abdomine nigro, capite pedibusque flavis; seta scutelli duæ; alarum pictura nigra, in apice radiata, prope marginem posticum paulo confertius, in disco rarissimo guttata, gutta cellulæ posterioris primæ nulla; vena longitudinalis tertia non setosa.

Yellowish-gray, abdomen black, head and feet yellow; scutellum with two bristles; the black picture of the wings with rays at the tip, more densely guttate in the vicinity of the posterior margin, very sparsely in the middle, and with a single drop in the first posterior cell; the third longitudinal vein is not bristly.　Long. corp. ♂ 0.09, ♀ 0mm terebra 0.12; long. al. 0.12.

Syn. *Trypeta melanogastra* Loew, Monographs, etc., I, p. 90.　Tab. II, f. 24.

Hab. Cuba (Poey).

Observation 1.—Two misprints must be corrected in the description in the first volume of these Monographs: the figure of the wing is quoted fig. 23, instead of 24, and on page 91, line 19, "fifth" must be read, instead of "first." Moreover, it must be added that the figure was drawn from a female specimen. The relation of *T. melanogastra* to *T. mexicana* Wied. will be explained under the head of the latter.

Observation 2.— *T. melanogastra* belongs, together with the

preceding species, to the genus *Euaresta*; it differs from them in
the presence of only two bristles upon the scutellum and in the
absence of bristles upon the third vein. In the system adopted
by me some time ago for the European Trypetidæ, this species,
on account of the somewhat prolonged flaps of its proboscis and
of the bareness of the third vein, would have to be placed in the
genus *Oxyna*. I do not believe that its generic separation from
the preceding species is to be recommended. A close relative
of this species is a Brazilian one, which differs, however, in its
wings being comparatively much narrower and its body more
slender. I let its description follow:—

T. tenuis n. sp. ♀. (Tab. X, f. 29.)—Angusta, luteo-cinerea, capite
pedibusque gracilimis flavis; setis scutelli duae; ala pro portione
angusta, pictura nigra in angulo postico elata, in apice radiata, prope
marginem posticum confertius, in disco rarissime guttata, gutta cellulæ
posterioris primæ unica.

Slender, yellowish-gray; the head and the slender feet are yellow; wings
comparatively narrow, with a black picture, which is faded on the
posterior angle, radiate on the apex, more densely guttate near the
posterior margin, very sparsely in the middle of the wing, where the
first posterior cell contains but a single drop; third longitudinal vein
not bristly. Long. corp. cum terebra 0.13; long. al. 0.13.

Body remarkably narrow and slender. Ground color blackish, but so
much covered with yellowish pile and pulverulence that thorax and
abdomen have a yellowish-gray appearance. Head, including antennæ,
palpi, and proboscis, yellow; occiput, on its upper half, with a large blackish-gray spot. The front a little more than of medium breadth; its usual
bristles blackish. Face somewhat excavated and narrower than the front.
Antennæ somewhat broad, not quite reaching the edge of the mouth, which
is somewhat drawn upwards, but does not project distinctly in the profile.
Eyes comparatively large and rounded; cheeks very narrow. The palpi
reach to the anterior edge of the mouth. The suctorial flaps seem to be
somewhat injured in the described specimen, so that I am not quite sure
whether the proboscis is geniculate or not; I believe that, in uninjured
specimens, it would look short-geniculate; the dark color which the flaps
have in the described specimen is certainly an unnatural one. The
ground color of the thorax is altogether blackish, even upon the humeral
corners; its upper side has a yellowish-gray appearance, in consequence
of its pulverulence and pile; on the metathorax and the pleuræ the
coloring is more blackish-gray. The scutellum is of the same coloring
with the upper side of the thorax, the extreme apex only somewhat
tinged with yellow; it bears only two bristles, which, like those of the

thorax, are blackish. Abdomen narrow, but little more gray than the upper side of the thorax, without any rows of dark spots, but on each side of the second segment with a but little apparent yellow spot; the short pile as well as the longer hairs upon the posterior margin of the last segment are yellowish. The flat, shining black ovipositor is as long as the whole abdomen, and basal with dark pile. The feet are slender and yellow, as well as the coxæ. Wings rather hyaline, with a brownish-black very continuous reticulation; the root of the wings is not distinctly spotted as far as the end of the small basal cells, but somewhat dusky; upon the middle of the costal cell there is a blackish-brown crossline; the stigma does not contain any hyaline drop, but its inner basal end is very slightly tinged with yellow; immediately beyond the stigma there are, near the anterior margin, two drop-like hyaline spots; each of them has a small hyaline drop under it, below the second longitudinal vein; the second one is smaller; before the end of the second vein there is no hyaline drop; near the tip of the wing the apex shows the usual five rays, which have a considerable breadth, and the last of which is connected by a bridge with the remaining brownish-black coloring, which thus isolates the inner end of the hyaline interval in the shape of a drop; the anterior side of the fourth vein shows two conspicuous spots, one immediately before, the other not far beyond, the small crossvein; in the discal cell there are three hyaline drops along the fifth vein, the middle one being the largest and lying almost under the small crossvein; above the last of these drops there is sometimes one little drop more; the extreme basis of the discal cell also shows an indistinct, sometimes double, little drop; the third posterior cell contains but a few large drops, which are partly coalescent in couples; the posterior corner of the wing is likewise guttate, but the drops are much less apparent here, owing to the pale ground color. The small crossvein is hardly half as distant from the end of the discal cell as from the basis; the third longitudinal vein is not bristly.

Hab. Brazil (collect. v. Winthem).

56. T. mexicana Wied. ♀. (Tab. X, f. 26.)—Luteo-cinerea, abdomine nigro, adversus basim interdum sordide luteo, capite pedibusque flavis; seta scutelli duæ; alarum pictura nigra in apice radiata, radiis tamen in marginem posticum excurrentibus minus explicatis et minus libera, prope marginem posticum confertius, in disco rarissime guttata, gutta cellulæ posterioris primæ unica; vena longitudinalis tertia non setosa.

Yellowish-gray, abdomen black, sometimes of a dingy clay-yellow towards the basis; head and feet yellow; scutellum with two bristles; the black picture of the wings is radiate on the apex, but the rays in the vicinity of the posterior margin are less developed and less free; the drops near the posterior margin are more numerous, those in the middle of the wing very sparse; the first posterior cell contains but a single drop;

third longitudinal vein not beset with bristles. Long. corp. 0.09—0.10;
long. al. 0.12.

6th. *Trypeta mexicana* WIEDEMANN, Ausw. Zweifl. II, p. 551.

Yellowish-gray. Front of a more vivid yellow, upon the lateral
margin with a rather indistinct whitish pollen; the usual bristles
upon it are black; those on the vertical margin pale yellowish.
Eyes rounded ovate; cheeks very narrow. Face distinctly
excavated, the anterior edge of the mouth is strongly drawn
upwards and rather projecting in the profile. The bristles of the
thoracic dorsum seem to be black, in reflected light they appear
brown; in the middle of the dorsum there are but two pairs, the
first of which is very much advanced. The short pile upon the
thorax and the bristles upon the pleura are pale yellowish.
Scutellum of a dingy-yellow at the tip, and with two bristles.
Abdomen black (a male from Texas shows a dingy yellowish
coloring at the basis), appearing almost grayish-black under a
very thin pulverulence, which does not prevent it from retaining
some lustre; its pile is almost without exception pale yellowish.
Feet and coxæ rather saturate yellow, the pile and bristles upon
them yellowish. Wings hyaline with a brownish-black picture,
which is almost completely radiate towards the end; however,
the rays ending in the posterior margin are less developed and
less separated from each other than is the case in a normal pattern
of this kind; the hyaline intervals between the rays distinctly
show that they owe their origin to confluent drops. The root
of the wings is but little spotted as far as the beginning of the
stigma and the end of the small basal cells; the adjoining portion
of the picture is almost without drops, so as almost to assume
the appearance of an oblique crossband, running towards the
posterior margin; the stigma at its basis contains a small hyaline
drop; immediately beyond it, in the marginal cell, there are two
square hyaline spots, separated by a brownish-black line; under
the first of them the submarginal cell contains a considerable
hyaline drop; the anterior side of the fourth vein shows two large
drops, the one a little before, the other a little beyond the small
crossvein; the discal cell, on the fifth vein, contains three drops,
the first of which is the smallest and the second the largest; the
third posterior cell contains, besides the small hyaline spot at the
basis, four drops of considerable size, three of which are placed
at the posterior side of the fifth longitudinal vein; in the poste-

rior corner likewise there are several drops. The third longitudinal vein is without bristles and the small crossvein corresponds to the second third of the discal cell.

Hab. Mexico (Berlin Museum); Texas (Belfrage).

Observation.—The above description, as well as the figure, are prepared after the specimen in the Berlin Museum, which is the original type of Wiedemann's description. Two males, sent by Mr. Belfrage from Texas, agree in all respects, with the only exception that, in one of them, the basis of the abdomen is dingy yellowish. I am in doubt whether *T. mexicana* is not the male of the Cuban species, which I described as *T. melanogastra,* and of which I possess a very imperfect soiled and faded specimen, not sufficient to enable me to form an opinion. A part of the apparent differences may be due to this condition of the specimen. The description of *T. melanogastra* in the first volume of the Monographs says that there is sometimes a clear drop immediately before the end of the second vein; I must complete this statement by saying that this drop exists in the two females of my collection, but not in the male; whether this difference in the picture of the wings is a constant, or at least an ordinary, sexual distinction, I am not prepared to say. The development of the rays ending in the posterior margin in the female of *T. melanogastra* is not even always as complete as Tab. X, f. 24 (drawn after a female specimen) represents it; and the male of my collection approaches very much in this respect the typical male of *T. mexicana.* The differences which fig. 24 and 28 show in the development of the drops in the vicinity of the posterior margin, are of not much importance for specific distinction, as the reticulation in that vicinity is very variable in many species. All these circumstances seem to militate very strongly in favor of specific identity. The only notable difference which I can perceive in the typical male of *T. mexicana* (in the Berlin Museum) as well as in the two males from Texas in my collection, when compared to my single male specimen and my two females of *T. melanogastra,* consists in the position of the hyaline drop in the submarginal cell, which in *T. mexicana* is placed under the first of the two hyaline indentations situated in front of it, while in *T. melanogastra* it is under the brown line which separates the two indentations. This difference is not important and not equally distinct in all specimens, and it is probable that the

comparison of a larger number of them will still more prove its
insignificance. There will be no reason then to maintain *T.
melanogastra* as a separate species.

57. T. pura n. sp. ♀.—Cinerea, thorace fusco-vittato, pilisque albidis
instructo, abdomine nigro-piloso, capite pedibusque ex fusco-luteis; seta
scutelli quatuor; alae albidae, praeter basim et angulum posticum colore
nigro guttato-reticulata, in apice radiata, guttis in dimidio posteriore
confertis, in anteriore rarissimis, tribus tamen majoribus ultra stigma
in triangulum dispositis; vena longitudinalis tertia non pilosa.

Gray, thorax with brown longitudinal stripes and white pile, abdomen
with black pile, head and feet brownish-yellow; scutellum with four
bristles; wings whitish, except the basis and the posterior angle, with
a black reticulation, which is radiate on the apex; it is somewhat
guttate upon the posterior region, sparsely on the anterior; immediately
beyond the stigma there are three large drops, disposed in a triangle;
the third longitudinal vein is not bristly. Long. corp. cum terebra
0.23; long. al. 0.19.

Gray; abdomen more blackish-gray. Head clay-yellowish;
the front more brownish-brick color (which may be due to a dis-
coloration of the described specimen); it is remarkably broad,
almost half as broad as the whole head; the usual bristles upon
it are black, the bristles on the vertical margin whitish.
Antennae almost brownish-brick color; the short pile on the
second segment is whitish; that on the third is blackish; the
third joint is gently excised on the upper side; arista blackish-
brown. Oral opening of medium size; its anterior edge somewhat drawn upwards and a little projecting in the profile. Proboscis not geniculate; palpi not quite reaching to the anterior
edge of the mouth, with black pile. Eyes rounded, their perpendicular diameter but little longer than the horizontal one. Cheeks
of a moderate breadth. Thoracic dorsum with indistinctly
limited, although well-marked, rather dark brown longitudinal
stripes; its short pile is whitish, the bristles black. Scutellum
grayish-brown, with a broad grayish border on the sides, and
with four black bristles. The ground color of the abdomen is
black, the posterior margin of each segment brick-red, especially
the last segment, where this border is the broadest; its pile is
yellowish-white in the vicinity of the basis only, elsewhere without exception black. Ovipositor flattened, rather broadly truncate at the end, shorter than the last two abdominal segments

taken together, red or brownish-red, with a black border at the
tip; its pile is black, whitish on the basal corners only; on the
under side there is some whitish pile, conspicuous for its greater
length. The whole venter has a brick-brownish coloring; the
pile upon it seems to be of the same color as that on the upper
side. Feet brownish clay-yellow, almost brownish, brick color.
Wings in the reflected light altogether milky-white, in a transmitted light whitish-hyaline. The picture of the wings is black;
it does not cover the whole posterior corner of the wing and the
longitudinal half of the third posterior cell, contiguous to it, with
the only exception of a very striking black border along the sixth
longitudinal vein; above this the reticulation begins a little
beyond the little basal cells, and, at the anterior margin, with the
black stigma, which contains no drops. The space thus left free
contains but a few isolated little black spots. The pattern of the
picture recalls the European *T. pulchra* Lw. (compare my
Trypetidæ, Tab. XXIV, f. 2); in the shape and position of the
two portions of it which are almost without any drops, it is still
more like *T. conjuncta* Lw. (comp. *Trypetidæ*, Tab. XXIV, f.
1), only the drops upon the posterior half of the wing are much
more numerous than in those two species; the first almost drop-
less space begins at the stigma and runs obliquely to the small
crossvein; the second is limited posteriorly by the fourth vein and
becomes completely confluent with the first space upon and
immediately behind the third vein; upon the anterior margin
both spaces are separated, immediately beyond the stigma, by a
large, somewhat triangular drop, and by a rounded drop which
follows it; a third drop, of considerable size, in the submarginal
cell, forms a triangle with the other two; the submarginal cell
contains, moreover, under the second drop near the anterior
margin, another little drop; the second almost non-reticulated
space contains two drops on the anterior margin, the first of
which is a little distance before, the second immediately beyond
the end of the second longitudinal vein, and sends four tolerably
well-developed rays towards the margin; the first two of these
coincide with the ends of the second and third longitudinal veins,
the last two are in the second posterior cell; the first basal cell
shows only a row of drops along its posterior side; the first
posterior cell contains, besides a few very small drops in the
vicinity of its posterior side, a large drop, placed a little before

the end of the discal cell; the numerous drops of the discal cell
are of very unequal size, show an inclination to be arranged in
two rows and leave more black space on the anterior than on the
posterior side; in the third posterior cell the somewhat lacerated
reticulation is confined in a very marked manner, to the somewhat larger longitudinal half of the cell, contiguous to the discal
cell; both crossveins are perpendicular and less distant from each
other than the length of the small crossvein; the third vein is not
bristly.

Hab. Massachusetts (Sanborn).

Observation.—I place this species in the genus *Euaresta*, on
account of the reticulation, which is radiate on the apex. While
*T. festiva, spectabilis, bella, obscuriventris, mexicana, melano-
gastra,* and *tenuis,* all closely related, form the solid nucleus of
the genus, the connection of *T. pura* with it is a purely artificial
one, based upon a resemblance in the picture of the wings; it has
more real relationship to those *Urellia*, the scutellum of which
has four bristles. But in order to place *T. pura* in that genus, it
will be necessary to modify its definition, which will have to be done
in further developing the system of the *Trypetina.* According
to the system adopted in my Monograph of the European *Trypetidæ,* this species would have to be placed in the genus
Tephritis.

334. T. abaterna Lw. ♂ ♀. (Tab. XI, f. 7.)—Cinerea, capite, pedibus
et scutello setis quatuor instructo, flavis; alarum dimidium basale
colore cinereo obsolete reticulatum, apicale macula nigra, pulchre radiata, ornatum.

Gray, head, feet, and the four-bristly scutellum yellow; the proximal half
of the wings with a faded gray reticulation, the distal half with a black,
handsomely radiated spot. Long. corp. ♂ 0.12—0.13, ♀ cum terebra
0.13—0.14; long. al. 0.12—0.13.

Syn. *Trypeta abaterna* Loew, Dipt. Amer. Cent. II, No. 77.

The ground color of thorax and abdomen is rather variable;
generally it is altogether blackish; the humeri, often also the
upper side of the pleura, the scutellum, the basis of the abdomen,
and the posterior margins of its segments usually are, to a greater
or lesser extent, clay-yellowish; sometimes the yellowish color is
so extended, that, except upon the thoracic dorsum and the metathorax, hardly any blackish is left; nevertheless the ground color
of the thorax and of the abdomen is so covered up by a pale

pulverulence and pale yellowish pile, that thorax and abdomen assume a uniform grayish-yellow hue. Head yellow, except the middle of the occiput, which shows a large blackish-brown spot. Front rather broad, attenuated anteriorly; the usual bristles very pale yellowish. Antennæ dark yellow, not quite reaching the somewhat projecting edge of the mouth; the anterior corner of the third joint rounded. The broad oral opening rather round. Proboscis and palpi short, not reaching beyond the anterior edge of the oral opening; proboscis not geniculate. The upper side of the thorax is beset with brown or brownish bristles. Scutellum yellow, with four bristles. Ovipositor reddish-yellow, flat, rather broad, somewhat shorter than the last two abdominal segments taken together, beset with whitish pile. Feet yellow, front femora with yellowish bristles. Wings hyaline; their proximal half is somewhat less limpid than the distal one, rather uniformly pictured with a loose, gray reticulation, which is faintest near the anterior margin; the distal half of the wing is occupied by the radiated black spot, characteristic of the genus *Urellia*, which extends from the anterior margin to the fourth vein; this spot emits two narrow oblique rays, running towards the anterior margin; the first begins at the anterior end of the small crossvein and runs to the end of the colorless stigma; the second, shorter one, reaches the middle between the tip of the stigma and beginning of the black spot itself; three rays run towards the apex, of which the ends of the two posterior ones coincide with the ends of the third and fourth veins, where they are somewhat expanded; the shortest, anterior ray, sometimes separated from the body of the black spot by two drops only, reaches the anterior margin between the ends of the second and third veins; the first two of the rays running towards the posterior margin cross the middle of the second posterior cell; the narrower third ray follows the posterior crossvein and is sometimes connected with the second by a gray bridge, which divides the hyaline indentation between them into two large drops; in the first posterior cell, above and a little before the posterior crossvein there is a large hyaline drop, which, upon its proximal side, is bordered with black or blackish. The third vein is not bristly.

Hab. North America (coll. Winthem); Cuba (Gundlach).

Observation 1.—I have described *T. abstersa* in the Dipt. Am.

Cent. II, after a North American female in the Winthem collection. I have received since several specimens of a Cuban *Trypeta* from Mr. Gundlach, which I suppose to be the same species.
They are somewhat smaller, have a more extended blackish
coloring, and the incomplete gray reticulation of the proximal
half of the wing is considerably darker towards the posterior
margin. Unfortunately, I have not the original specimen of the
Winthem collection at hand for comparison, and, therefore, cannot finally decide about the specific identity. In the figure of
the wing, the gray reticulation of its proximal half is represented
by the engraver me too distinctly guttate, in fact more so than is
the case in either the Cuban or in the typical specimen.

Observation 2.— T. abstersa belongs in the genus *Urellia*, and
in the group of species having four bristles upon the scutellum.
The more developed picture on the basal half of the wing requires,
however, that it should be placed on the limit of this genus and
in the close relationship of *T. pura* and similar species.

59. T. polyclona n. sp. ♀.—Albido-cinerea, capite pedibusque
flavis; setis scutelli quatuor; alis hyalinis, praeter dimidii apicalis
maculam magnam nigram, radios novem emittente, duos in costam,
duos in apicem et quinque in marginem posticum emorrentes.

Whitish-gray, head and feet yellow. Scutellum with four bristles; wings
hyaline, upon their distal half with a large black spot, which emits
nine rays, namely, two to the anterior margin, two to the apex, and five
to the posterior margin. Long. corp. cum terebra 0.15; long. al. 0.14.

Of this handsome species I possess only a single, rather worn,
specimen. Head yellow, of the same structure as in *T. abstersa*,
only the front comparatively narrower. Thorax, scutellum, and
the whole abdomen whitish-gray. The bristles on the scutellum
are broken off, nevertheless it is apparent that they were four in
number. Ovipositor black, somewhat longer than the last two
abdominal segments taken together. Feet yellow. Wings
whitish-hyaline, upon their distal half with a large spot, emitting
nine rays towards the margin of the wing; the spot is a little
removed from the small crossvein, near which, in the first basal
cell, there is an irregular blackish spot; the first ray runs from
the anterior end of the small crossvein in an oblique direction
through the otherwise colorless stigma, to the costal vein, which,
at the place where it is thus reached, has a conspicuously black

color; the second ray also runs obliquely to the anterior margin, which it reaches before the middle of the distance between the ends of the second and third longitudinal veins; the third and fourth rays run towards the apex and end upon the ends of the third and fourth veins; among the five rays running towards the posterior margin, the first two cross, as usual, the second posterior cell, and the third follows the posterior crossvein; the fourth originates but little beyond the posterior crossvein, exactly at the place where the spot incloses a large drop, placed on the anterior side of the fourth vein; it runs almost parallel to the preceding ray as far as the posterior margin; the last ray finally originates at the posterior end of the small crossvein, and runs in a very oblique direction, diverging from that of the preceding ray, towards the margin, in the vicinity of which the intensity of its coloring is diminished; the drops, through the coalescence of which the hyaline intervals between the last three rays are formed, are indicated by the irregular outlines of the last two rays; besides the drop already mentioned, which is situated on the anterior side of the fourth vein, the black spot contains a second drop immediately beyond the end of the second vein.

Hab. Cuba (Gundlach).

Observation 1.—*T. polyclona* is a typical *Urellia*, and belongs, as well as *T. abstersa*, to the division with four bristles on the scutellum.

Observation 2.—One would almost be tempted to recognize in this species the *T. uncinrna* Walker, List, etc., IV, p. 1033, from Florida, which is an *Urellia*. But a positive identification is prevented by the circumstance that Walker mentions the feet as having black pile, which is not at all the case in my species.

60. T. solaris Lw. ♀. (Tab. X, f. 19.)—Albido-cinerea, capite pedibusque flavis, setis scutelli duabus; alis albo-hyalinis, prope venam transversalem medianam sublinfuscatis, in dimidio apicali macula magna nigra ornata, guttas duas incidentes et radios septem integros, quinqueque abbreviatum emittente.

Whitish-gray, head and feet yellow; scutellum with two bristles; wings whitish-hyaline, brownish in the vicinity of the small crossvein, upon the distal half with a large black spot, which contains two drops and emits eight rays, the last of which alone is shortened. Long. corp. cum terebra 0.17; long. al. 0.18—0.17.

Syn. *Trypeta solaris* Loew, Monogr., etc., I, p. 84. Tab. II, f. 19.

Hab. Georgia (Osten-Sacken).

Observation.—To the above-quoted description I must add, in order to facilitate the distinction from the following species, that the rays running towards the posterior margin are strongly marked, and that the last of them ends abruptly at the fifth vein (the distance is too large in the figure); that there is no trace of a blackish spot near the fifth vein, but that, in the discal cell, immediately beyond its middle, there is an exceedingly minute gray mark. This species is a typical *Urellia*, of the group with two bristles on the scutellum.

61. T. actinobola n. sp. ♀.—Albido-cinerea, capite pedibusque flavis, setis scutelli duae, alis totis albo-hyalinæ, præter punctum nigrum venæ quintæ oppositum in dimidio apicali maculâ magnâ nigrâ ornatæ, guttas duas includente et radios septem integros, octavamque abbreviatam emittente.

Whitish-gray, head and feet yellow, scutellum with two bristles; wings altogether whitish hyaline, with the exception of a punctiform dot on the fifth longitudinal vein and of a large black spot upon the distal half of the wing; the latter contains two drops and emits eight rays, the last of which alone is abbreviated. Long. corp. 0.13—0.14; long. al. 0.15.

This species is so very like the preceding that the mention of the differences in the picture of the wings will be sufficient for its recognition. There is no trace here of the brownish coloring which, in *T. solaris*, surrounds the small crossvein, and likewise none of the minute mark in the first basal cell, near the small crossvein; the little dot beyond the middle of the discal cell which occurs in *T. solaris* is likewise wanting here; but instead of these, there is, on the posterior side of the fifth vein, nearly under the end of the first vein, a very well-marked punctiform blackish dot; the large black spot on the apex is very like that in *T. solaris*, with the following differences: the first ray is not extinguished within the stigma, but crosses it without being discolored and reaches the margin; the rays running towards the apex and the posterior margin are very much narrower; the same applies to the last ray, which, moreover, is interrupted already in the discal cell, before reaching the fifth vein.

Hab. Texas (Belfrage).

ANALYTICAL TABLE OF THE SMALLER GENERA,

ADOPTED FOR THE NORTH AMERICAN TRYPETÆ.

1 { A picture on the wings is extant, but it is never reticulate.　　3
    The picture is entirely or partly reticulate, sometimes altogether
    wanting.[1]　　15

2 { Scutellum with six bristles.[2]　　I. HEXACHÆTA.
    Scutellum not with six bristles.　　3

3 { The third vein conspicuously curved forwards at the tip.
    　　II. ACROTOXA.
    The third vein not curved forwards at the tip.　　4

4 { The picture of the wings is on the rivulet-pattern.　　5
    The picture of the wings is not on the rivulet-pattern.　　6

5 { Body elongate, abdomen narrower than thorax.　VI. STRAUZIA.
    Body short, abdomen as broad as thorax.　　6

6 { Horizontal diameter of the eyes remarkably short.　III. STENOPA.
    Horizontal diameter of the eyes not shorter than usual.　　7

7 { The antepenultimate section of the fourth vein straight. IV. ACIDIA.
    The antepenultimate section of the fourth vein curved. V. EURIBIA.

8 { Coloring of the body generally light, never black.　　9
    Coloring of the body black.　　13

9 { Upon the middle of the wing there are two crossbands converging
    towards the posterior margin.　　10
    No crossbands converging posteriorly upon the middle of the wing.
    　　11

10 { The third longitudinal vein is gently curved backwards towards the
     end; head not tumid.　　VII. SPILOGRAPHA.
     The third longitudinal vein is straight, up to its tip; head perceptibly
     swollen.　　VIII. OEDASPIS.

11 { Wings with four very oblique crossbands and with very oblique
     approximate crossveins.　　12
     Wings with crossbands which are rather perpendicular or dissolved
     in spots and with very steep crossveins.　　XI. TRYPETA.

---

[1] Among these species is *T. Lichtensteinii*, the picture of which cannot
well be called reticulate, but rather spotted.

[2] Compare also *Ensina*.

12 { Scutellum tumid, bituberculate.   IX. PAROXYNA.
   { Scutellum of the ordinary structure, not swollen, although convex.
                                                                          X. PLAGIOTOMA.

13 { Crossveins conspicuously approximate, scutellum generally swollen.
                                                                          XII. OXDASYA.
   { Crossveins not approximate, scutellum not swollen.   14

14 { Scutellum yellow, with four bristles, wings with black crossbands.
                                                                          XIII. RHACOLEPIS.
   { Scutellum black, with two bristles, wings black, with hyaline inden-
      tations along the margin.   XIV. ACIDIA.

15 { Fifth vein strongly bristly; scutellum with six bristles.
                                                                          XV. BLEPHARONEURA.
   { Fifth vein not bristly; scutellum with six or two bristles.   16

16 { Wings banded on the apex.   XVI. ACROTAXIA.
   { Wings not banded on the apex.   17

17 { Face spotted.   18
   { Face not spotted.   19

18 { Wings very much dilated; pattern of the picture not radiating.
                                                                          XVII. EUTRETA.
   { Wings not dilated; the pattern of the picture radiating along the
      margin (Tab. XI, f. 3).   XVIII. CARPHOTRICHA.

19 { Front remarkably broad.   20
   { Front narrow, or of medium breadth.   21

20 { Third antennal joint short, rounded at the tip, ovipositor conical.
                                                                          XIX. ROBERTA.
   { Third antennal joint remarkably long, with a very sharp anterior
      angle, ovipositor flattened.   XX. ACINOCERA.

21 { Wings without picture, or on the apical half only, with a reticulation
      dissolved in crossbands.   XXI. ASPILOTA.
   { Wings neither without picture, nor, on the apical half, with a retic-u-
      lation dissolved in bands.   22

22 { Wings of an evenly broad shape, and with an unusually blunt apex.
      (Tab. X, f. 18, and Tab. XI, f. 9.)   XXII. ICTERICA.
   { Wings of the usual shape or dilated.   23

23 { Flaps of the proboscis very much prolonged.   XXIII. ENSINA.
   { Flaps of the proboscis short, or but little prolonged.   24

24 { Pattern of the picture not radiating.   XXIV. TEPHRITIS.
   { Pattern of the picture radiating.   25

25 { The whole or nearly the whole surface of the wings with a unicolor-
      ous reticulation.   XXV. ECARSTA.
   { A star-shaped black picture on the apex, the remaining surface
      immaculate, or with very few spots, at the utmost with a very
      faded reticulation.   XXVI. URELLIA.

DISTRIBUTION OF THE NORTH AMERICAN TRYPETÆ AMONG THE ADOPTED SMALLER GENERA.

Gen. I. HEXACHÆTA.
  1. eximia *Wied.*
  2. amabilis nov. sp.

Gen. II. ACROTOXA.
  3. anapheta *Lw.*
  4. fraternulus *Wied.*
  5. ludens nov. sp.
  6. tricincta nov. sp.

Gen. III. STENOPA.
  7. vulnerata nov. sp.

Gen. IV. ACURA.
  8. fratria *Lw.*
  9. suavis *Lw.*

Gen. V. EPOCHRA.
  10. canadensis nov. sp.

Gen. VI. STRAUZIA.
  11. longipennis *Wied.*

Gen. VII. SPILOGRAPHA.
  12. electa *Say.*
  13. flavonotata *Macq.*

Gen. VIII. OEDICARENA.
  14. tetanops nov. sp.

Gen. IX. FEROXYMA.
  15. marginata *Lw.*

Gen. X. PLAGIOTOMA.
  16. discolor *Lw.*
  17. obliqua *Say.*

Gen. XI. TRYPETA.
  18. palposa *Lw.*
  19. florescentiæ *Lin.*

Gen. XII. OEDASPIS.
  20. polita *Lw.*
  21. atra *Lw.*
  22. gibba nov. sp.

Gen. XIII. EUAGGLETIS.
  23. cingulata *Lw.*
  24. tabellaria *Fitch.*
  25. pomonella *Walsh.*

Gen. XIV. ACIURA.
  26. insecta *Lw.*

Gen. XV. BLEPHARONEURA.
  27. parvilugastra nov. sp.

Gen. XVI. ACROTÆNIA.
  28. testudinea nov. sp.

Gen. XVII. EUTRETA.
  29. sparsa *Wied.*
  30. rotundipennis *Lw.*

Gen. XVIII. CARPHOTRICHA.
  31. culta *Wied.*

Gen. XIX. EURIBIA.
  32. solidaginis *Fitch.*
  33. comma *Wied.*
  34. latifrons *Lw.*

(820)

COMPARISON BETWEEN THE EUROPEAN AND THE AMERICAN FAUNA OF TRYPETINA.

INCOMPLETE as our knowledge of the North American Trypetina is, our scanty materials are, nevertheless, sufficient to enable
us to form an approximate idea of their relation to the European
fauna. Even a superficial comparison of a North American with
a European collection of *Trypeta* will show, that certain subgenera, characteristic for Europe by the number of species which
represent them, are absolutely or almost wanting in America,
while, on the contrary, North America possesses other, very
peculiar forms, which do not occur in Europe.

We will notice, in the first place, that the subgenus *Urophora*,
which, in Europe, embraces fully one-eighth of all the species, is
not represented at all in North America.[1] Next to this, we
become aware of the fact that the subgenus *Trypeta*, containing
another eighth of all the European species, is represented in
North America by *Trypeta palposa* only, besides *Trypeta florescentiæ* Lin., which is very probably imported from Europe.

As forms peculiar to North America and entirely foreign to
the circles of relationship of the European *Trypetina*, the species
of the subgenera *Hexachæta, Acrotoxa, Blepharoneura, Acrotænia, Eutreta,* and *Acidogona* deserve especial attention.

Besides these two very striking differences between the two
faunas, a close comparison reveals other discrepancies; as, for
instance, that less characteristic European subgenera are entirely
wanting in North America, while subgenera occurring in North

---

[1] In South America likewise, no species of *Urophora* have as yet been
found; all the South American species published by European authors as
Urophora do not belong to this genus at all; most of them are not even
Trypetida, but *Ortalida*, with black crossbands on the wings.

America, although wanting in Europe, are found to be closely related to European forms.

Subgenera with a small number of species, occurring in Europe and wanting in North America, are: 1. *Platyparea* (two species; the larva of the typical *Pl. poecilopotera* lives in the stems of *Asparagus officinalis*); 2. *Euphranta* (one species, on *Asclepias* and *Vincetoxicum*); 3. *Hemilea* (one species); 4. *Hypenidium* (one species); 5. *Chætostoma* (one species, distinguished by the bristly sides of the face); 6. *Anomœa* (one species, in the fruits of *Cratægus*); 7. *Zonosema* (two species, related to *Rhagoletis*; in the fruits of *Rosa* and *Berberis*); 8. *Rhacochlæna* (one species); 9. *Myopites* (several, but as yet not well separated species; the larvæ live in the flowers of *Inula* and of the related genera); 10. *Sphenella* (one species; larvæ in the flowers of *Senecio*). If we accept the sufficiently well-founded division of the genus *Ortalis*, in *Ortalis* and *Orellia*, we have, moreover: 11. *Orellia* (three species; one on *Bryonia*, another on *Zizyphus*), to add to those small European subgenera, which have no representatives in North America.

The subgenera peculiar to North America, but allied to some European forms, are; the subgenera *Straussia* and *Oedicarena*, which resemble *Spilographa*; *Eparhra* and *Stenopa*, which stand very close to *Acidia*; *Aspilota*, *Plagiotoma*, and *Peronyma*, which all approach *Trypeta*; *Icterica*, related to *Oxyphora*; and finally *Eurosta*, closely allied to some species of *Oxyna*.

Such are the differences between the two faunæ; I will now show the resemblances, as far as observed, between them.

The most striking coincidence and the most remarkable for the great number of analogous species, between the two faunas, occurs within the circle of relationship of the European species belonging to the subgenera: *Carphotricha, Oxyphora, Oxyna, Tephritis, Ensina, Urellia*. Another point of coincidence of the same kind, although less well represented as to the number of species, occurs within the closely related subgenera *Spilographa, Acidia*, and *Rhagoletis*. A third one may be noticed within the genus *Ortalis*. Moreover, the North American species of the subgenera *Trypeta* and *Aciura*, a single one in each, are very much like European species of the same subgenera in their general appearance   Two species, common to both continents, have, until now, been ascertained: *Trypeta florescentiæ* (living on

Sonchus) and *Tephritis angustipennis* (occurring in Europe on *Achillea ptarmica*). The specific identity of the American *Acidia fratria* and the European *Acidia heraclei* is not impossible, although as yet not certain.

It must be borne in mind, however, that all the comparative statements, given above, are founded upon a very imperfect knowledge of the North American fauna, and may be considerably modified with an increase of this knowledge.

If the European *Trypetina* be compared, not with those of the whole North American continent, but with the fauna occurring in America within the European latitudes, then some of the more striking differences between the two faunas at once disappear, as those subgenera which are absolutely foreign to Europe (*Hexachaeta, Acrotoxa, Blepharoneura,* and *Acrotaenia*) do not reach so far north. The occurrence of all four of them subgenera in Brazil proves that they are South American forms, which extend to the southern portions of the North American continent.

It was to be expected that the knowledge of the North American species should exercise an influence upon the subdivision of the old genus *Trypeta* in subgenera, a subdivision hitherto based almost exclusively upon European species. Those North American subgenera, which have no relationship whatever to European forms, of course merely increase the number of subgenera, without influencing in any manner the already existing subdivision. But it is different with those subgenera which contain forms common to both continents, and here the modifying influence of the American fauna becomes apparent. Thus we can already recognise: 1. That the definition of the subgenus *Carphotricha*, founded upon European species, has to be modified, in order to include all the species belonging to it; 2. That the genus *Oxyphora*, in its present acceptation, contains, besides a number of closely allied species, several far too aberrant forms; moreover, that it can no more be separated from the neighboring subgenera merely by the presence of bristles upon the third vein, a character which hitherto has been found sufficient for the distinction of the European species; 3. That the subgenus *Ensina* must be taken in a broader sense than has been done in my Monograph of the European *Trypetae*, especially through the addition of some species which, in the same Monograph, were placed in *Oxyna*; 4. That the remaining portion of *Oxyna*

must be united generically with the subgenus *Tephritis*, or else
that it should be separated from it in some other manner than
has been hitherto done; and that, in order to facilitate the identification of species, a new genus, closely allied to the two above
named ones, should be founded, for which I have already proposed the name of *Euaresta*.

I reserve for another place to carry out in detail the improvements of the system of *Trypetina* of which I have here given
the outline, and I intend, at the same time, to take in consideration the known species from all the other continents.

APPENDIX I.

CRITICAL ENUMERATION OF ALL THE NORTH AMERICAN TRYPETINA
DESCRIBED BY OTHER AUTHORS.

---

1. aciduaa *Walk.* very probably belongs to the subgenus *Acrotoxa*; what Mr. Walker says of the curvature of the end of the third longitudinal vein is evidently to be referred to the fourth vein, and the same remark applies to *Trypeta Ethalea* Walker, from Para, which follows upon the former in the text.

2. acutangula *Thoms.*, unknown to me; probably belongs to the subgenus *Tephritis*.

3. ancea r. d. *Walp* (Tijdschr. voor Ent. 2 Ser. II, p. 167), described as *T.* (*Aciura*) *ancea*; does not belong to the *Trypetidae* at all, but to the *Ortalidae*, and is synonymous with *Chaetopsis ancea* Wied.

4. albiacutellata *Harr.* has never been described, and, hence, is to be stricken out.

5. antillarum *Macq.*, described by Macquart as *Urophora* does neither belong to this genus nor to the *Trypetidae* in general, but to the *Ortalidae*; figure and description agree so little that the identification will be difficult.

6. arcuata *Walk.* is synonymous with *Tritoxa flexa* Wied. (Ortalidae).

7. armata *R. Desv.*, published as a *Straussia*; this is the male of *T.* (*Straussia*) *longipennis* Wied.

8. asteria *Harris* is identical with *T.* (*Eurosta*) *solidaginis* Fitch, as Baron Osten-Sacken has shown; the choice of the name depended on an erroneous assumption as to the plant on which the larva lives.

9. aurifera *Thom.*, a species unknown to me, belonging to the subgenus *Eutreta*.

10. avata *Walk.*; the very insufficient data given by the author do not even enable me to decide whether this is a *Trypetida* or an *Ortalida*; even the location of the species in the genus *Urophora* does not help through this dilemma, because *Myennis fasciata* Fab. is placed in the same genus, thus proving that Mr. Walker was not cognisant at all of the characters of this genus.

11. Beauvoisii *R. Desv.*, described as *Priscella Beauvoisii*; unknown to me, so far that I am unable to decide whether it is a *Trypetida* or

an *Ortalida*; the former, however, seems more probable. Its occurrence in America is uncertain, and is only supposed by R. Desvoidy, because the described specimens belonged to *Palisot de Beauvois* collection.

12. **calliptera** *Say* is synonymous with *T. (Eutreta) sparsa* Wied.

13. **cinctipes** *Harris* is to be stricken out, as undescribed.

14. **comma** *Wied.*, an *Eutreta*, has been described in this volume.

15. **cornigera** *Walk.*, an unimportant variety of the male of *T. longipennis* Wied.

16. **cornifera** *Walk.*, same remark as the preceding.

17. **cribrata** *v. d. Walp* (l. c. p 198), syn. with *T. (Eutreta) latifrons* Lw.

18. **culta** *Wied.*, a *Carphotricha*, described above.

19. **dinia** *Walk.* In the Monographs, Vol. I, I expressed the supposition that it may belong to the relationship of *T. (Acinra) tibialis*; but in doing it, I paid too little attention to the coloring of the body. I think it more probable now that this is a species closely allied to *T. (Hexachaeta) eximia* Wied., perhaps even only a badly described variety of this very species.

20. **electa** *Say*, a *Spilographa*; has been described in Monographs, Vol. I.

21. **eximia** *Wied.*, a *Hexachaeta*, described above; known long ago as a Brazilian species; its occurrence in Mexico has been discovered recently.

22. **fasciventris** *Macq.*, synonymous with *T. (Hexachaeta) eximia* Wied.

23. **femoralis** *Thoms.*, an unknown *Urellia* from the group with two bristles on the scutellum.

24. **fimbriata** *Macq.* is the same as *T. (Carphotricha) culta* Wied.

25. **flavonotata** *Macq.*, a species closely allied to *T. (Spilographa) electa* Say, but not a mere variety of this species, as I formerly supposed. It is described in this volume.

26. **flexa** *Wied.* is a *Tritoxa* (Ortalida).

27. **fraterculus** *Wied.*, described by Wiedemann as *Dacus fraterculus*, after a specimen from Brazil; occurs likewise in Peru, New Granada, and Cuba. Belongs to the genus *Acrotoxa*, and is the same as *Trypeta unicolor* Lw., Monographs, Vol. I. Wiedemann's description did not enable me to recognise this identity, which I have, however, found out since, by comparing the original specimen. As a matter of course, Wiedemann's name has to be maintained.

28. **fucata** *Fabr.* may be referred to *Tephritis*, and has been described above.

29. **fulvifrons** *Macq.* is *Chetopsis aenea* Wied. (Ortalida).

30. **genalis** *Thoms.*, from California; unknown to me; probably a *Tephritis*.

31. **inermis** *R. Desv.*, published as a *Straussia*, is *T. (Straussia) longipennis* female.

32. **interrupta** *Macq.*, described as *Urophora*, is not a *Trypetida* at all, but a *Rivellia* of difficult identification.

33. **latipennis** *Macq.*, published as a *Platystoma*, is most certainly a *Trypetida*, in which I cannot recognize anything else but *T.* (*Eutreta*) *sparsa*.

34. **Lichtensteinii** *Wied.*, described above after the types of Wiedemann's work, and provisionally placed in the genus *Icterica*, from the typical species of which, however, it is somewhat different.

35. **Megaster** *Thoms.* is the same as *T.* (*Acidia*) *fratria* Lw.

36. **longipennis** *Wied.* is the typical species of the genus *Stenssia*, and, as it seems, undergoes considerable variations. In Monographs, Vol. I, I have given a description of this species, and in the present volume have enumerated the varieties which I have had occasion to see, some of which, however, may be distinct species.

37. **marginepunctata** *Macq.*, almost certainly a *Trypetida*, but which it would be premature to identify with *T.* (*Carpholricca*) *culta* Wied. Macquart's data are so very insufficient that the identification will be very difficult.

38. **melliginis** *Fitch* is a *Rivellia*, under which head it has been discussed.

39. **mevarna** *Walk.*, an *Urellia*, unknown to me.

40. **mexicana** *Wied.*, an *Eutreta*; the above description has been prepared from Wiedemann's typical specimen.

41. **narytia** *Walk.*; the remarks appended above to *arula* Walk. may be repeated here.

42. **novaboracensis** *Fitch* is synonymous with *T.* (*Eutreta*) *sparsa* Wied.

43. **nigriventris** *Macq.*, erroneously described as *Urophora*; it is a *Trypetida*, which I do not know, and concerning the systematic position of which I am in doubt.

44. **obliqua** *Macq.* is an *Acrotora*; I do not know it.

45. **obliqua** *Say* is the type of the subgenus *Plagiotoma*; is described in Monographs, Vol. I.

46. **ocresia** *Walk.* belongs to the subgenus *Acrotora*; I am unable to identify it among the species known to me.

47. **picciola** *Bigot* (R. de la Sagra, Hist. fis. Cub. Tab. XX, f. 10). This species, described as *Acinia*, is the same as *T.* (*Eusina*) *humilis* Lw.

48. **picta** *Fabr.*, type of the genus *Campiosoura* (*Ortalida*).

49. **pomonella** *Walsh*, subgenus *Rhagoletis*, is described in this volume.

50. **quadrifasciata** *Macq.* I suppose that this species will be found to be identical with *T.* (*Peronyma*) *sarcinata* Lw.

51. **quadrivittata** *Macq.* is an *Ortalida*.

52. **scutellaris** *Wird.* is an *Ortalida*.

53. **scutellata** *Wied.* is a *Trypeta* the position of which cannot be made out of Wiedemann's description; Wiedemann's typical specimen unfortunately is no more in existence.

54. **septenaria** *Harris* is to be stricken out, as undescribed.

22

55. solidaginis *Fitch*, an *Eurosta*, sufficiently described in Monographs, Vol. 1.

56. sparsa *Wied.*; described in Monographs, Vol. 1; typical species of the genus *Eutreta*.

57. tabellaria *Fitch*; described as a *Tephritis*. In Monographs, Vol. I, I have expressed the erroneous supposition that this species belongs to the Ortalidæ. It is a Trypetida of the subgenus *Rhagoletis*, and has been described in the present volume.

58. tribulis *Harris* is not described, and hence must be stricken out.

59. trimaculata *Macq.* is *T. (Straussia) longipennis* Wied.

60. trifasciata *Harris*; not described.

61. villosa *R. Desv.*; described as *Prionella*; the remark appended above to *Prionella Beauvoisii* may be repeated here.

———————

The result of the above remarks may be summed up as follows:—

1. *Five* of the above-quoted species named by Mr. Harris must be stricken out, as their descriptions have never been published:—

albiscutellata *Harris*.	tribulis *Harris*.
cinctipes *Harris*.	trifasciata *Harris*.
septenaria *Harris*.	

2. *Ten* species must be transferred to the *Ortalidæ*:—

ænea *v. d. Wulp.*	interrupta *Macq.*
antillarum *Macq.*	meliginis *Fitch.*
arcuata *Walk.*	picta *Fabr.*
flexa *Wied.*	quadrivittata *Macq.*
fulvifrons *Macq.*	scutellaris *Wied.*

3. *Fifteen* species are merely synonyms of other Trypetidæ; the two marked with an interrogation are not as certain as the others:—

armata *R. Desv.*	=	longipennis *Wied.*
asteris *Harr.*	=	solidaginis *Fitch.*
caliptera *Say*	=	sparsa *Wied.*
cornigera *Walk.*	=	longipennis *Wied.*
cornifera *Walk.*	=	longipennis *Wied.*
cribrata *v. d. Wulp*	=	latifrons *Lw.*
fasciventris *Macq.*	=	eximia *Wied.*

fimbriata *Macq.* = culta *Wied.*
? llogaster *Thoms.* = fratria *Lw.*
inermis *R. Desv.* = longipennis *Wied.*
latipennis *Macq.* = sparsa *Wied.*
novemboracensis *Fitch* = sparsa *Wied.*
picciola *Bigot* = humilis *Lw.*
trimaculata *Macq.* = longipennis *Wied.*
? quadrifasciata *Macq.* = sarcinata *Lw.*

4. *Fifteen* species are recognized by me and described in detail in Monographs, Vol. I, and in the present work:—

comma *Wied.*
culta *Wied.*
electa *Say.*
eximia *Wied.*
flavomaculata *Macq.*
fraterculus *Wied.*
incisa *Fabr.*
Lichtensteinii *Wied.*

longipennis *Wied.*
mexicana *Wied.*
obliqua *Say.*
pomonella *Walsh.*
solidaginis *Fitch.*
sparsa *Wied.*
tabellaria *Fitch.*

5. *Sixteen* species consequently remain, which I have never seen or have not been able to identify; most of them are undoubtedly *Trypetidæ*; the doubtful ones I have marked with an interrogation:—

acidusa *Walk.*
acutangula *Thoms.*
aurifera *Thoms.*
? avala *Walk.*
? Beauvoisii *R. Desv.*
Dinia *Walk.*
femoralis *Thoms.*
genalis *Thoms.*

marginepunctata *Macq.*
mevarna *Walk.*
? narytia *Walk.*
nigriventris *Macq.*
obliqua *Macq.*
ornata *Walk.*
scutellata *Wied.*
? villosa *R. Desv.*

APPENDIX II.

THE descriptions of North American species of *Trypeta*, published by previous authors, but not identified in the foregoing Monograph, are reprinted *verbatim* in the Monographs, etc., Vol. I. p. 94. The following are Californian species of Mr. Thomson, were published since the issue of that volume (*T. liogaster* Thoms. is left among them, as its synonymy with *T. fratria* Lw. is not quite certain).

Thomson, Eugenies Resa, etc., Zoologi, VI, p. 578.

Genus TRYPETA.

A. Ala cubiti ramo submarginali setaloso, cellula anali postica angulo infero breviter sed acute producta, abscissa costali 2a spinula fere nulla. Frons serie laterali 6-setosa. Thorax setarum dorsalium pari pone medio sita. Scutellum 4-setosum. Proboscis brevis.

251. Trypeta liogaster.—Ferruginea nitida, abdomine glabro; alis albis, fusco-flexuo-o-variegatis; postscutello macula magna didyma nigra. ♀. Long. 5 mill.

Patria. California.

T. Onopordi colore et alarum pictura simillima, abdomine glabro mox distincta. Caput rotundum, fere globosum, ferrugineum, occipite haud excavato; fronte subopaca, subtilissime puberula, serie laterali 6-setosa, setis 2 posterioribus magis ab oculis remotis; epistomate haud brevi, fovels antennalibus minus determinatis, divergentibus, genis angustis, inferne paullo latioribus; peristomio magno, rotundo, utrinque medio seta una validiore nigra instructo, proboscide brevi, capitulo crasso; oculis nudis, fere ovalibus, inferne sat longe descendentibus, orbita frontali parallela, faciali minus divergente. Antennæ subdeflexæ, basi vix distantes, articulo 3o ovali, apice haud mucronato,

epistomatis apicem haud attingente, seta nuda. Thorax ferrugi-
neus, nitidus, glaber, setarum dorsalium pari pone medium sito;
scutellum subtriangulare, 4-setosum, postscutello macula magna
nigra nitida utriaque ornato. Alæ longæ, margine infero vix
sinuato, albo-brunneoque flexuoso-variegatæ, macula nempe ob-
longo-quadrata cellulam totam mediastinam fere occupante alter-
que costali triangulari ad cubiti ramum submarginalem usque
descendente, pone postcostæ exitum sita, cum maculis duabus
disci sinubusque profundis marginis inferioris ante apicem albis,
imel inferne late albida; nervis costali abscissa 2a spinula fere
nulla, 3a 2a baud duplo breviore, 6a sextæ fere æquali; media-
stino apice sub angulo recto costam versus abscendente ibidemque
obsoleto; postcostali toto dense setuloso, medium alæ vix attingente; cubiti furca sat longe ante apicem cellulæ humeralis sita,
ramo submarginali parce vix ultra nervum transversum ordinarium setuloso, postice leniesimo curvato et brachiali plane
parallelo; humerali mox pone nervum transversum discoidalem
desinente; cellula discoidali postice recta truncata nervum
transversum ordinarium perpendicularem, longe pone postcostæ
exitum sitam, in sua tertia posteriore parte excipiente; anali
inferne haud longe, sed acute producta, quam humerali breviore.
Abdomen ovali-rotundum, supra leviter convexum, glabrum,
nitidum, segmento 5o margine postico utriaque setis 4 ornato,
6o parvo fere triangulari, apice truncato, brunneo-nigro, tere-
bram includente. Pedes haud validi, coxis anticis medium
mesosterni vix attingentibus; femoribus anticis subtus setosis;
tibiis intermediis apice calcari nigro armatis; mesosternum, ut
in omnibus, seta in angulo posteriore instructum; epimeris etiam
sub alis seta nigra præditis.

B. Alæ ramo cubiti submarginali nudo.
　　cc. Alæ cellula discoidali postice quam nervi transversi ordinar.
　　　　longitudine vix latiore.
　　　b. Proboscide haud hamato-reflexa.
　　cc. Alæ cellula discoidali angulo infero recto.
　　dd. Alæ minus angusta, cellulis brachiali et humerali haud brevibus,
　　　　nervo transverso discoidali margine infero alæ approximato,
　　　　abscissa costali 5a 6a haud duplo longiore.
　　ev. Alæ albidæ vel hyalinæ, fusco-maculatæ, vel reticulatæ.
　　　f. Scutellum bisetosum. Alæ angulo inferiore cellulæ analis
　　　　recto. Thorax setarum dorsalium pari ante medium sito.
　　　　Femora plerumque tenuia, antica setis 3-4 subtus ornata.
　　gg. Cellula postcostali nigra vel nigro-fusca.

259. Trypeta femoralis.—Nigro-fusca, glauco-pruinosa, capite cum antennis pedibusque flavis, femoribus intermediis subtus setulis 4–5 munitis; alis albidis, macula posteriore fusca apicem versus nullam ramum sed inferne ramum integrum nervum transverso-discoidalem transsecantem emittente, cum cellula posticostali per plagam obliquam connexa. ♂. Long. 4 mill.

Patria. California.

Præcedentibus[1] similis et affinis, femoribus intermediis subtus setis 4–5 validioribus munitis, alis macula posteriore nigro-fusca guttulas 3 majores includente, ramum apicalem nullum sed inferne ramulos 2 abbreviatos auto ramum nervum transverso-discoidalem transsecantem emittente, ramis 2 posterioribus basi tantum indicatis, nervo humerali longitudinaliter ultra medium infuscato distincta.

ff. Scutellum 4-setosum. Alis angulo inferiore postico cellulæ analis acuto subproducto.

260. Trypeta acutangula. Nigricans, cano-pruinosa, capite, scutelli apice pedibusque flavis; alis parce fusco-reticulatis, macula majore nigricante, fusco-radiata, cellula posticostali flavescenti. ♂. Long. 4 mill.

Patria. California.

Alis pictura fere *T. cometa*, sed disco et antice parce fusco-reticulatis, cellula postcostali fere tota flavescenti, serie frontali 5-setosa mox distincta. Caput thoracis latitudine, flavo-testaceum, occipite superne fusco, fere truncato; fronte fere transversa, serie utrinque 5-setosa; epistomate brevi, foveis antennalibus fere parallelis, sat discretis; peristomio subrotundo, proboscide haud geniculata; oculis sat magnis, inferne sat longe descendentibus, orbita frontali antrorsum fere convergente. Antennæ breves, subdeflexæ, articulo 3o ovali-rotundo, epistomatis apicem fere attingente, nigro-fusco, seta nudiuscula. Thorax cano-pruinosus, setarum dorsalium pari pone suturam transversam sito; scutello apice lato testaceo, 4-setoso, setis apicalibus minoribus approximatis. Alæ sat latæ, obscure hyalinæ, parcius, disco medio evidentius, fusco-reticulatæ, macula posteriore nigricante, subrotunda, guttas 2 costales includente, quarum posteriore paullo

---

[1] The two preceding species are: *T. glauca* from Sidney, which the author calls "*T. solari* Loew similis et affinis," and *T. meteorica* from Buenos Ayres, described as "præcedenti simillima." O. S.

ante rami marginalis exitum alia, apicem versus ramum bifurcatum, inferne ramos 3 angustos integros fuscos emittente; fuscedine nervi trausveral ordinarii aat lata, postice guttis 2 majusculis
a macula posteriore magna sejnncta, per strigam obliquam cum
cellula postcostall flavescenti connexa et in cellulam discoidalem
lobum triangularem emittente; cellula marginall postice guttis 2
magnis albidis, linea transversa fusca separatis ornata; nervis
costali alaciaa 2a spinula distincta armata, 5a 6a plus qnam
sesqui longiore; postcostali medium alae attingente; cubiti ramo
submarginall postice cum brachio plane parallelo, hoc pone
nervum transverso-discoidalem lenissime curvato; cellula discoidali nervum transversum ordinarium, sat longe pone postcostae
exitum, nonnihil pone medium alae situm, in sua 5a posteriore
parte excipiente; quali angulo inferno postico acute subproducto.
Abdomen unicolor, nigricans, cano-puberulum et pilis depressis
parvis rigidis pallidis vestitum, segmento 4o praecedente plus
quam duplo longiore. Pedes toti flavi, femoribus hand validis,
anticis subtus setulis 3-4 flavidis longioribus et basi nonnullis
brevioribus ornatis.

  bb. Probuscida hamato-reflexa. Epistomate brevi, inferne promi
   nente; peristomio antice exciso-assurgente. Palpis prominulis.
   AA. Ala fascia recta nervum transversum ordinarium transennata haud
    ornala sed fusco reticulata.
   i. Scutellum 4-setorum.

264. Trypeta aurifera.—Nigricans, capite cum antennis pedibusque testaceis, femoribus ultra medium nigris; alis subhyalinis, obsolete
fusco-reticulatis, macula costali quadrata pone spinulam alta, determinate nigricante. ♂ ♀. Long. 3-4 mill.

Patria. California.

T. elongatulae simillima, femoribus ultra medium nigro-fuscis,
alis adhuc obsoletius fusco-reticulatis, cellula postcostall nigrofusca, guttam albidam haud includente mox distincta. Caput
hand transversum, thoracis latitudine, testaceum, occipite fusco,
inferne tumido; fronte subdeclivi, latitudine sua dimidio longiore,
utrinque albida 4-setosa, acuto ocelligero nigro-fusco; epistomate
brevi, verticali, genis inferne haud latis, superne angustis; peristomio oblongo, antice angulato-exciso, proboscide elongata,
geniculata, capitulo longissimo, tenui; oculis magnis obliquis.
Antennae basi contiguae, testaceae, breves, epistomatis apicem

attingentes, articulo 3o breviter ovali, seta nuda. Thorax
nigricans, cano-pruinosus et pube brevi rigida pallida vestitus,
setarum dorsalium pari mox pone suturam sito; scutello
4-setosum, setis apicalibus parvis. Alæ subhyalinæ, obsolete
fusco-reticulatæ, macula quadrata pone spinulam nigricante,
determinata: nervis costali abscissa 2a spinula munita, 6a 6a
paullo longiore; postcostali medium alæ haud attingente; brachiali et ramo submarginali cubiti parallelis; cellula discoidali
nervum transversum ordinariam, longe pone postcostæ exitum
paullo pone medium alæ sitam, in sua 4a posteriore parte excl-
plente; anali angulo inferno acuto. Abdomen subdepressum,
pruinosum et pube rigida pallida vestitum, segmentis 4o et 6o
apice setulis nonnullis marginatis, 6o depresso, nitido, glabro. ♀
præcedentibus simul sumptis longitudine æquali. Pedes haud
validi, femoribus anticis subtus setis 2-3 ornatis, omnibus nigris,
apice cum tibiis tarsisque testaceis.

265. Trypeta genalis.—Nigricans, capite pedibusque flavis, femoribus ultra medium nigris; alis byalinis, fusco-reticulatis, striga obliqua
pone spinulam apiceque magis fuscis; abdomine bifariam fusco-macu-
lato, tenebra brevi depressa. ♂ ♀. Long. 3—4 mill.

Patria. California.

T. *tessellatæ* Loew, simillima genis superne angustioribus; alis
obscure byalinis, gutta minoribus, disco interiore basali magis
fusco-reticulato distincta; a præcedente capituli labiis brevioribus,
alis evidentius fusco-reticulatis discedens. Caput ut in præcedente, fronte paullo latiore, epistomate parum prominulo, proboscide capitulo minus elongato. Thorax et scutellum ut in
præcedente constructa. Alæ subhyalinæ, fusco-reticulatæ, striga
nigro-fusca pone spinulam guttam albam costalem includente,
oblique nervum transversum ordinarium transeunte, apice fusco,
guttis pluribus majoribus albidis, quarum 5 arcum ante apicem
formantibus ornato; nervis omnino ut in præcedente directis, sed
postcostali medium alæ attingente, transverso ordinario paullo
pone postcostæ exitum sito. Abdomen bifariam fusco-macula-
tum, pilis brevibus rigidis albidis in margine apicali segmentorum
evidentioribus vestitum. Pedes ut in præcedente, sed femoribus
anticis subtus setis 4-5 ornatis.

INDEX OF THE TRYPETINA.

(345)

EXPLANATION OF THE PLATES.

ORTALIDÆ.

PLATE VIII.

1. Amphicnephes pertusus nov. sp.
2. Himerocssa pretiosa nov. sp.
3. Rivellia conjuncta nov. sp.
4. Rivellia viridulans Rob. Desv.
5. Rivellia quadrifasciata Macq.
6. Rivellia variabilis nov. sp.
7. Rivellia flavimana nov. sp.
8. Rivellia pallida nov. sp.
9. Myrmecomyia myrmecoides Lw.
10. Tritoxa flexa Wied.
11. Tritoxa cuneata nov. sp.
12. Tritoxa incurva nov. sp.
13. Camptoneura picta Fbr.
14. Diacrita costalis Gerst.
15. Diacrita æmula nov. sp.
16. Idana marginata Say.
17. Tetanops luridipennis nov. sp.
18. Tetanops integer nov. sp.
19. Anacampta latiuscula nov. sp.
20. Ceroxys obscuricornis nov. sp.
21. Ceroxys ochricornis nov. sp.
22. Ceroxys canus Lw.
23. Ceroxys similis nov. sp.
24. Tephronota humilis nov. sp.
25. Stictocephala cribrum nov. sp.

(349)

26. Stictocephala cribellum nov. sp.
27. Callopistria annulipes *Macq.*
28. Stictocephala corticalis *Fitch.*
29. Stictocephala vau *Say.*
30. Pterocalla strigula nov. sp.

PLATE IX.

1. Oedopa capito *Lw.*
2. Oedopa capito *Lw.*
3. Oedopa capito *Lw.*
4. Euphara cærulea *Macq.*
5. Notogramma stigma *Fbr*
6. Scoptera colon *Lw.*
7. Euxesta spoliata *Lw.*
8. Euxesta pusio *Lw.*
9. Euxesta notata *Wied.*
10. Euxesta costalis *Fbr.*
11. Euxesta quaternaria *Lw.*
12. Euxesta binotata *Lw.*
13. Euxesta annonæ *Fbr.*
14. Euxesta Thomæ *Lw.*
15. Euxesta abdominalis *Lw.*
16. Euxesta alternans *Lw.*
17. Euxesta stigmatias *Lw.*
18. Euxesta eluta *Lw.*
19. Chætopsis ænea *Wied.*
20. Chætopsis debilis *Lw.*
21. Stenomyia tenuis *Lw.*
22. Eumetopia rufipes *Macq.*
23. Eumetopia varipes *Lw.*
24. Epiplatea erosa *Lw.*
25. Stenomacra Guerinii *Bigot.*
26. Idiotypa appendiculata nov. sp.
27. Celometopia bimaculata nov. sp.
28. Hemixantha spinipes nov. sp.
29. Melanostoma affinis nov. sp.

TRYPETIDÆ.

PLATE X.

TRYPETA.

1. discolor *Lw.*
2. longipennis *Wied.*, ♂.
3. longipennis *Wied.*, ♀.
4. fratria *Lw.*
5. suspensa *Lw.*
6. fraterculus *Wied.*
7. electa *Say.*
8. insecta *Lw.*
9. palposa *Lw.*
10. suavis *Lw.*
11. cingulata *Lw.*
12. polita *Lw.*
13. sparsa *Wied.*
14. rotundipennis *L.*
15. clathrata *Lw.*

16. solidaginis *Fitch.*
17. humilis *Lw.*
18. seriata *Lw.*
19. solaris *Lw.*
20. æqualis *Lw.*
21. festiva *Lw.*
22. latifrons *Lw.*
23. bella *Lw.*
24. melanogastra *Lw.*, ♀.
25. timida *Lw.*
26. obscuriventris nov. sp.
27. spectabilis nov. sp.
28. mexicana *Wied.*
29. tenuis nov. sp.
30. peregrina nov. sp.

PLATE XI.

TRYPETA.

1. geminata *Lw.*
2. comma *Wied.*
3. culta *Wied.*
4. finalis *Lw.*
5. albiceps nov. sp., ♂.
6. melanura nov. sp.
7. abstersa *Lw.*
8. Vernoniæ *Lw.*
9. Lichtensteinii *Wied.*
10. albidipennis *Lw.*
11. alba *Lw.*
12. phænicura nov. sp.
13. testudinea nov. sp.
14. obliqua *Say.*

15. tetanops nov. sp.
16. sarcinata *Lw.*
17. atra *Lw.*
18. nigerrima *Lw.*
19. ludens nov. sp.
20. parallela *Wied.*
21. consobrina nov. sp.
22. hamata nov. sp.
23. integra nov. sp.
24. pseudoparallela nov. sp.
25. serpentina *Wied.*
26. grandis *Macq.*
27. bivittata *Macq.*

VAI 1524350

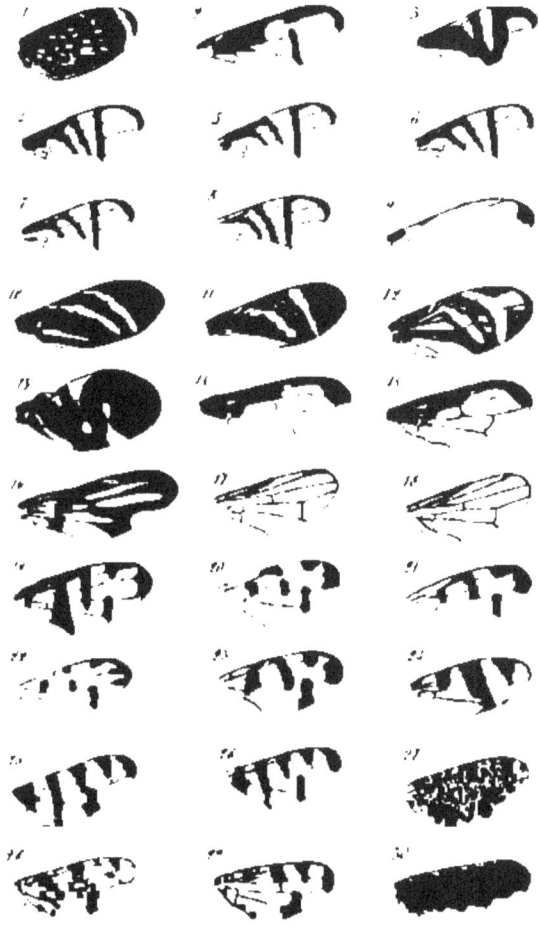

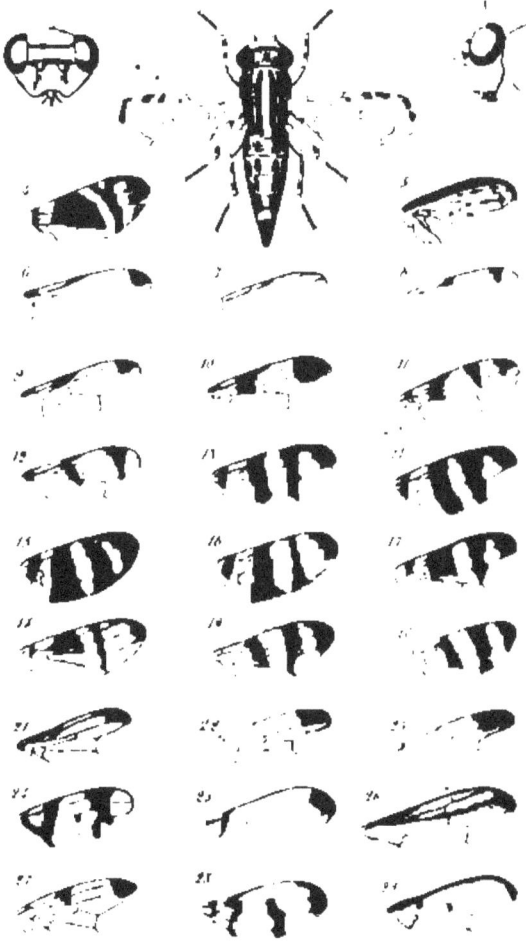

Pl. X.

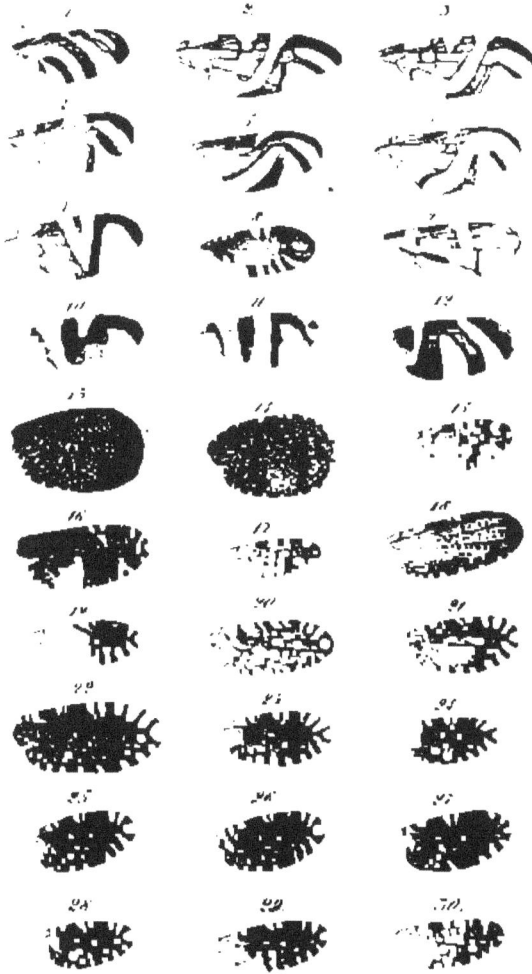

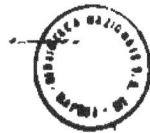

Pl. XI

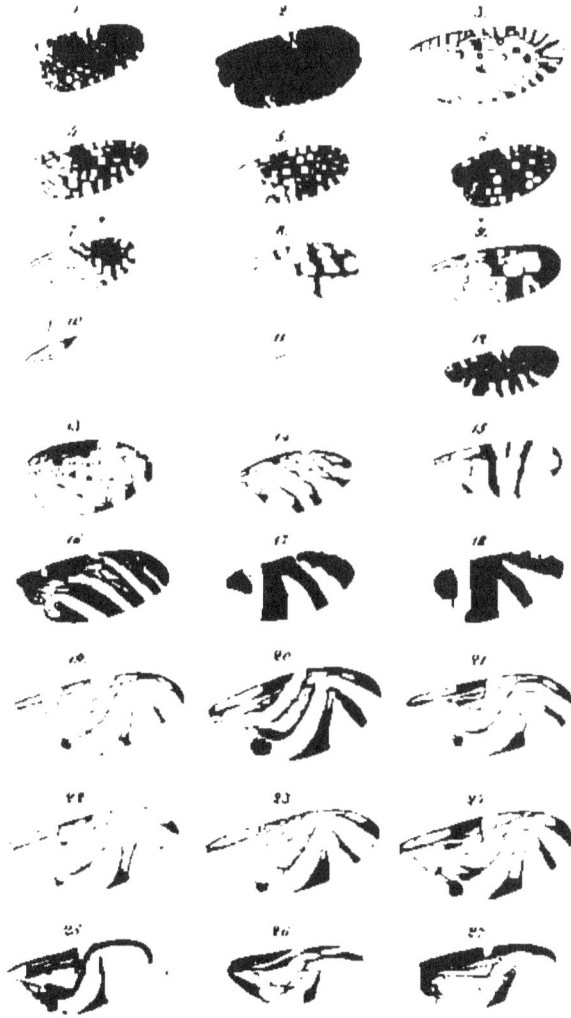

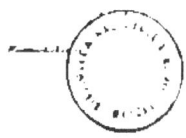

CORRECTIONS TO VOLUME III.

Page 283, as a synonym of *T. latifrons* insert:—

Trypeta cribrata v. d. WULP, Tijdschr. v. Entom. 2 Ser. Vol. II, p. 158. Tab. V, f. 15.

Observation (by the Editor) to page 153.—This volume was already printed when I received from Mr. E. Burgess specimens taken near Beverly, Mass., and showing the characters of *Sciptera vibrans* Lin., as distinguished from *S. calva* Loew. Immediately afterwards I found in the Museum of Comparative Zoölogy a precisely similar specimen, apparently taken near Cambridge, Mass.—O. S.

ADDITIONS AND CORRECTIONS

TO THE PREVIOUSLY PUBLISHED VOLUME.

Corrections to Volumes I and II, furnished by Mr. Loew.

VOLUME I.

Page 10, line 3 from bottom, instead of *Cylindrotoma Mrig.* read *Macq.*

" 17, " 15 from top, instead of *wing*, read *margin of the wing.*

" 17, " 14 from bottom, *Mctoponia* (*=Inopus*), strike out *Inopus.*

" 18, " 20   "   instead of *Aissa*, read *Antuno.*

" 19, " 15 from top, instead of *fourth cell of posterior margin*, read *fourth posterior cell.*

Page 21, lines 17 and 13 from bottom, instead of *Osscbius*, read *Opschius.*
   (The same name must be corrected in the Index.)

Page 38, line 17 from bottom, instead of *legs proportionately short*, read *legs very long and slender, with the tarsi proportionately short.*

Page 39, line 12 from bottom, instead of *generally*, read *mostly.*

" 40, " 12   "   instead of *with no* read *without.*

" 42, " 6   "   instead of *tarsi* read *tibiæ.*

" 47, *Asteina*; add at the end: (*Sigalodaea signa has a posterior cross-vein*).

Page 55, line 4 from top, instead of *is*, read *it is.*

" 56, " 4 from bottom, instead of *and*, read *or.*

" 57, " 8 from top, instead of *and*, read *or.*

" 70, " 10   "   instead of *short*, read *thin.*

" 75, " 4   "   instead of *edge*, read *border.*

" 80, " 12 from bottom, instead of 23, read 24.

" 91, " 20 from top, instead of *first* read *fifth.*

" 173, " 10 from bottom, before the word "*longitudinal*, add *fourth.*

VOLUME II.

Page 279, lines 7 from top and 13 from bottom, instead of *Nordhawira*, read *Nordshausen.*

(III)

CORRECTIONS TO VOLUME IV.

(By C. R. Osten-Sacken.)

Page 2, line 6 from bottom, instead of *general*, read *common*.

" 16, " 9 from top, instead of p. 11, read p. 387.

" 23, " 8 " instead of *auxiliary*, read *subcostal* (this error occurs twice on the same line).

Page 129, line 3 from bottom, instead of *all the*, read *most*.

" 132, lines 2, 4, 14, 15 from bottom, instead of *Paratropesa*, read *Paratropesa*.

The same error occurs on page xi, line 4 from bottom.

" 49, " 18 "

" 333, " 2 from top.

" 343, " 3 from bottom, column first.

" 345, " 6 "

Page 134, line 4 from bottom, strike out *lin*.

" 159, " 15 " instead of *is*, read *are*.

" 179, " 19 from top, instead of 1823, read 1829.

" 219, " 4 from bottom, before *yellowish*, insert *femora*.

" 249, lines 15 and 16 from bottom: the quotation from Doleschall given here refers to his paper in pamphlet form; the full quotation may be found on page 16, line 5 from top, where p. 367 should be read, instead of p. 11.

Page 275, line 11 from top, instead of *paupera*, read *pauper*.

The same error occurs on page x, line 4 from top, column first.

" 277, " 5 "

" 278, " 3 "

" 344, " 4 from bottom, column sec'd.

Page 293, line 13 from top, instead of *ruficornis* Wied. and *erythrocephala* Macq., read *ruficornis* Macq. and *erythrocephala* Wied.

Page 295, line 3 from bottom, instead of p. 19, read p. 391.

" 331, " 18 from top, instead of 17, read 14.

ADDITIONS TO VOLUME IV.

(By C. R. Osten-Sacken.)

Page 4. Ptychoptera. The larvæ of this genus examined by Brauer, differ from all the known larvæ of Tipalidæ in having the head and imbedded up to the mouth in the first thoracic segment, but entirely free. This observation justifies the isolated position which I have given to this group in the family. Compare Verh. Zool. Bot. Ges. 1869, p. 644.

Page 23. The analytical table, given here, would be improved by being modified thus:—

I. A single submarginal cell.

Antennæ 14-jointed.	Antennæ 16-jointed.
Empodia indistinct or none.	Sect. II. Limnobina anomala.
Sect. I. Limnobina.	

II. Two submarginal cells. Empodia distinct, etc. etc.

Page 49. The same modification may be made on this page.

Page 57. Dicranomyia. My remarks concerning the differences between this genus and *Limnobia* apply to those North American and European species which I had occasion to compare. I have accumulated as many distinctive characters as a careful comparison of the material before me could disclose; but I should not wonder at all if forms occurred the location of which remained doubtful, all the enumerated distinctive characters notwithstanding.

Page 81. Mr. Loew draws my attention to the fact, that the antennæ of *Rhipidia* cannot be properly called *pedicelled*, because the short stems, connecting the joints, are processes of the anterior part of the joint and not of the posterior one.

Page 102. Styringomyia. During my passage through Stockholm in 1872, I made the interesting discovery that this genus, besides its occurrence in amber and copal, is found living in Africa. I saw several specimens among the unnamed diptera from Caffraria (from Wahlberg's voyage) in the Stockholm Museum. The species was apparently different from that included in copal, which I possess.

(vii)

Page 115. **Toxorrhina** *m–lidris* O. S. ♂ . I found three males and one female near Tarrytown, N. Y., in July, 1871. They all have the discal cell *open*, which, therefore, seems to be the rule in this species. The stripes of the thorax are dark brown; the position of the great crossvein is variable, sometimes at the very base of the discal cell, sometimes before it.

Page 133, at the bottom. **Sigmatomera.** I described this new genus, from Mexico, without adding the description of the typical species, which, as I anticipated, would be soon published in a new fascicle of Mr. Bellardi's *Saggio*, etc. This publication having been, in the mean time, indefinitely postponed, it becomes necessary to supply the above mentioned omission.

Sigmatomera flaripennis n. sp.—Yellow, antennæ long, black, except the first joint, which is yellow; front feet and middle femora yellow (the remaining feet as well as the middle tibiæ and tarsi, are wanting). Wings tinged with yellowish; central crossveins and 5th vein slightly bordered with brown. Long. corp. 0.50–0.6; long. al. 0.64. *Hab.* Mexico (Sumichrast).

Page 173. **Psilocenopu.** I had occasion to examine specimens of *P. Meigenii* Zett., since the publication of Vol. IV, and have become aware that my opinion about its location was erroneous. This genus is related to *Trimicra*, and its venation is exactly like the latter genus, the subcostal crossvein being quite remote from the tip of the auxiliary vein. The two other European species, mentioned on pages 173 and 174 as *Psilocenopu*, do not belong to this genus at all, and are much better placed in the genus *Goniomyia*. The above correction will necessitate changes in all the passages, where the genus *Psilocenopu* is mentioned. Such passages are the following:—

Page 21, line 4 from bottom, instead of *Psilocenopu?*, read *Goniomyia?*.
 " 36, " 7 from bottom, strike out the whole passage beginning with *is represented*.
Page 36, line 3 from bottom, add *Psilocenopu*.

 " 47, modify the analytical table thus:—

	30
29 { The distance, etc.	
{ The distance, etc.	Gen. XXII. Gnophomyia.
30 { Seventh longitudinal vein straight; Tab. II, f. 1.	31
{ Seventh longitudinal vein conspicuously bisinuated; Tab. I, fig. 20.	Gen. XXI. Styringa.
31 { Three terminal joints of the antennæ abruptly smaller.	Gen. XVIII. Trimera.
{ Three terminal joints, etc., *not* abruptly smaller.	Gen. XX. Psilocenopa.

(xx)

Page 49, line 14 from bottom, transfer Gen. XXII, *Psilocnops*, as Gen. XX, after *Chiona*.

Page 135, line 2 from bottom, strike out the passage beginning with "I believe now" and ending with "typical Eriopterina."

Page 137, line 11 from top, instead of *Psilocnops*, read *Goniomyia*.

" 173, line 13 from bottom, strike out the whole paragraph beginning with the words: "A genus closely allied, etc.," as well as its continuation on the next page, down to the "Description of the species."

Page 176. Gen. XXII. *Psilocnops* should be placed between *Chiona* and *Symplecta* as Gen. XX. with the following notice: Established by Zetterstedt in 1840 (*Fauna Lapponica*, p. 847), and later in *Dipt. Scand.* X, p. 4007, upon a single species, found in Sweden. This genus, as far as I have been able to study it upon a dry specimen, is related to *Trimicra*, and its venation is exactly the same, the subcostal crossvein being quite remote from the tip of the auxiliary vein, etc. However, it does not have the last three external joints abruptly smaller, and its general appearance is altogether different.

Page 177, line 10 from bottom, strike out the passage beginning with the words: "The majority" down to the bottom of the page, and read as follows instead: Some European species differ from the American ones in the following characters: in their coloring the black prevails over the yellow; only a few traces of the latter color are left; the auxiliary vein seems to extend much farther beyond the origin of the præfurca than is the case in the American species; the structure of the male forceps seems also to show some differences, which, however, I have not been able to ascertain, not having had fresh specimens for comparison. Such species are the *Erioptera lateralis* Macq., *Hist. Nat. Dipt.* II, p. 653 (Syn. *Limnobia flaccilimbata* Hal., in Walker's *Ins. Brit. Dipt.* III, p. 304) ; the *Goniomyia scutellata* Egger and *G. cincta* Egger, in Schiner's *Fauna Austriaca*, Diptera. One of the latter may be synonymous with the former, and Dr. Schiner was perfectly right in referring them to the genus *Goniomyia*. All these species are not unlike the American species of *Gnophomyia* in their general appearance; they differ, nevertheless, in the absence of the marginal crossvein, in the shortness of the first submarginal cell, in the diverging direction of the branches of the fork which form it, and in the presence of yellow in the coloring. It is not impossible, however, that forms of transition may be discovered between these two genera, as well as between them and *Empeda*.

(xi)

Page 218. *Limnophila inornata* O. S. ♂.—This species was quite common near Tarrytown, N. Y., in June, 1871. Two females which I have before me have the stigma somewhat tinged with brown; the brown at the tip of the femora is more abruptly marked. In the above-quoted description, p. 219, line 4 from bottom, the word *femora* must be added before the word *yellowish*. On the following page, line 5 from top, instead of *about*, read *somewhat less than*. The fore tarsi of the females are shorter than those of the male. The length of the second posterior cell is variable.

Page 260. **Polymera.** This South American genus, never seen by me before the publication of my volume, was doubtfully mentioned among the *Amalopina*. Mr. Loew had opportunities of examining good specimens recently, and published the result in a paper entitled *Über die systematische Stellung d. Gatt. Polymera* Wied. (Zeitschr. f. d. gesammten Naturwiss. Neue Folge, 1871, Bd. III, Tab. V, f. 1, 2). It appears now that the antennæ of *Polymera* are *not* 28-jointed, as was stated by former authors, but 16-jointed, and that there cannot exist the slightest doubt about its location among the *Limnophilina*. It has peculiarities, however, which distinguish it from the ordinary *Limnophilina* of Europe and North America: a remarkably elongated third antennal joint, a structure of the following joints, in the male, which makes them appear double (hence the error of former authors), an open discal cell, and both branches of the fourth longitudinal vein forked (contrary to the rule stated on page 201, No. 2); the wingveins have a rather conspicuous pubescence. Mr. Loew ends his article with a statement of the principal characters of *Polymera*, as recognized by him, which I reproduce here, with a slight modification :—

Polymera.—The number of antennal joints is normal, 16; the first joint of the flagellum is remarkably elongated, cylindrical, beset with long, erect hairs; each of the following joints, in the male, shows two consecutive knots, or swellings, every one of which is provided with a distinct vertical of hairs; in the female, three joints are simply cylindrical, and beset with hairs like the first joint of the flagellum. Wingveins beset with a long pubescence; subcostal crossvein only a short distance from the tip of the auxiliary vein; marginal crossvein distinct, inserted on, or a little beyond the middle of the very long submarginal cell; basal cells comparatively rather short; discal cell open, coalescent with the third posterior cell; five posterior cells; the second with a petiole of a very great length; feet long and slender; tibiæ with very small but distinct spurs; ungues and empodia very small.

(xiii)

www.ingramcontent.com/pod-product-compliance
Lightning Source LLC
Chambersburg PA
CBHW030908270326
41929CB00008B/616